The Nuclear Dilemma and the Just War Tradition

The Nuclear Dilemma and the Just War Tradition

Edited by

William V. O'Brien
Georgetown University

John Langan, S.J.
Woodstock Theological Center,
Georgetown University

Lexington Books
D.C. Heath and Company/Lexington, Massachusetts/Toronto

Library of Congress Cataloging-in-Publication Data

Main entry under title:

The Nuclear dilemma and the just war tradition.

Includes bibliographical references and index.
Contents: Ethics in distress : can there be just wars in the nuclear age? / David Hollenbach—Threats, values, and defense / James Turner Johnson—Justice, war, and politics / Gerald M. Mara—[etc.]
1. Nuclear warfare—Moral and ethical aspects—Addresses, essays, lectures. 2. Just war doctrine—Addresses, essays, lectures. 3. Deterrence (Strategy)—Moral and ethical aspects—Addresses, essays, lectures.
I. O'Brien, William Vincent. II. Langan, John, 1940–
U263.N754 1986   172'.42   85–45946
ISBN 0–669–12599–7 (alk. paper)

Published simultaneously in Canada
Printed in the United States of America
Casebound International Standard Book Number: 0–669–12599–7
Library of Congress Catalog Card Number: 85–45946

The paper used in this publication meets the minimum requirements of American National Standard for Information Sciences—Permanence of Paper for Printed Library Materials, ANSI Z39.48–1984.
∞ ™

The last numbers on the right below indicate the number and date of printing.

10 9 8 7 6 5 4 3 2 1

95 94 93 92 91 90 89 88 87 86

Contents

Part V Conclusion 221

Acknowledgments

The papers which make up the core of this volume were presented at a conference entitled, "Justice and War in the Nuclear Age," held at Georgetown University, March 15–17, 1984. While the immediate stimulus was the series of debates surrounding the U.S. Catholic bishops' Pastoral Letter, *The Challenge of Peace: God's Promise and Our Response*, the overall goal of the conference was the much broader one of fostering more analytic and critical reflection on the significance of nuclear weapons for the religious *and* secular variants of the just war tradition.

The editors are particularly grateful to Associate Dean Gerald Mara who first suggested that a scholarly conference on these issues would be both necessary and significant, to James Turner Johnson of Rutgers University who contributed substantially to the definition and planning of the conference, and to Graduate Dean Richard B. Schwartz who committed financial support to this scholarly treatment of a highly significant political and moral issue. The Graduate School's support was then generously supplemented by Georgetown's Center for Strategic and International Studies.

The success of the conference discussions was due, in large measure, to the efforts of a number of eminent commentators. Considerations of space, as well as a desire to produce a more ordered volume than the usual set of conference proceedings, have prevented us from reproducing their comments here. We have tried to recognize some of their principal concerns in our introductory and concluding chapters. The commentators, whose prominence and diversity matched those of our contributors, included Michael Howard, Oriel College, Oxford University; Norman Birnbaum, Georgetown University Law Center; Thomas Garwin, Office of Technology Assessment; Michael Mandelbaum, Columbia University and the Lehrman Institute; James Childress, the University of Virginia; Robert Osgood, the Johns Hopkins School of Advanced International Studies and the U.S. Department of State; and the Reverend J. Bryan Hehir of the U.S. Catholic Conference and Georgetown University's Kennedy Institute of Ethics. Special thanks in this category go to Professor Osgood, who led a very provocative session, on very short notice, in substitution for an ailing John Keegan.

The same considerations as those noted above also prevented us from including the very fine policy responses to these papers which served to conclude the conference. The panel of policy representatives—chaired by Former United Nations Ambassador Donald F. McHenry and consisting of James Leonard, Former Deputy Special Negotiator for the Middle East; Walter Slocombe, Former Deputy Undersecretary of Defense for Policy Planning; and General William Y. Smith (USAF-Retired), Former Deputy Commander-in-Chief, U.S. European Command—served to remind us of how much and how well practitioners can stimulate, amplify, and correct what academics have to say on these issues.

The final success of the conference, however, depended on the contributions of the more than one hundred academics, policymakers, military officers, and religious leaders who attended the two and one-half days of sessions. They and their colleagues, who continue these discussions daily in academic and practical contexts, are those to whom this volume is most appropriately dedicated.

The publication of these papers would have been impossible without the competent, gracious, and highly tolerant efforts of Mary Ellen Timbol and her staff at Georgetown University and Jaime Welch-Donahue, Karen Maloney and their staff at Lexington Books.

The editors gratefully acknowledge permission to reprint excerpts from the following sources: "President's Speech on Military Spending and a New Defense, *New York Times*, March 24, 1983; "Star Wars—Pie in the Sky" by Robert Bowman, *New York Times*, Dec. 14, 1983; "Nuclear Fantasies," *The New Republic*, April 18, 1983; *The Challenge of Peace*, U.S. Catholic Conference; "Nuclear Weapons and the Atlantic Alliance" by McGeorge Bundy et al., *Foreign Affairs* (Spring 1982); *Thinking about National Security* by Harold Brown, Westview Press; "Area Bombing in World War II: The Argument of Michael Walzer" by Stephen E. Lammers, *The Journal of Religious Ethics* (Spring 1983); *Just and Unjust Wars* by Michael Walzer, Basic Books; "Thinking About Nuclear Weapons" by H.A. Feiveson, *Dissent* (Spring 1982); "To Cap the Volcano" by McGeorge Bundy, *Foreign Affairs* (October 1969); and "The Countervailing Strategy" by Walter Slocombe, *International Security* (Spring 1981).

Part I
Introduction

1

The Nuclear Dilemma and the Just War Tradition

John Langan, S.J.
Woodstock Theological Center
Georgetown University

S cripture informs us that "Of making many books there is no end." (Ecclesiastes 11,6) Depending on your point of view and on the nature of your involvement in the process of writing, editing, reading, assessing, and using books, this is either encouraging or discouraging—a word of hope or a cry of frustration. Since most books are gratuitous productions, not the result of law or of dire necessity, it may seem that a strong justification is necessary before imposing yet another volume of essays on the reading public.

In reply, one can point to the overwhelming importance of the questions that this set of reflections addresses. No problem seems more intractable or more ominous than the problem of political violence in our world of technological complexity, social vulnerability, and political division. The moral stakes are so high, the visions of what we might do and what we might suffer are so repellent and so distant from our ordinary experience and even from the sufferings of previous wars, that we should spare no effort of intellect or imagination in our efforts to comprehend and to avoid this dread reality. Surely in the nuclear predicament in which the world has placed itself, it behooves both strategists and moralists, both citizens and leaders, both soldiers and clergy always to bear in mind the famous injunction of Oliver Cromwell, "I beseech you, in the bowels of Christ, think it possible that you may be mistaken," and to seek out opportunities for testing and improving our analyses of this predicament and our recommendations for dealing with it.

As students of freshman composition soon discover, however, a weighty or difficult subject alone is not enough to make a worthwhile or useful book. There must also be some distinctive angle of vision, some particular point to be made, some occasion or development that gives the work a special timeliness or utility. The first two conditions are never easy to meet in a collection of essays by different authors. It is commonly thought to be a virtue in such collections that there should be a great diversity of points of view and that the general argument is best advanced through the making of points that are in conflict with each other.

This book in fact achieves something midway between the unitary viewpoint naturally found in the work of a single author and the unstructured confusion characteristic of debates in which there is consensus neither on premises nor on methods of argument. Although it is rash for any editor to generalize about his colleagues in such a venture as this, it is important to underline the fact that all the contributors to this volume approach the issues of contemporary warfare from within the perspective of the just war tradition and that all share a common conviction about the moral importance of defending free political communities and a common concern about the moral character of the means by which this is to be done. It should also be remembered that the authors think of themselves as participating in a U.S. and Western debate over the shape of a morally acceptable policy with regard to nuclear weapons, not in all their possible functions but as they affect the defense of the United States and its principal allies. These two points mean that some of the major positions or points of view that influence public debate or that are worth considering on matters of national security and the use of force in international affairs are not represented in this book. Thus there is no one writing as a Christian pacifist or as a radical critic of Western democratic institutions or as the proponent of a strict *Realpolitik* approach for which moral considerations are irrelevant. There is no one writing from the perspective of the Soviet Union or of a power involved in intense regional conflict and interested in the effect of nuclear weapons on itself and its adversaries. These limitations do not arise from a belief that nothing interesting or illuminating will come from such sources, but rather from an effort to bring about an extended and focused reflection on the perplexities and opportunities that confront thinkers and policymakers in the just war tradition at this point in its development.

The conference on "Justice and War in the Nuclear Age," held at Georgetown University on March 15–17, 1984, and the source of this book, was conceived with precisely this objective in mind. There have been, we believe, three factors that make this period a particularly important one for the development of the just war tradition. The first was the surge in public debate and political activism in both western Europe and the United States centered around NATO's deployment of Pershing 2 and cruise missiles in 1984 and around the nuclear freeze movement. In the year since then, there has been a certain decline in public expressions of concern over nuclear arms: certainly in the short term, the antinuclear forces failed to achieve their political objectives. Conservative governments in the United States, the United Kingdom, and West Germany, along with the socialist-led coalition government in Italy and the socialist government in France, have beaten back both protests and legislative initiatives that would have prevented either the deployment or the new development of nuclear weapons systems. But all participants in the political decisions have been reminded of the open democratic context in which national security policy is shaped in the West. This is both a potential source of disruption and distraction for policymakers and a powerful source of legitimacy for decisions once reached by governments with a popular mandate.

The second shaping factor for current discussions has been technological change and innovation in weapons systems. This has, of course, been a fundamental condition from the beginning of the nuclear age. But the readiness of the Reagan administration and of the U.S. public to increase the military budget, the North Atlantic Treaty Organization (NATO) decision to proceed with deployment of intermediate-range ballistic missiles in response to Soviet deployments, and the continuing inventiveness of military engineers all have meant that the current period is one in which decisions about new weapons systems occupy a central place in the making of military policy. An even more wide-ranging and fundamental development in this area has been President Reagan's proposal of the Strategic Defense Initiative (SDI) in his celebrated "Star Wars" speech of March 1983. This continues to provoke vigorous controversy that deals not only with the cost and the effectiveness of the various programs included but also with the extent to which SDI can or will alter the fundamental condition of mutual deterrence under which both the United States and the USSR have lived for the last generation.

It is clear that this debate is more than the standard struggle over the size and composition of the military budget. It raises pointed questions about the desirability of U.S. adherence to both past and future arms control agreements, and it challenges many of the basic assumptions of national security policy. The debate also puts in question one of the most fundamental commitments of post-Enlightenment Western civilization (and of many modernizing movements in the rest of the world)—namely, the commitment to ride the tiger of technological innovation wherever it may lead. It will be impossible for the next few years to conduct any serious debate on the moral aspects of nuclear weapons without consideration of the terms in the argument that may (or may not) be transformed by likely technological innovations.

A third factor that has made this a time of particular importance has been the development and final acceptance of the U.S. Catholic bishops' Pastoral Letter, *The Challenge of Peace.* This was a process that lasted from November 1980, when the bishops decided to undertake the preparation of the letter, to November 1983, when the final version of the letter was approved. The process was unprecedented in the history of Catholicism by reason of the diversity of outside experts who were consulted and the public discussion of the document in its successive drafts. The process attracted remarkable attention for a religious document belonging to a genre that normally draws only perfunctory treatment from the press. The decisive debates at the bishops' meetings in Washington and

Chicago drew hundreds of journalists from around the world. The document that resulted attracted both editorial comment and scholarly scrutiny and won the support of various non-Catholic religious groups. Though seemingly at odds with the policies of the Reagan administration, it drew little in the way of criticism from the highest levels of military and political leadership in the country. In the short run, it seems to have done little to alter the course of U.S. national security policy or to improve relations between the superpowers. It clearly marked an important turning point in the history of U.S. Catholicism, which showed a new venturesomeness in criticizing the government on essential matters of public policy and which at certain times seemed to rejoice in an adversary or "prophetic" stance.

But why should such a change be of more than parochial interest? After all, anxiety about nuclear weapons has been common since they were first used in 1945. Such prominent moralists as Paul Ramsey and Michael Walzer have addressed themselves to the problems that nuclear arms create for traditional just war theory without checking the increasing dependence of the superpowers on these weapons of mass destruction. What would a document of the U.S. Catholic church—a church not distinguished for the renown of its scholars or for the intellectual acumen of its bishops—add to the reflections of experts on this difficult topic?

There are three things I would point to as indicators that the U.S. bishops made a distinctive contribution to the debate on moral aspects of contemporary military and security policy. First, Roman Catholicism is far and away the largest religious group in the United States, and on these issues it has the support of very significant elements in what are commonly referred to as the "mainline" Protestant churches. It is also a church with considerable institutional cohesion and extensive international links. Second, the document provoked a series of similar documents issued by Catholic hierarchies in nations ranging from Japan to Ireland; of these the most important were the letters published by the German and French bishops.[1] The result was a spectrum of opinions, some manifesting revulsion at nuclear weapons and the threat to civilization they present, others the resolution to defend free societies, both of which tendencies are clearly present in the U.S. bishops' letter. All these documents are formulated within the just war tradition, while at the same time they are expressions of the church's revulsion at the prospect of war, especially in its most destructive contemporary forms.

The Pastoral Letter did not evoke universal agreement, particularly not in the details of its argumentation; but it did draw forth a very wide response, touching as it did on matters of such fundamental importance to so many different societies. It gave the concern over these matters a form and a direction, along with a recognized place in the institutional life and memory of Roman Catholicism. The Second Vatican Council (Vatican II) had, of course, touched on these matters;[2] but it is safe to say that the Pastoral Letter made the connections in such a way that the religious values and moral concerns could guide choices in the public policy debate while at the same time the public policy options could be comprehended and assessed by individuals within the religious tradition.

Third, the letter of the U.S. bishops constitutes a fusion of ecclesiastical and secular elements, both academic and political; at the same time, it is an effort by groups (the ad hoc committee chaired by Cardinal Bernardin and the bishops' conference itself) to express the concerns and shape the beliefs of much larger groups (American Catholicism and the U.S. public). It is an *opus mixtum,* a complex product lacking both the purity and the characteristic virtues of more individual and more narrowly defined contributions to the discussion. The crucial point is not that the final product is better than the work of the individual moral or strategic theorists, but that it is the institutionalization of a certain way of arguing about the moral problem of war in the nuclear age. It takes its place in relation to previous church documents and to the tradition of Catholic theology; it is amended, and compromises are made on various points, while accommodations are made to different criticisms. What emerges is both more and less than a scholarly effort by an individual or even by a team of individuals. It is an object of institutional commitment and of the exercise of institutional authority (though not in a coercing or definitive way). At the same time, it is a body of assertions, conclusions, and recommendations held together by the backbone of a complex argument. As such, it can be subjected to searching intellectual criticism and evaluated for the consistency and the adequacy of its treatment of the nuclear dilemma.[3] The merit of the U.S. bishops' letter (as well as of the German letter) is that it captures enough of the diverse values present in the nuclear dilemma and that it is appropriately complex and reflective in its treatment of the issues so that it repays careful study even when one disagrees. It thus makes a suitable reference point for the future development of the debate in this area.

One can present the ongoing debate on nuclear weapons and defense policy as a triangular affair. At one apex of the triangle are the technical and military specialists, the people who understand how nuclear weapons are to be made and used, deployed and counteracted—how they are in fact integrated into the Western military system, as well as what alternative patterns of production and deployment might be practicable. These specialists deal in matters of fact, but also in some more or less speculative opinions (for instance, when they predict the results or costs of new weapons systems or research programs or when they estimate adversary capabilities or intentions). At a second apex of the triangle are the formulators and makers and critics of security policy. They include political leaders, Pentagon bureaucrats, some of the military leadership, and those professionally involved with making foreign policy and with the effects of nuclear weapons on international relations. Their concern is primarily with the political values and objectives that are protected or jeopardized by possessing, deploying, and possibly using nuclear weapons, rather than with weapons systems and their physical properties and military effectiveness. The remaining apex of the triangle is occupied by those persons who are concerned about the moral and religious values that can be violated or affirmed by our national security policy and by the threat to use nuclear weapons, which is a central element in that policy.

I think it can safely be said that, before the U.S. bishops' Pastoral Letter, that third apex did not have institutional weight and definition at all comparable with what could be found at the other two. Valuable and distinguished work had been done by various moralists, notably by Paul Ramsey in the earlier years of the nuclear age and, more recently, by Michael Walzer and James Johnson and consistently over the years by William O'Brien. Various protest movements, assemblies of clergy and citizens, and official church bodies had expressed concern and disapproval with regard to U.S. defense policy. Without these contributions and the learning that came from them, the Pastoral Letter would have been much impoverished. Academic debates, however, especially in the humanities, often have a way of petering out with key issues still unresolved (since the responsibility of intellectuals and academics is to understand rather than to decide). Protest movements and pacifist groups are notoriously prone to internal division and are often uncertain about whether they wish to have a continuing involvement with the messy uncertainties of political power and its military instruments. Roman Catholicism, with its massive presence in U.S. life, its churchly rather than sectarian character, and its mode of arguing moral issues in a way that values consistency and respects the precedents formed with respect to earlier and related issues (a mode that is similar in many ways to the patterns of reasoning employed in appellate courts in the United States), provides an appropriate institutional base for this third apex. The Pastoral Letter is the first expression of that new function of U.S. Catholicism in the national security debate.

It should be clear from what I have said that I do not regard the three corners of the national security debate as three positions or doctrines, but rather as three different social locations within which the issue of nuclear weapons is raised, on which individual participants in the debate are based, and among which there must be at least some effective cooperation if policy is to be made and legitimated. All three apexes of the triangle are marked by fierce struggles about the direction and control of policy; and actors based on any one apex of the triangle are frequently at odds with dominant tendencies of other apexes. Thus the Pastoral Letter is critical of policies of both the Reagan and Carter administrations, which were in disagreement with each other; and it is itself criticized by pacifist church members, by moral philosophers, and by proponents of new weapons systems. The moral-religious apex of the triangle is normally the weakest, since it draws on many fewer people with a vital career commitment and genuine expertise and since it plays the role of critic rather than decision maker. On the other hand, it can appeal to values and concerns that are important to thoughtful persons who are professionally identified with other corners of this triangular debate. From the beginning of the nuclear age we have been blessed in having many persons in the scientific and technical communities as well as in military and political life who have been perplexed over the moral dilemmas presented by nuclear weapons and have been willing to contribute to the public debate on these matters.

It would be a mistake to treat the Catholic bishops' Pastoral Letter as in any sense a definitive expression of what can be said from this third apex of the triangle. Rather, it serves as a common reference point and is likely to do so until the next change occurs in the basic terms of the security debate. It certainly does not elicit universal consent, even within the Catholic community, but it attracts and merits universal scrutiny. The letter also deserves attention because of its interesting political relationship to the policies of the Reagan administration. The letter was developed and adopted at a time when an administration was in power that affirmed the necessity of a massive arms buildup, that was profoundly suspicious of the direction of Soviet policy and openly skeptical of the value of arms control agreements, and that articulated a nationalistic approach to many issues of international life. The bishops' letter deprecates the arms buildup, avoids any detailed criticism of the Soviet Union and its actions, urges new arms control agreements, and uses much of the internationalist rhetoric of the last forty years. Interestingly, there was no direct confrontation on the policy issues or on the basic assumptions between the Reagan administration and the Catholic bishops. I would not suggest that no significant disagreements exist between the bishops and the administration but, rather, that the key proponents of two quite different approaches to security policy understand that the U.S. public is unlikely to move to a wholesale rejection of either approach—that as a people we desire both security through strength and reassurance that moral constraints are being observed in the protection of national security.

Recognition of these key factors changes the terms of national security debate: greater public involvement, the increased pace of technological change, and the statements of the churches lay behind our planning of the conference at Georgetown in March 1984 and behind the organization of this book, which includes the papers presented at that conference. We were also particularly concerned that two important systematic issues had not received adequate attention in the bishops' letter or in the subsequent public discussions: (1) the moral justification for the defense of a free political community—the fundamental *jus ad bellum* in our present situation—and (2) the interconnections between nuclear and conventional war.

Attempting to summarize the various chapters here is neither appropriate nor necessary, but a synoptic view may be helpful. Taken together, the chapters are an effort to understand the problem of justice in war in the nuclear age on the part of a moral theologian (Hollenbach), a historian of the just war tradition (Johnson), a political scientist (Dougherty), a moral philosopher (Langan), an expert on international law (O'Brien), a military historian (Keegan), and two political theorists (Mara and Walzer). This came to be a common effort to think through the problems of just war theory for our time in a way that takes account of the current situation. The chapters are not conceived as replies to or comments on the U.S. bishops' Pastoral Letter, although for reasons that I have mentioned the Pastoral Letter does figure prominently in some chapters (Hollenbach, Langan, and O'Brien). It is our hope that, taken together, they show both the relevance and fruitfulness of the traditions of religious, moral, and political thought from which the contributors came and that, taken separately, they show the value of studying so complex and troubling a phenomenon as contemporary warfare from the standpoint of a variety of disciplines.

Beyond the enterprise of writing books and scrutinizing academic studies and moral reflections, there is the greater and more perilous task of guiding public affairs in a just and prudent way. In the years since 1945, this task has grown even more difficult. Since the time of Plato, academics have felt both the desire and the responsibility to provide guidance for the problems of public life. This guidance has not always been welcomed, nor has it been seen as genuinely useful or necessary. But one constant theme in the nuclear age has been the raising of fundamental questions of moral and political order. This is the natural result of public awareness of the magnitude of the threat to the continuity of Western civilization that nuclear weapons present and of the starkness of the ideological opposition between the two great political systems that rely on the possession of nuclear weapons. When we contemplate the dreadful possibilities of nuclear warfare, we are impelled to ask: Why do we carry this risk? What could make it necessary or legitimate? Is there any way beyond this impasse? In this frame of mind, the most urgent practical crises are seen to raise fundamental issues of moral and political theory, and old solutions to practical problems are challenged as never before. This book may be of most help to those among us, both citizens and leaders, who are willing to think about their immediate decisions in ultimate terms and to test their deepest thoughts in the crucible of public debate in an anxious and troubling time. If these essays can deepen understanding and help to sustain resolution and hope in the face of threats and uncertainties, they will have done a worthy service of the type that academic reflection can give to public life.

Notes

1. For a useful review of these episcopal statements, see Mark Heirman, "Bishops' Conferences on War and Peace in 1983," *Cross Currents* 33(1983):275–287.

2. A discussion of the treatment of the problem of nuclear warfare in Vatican II can be found in John Langan, "Between Religion and Politics: The Morality of Nuclear Deterrence," chapter 6, this book.

3. A particularly challenging reading of the pastoral is given by Susan Moller Okin, *World Politics* 36(1984):527–554.

Part II
Theory

2

Ethics in Distress: Can There Be Just Wars in the Nuclear Age?

David Hollenbach, S.J.
Weston School of Theology

In the recent literature on the ethics of war, a vocabulary has come increasingly into use that provides a point of entry into the current debate on justice and war in the nuclear age. If an index of key words in the recent ecclesiastical pronouncements and scholarly analyses of the ethics of warfare were available, the references under *crisis, emergency, tension,* and *distress* would direct one to some of the most challenging passages of these documents. Every sane person knows, of course, that the employment of a significant number of the nuclear weapons deployed today would be a crisis or emergency for humanity of extreme magnitude. My interest in this vocabulary, however, has a different and less apocalyptic focus. These words are used in contexts that suggest not only that the realities of contemporary nuclear strategy may be in conflict with the traditions of Western and Christian ethical thought, but also that we may be faced with policy choices that are simply not analyzable in terms of traditional moral categories. If this is the case, we would be confronted not only with the possible crisis of an actual nuclear war, but also with a crisis of moral reason itself. Ethics would itself be in distress. It is my intention in this chapter to examine the reasons that have led to the emergence of this language of distress, to ask whether these reasons really imply a crisis of moral reason, and to explore what can be done about this situation.

The Situation of Distress

It will be useful to begin by pointing out some of the passages I have in mind in the recent literature. They occur principally in the context of the discussion of the morality of nuclear deterrence, especially those forms of deterrence that threaten to attack urban populations. For example, the Roman Catholic bishops of France, in their pastoral letter of November 8, 1983, were willing to justify the threat to use the French *force de frappe* as a means of deterring both nuclear blackmail and actual Warsaw Pact aggression against France. They argued that a smaller power like France can achieve a "deterrence of the strong by the weak" through possession and threat to use weapons capable of inflicting "intolerable damage upon a much more powerful aggressor."[1] The bishops acknowledge that the French strategy involves a threat to attack cities, and point out that such countercity attacks were "condemned, clearly and without appeal" by the Second Vatican Council.[2] They then note that "threat is not use" and reply to the question of whether the immorality of use makes the threat immoral with a rather vague response: "That is not evident."[3] They are pressed to this conclusion by what they call "a logic of distress."[4] Indeed, they state that their conclusion embodies an "ethic of distress."[5] Their exact meaning is not spelled out, but it does seem to imply the existence of an inner moral tension in their conclusion. It may even contain a moral contradiction that is made tolerable only by the present lack of more acceptable alternatives and that must be overcome as soon as possible. A "situation of distress" makes bedfellows of moral purpose and the threat to do the immoral.

The Catholic bishops of West Germany have been led to a similar sort of conclusion. They characterize their temporary tolerance of a threat to do that which they judge to be immoral as acceptance of an "emergency system (*Notordnung*)" that is needed until we can find an alternative.[6] The realities of the conflict between East and West press them to adopt an "emergency set of ethics (*Notstandethik*)."[7] The emergency to which they refer is the "immense tension" at the heart of nuclear strategy. This cord of tension has two strands.

The first concerns the *goals* of policy. Nuclear strategy seeks to defend against "injustice, oppression and totalitarian extortion." It also seeks to prevent the "horror" that war, conventional or nuclear, between the superpowers would bring.[8] These twin goals of the protection of justice and the prevention of war cannot be considered a single unified objective. Indeed, a single-minded pursuit of one of them can threaten the other. The relation between the dual ends of justice and peace has been analyzed extensively through the history of the just war tradition. The German bishops suggest, however, that the nuclear weapons deployed on both sides of the East-West divide have raised it to a level that deserves to be called an emergency.

The second strand of policy concerns the *means* employed in nuclear strategy. Here the tension is between the direction in which these means carry us and the ends that have pressed us to develop these means. Nuclear force structures and targeting doctrines are designed to protect justice and secure peace. There is a serious danger, however, that these means could subvert one or both of the goals they seek to secure. In fact, present nuclear strategies are based on means that, if used, would violate both just war norms and fundamental human rights. The emergency ethic of which the German bishops speak is based on an acknowledgment that such a subversion of the ends of strategy by its means is a distinct possibility in the nuclear age. Their toleration of the legitimacy of these means, despite the risks entailed, is anguished: "By virtue of this decision we are choosing from among various evils the one which, as far as it is humanly possible to tell, appears as the smallest."[9] Their dissatisfaction with this "emergency ethic" is evident in their repeated plea that some better arrangement must be created. Although they express a true Christian trust that "with God all things are possible," nevertheless, their optimism on the political level is not great:

> Those who rely on this will never be able to accept the existing conditions (cf. Mk 9:23). Such people are summoned to hope against hope (cfc Rom 4:18). . . . We know from the gospel that this emergency situation is not the final word in worldly wisdom, for God's wisdom is not our wisdom.[10]

Here the German bishops come close to saying that efforts to bring nuclear strategy under the direction of moral reason have not succeeded and that our only recourse is to a religious trust that God will extract us from this situation of distress. This response, though understandable, is a curious one, for although Roman Catholic theology has a very strong doctrine of divine providence, it has never viewed God's providence and human responsibility as antithetical to each other. As Thomas Aquinas stated, human beings are rational beings and, as such, "participate in providence by their own providing for themselves and others."[11] The problem that leads the German bishops to this transmoral religious *cri de coeur* is that is is far from clear just how we are to provide for ourselves and others under the nuclear shadow.

Michael Walzer has stated the problem in the most explicit and challenging terms. Walzer, no utilitarian, therefore strongly rejects most tendencies to collapse the moral criteria for the justice of warfare into the single norm of proportionality. He sees efforts to determine the morality of warfare solely on the basis of a comparative weighing of goods and evils as stumbling on the difficulty of weighing different kinds of incommensurable values against each other.[12] Further, the norm of proportionality is a "weak constraint,"[13] lacking the "creative power"[14] to set definite limits on war. It must therefore be supplemented, as the just war tradition has long known, by a firm principle of noncombatant immunity from direct attack.

Walzer, however, is prepared to suspend this noncombatant immunity constraint in the situation he calls "supreme emergency." The phrase, borrowed from Churchill, refers to military-political circumstances where the fundamental values of civilization are in imminent danger of being destroyed or overthrown.[15] Walzer appealed to this line of reasoning to justify the initial instances of British saturation bombing of German cities during World War II. In his view, there was simply no alternative way to resist the massive evil being perpetrated by the Nazi regime. Walzer argued that this justification ceased as soon as other means for defending the fundamental values of civilization became available.

The status of the moral justification Walzer offers for these indiscriminate area bombings, however, remains ambiguous. On the one hand, he declares them to be legitimate. On the other hand, he states that those who ordered and carried out the bombings must be willing to "accept the burdens of criminality here and now."[16] This criminality is not only a violation of a legal code but also a transgression of moral norms:

> The deliberate killing of the innocent is murder. Sometimes, in conditions of extremity (which I have tried to define and delimit) commanders must commit murder or they must order others to commit it. And then they are murderers, though in a good cause.[17]

Walzer is fully aware that this conclusion is self-contradictory. Although not all killing is immoral according to just war tradition, all murder surely is. Murder, by definition, is unjustified killing. To declare it morally legitimate is to make a nonsensical statement: this act is both justified and unjustified at the same time. It is to state, in Walzer's own words, "that what was necessary and right was also wrong."[18] Such a conclusion brings ethics itself into a state of emergency or distress, and Walzer's otherwise highly regarded study has been criticized for it.[19]

Coherent and consistent moral reasoning on the British decision to bomb German cities would, if just war norms are really binding, press one to the conclusion which John C. Ford reached while the war was still being fought:

> If anyone were to declare that modern war is necessarily total, and necessarily involves direct attack on the life of innocent civilians and, therefore, that obliteration bombing is justified, my reply would be: So much the worse for modern war. If it necessarily includes such means it is necessarily immoral itself.[20]

Although Walzer does not believe that all modern war is necessarily total, his book seems to suggest that when the defense of truly fundamental values can only be achieved through the violation of moral norms, we should say "so much the worse for morality." Supreme emergency seems to provide temporary license to go "beyond good and evil"; that is, it grants license to commit immoral acts in the defense of the truly basic values of civilization. Supreme emergency confronts us with a fundamental moral antinomy or aporia in which we cannot seek justice without performing injustice, or in which we cannot remain just without allowing injustice to destroy the very foundations of a just society.

Walzer's position on the saturation bombing of World War II is consequently imbued with a deep sense of tragedy. He struggles mightily to hedge it around with stringent limits in an attempt to prevent the principle of noncombatant immunity from becoming another casualty of modern war. As Lawrence Freedman and others have pointed out, however, the doctrines that have governed plans for the use of nuclear weapons had their origins in the pre-Hiroshima theories on the strategic use of air power that led to bomber attacks on cities.[21] From a moral point of view, the key debates about the morality of the use of nuclear weapons through much of the nuclear age has a shape similar to that of the debate about the legitimacy of these bombardments of cities with conventional weapons. It is undoubtedly true that the advent of nuclear weapons in 1945 and their subsequent development must be regarded as a qualitative transition in the moral problem of warfare.[22] Nevertheless, the decision to resort to strategic bombardment during World War II provided a precedent for the development of strategies of counterpopulation nuclear warfare. In his critique of Walzer's argument from supreme emergency—a critique that is directed at Walzer because his position represents the most analytically precise version of a view held by a number of others—Stephen Lammers highlights the significance of this moral (or immoral) precedent:

> It is true that politics includes single, unrepeated acts, the effects of which are quite limited. Politics also includes policy decisions which are implemented over time and which, when implemented, take on a life of their own. ... In politics, a policy decision may lead to the creation of a social practice which becomes part of political life in the future. The evil that was supposed to be done at a given time may live on long after the conditions which made the policy "necessary" are past. Thus an evil determinate in kind may become indeterminate in duration.[23]

In fact, this is just what has happened to the temporary suspension of the principle of noncombatant immunity since World War II. Although there have been repeated efforts to provide alternatives to counterpopulation threats, the ultimate threat to attack cities has remained a permanent feature of the plans and the strategies of the nuclear powers. It is indeed fortunate that these strategies have not yet been carried into action; nevertheless, the mainstream version of nuclear strategy has continued to rely on a threat to violate this basic principle of the just war tradition.

The dilemma posed by these strategies is evident in the discussions of nuclear deterrence in the recent European bishops' statements. Once again, however, Walzer's writing has the advantage of making this dilemma more explicit than do either the French or German bishops. He argues forcefully that the threat to attack civilians is itself immoral, even when this threat is part of a strategy of deterrence. It embodies a "commitment to murder."[24] Although he acknowledges that the threat to kill the innocent and the carrying out of this threat are very different things, they are very close on the level of intention. Counterpopulation deterrence—mutual assured destruction (MAD), for example—must therefore be judged morally perverted even if it succeeds in preventing the outbreak of war. Here, however, what Lammers is worried about becomes most relevant: once noncombatant immunity is set aside in a situation of supreme emergency, a social practice is legitimated that will be very difficult to delegitimate in the future. This is so because technological capacities and ideological rivalries have created social conditions in which the great nuclear adversaries of today feel supremely threatened and this threat bodes to be of indeterminate duration. As Walzer puts it:

> Supreme emergency has become a permanent condition. Deterrence is a way of coping with that condition, and though it is a bad way, there may be no other that is practical in a world of sovereign and suspicious states. We threaten evil in order not to do it, and the doing of it would be so terrible that the threat seems in comparison to be morally defensible.[25]

Here the same questions must be put to Walzer's approach to the ethics of deterrence that were raised concerning his legitimation of the early saturation bombing attacks of World War II. Is it based on a utilitarian moral theory, or is it really a suspension of morality itself? If the former is the case, he must bid adieu to the principle of noncombatant immunity as a relevant moral criterion in the current nuclear debate. Such an outcome would undermine his entire project of rethinking and developing the just war tradition as an expression of a human rights ethic. If, on the other hand, he sees it as a suspension of morality, then there is little point in discussing the ethics of nuclear strategy at all. In either case, a wide chasm has been opened up between the traditional ethics of warfare and the contemporary policy arguments. Walzer sees no way out of this: "Nuclear weapons explode the theory of just war. They are the first of mankind's technological innovations that are simply not encompassable within the familiar moral world."[26] Unless an alternative can be found to this situation, ethics itself will succumb to the incubus of nuclear distress.

The Pacifist Alternative

There are two different kinds of possible response to this distressing analysis. Both call for recasting the presuppositions that lead Walzer and the European bishops to adopt this questionable emergency ethic. The first calls for an abandonment of the presupposition that moral responsibility necessarily demands the taking up of the burdens of political responsibility. This position is, broadly speaking, pacifist and sectarian. It is represented in the current debate by theologians such as John Howard Yoder and Stanley Hauerwas. The second alternative rests on the view that the situation of distress created by nuclear weapons can be transformed by replacing deterrence based on the threat to attack population centers with deterrence based on a credible, counterforce war-fighting capacity. This alternative appears today in a variety of versions, represented by moral and strategic thinkers such as James Johnson, Albert Wohlstetter, and William O'Brien.

The pacifism of Hauerwas and Yoder is based on an interpretation of the religious foundations of Christianity in the story of the people of Israel and the life, teaching, death, and resurrection of Jesus Christ. No moral thought that claims to be Christian can have any other ultimate basis. It is clear, however, that Hauerwas's version of an ethic of nonviolence is also based on an interpretation of our contemporary social, intellectual, and political situation. It is this latter interpretation that has led him to the conclusion that it is quite literally *impossible* to embody the ethical meaning of the Christian story in the political institutions and cultural patterns of modern Western society.

Here Hauerwas relies heavily on the reading of the development of modern Western intellectual and social history proposed by Alasdair MacIntyre, a philosopher who, though not religious himself, shares a strong sensitivity to the traditions of Western religious thought. In MacIntyre's view, post-Enlightenment ideas and institutions have destroyed the possibility of giving any universally plausible and rational account of the foundation of morality. He describes our situation today as one in which moral language is frequently used in public debate, but this usage is most often to express disagreement. There seems to be "no rational way of securing moral agreement in our culture."[27] As an example of moral disagreement for which there seems no terminus, MacIntyre cites the debate between those who regard the threat of nuclear war as a reason that we all ought to be pacifists today and those who argue that we must be prepared to fight nuclear war if we wish to maintain peace. The impossibility of adjudicating these disagreements is the result of the fact "that modern moral utterance and practice can only be understood as a series of fragmented survivals from an older past and that the insoluble problems which they have generated for modern moral theorists remain insoluble until this is well understood."[28] We have lost a coherent moral vision as a result of the culturally fragmenting effect of modernity, and we have also lost the kind of coherent institutions of communal life tht are necessary to sustain such a vision.

MacIntyre regards the present situation as a kind of new "dark ages," and he prescribes a remedy that is analogous to the creation of monasticism and the revived emphasis on virtuous life in community during the dying years of the Roman Empire:

> What matters at this stage is the construction of local forms of community within which civility and the intellectual and moral life can be sustained through the new dark ages which are already upon us. And if the tradition of the virtues was able to survive the horrors of the last dark ages, we are not entirely without grounds for hope. This time however the barbarians are not waiting beyond the frontiers; they have been governing us for quite some time. And it is our lack of consciousness of this that constitutes part of our predicament. We are not waiting for Godot, but for another—doubtless very different—St. Benedict.[29]

Although the cogency of MacIntyre's interpretation of our intellectual and social history need not detain us here (in my view it has both strengths and weaknesses), it is clear why Hauerwas appeals to it as a secular, philosophical warrant for the revival of a form of Christian sectarian pacifism. The "explosion" of the just war theory is the result of the head-on collision of the principle of noncombatant immunity, which is rooted in a theory of human rights, with the principle of proportionality, which calls for the comparative weighing of relative goods and evils. The collision is evident in Walzer's writings, where a human rights–based just war theory conflicts with a form of utilitarianism in the situation of supreme emergency. It has become impossible to reconcile these two principles as long as our world is one where threats against populations are deterred by proportionate counterthreats of the same sort. Discrimination and proportionality in the present circumstances are but "fragmented survivals" uprooted from the moral tradition in which they initially germinated by the force of modern political and military realities.

The tradition that gave rise to classical just war theory shares a common presupposition with the pacifist perspective advocated by Hauerwas. The common ground on which just war theory and pacifism stand is the conviction that survival—even the survival of the most fundamental of this-worldly values—is not an absolute value.[30] Both the biblical eschatology that sees the Kingdom of God as the ultimate reference point for ethical choice and the Christianized version of the Aristotelian teleological ethic developed by Thomas Aquinas relativize intraworldly values. They envision the possibility that these values may sometimes have to be sacrificed. Fidelity to the call of the Kingdom of God or to the teleological ordering of human nature to union with God can come into conflict with the political values of justice and human rights in ultimately tragic circumstances, and these later values must sometimes give way.

It is fair to say, I think, that neither social contract theory nor utilitarianism shares this perspective. For example, a perpetual problem with social contract theories has been the difficulty of providing reasons that the contract should be kept when doing so will subvert the reasons that support the obligations to adhere to the contract in the first place—that is, universal protection of freedom and enlightened self-interest, including my own.[31] At the same time, contract theory cannot advance cogent reasons why the contract should be broken, for to do so would also deny the universally normative rationality on which it rests. This bind is evident in Walzer's conclusion that the suspension of noncombatant immunity in the supreme emergency is both right and wrong at the same time.

This sort of problem inevitably arises when an ethic is based on universal, rational principles that lack an eschatological or teleological point of reference. Both contract theory and utilitarianism force us into antinomies where we simply cannot know what we ought to do, not because of a lack of social or political knowledge, but because of the limits of the moral theories themselves. The upshot is an increased fragmentation of the human moral community as diverse solutions are asserted from different quarters. Hauerwas concludes, therefore, that modern intellectual categories and social institutions make it impossible to develop an argument about the morality of nuclear strategy that has a chance of universal acceptance. He believes we must be prepared to accept the "divided-ness" of the world, even on this fundamental moral level. He goes farther than MacIntyre here, for it is not simply the loss of an Aristotelian teleological framework that has brought this dividedness about. From a Christian perspective, it must be this way, since the hope for a reconciled world is necessarily eschatological—it can be realized only beyond history. Therefore, the quest for a universal set of moral norms that can order a divided community in accord with reason is illusory.[32]

One can therefore interpret Hauerwas as implying that *all* contemporary normative ethical systems are in some sense sectarian. Or, better, there is no universal moral rationality to opt out of as the Troeltschian typology suggests "sect-type" religious groups are wont to do. All moral traditions are history-bound and tied to the narratives and traditions of the communities that form them. Therefore, Christian pacifism cannot be charged with being morally deficient because it does not propose a political ethic capable of regulating the life of society as a whole on the basis of universal rational principles. In Hauerwas's view, all the competing normative visions available are subject to this charge as well. In addition, Christian pacifism has a distinct advantage over those systems that would justify violence for the enforcement of a partial ethical vision. It does not claim to be operating on the basis of universal rationality, but it acknowledges that it is shaped by a particular narrative tradition: the story of Israel and of Jesus Christ. It does not abandon the *hope* for universal reconciliation and the full achievement of justice and peace in society, but it regards this hope as eschatological and to be fulfilled by the action of God, not by human force of arms.

Neither does this sort of Christian pacifism believe that all normative visions are equally true. Rather, it holds that the ethics of nonviolence is in fact the true perspective, and that this truth is verified in the experience of the nonviolent community. Such a concrete historical experience of justice and peace in community is in fact the only basis for judging the truth or falsity of normative frameworks. Thus convincing those with other convictions to change their stance can only be done by inviting them to share this experience and providing an alternative community in which this experience is available to them. As Hauerwas puts it:

> We have no guarantee, of course, that others will accept such a way of life, but Christians must live with the confidence that others will find that such a life frees them from the fears that give birth to slavery and injustice. God has promised the church that if we are faithful our life will not be without effect. The church's task does not depend on nor is it sustained by such effectiveness, however; it is sustained by our experience that by living faithfully we do find God in the truth of our existence.[33]

This, I take it, is the sort of thing MacIntyre has in mind when he says that modern society, living under the threat of insoluble moral conflicts, is waiting for a new St. Benedict.

I have discussed Hauerwas and MacIntyre at some length for two reasons. Their interrelated viewpoints are a relatively sophisticated reflection of an attitude that is increasingly present on the popular level of the nuclear debate—namely, that it is next to impossible consistently to relate moral norms to today's highly complex strategic arguments. For Hauerwas and MacIntyre, that is simply a particular case of the problem of relating moral norms to a form of rationality that has lost its teleological connection with ends and its religious connection with eschatological hope. On this level I am in full agreement with them. This is not to say that morality is impossible without religion (an issue that I prefer to leave to another occasion). Rather, it reflects a conviction that a loss of a sense of the historical possibilities for changing the present terms of the debate leads to an ethical dead end. Teleological and eschatological dimensions in ethics keep this from happening as neither social contract theory nor utilitarianism can do. An ethic that starts and ends within the boundaries of the present conflict-ridden situation cannot fail to lead to insoluble puzzles. Ethics is meant to transform the human condition from what it is to what it could be, not simply to help us better understand the conflicting values of our world. For this reason I welcome the challenge from this quarter.

The second reason for considering this approach is to criticize it constructively in the hope of moving the debate on the relation of morality and nuclear policy to a more fruitful level. Despite Hauerwas's strong desire to move us out of the present bind by his appeal to an eschatological hope, he lacks principles that can guide policy in a historically incremental way. His view goes beyond an "ethics of distress" to the proclamation of the death of political ethics as this term is normally understood. This is because Hauerwas, in contrast to Augustine and Paul Ramsey, rejects the value of norms for distinguishing between more and less perfect forms of justice and peace in the earthly city.[34] He draws a stark contrast between the absolute peace and justice of the kingdom of God and the injustice and violence of the world of power politics. For Ramsey, following Augustine, the picture is considerably more complex than this.

In Augustine and Ramsey, the city of God and the earthly city cannot be identified with distinct communities in history—for example, the church and the Roman Empire or a contemporary pacifist community and the superpowers. The two "cities" coexist together in all things human, whether these be nation-states, churches, or even individuals. The ethical task, then, is transformation, not a division into sheep and goats. And it is the norms of the just war tradition that guide us as we seek this transformation of a world that is a mixture of good and evil. This tradition situates conflict in a historical, developmental framework and demands that we seize every opportunity to further this transformation, while recognizing that it will always be incomplete within history. This Augustinian perspective, in other words, does not deny the moral tensions inherent in political life, but it does refuse to allow tension to become dualism or to explode into self-contradiction.

Ethics and Limited War

This transformationist Augustinian interpretation of political ethics and just war theory may provide a clue to how we can move beyond the distressing state of the current debate on the relation of morality and nuclear war. The explosion of the just war theory described by Walzer is the result of the presence of immoral intentions in MAD deterrence theories. The strategic debates of the 1960s had sought to find an alternative to this sort of deterrence by proposing a variety of counterforce strategies that could in fact serve as a credible deterrent without threatening to attack civilians directly. That debate, Walzer concludes, petered out in the mid-1960s when the extent of collateral damage to civilians by most imaginable counterforce attacks and the high likelihood of escalation of any superpower conflict to a catastrophic nuclear war became clear.[35] Walzer's conclusion in 1977 was similar to the one reached more recently by Lawrence Freedman:

> The position we have reached is one where stability depends on something that is more the antithesis of strategy than its apotheosis—on threats that things will get out of hand, that we might act irrationally, that possibly through inadvertance we could set in motion a process that in its development and conclusion would be beyond human control and comprehension.[36]

Nuclear strategy is a mixture of good intentions and evil threats. It is a construct of human rationality that only "works" because of our fear that human beings will act irrationally and immorally. Its consequences might be peace of a sort, a catastrophic war, or a long twilight struggle of uncertainty and doubt.

Nuclear strategy, we might say, is a quintessentially Augustinian phenomenon. It is virtually impossible to untangle the good and the evil elements in it. The good is an aspect of the evil, and the evil both the source and the possible outcome of the good it seeks to achieve. Just as Augustine's well-known robber bands had their own form of justice, so the darkness of nuclear strategy does contain a measure of rational purpose within it. But they *were* robbers, and the strategy *remains* full of demonic potential. We cannot simply accept it, nor can we simply reject it. The pacifist risks the loss of the good it can achieve by making aversion to the evil in it the sole basis of decision. Walzer and the European bishops are more cautious, because their basic adherence to just war tradition has given them a more Augustinian political sensibility. They recognize that rejection of deterrence could have a terrible price, and their acceptance of it is reluctant and even tortured. They call for the creation of alternatives to a system that seeks to "win the peace" by threatening civilian populations. But neither really says much about what these alternatives might be. This is understandable in Walzer's case, I believe, because the alternatives that are currently being proposed were still in gestation as he wrote his book. I am less willing to grant the

French bishops this excuse, for when they wrote their letter in 1983 a wide array of alternatives to MAD not only were under discussion but were being translated into policy. As Stanley Hoffmann has noted, the French bishops seem insufficiently aware of the new technologies and strategic doctrines that make counterforce deterrence and defense the moral point at issue in the current debate.[37] By provisionally legitimating countervalue deterrence, they not only acquiesce in the explosion of the just war theory, but also, because they do not take the newer strategic proposals into account, implicitly legitimate policies they seem not to have considered. The lack of attention to the specifics of these new strategic doctrines is also a problem with the German bishops' document, although I suspect the reasons for it were more political than in the case of the French.

The Augustinian view of political ethics should put us on guard against this sort of reluctance to take seriously the concrete possibilities of changing the dangerous situation we are in. Augustinian thinking does not expect to be able to untangle all the moral threads of political life. But it is equally insistent that history is an open system, capable of change and movement. The way we respond to the openings for the enhancement of justice and community among peoples and for the reduction of injustice and violence is an index of whether our polity is simply a band of murderers and robbers or something better than this. MAD seeks to establish a form of justice, but it is the justice of a murderous world. The issue is this: What can be done to transform it?

It is here that the various counterforce nuclear strategies under consideration today demand scrutiny from a moral perspective. I have argued elsewhere that it is impossible to reach moral conclusions about nuclear deterrence and defense in the abstract.[38] It is the abstraction from actual and concrete policy choices that induces the internal emergency or distress within ethics itself. If we fail to consider actual concrete alternatives to the morally self-contradictory strategy of MAD, we foreclose the possibility that ethical principles can transform the situation into one that is less dangerous and more just.

It is precisely this search for alternatives that can be found in contemporary discussions of whether there is a possibility of creating a strategy for the deterrence of war through a credible, counterforce threat that would itself meet the norms of discrimination and proportionality proposed by the just war theory. The advocates of such limited nuclear war strategies all admit that there is a grave level of uncertainty over whether these limits would in fact be respected should deterrence fail. They differ in how they actually conceive these limits. Albert Wohlstetter believes that targets should be limited to the military and that strict limits on collateral civilian damage are necessary.[39] Colin Gray would expand these limits to include the military and political leadership of the adversary, an expansion that renders a "decapitating" first strike at least imaginable.[40] William V. O'Brien stretches the limits even further, when he argues that strategic attacks on cities could conceivably be part of a "limited" war where they were carried out for purposes of intrawar deterrence—that is as a means of dissuading an adversary from taking further escalating steps that will likely lead to holocaust.[41]

In considering these proposals for moving away from MAD and toward a strategy that seeks to adhere to just war norms, the problem is evident: the boundaries between counterforce and countervalue strategies are very tenuous indeed. We seem almost inevitably pushed to the conclusion, reached by Walzer and Freedman, that any sort of deterrence works only because of the fear that things will get out of control. In my view, the proposals of both Colin Gray and William O'Brien are virtually indistinguishable from MAD. If actually carried out, both seem certain to produce a form of spasmodic or indiscriminate response and counterresponse that would be impossible to distinguish from the failure of MAD. The danger of both proposals is increased by the fact that both Gray's decapitation strategies and O'Brien's limited-war proposals depend on the deployment of first-strike-capable weapons—a sure formula for making deterrence less stable. Therefore, neither of them, in my view, really represents the desired transformation of our political/military circumstances in accord with the Augustinian imperative. Both leave the situation of distress much as it was.

The case of Wohlstetter is more complex. His statement that we must "face up to evasions making 'murder respectable' in such chaste phrases as 'countervalue attacks'" seems clearly to rule out O'Brien's rather expansive version of the nature of limited war.[42] His view that Soviet leaders value military power as much as they do civilian populations has analogies with Colin Gray's emphasis on the value of political control in the Soviet system, a valuation that leads Gray to think that threat of decapitation will be such a strong deterrent to Soviet adventures. Wohlstetter does not seem to advocate this approach, but neither does he rule it out. His real concern is that MAD not only is an immoral strategy but is actually incredible as a deterrent, because it rests on an insane threat to commit suicide. His desire to develop a limited-war strategy as an alternative to MAD is supported by both moral and political reason. In this he is on solid Augustinian ground.

One of the chief problems with his approach, however, is his tendency to identify "minimum deterrence" with MAD. This use of language, which is not Wohlstetter's creation, introduces a conceptual confusion into the contemporary debate. It suggests that *increases in our war-fighting capacity* necessarily move us away from the specter of mutual destruction. This is not necessarily so. In fact, it may have the opposite effect, depending on *what kind* of war-fighting capacities are developed. For example, the Scowcroft commission proposed the development and deployment of both the MX and single-warhead mobile missiles. These two systems are both war-fighting weapons, designed for deterrence through a credible threat. But the threat posed by the two weapons to an adversary is significantly different. In my view, the replacement of MIRVed Minuteman missiles with the single-warhead mobile missile would be a step toward a "more minimal" deterrent than the one we now have, whereas MX is a move toward a "more maximal" one, if *minimal* and *maximal* are used to refer to the dangers they present. This would still entail a severe danger that nuclear war could occur. But the danger would be less than under the present arrangement and much less than in the world of vulnerable first-strike weapons we are moving into. Wohlstetter's polemic against minimal deterrence needs to be refined by distinctions like these. One can also ask: do not such distinctions enable us to imagine ways that large numbers of currently deployed nuclear weapons in our supposedly minimal deterrent could be replaced by conventional forces, including conventionally armed precision-guided missiles. Wohlstetter himself suggests this, but I would be much happier if he had more carefully explored the possible meanings of minimal deterrence before accepting the convention of identifying the idea with MAD. Such an exploration could open the way for us to seize opportunities to transform the grossly murderous logic of present strategy into something that is at least less murderous if not truly pacific.

In my opinion, this is the avenue that the U.S. Catholic bishops have taken in the Pastoral Letter *The Challenge of Peace*. This is not the place for a detailed analysis of this complex document.[43] One point, however, is notable in the context of this discussion. The U.S. bishops do not advocate minimal deterrence in the sense presupposed by Wohlstetter—that is, MAD. Indeed, they oppose it vigorously: "it is not morally acceptable to intend to kill the innocent as part of a strategy of deterring nuclear war."[44] At the same time they argue against forms of deterrence that will increase the danger of nuclear war or that target military forces in ways that are likely to produce disproportionate collateral damage:

> While we welcome any effort to protect civilian populations, we do not want to legitimize or encourage moves which extend deterrence beyond the specific objectives of preventing the use of nuclear weapons or other actions which could lead directly to a nuclear exchange.[45]

With these criteria as background, they consider specific alternatives to MAD and their implications for the quest for the goals of nuclear war prevention and the defense of justice and human rights.

Their specific conclusions are an attempt to direct policy into avenues that are less dangerous than some of the war-fighting strategies being proposed (for example, that of Colin Gray); less open-ended than others (for example, those of Wohlstetter); and less inconsistent with just war norms than a third type of limited-war doctrine (for example, those of O'Brien). The conclusions they draw are largely negative: no "hard-target kill weapons, no protracted war scenarios, no quest for superiority, no systems which make disarmament more difficult to achieve."[46] They also make a number of positive recommendations, largely in the areas of the need for negotiated arms control treaties; removal of nuclear forces from forward-based positions in Europe; and improved command, control, and communication systems.[47]

Some have argued that the U.S. bishops have moved to a level of specificity that goes beyond their competence as moral teachers in making recommendations of this sort. On the contrary, attending to the actual proposals being made today is really the *only* way to reach conclusions about the relation of morality to nuclear strategy. To argue against this level of specificity in addressing nuclear questions would be analogous to saying that moral teachers should speak about the morality of medicine but should never discuss any specific medical procedure. This would be absurd, for there is no such thing as the morality of medicine as such. One could say, of course, that if there had never been a fall from grace by Adam and Eve, there would be no sickness and death in our world, as Genesis, St. Paul, and the Christian tradition have long taught. But in a fallen and divided world, sickness exists, doctors are needed, and ethical perspectives on their practice are a legitimate concern of theologians, philosophers, and bishops, not just of the physicians themselves. The same can be said of the ethics of warfare. It depends on an analysis of the pathways that are open to us for healing political conflict and avoiding actions that make the illness worse.

In my view, the U.S. bishops have done as good a job as anyone has in synthesizing the religious, philosophical, political, and military dimensions of the nuclear issue. There are, however, limits to their achievement. In particular, I think more needs to be said about defensive systems and the various types of weapons proposed as replacements for MIRVed missiles. Can any of these serve the purposes of minimal deterrence as the term has been redefined here—that is, as minimally dangerous. Despite these limits, the U.S. bishops' letter serves as an example of moral reasoning that seeks to avoid the self-contradiction of the "ethics of distress." As good practitioners of Augustinian moral theory, they seek to transform and redeem a broken polis by seizing those opportunities for peace, order, and justice that history has given us today. Although their work hardly closes the debate, it does provide a model for avoiding some of the dead ends into which we have wandered.

Notes

1. "The French Bishops' Statement: Winning Peace," *Origins* 13, no. 26 (December 8, 1983):442, col. 3.
2. Ibid., p. 443, col. 2.
3. Ibid., p. 443, col. 2.
4. Ibid.
5. Ibid., note 20.
6. Joint Pastoral Letter of the German Bishops, *Out of Justice, Peace* (Dublin: Irish Messenger Publications, 1983), p. 61.
7. Ibid., p. 39.
8. Ibid., p. 61.
9. Ibid., p. 61.
10. Ibid., pp. 61–62.
11. Thomas Aquinas, *Summa Theologiae,* Ia IIae q.91, art. 2.
12. Michael Walzer, *Just and Unjust Wars* (New York: Basic Books, 1977), p. 129.

13. Ibid., p. 153.

14. Ibid., p. 133.

15. Ibid., p. 252.

16. Ibid., p. 260.

17. Ibid., p. 323.

18. Ibid., p. 324.

19. See, for example, the recent study by Stephen E. Lammers "Area Bombing in World War II: The Argument of Michael Walzer," *Journal of Religious Ethics* 111(1983): 96–113.

20. John C. Ford, S.J., "The Morality of Obliteration Bombing," *Theological Studies* 5(1944):268.

21. Lawrence Freedman, *The Evolution of Nuclear Strategy* (New York: St. Martins Press, 1981), p. 3ff.

22. For a helpful discussion of some of the dimensions of this qualitative transition, see Michael Howard, "Bombing and the Bomb," in his *Studies in War and Peace* (New York: Viking Press, 1971), pp. 141–153.

23. Lammers, op. cit., p. 104.

24. Walzer, *Just and Unjust Wars*, p. 272.

25. Ibid., p. 274.

26. Ibid., p. 282.

27. Alasdair MacIntyre, *After Virtue: A Study in Moral Theory* (Notre Dame, Ind.: University of Notre Dame Press, 1981), p. 6.

28. Ibid., pp. 104–105.

29. Ibid., pp. 244–245.

30. See Stanley Hauerwas, "On Surviving Justly: An Ethical Analysis of Nuclear Disarmament," in Jill Raitt, ed., *Religious Conscience and Nuclear Warfare*, the 1982 Paine Lectures in Religion, privately printed by the University of Missouri–Columbia, p. 19.

31. For a helpful discussion of this, see Ronald Green, *Religious Reason: The Rational and Moral Basis of Religious Belief* (New York: Oxford University Press, 1978), chap. 3.

32. See Hauerwas, *A Community of Character* (Notre Dame: University of Notre Dame Press, 1981), p. 101.

33. Ibid., p. 106.

34. See Paul Ramsey, *War and the Christian Conscience: How Shall Modern War Be Conducted Justly?* (Durham, N.C.: Duke University Press, 1961), chaps. 2, 3.

35. Walzer, *Just and Unjust Wars*, p. 278.

36. Freedman, *Evolution of Nuclear Strategy*, p. 400.

37. Stanley Hoffmann, "Le cri d'alarme de l'église américaine," *Le monde*, November 19, 1983, p. 1.

38. David Hollenbach, S.J., *Nuclear Ethics: A Christian Moral Argument* (New York: Paulist Press, 1983), pp. 73–77.

39. See, most recently, Wohlstetter's reply to his critics in "Morality and Deterrence: Wohlstetter and Critics," *Commentary*, December 1983, pp. 13–22.

40. See Colin Gray and Keith Payne, "Victory is Possible," *Foreign Policy* 39 (Summer 1980):14–27.

41. William V. O'Brien, *The Conduct of Just and Limited War* (New York: Praeger, 1981), p. 135.

42. Albert Wohlstetter, "Optimal Ways to Confuse Ourselves," *Foreign Policy* 20(Autumn 1975):198.

43. For several views of it, see Philip J. Murnion, ed., *Catholics and Nuclear War: A Commentary on "The Challenge of Peace," The U.S. Catholic Bishops' Pastoral Letter on War and Peace* (New York: Crossroad, 1983); and Michael Novak, *Moral Clarity in the Nuclear Age* (Nashville, Tenn.: Thomas Nelson, 1983).

44. National Conference of Catholic Bishops, *The Challenge of Peace: God's Promise and Our Response* (Washington, D.C.: United States Catholic Conference, 1983), no. 178.

45. Ibid., no. 185.

46. Ibid., nos. 188–190.

47. Ibid., no. 191.

3
Threats, Values, and Defense: Does the Defense of Values by Force Remain a Moral Possibility?

James Turner Johnson
Rutgers University

The Just War Tradition

Two deep and broad streams of moral reflection on war run through Western history. These streams have their thematic origin in a single fundamental question: Is it ever morally allowable to employ force in the protection and preservation of values? The moral tradition of pacifism has resulted from a negative response to this question, given in various ways under various historical circumstances. A positive answer, given in ways no less conditioned by historical circumstances yet with a similar depth of underlying consistency and wholeness, has produced the other moral tradition on force and violence, which it is both convenient and proper to call by a familiar name: *just war tradition.* We should note two characteristic facts about this tradition.

First, it is a moral response to the question of value and force that is not only historically deep but is a product of reflection and action across the whole breadth of this culture's experience. It is not a moral doctrine in the narrow sense, reflecting the attitudes only of those sectors of the culture, like religion, often conceived as having a specialized function of moralizing cut off from the rest of human existence. To be sure, this tradition has often found expression in church law and theological reflection; yet it also appears in codifications and theories of international law, in military manuals on how rightly to conduct war, and—as Michael Walzer has shown in *Just and Unjust Wars*—in the judgments and reactions of common people.[1] In short, this tradition encapsulates something of how we in this culture respond morally to the question of protection of value by force. It is not the only response—pacifist rejection of force parallels it through history—but it is a fundamental one, revealing how we characteristically think

From "Threats, Values, and Defense: Does the Defense of Values by Force Remain a Moral Possibility?" by James Turner Johnson, *Parameters* (Spring 1985). Reprinted with permission.

about morality and war and defining the terms for our reflections in new or changing circumstances.

The second characteristic fact about just war tradition is that it preserves not one but two kinds of moral response to the question of value and force: limitation always accompanies justification. The response that says, yes, here are some conditions in which it is morally right to use force to protect value, goes on to set limits to what may rightly be done toward that end. This second element in the response is determined by the nature of the value or values to be protected; thus the need for limitation is built into the need to protect value as a necessary correlate. This means in general that unlimited or even disproportionately large amounts of force are not what is justified when the use of force to protect values is itself justified. Just war tradition, as recognized by such contemporary commentators as Paul Ramsey, William V. O'Brien, and Walzer, is a moral tradition of justifiable and limited war.[2] What has come to be known as the *jus ad bellum* has to do with the question of justification; that of limitation is addressed by the *jus in bello*. These are interconnected areas, but the priority, logical as well as historical, is with the former: only after the fundamental question is answered about the moral justification of employing force to protect values does the second question, about the morally requisite limits governing the use of that force, arise in turn. Problems arising in the *jus in bello* context may cause us to want to reflect further about the nature of the values we hold, the threat against them, and the means we may use to defend them; yet such further reflection means only that we must again enter the arena of the "war decision," the *jus ad bellum*.[3]

It is often claimed that the development of nuclear weapons has made this traditional way of thinking about morality and war obsolete and irrelevant.[4] From what I have said, it should be clear that I think this is not the case. Indeed, my claim is that we naturally think in the same terms that are encountered in the tradition, whether we want to or not. A pacifist critic like James Douglass employs one part of the tradition to reject the whole of it.[5] No sooner has another critic, Stanley Hoffmann, rejected it than he reinvents it point by point.[6] Such phenomena should be instructive. We would do well not to repudiate this tradition of moral reflection from the past; to do so merely isolates us from the wisdom of others surely no less morally or intellectually acute than we—others who in their own historical contexts have faced problems analogous to our own about whether and how to employ force in the defense of values. It is thus better to use this tradition consciously—trying to learn from it and with it, even in the nuclear age—than to forget it and subsequently have to reinvent it.

Defense of Values by Force as a Moral Possibility

To protect and preserve values is the only justifying cause for the use of force that is admitted in Western moral tradition. Classically, the use of force in response to a threat to values was justified in four ways: to protect the innocent, to recover something wrongly taken, to punish evil, and to defend against a wrongful attack in progress. Let us look briefly at each of these and inquire what we may derive from them in our present context.

Defense of the innocent is an idea that can be traced at least as far as Augustine in Christian thought.[7] It also has a history in military traditions back through the code of chivalry into the customs of premedieval Germanic societies.[8] By itself it implies an interventionist model of the justified use of military force and, more broadly, of national power. This not only flies in the face of much contemporary moralizing but also challenges such neoisolationists as Laurence Beilenson who argue for a retreat from foreign involvement by this country and the creation of a new "fortress America."[9] It is also at odds with the individualistic ethics fostered domestically in our society with the demise of close ties of community, an ethic that implies "not getting involved" perhaps even in extreme cases like mugging or rape.[10] Granted that it is extremely dangerous to throw military power around in a world that has the capability of destroying itself by global war; granted also that national *hubris*, if unrestrained, could use defense of others as an unwarranted excuse for a new round of imperialistic conquests;[11] there still, I submit, remain in the contemporary world cases in which limited and proportionate use of force may be the appropriate means to preserve the value referred to in the phrase "defense of the innocent." The case of Grenada was not morally the same as that of Afghanistan; intervention in Hungary by the West at the time of the 1956 uprising would not have been the moral equivalent of the Soviet invasion that did in fact occur; intervention in Uganda by neighboring Tanzania to depose Idi Amin and put an end to his bloodthirsty and self-aggrandizing rule was not the same as would have been an invasion aimed simply at increasing Tanzanian territory. Clearly, not every case where the rights of innocent persons need to be protected should become an occasion for military intervention; the case of Hungary offers a clear instance when following out this line of implication from just war tradition to the exclusion of other considerations would have led to the wrong decision. But my point is that the moral distinctions assumed by the classical formulation of just war tradition still remain, and the necessity to tread warily (which was no less an obligation in any previous age of human history) does not remove either the moral outrage that comes from violation of the innocent,[12] the obligation to prevent or stop such violation if at all possible,[13] or the possibility that among all the means available, military ones may be the best.

The recovery of something wrongly taken is a necessary counterpart to the idea of defense against aggression in progress.[14] If such after-the-fact reaction were not allowed, the result would be that expansion or other aggressive acts would, if speedy and effective, be tacitly accepted. There must be, of course, some consistent and agreed-on means of identifying what belongs to one society or one polity and what to another; but even in the absence of complete consensus on this, it is not necessary to reduce everything to a matter of different ideological or national perspective, so that what is one's own is simply whatever one says is one's own. The Falklands conflict provides an instructive contemporary example of the relevance of such reflection. The Argentine claim to the islands was not without some merit, but this was hardly of sufficient value to justify military invasion and occupation against the will of the inhabitants. The principle of self-determination, often cited to protect weak nations against military and other forms of aggression by stronger ones, though not the only meaningful principle here, was certainly violated by Argentina's action. If only defense against an aggression in progress were justified, then Britain and the British inhabitants of the islands would have had no recourse, after the failure of the intensively pursued negotiations, but to accept the newly established status quo of Argentine military rule. The allowance of after-the-fact use of force to regain something wrongly taken is the source of moral justification for Britain's military actions in the Falklands war.

The punishment of evil is, in my judgment, the least useful of the classic formulations of just cause in the present context.[15] One reason for this is the prevalence of ideological divisions in the contemporary world. This line of justification for the use of force to protect value is all too easily changed into a justification for ideological warfare by one's own "forces of light" against the "forces of darkness" with their different ideological beliefs. This problem is not as acute among the superpowers as it once was, although it still exists and might still be fanned back to its former heat; more pressing immediate instances are to be found in the conflicts of the Middle East and Northern Ireland. Yet classically the punishment of differences of *belief* was not what was implied by this idea of just cause; what was to be punished was the kind of *action* identified in the other three kinds of justifying cause.[16]

What is unique to this concept of punishment taken alone is that it implicitly allows going beyond what these other concepts justify to further action aimed at insuring that the same thing does not happen again. Because such an allowance can easily be pushed too far, we should be cautious in citing this reason to justify force for the protection of value in the present age. Nuclear deterrence depends on the threat of punishment above all else; yet the use of current types of strategic nuclear weapons kept for deterrence purposes could itself threaten the very values such use would ostensibly seek to preserve. This is, of course, the heart of the nuclear dilemma, and I will return to it later. For now, my only point is that the justification of force as punishment for wrong done must not be allowed to become isolated from the general question of the protection of value or from the other justifying moral reasons for the use of force to protect value. Yet even with this caveat, if the goal of permitted military action is, as another part of just war tradition insists, the end of peace, then it is not proper to rule out the morality of punishment entirely.

If we had begun with twentieth-century international law and some other aspects of contemporary moral, political, and legal thought, we would have started with the justification of *defense against aggression in progress*—and perhaps got no further.[17] By keeping this classic idea of justifying cause for the use of force until last, I mean to symbolize that this idea is not as fundamental over the whole history of Western moral reflection on war as it has become in contemporary thought. Indeed, when we set this justification for the use of force alongside the others just identified and discussed, we discover that the right of self-defense is not in fact a moral absolute. One may oneself be in the wrong in a particular conflict. Rather than to exalt one's own righteousness and well-being over that of others, the better moral course is to deflate somewhat this allowance of self-defense to more appropriate proportions alongside the other *jus ad bellum* provisions.

In short, self-defense is not an absolute right, and the means of self-defense may therefore not be unlimited; there are other values to consider than the integrity of the self or one's own national polity. It is this consideration from just war tradition that points to the wrongness of schemes of national defense based on a threat of catastrophic annihilation, even if that threat is mutual. The irony of the present situation is that the very legal and moral efforts that attempt to restrict the incidence of the use of force by allowing only its defensive use—I am thinking of the Kellogg-Briand Pact of 1928 and Article 2 of the United Nations Charter, as well as current ostensibly moral arguments that the more terrible the deterrent threat, the less likelihood there will be of war—have the effect of insuring that should war come, despite these efforts, it will be of the most immoral and value-destructive kind attainable through military technology. That is, concentrating solely on the rightness of defense against aggression, though admittedly a moral justification for the use of force, has led us to think of strategic nuclear deterrence by threat of catastrophe as morally right, while ruling out lesser levels of force as possible responses to threats to value, even when these latter are more justifiable from the broader perspectives of just war tradition.[18]

In short, we would do well to remember what many in our present debate have either forgotten or systematically ignored: that circumstances may come into being in human history in which the use of force, at appropriate levels and discriminatingly directed, may be the morally preferable means for the protection and preservation of values. In forgetting or ignoring this, sometimes in the name of ostensibly moral considerations, those who would reject such a use of force are in fact choosing a less moral course than the one historically given form in the tradition that says that just war must also be limited war.

The Question of Values

May values ever be defended by forceful means? Answering this question requires us to think, first, about the nature of the values to be protected and the interrelation among values. We do this normally not by reflection but by affirmation. Hence the following from John Stuart Mill:

> War is an ugly thing, but not the ugliest of things. The decayed and degraded state of moral and patriotic feeling which thinks nothing *worth* a war, is worse. ... A man who has nothing which he cares about more than he does about his personal safety is a miserable creature who has no chance of being free, unless made and kept so by the existing of better men than himself.[19]

Mill in this context alludes to the values from which he speaks, but the salient fact about this statement is his ranking of relative values. He does not deny the value of personal safety; yet it is not for him the *highest* value. He does not deny the ugliness of war; he only affirms that in the ranking of priorities it is not the *worst* evil. Mill was, of course, a utilitarian in ethics; yet such priority ranking of values is not a feature unique to utilitarianism and to be dismissed by all nonutilitarians. Such ranking is indeed a feature of *any* ethic, for the service of one value often conflicts with the service of another, and there must be some way of deciding among them. Consider the following from Erasmus, a figure who was anything but a utilitarian:

> Think ... of all the crimes that are committed with war as a pretext, while "good lawes fall silent amid the clash of arms"—all the instances of sack and sacrilege, rape, and other shameful acts, such as one hesitates even to name. And even when the war is over, this moral corruption is bound to linger for many years. Now assess for me the cost—a cost so great that, even if you win the war, you will lose much more than you gain. Indeed, what realm ... can be weighed against the life, the blood, of so many thousand men?[20]

This passage is replete with priority ranking of values. Erasmus begins by identifying war rhetorically with criminal activity, thus locating it at the bottom of the value scale. He then turns explicitly to proportional counting of relative costs: "even if you win the war, you will lose much more than you gain"; "what realm ... can be weighed against the life, the blood, of so many thousand men?" Such comparative weighting of goods is as central to the ethics of Erasmian humanism as it is to Mill's utilitarianism; indeed, it appears as a core feature of moral argument as such. Ultimately, there is no way to get to the truth or falsity of various perceptions of value. This is why, finally, there can be no real argument between absolute pacifists, who reject all possibility of the use of force to protect value, and those who accept some possibility of such use of force.[21] But this is not a problem in most of the current defense debate, which is a debate over ranking of values among persons who weight their values as differently as do Mill and Erasmus.

Recognizing values where they exist and sorting them according to priorities where there are conflicts among them is the function of moral agency, an art learned in one's community of moral discourse.[22] Without going into a full theory of moral agency, which is far beyond the scope of this chapter, the most we can say here is that affirmations like those of Mill and Erasmus allow us to glimpse the structure of relative values held by each participant in a moral debate and to relate those structures of value both to a larger normative conception of common life and to our own personal rankings of value. For our present purposes this is enough.

One interesting thing about Erasmus and Mill on war is how contemporary they sound; by thinking about them, we may learn something about ourselves. Erasmus counted costs both great and small in his rejection of war. A glimpse of the latter appears elsewhere in the letter quoted earlier, where he complains that preparations for war have dried up the sources of patronage on which he depended for support.[23] This was purely personal injury, but the complaint is not unlike contemporary arguments against military spending as subtracting from resources available for feeding the hungry, healing the sick and—in direct continuity with Erasmus—supporting humanistic scholarship. The value ranking is obvious.

The real meat of Erasmus' objection to war is found, however, in his idealistic vision of world community, which he conceived as both good in itself beyond the goods of any national community and achievable by the right kind of human cooperative interaction.[24] Again, this way of thinking has parallels in current debate, where rejection of force to protect values associated with the nation-state is coupled to a new vision of world order in which the nation-state system has no place.[25] The preservation of peace among nations, both in Erasmus and in contemporary debate, appears as the highest instrumental value, on which the maintenance of all other values depends. This is a different sort of reasoning from that of the pacifism of absolute principle; even the latter, however, may engage in priority ranking, as in these words of Mennonite theologian John Howard Yoder: " 'Thou shalt not kill' . . . is an absolute . . . immeasurably more human, more personalistic, more genuinely responsible than the competitive absolute, 'Thou shalt not let Uncle Sam down' or 'Thou shalt fight for freedom' or 'Never give up the ship.' "[26] What we may note here is the tendency to diminish rhetorically the values being downgraded; similarly, Erasmus in all his works against war represents war-making as nothing more than the result of frivolous and misguided rivalry among sovereigns. War, Yoder and Erasmus alike suggest, may never be anything more than frivolous and misguided; the possibility that it might be an instrumental means of protecting value is dismissed out of hand. Contemporary examples of such reasoning abound, centering around the dismissal of any form of military preparedness as "militarism" and rejection of "war-fighting" strategic planning as opposed to deterrence strategy.[27]

The influence of Erasmian humanistic pacifism on contemporary debate runs deep, and I cannot here chart its full extent, but one more example of this presence must be noted for what it is. Erasmus rejects war as the *summum malum*, assimilating it to criminality; in contemporary debate the counterpart is the assimilation of all war to the evil of castastrophic nuclear holocaust. Erasmus cites "sack, sacrilege, and rape"; Jonathan Schell, in the idiom of our own age, cites "the biologic effects of ultraviolet radiation with emphasis on the skin,"[28] while piling up evidence of "the likely consequences of a holocaust for the earth"[29]—as if anyone had to be reminded that a holocaust is, by definition, evil.

It should be clear that Erasmus, Schell, and Yoder are simply moving in a different sphere from Mill and the main line of just war thinking (which I also share). It is simply impossible, given the assimilation of war to criminality and holocaust, for Erasmus and Schell to share Mill's judgment that "[w]ar is an ugly thing, but not the ugliest of things." No more could Yoder, for whom the use of force is trivialized into the maxim, "Never give up the ship," or those who, like Erasmus, regard war as the result of frivolous self-assertion by political leaders or, in the current phrase, "militarism." Between these and the position represented by Mill there would seem to be an impassible gulf. Yet it is possible at least to see across that gulf, if not to bridge or remove it. And from the perspective of just war tradition, there is something fundamentally wrong with the perception of value found on the other side.

First, although there is no need to deny the charm of an idealistic vision of world community, such a conception of an ideal that is not yet a reality (and may never become one) should not subtract from the quite genuine value to be found in the nation-state system or, more particularly, in a national community like our own. Historically, the roots of the nation-state system lie in the need to organize human affairs so as to minimize conflict while preserving the unique cultural identities of different peoples. It can be argued plausibly that it still fulfills these functions—imperfectly, to be sure, but with nothing better currently at hand. Likewise, the personal security, justice, freedom, and domestic peace provided in a liberal democratic nation-state like the United States are not to be dismissed lightly by reference to a utopian vision in which these and other values would all be present in greater measure. We must always, as moral beings, measure reality against our ideals; yet to reject the penultimate goods secured by the real because they do not measure up to the ultimate goods envisioned in the ideal is to ensure the loss of even the penultimate goods that we now enjoy. The ultimate would certainly be better; yet in the meantime, we have the obligation to hold as fast as possible to the value at hand, even though doing so must inevitably incur costs. A positive response to the original just war question recognizes this, as did Mill; Erasmus and his contemporary idealistic descendants did not.

Second, if force is to be used to protect values, it is not trivia that are to be protected but values of fundamental worth. Mill's allusion to the value of "being free" is on a quite different level from Yoder's maxim, "Never give up the ship," or Erasmus' collapsing of all reasons for war into the venality of princes. Equally, I believe, not to be reduced to the trivial or frivolous is Walzer's perception, expressed throughout *Just and Unjust Wars*, that the justification for fighting lies in the recognition of evil and revulsion against it.[30] Walzer's negative way of putting the matter is important for another reason: it reminds us that we do not have to be able to give an extensive and comprehensive listing of all values that may be protected and in what ranking in order to know *that there are* such values; they will be apparent when they are violated or threatened with violation.

Third, knowing that some wars have resulted from the aggressively self-assertive characters of rulers does not mean that war may never be anything else. It is doubtful that Erasmus was right even about the rulers of his own time. In our own age we must surely make a distinction between, for example, the war made by Hitler and that made by Churchill; nor is it particularly useful to reduce the rise and fall of relations between the United States and the Soviet Union to the personalities of a Carter and a Brezhnev, Gorbachev and a Reagan. A manichaean dismissal of everything military as "militaristic" is also an uncalled for reductionism that makes military preparedness itself an evil, not an instrument for good or ill in ways to be determined by human choices.

Finally, neither in Erasmus' time nor in our own is it right to represent war as the irreducible *summum malum*. I have already suggested why I think Erasmus was wrong in making this claim; more important for our current context is the wrongness of assimilating all contemporary war to catastrophic nuclear war. Let us dwell on this for a moment.

Who could want a nuclear holocaust? Yet the effort to avoid such a catastrophe is not itself justification for rejection of the possibility that lower levels of force may justifiably be employed to protect value. This is, nonetheless, the clear import of the argument when limited conventional war is collapsed into limited nuclear war by reference to the threat of escalation and when nuclear war of any extent is collapsed into catastrophic holocaust on a global scale.[31] Such an argument has the effect of making any contemporary advocate of the use of force to protect values an advocate instead of the total destruction of humankind or even of all life on earth. It should hardly need to be said that such rhetorical hyperbole is unjustified; no one who argues from just war tradition, with its strong emphasis on counting the costs and estimating the probability of success of any projected military action, should be represented as guilty of befriending the idea of nuclear holocaust.

Yet this collapsing of categories is also wrong historically. War in the nuclear age has not been global catastrophe but a continuation of conventional warfare limited in one or several ways—by geography, goals, targets, means. This arena of contemporary limited warfare is one in which traditional moral categories for judging war are very much at home, as such different writers as William V. O'Brien and Michael Walzer have, in their respective ways, both recognized. The issue, then, is not of the prohibition of all means of defense in the nuclear age, because the assimilation of all contemporary war to the *summum malum* of nuclear holocaust is invalid; it is, rather, the perennial question of when and how force may be used for the defense of values.[32] We will return to this question later.

The Problem of Threats to Values

For there to be a need to defend values, there must be a threat to those values. To anyone with a modicum of objectivity, however, it must be apparent that in the current defense debate there is no agreement about the nature of the threat, and so there can be little hope of agreement about the means of preserving values in the face of the menace identified. Speaking broadly, I find in the present debate three distinct identifications of the threat to values that must be met. For some, there is no danger worth mentioning beyond that of nuclear holocaust, which is defined as threatening everything that is of value. For others the principal challenge to the values that matter for them is the arms race as such, with its diversion of resources to military ends and a perceived tranformation of values toward those of militarism. Finally, a third perspective identifies the principal threat to values in the rivalry between the United States and the Soviet Union, West and East, two different and competing social, economic, political, and moral systems. This last is the most easily identifiable in terms of traditional interstate political analysis and in terms of just war tradition. All three perspectives have many forms and are somewhat fluid, so that in painting them with broad strokes of the brush I cannot render the inner details of each. Yet the broadly painted pictures of these different perspectives are themselves interesting morally, and it is on these that I will focus in this brief context.

Let us begin by exploring what is distinctive about each of the first two positions I have identified. These clearly overlap, but their emphases are importantly different, as are their respective histories and implicit value commitments. One way of recognizing this quickly is by noting that the anti–nuclear-holocaust position can be expressed in a commitment to increased military spending for a strengthened deterrent, quite contrary to the anti–arms race position, which finds typical expression in the nuclear freeze movement and support for disarmament programs. Similarly, part of the historical case for tactical and theater nuclear weapons has been that they cost less to provide than equivalent conventional forces, thus tending to free economic and manpower resources for nonmilitary purposes; yet many from the anti–nuclear-holocaust position view such war-fighting weapons as inherently destabilizing and dangerously likely to lead to catastrophic nuclear war.[33] Within the anti–nuclear-holocaust position, opposition to the arms race and military spending is but an instrumentality, whereas within the anti–arms race position opposition to nuclear arms is only an instrumentality. When there is convergence between these two positions (as there has been in the most recent stage of the defense debate), it is a mixed marriage that is as likely to end in divorce as in conversion of one or both partners.

These two positions also have different historical and ideological roots. The anti–nuclear-holocaust position is, of course, a product of the nuclear age and specifically of the period in which the United States and the Soviet Union have practiced strategic nuclear deterrence against each other. It is thus the child of nuclear deterrence theory and finds a characteristic expression in one such theory, the deterrence-only position. Clearly, however, there has been a transformation of values from parent to offspring. Thus when Philip Green wrote *Deadly Logic* in the mid-1960s, he cited "resistence to Communism" as the fundamental "ethical root of deterrence theory,"[34] but the ethical root of the contemporary deterrence-only position is the perception of *nuclear warfare*, not the menace to values posed by a totalitarian political system, as the evil to be avoided by the possession of a nuclear deterrent.[35]

The historical roots of the anti–arms race position are at least a century old; they lie in opposition to the increasing practice in nineteenth-century European states of sustaining a standing army built up by universal or nearly universal conscription, and in opposition to the social and economic costs of sustaining such armies. Religious groups have been the chief enunciators of this position and they are so today. A direct line runs between the *Postulata* on war prepared for Vatican Council I in 1870, which deplored the "intolerable burden" of defense spending and the social costs of "huge standing and conscript armies,"[36] and the 1983 pastoral of the U.S. Catholic bishops with its deploring of the "economic distortion of priorities" due to the "billions readily spent for destructive instruments,"[37] or, to take a Protestant example, the 1980 statement on the arms race by the Reformed Church in America decrying "the devastating social and personal consequences of the arms race."[38] Two ethical roots of this position are visible in the sources cited: an opposition to war and weapons as contrary to the biblical vision of peace, and an identification with the needs of the poor as best expressing Christian conformity to Christ. Both themes have secular counterparts in contemporary debate, and the first obviously parallels the utopian vision of Erasmian humanism.

If nuclear holocaust is the danger against which values must be protected, then deterrence theory is one rational response, but so would be general nuclear disarmament. If the arms race itself is the menace to values that must be defended against, then a freeze on military expenditures followed by a general scaling down of military establishments is the clear implication. Both these perspectives on the contemporary threat to values incorporate truths about the present historical situation; both are rooted in important perceptions of moral value; each offers, in its own way, a response to the problem of threat to values as it perceives that threat. Yet neither of these perspectives is really about the question with which we began this chapter, the fundamental question that is the root of our moral tradition on war: When and how may force justifiably be employed for the defense of values? Rather than approaching seriously the problem of possible moral justification of force, each of these perspectives has, in its own way, *defined that possibility out of existence* in the search for a general rejection of the use of force as a moral option in the contemporary age. The reason is that neither of these perspectives is able to comprehend the possibility of significant threats to value alongside the one on which each of them is fixed.

The problem, however, is that what is thus ignored does not for this reason cease to exist. International rivalries persist, as they did in the prenuclear era;

ideologies and realistic perceptions of national interest continue to influence the actions of nations, and these actions are often played out through projections of force. Terrorism, civil war, and international war continue to be plain realities of our present era, and there is no reason to suppose either that aggression will no longer take place in human history or that it can effectively be opposed by means other than military ones.[39] Indeed, prospective victims of aggression today might reflect with Clausewitz: "The aggressor is always peace-loving; he would prefer to take over our country unopposed."[40] The just war perspective, the third perspective in the contemporary debate, views the problem of threats to value in this light, in continuity with the main line of statecraft over history, and conceives the problem of defense against such threats also in terms continuous with that historical experience.

Let it be clear: the rivalry between the Soviet Union and the United States is not the only source of danger to American values; yet it would be blindness to wish away the existence of this rivalry, which is rooted in more than common possession of mutual annihilative power; more than competing ideologies; more than national interest; more than global competition for friends, allies, and trading partners—and yet in all of these. And this rivalry is more than simply a product of adverse perceptions; it is real. Where it takes military form, as for example most unambiguously along the NATO–Warsaw Pact border, thinking about the menace to values must go beyond efforts to avoid catastrophic nuclear war and to end the arms race to include efforts to define and mount a credible, effective, and moral defense against the particular military threat manifest there.

At the same time, however, potential military defense of values is not limited to this confrontation or to the global East–West rivalry; it may be a matter of attempting to secure a weak Third World nation against the power of a nearby predator, of deterring or responding to terrorist attacks, or of maintaining the traffic of oil tankers through the Strait of Hormuz. All these possible uses of force involve the defense of value; all are, in general terms, the kind of resort to force regarded as justified in just war tradition. This third perspective on the threat to values, then, is the one I wish to address in my concluding section.

The Problem of Defense against Threats to Value

I wish now to return to a reflection with which this chapter began—that in general the nature of values to be protected and the threats against them are such that unlimited or even disproportionate amounts of force are not what is justified when the use of force to defend values is justified. When defense of values by force appears to require transgressing the boundaries set by the *jus in bello* concepts of proportionality and discrimination, this necessitates that we look again to see whether this is an occasion when the defense of values by force is morally justified. The answer may be no; yet it may also be yes, and this is the possibility I wish to explore in this section.

In fact there are two directions of thought, not one, that lead toward a renewal of the justification of value protection by force in such a situation. The first drives toward restructuring the application of force and beyond that to creating new kinds of force capabilities suited to limited application in the defense of value. The second leads into the far more dangerous consideration of whether values may ever be protected by means that themselves violate important values. I will discuss these in turn.

Clausewitz in his time understood well the difference between "absolute war"—war pushed to the limits of the destructive capacities of the belligerents—and "real" wars carried on by less than absolute means for limited purposes as an extension of politics. In the twentieth century many others have forgotten or ignored this difference.[41] Typically, the values threatened by war are less than ultimate, and so the threat; it is wrong to defend these values against such challenges by totalistic means disproportionate to both the values to be defended and the evil that menaces them. When we add that total war implies also the indiscriminate targeting of noncombatants, a violation of the fundamental idea of protection of the innocent, the indictment of such use of force in response to threats against values grows yet more damning.

Nevertheless, the problem of limitation of force in contemporary warfare is different from that which existed earlier. Today limitation must be accomplished first and foremost by human choice; in previous ages such limitation was also a product of the nature of weapons available, the restraints imposed by the seasons of the year, and the economic and social bases on which war was waged. Limitation in the use of force was relatively easy when the means were battle-axes or smooth-bore muskets, when three-quarters of the year was closed to military actions, and when soldiers were themselves units of economic production who could not be in arms year round. Today the problem is more complex: the structuring of force capabilities to defend against possible menaces to value must at the same time provide an effective deterrent and an effective means of active defense while still honoring the moral identity manifest in the society or culture in which the threatened values are known and maintained. Among the recent nuclear strategies that did not meet this dual test is massive retaliation, conceived as a strategy for use, since it allowed so-called brush-fire wars to erupt unchecked and threatened disproportionate and indiscriminate nuclear devastation as a response to aggression on a much lower scale. Nor does contemporary mutual assured destruction doctrine, for reasons already given. But the issue is not simply one of the disproportionateness of nuclear arms. The same moral problems exist, for example, with the strategic conventional air strikes against population centers of World War II. Similarly, in the context of current history one of the most acute problems is how to frame a moral response against terrorist activity without oneself being forced into the characteristic patterns of terrorism.

Though complicated, this problem is not insoluble. If the use of force is justified in response to threats against value, but the only means of force available are such that they contravene important values themselves, then the preferred moral alternative is the development of different means of force. If tactical and theater nuclear weapons are judged too destructive to use or deemed too likely to result in escalation to all-out nuclear war if employed, then the moral choice is to devise nonnuclear defenses to replace them and to pay the costs, economic and social, of such defenses.[42] If the strategic nuclear deterrent is deemed immoral to employ, then the right response is not to engage in the self-deception of deterrence-only reasoning but to explore possible means of defense against nuclear strikes that would not require a preemptive first strike by this nation or a possibly indiscriminate and disproportionate punitive second strike.[43] The justification of using force to defend value certainly means, as I have said earlier, more than *defense* in its narrow sense, the warding off of attacks in progress; yet it certainly also means at least that, and to claim the moral high ground for a rejection of steps toward creating such defense is simply to twist moral reasoning out of shape.

Finally, however, there remains the possibility that values must be protected and preserved by force, and by force that itself contravenes at least some of the values it intends to protect and preserve. This is the possibility that, at the extreme, has been called "supreme emergency,"[44] and only at this extreme is it a morally unique case. Must one fight honorably and die, even knowing that one's ultimate moral values will thus die also? Or may one sin for the moment in order to defeat the evil that threatens, hoping for time to repent later and making the commitment to pass on undiluted to future generations the values that have been transgressed in the emergency?[45] Some of the lines of argument already advanced bear on this dilemma. I have suggested that ideological claims ought not to be inflated to the point of seeming to justify unlimited warfare; I have argued against disproportionate and indiscriminate warfare as morally evil in themselves; and I have suggested that part of the trouble in responding to an immoral form of warfare like terrorism is that in making such a response one's own humanity may be diminished to the level of that of the terrorist. In short, I tend to be dubious of supreme-emergency claims and am inclined to hold the moral line for preservation of value in the means chosen as well as in the decision to offer a defense. Even so there remains a possibility of a genuine supreme-emergency situation. What is to be said about this?

First, it is not a newly recognized kind of situation. In the early Middle Ages Christian soldiers were required to do penance after participating in war because of the possibility that they might have acted sinfully in that war, killing perhaps out of malice toward the enemy rather than with a feeling of regretful duty in the service of justice. Here we encounter a case in which the possibility is admitted that protection of values may involve violation of values. When in the sixteenth century Vitoria considered what might be done in a just war, he allowed that a militarily necessary storming of a city could be undertaken even though this would inevitably result in violations of the rights of noncombatants in the city.[46] Such historical evidence suggests a moral acceptance of the possibility of preserving value by wrong means; yet this evidence also implies the limits on that acceptance.

Second, the transgression of value in the service of value must be approached through the general recognition that value conflicts are the stuff with which human moral agency has to deal. Every moral system provides means for handling such conflicts, and that a genuine supreme emergency might come to exist is by definition such a conflict, in which higher values must in the last analysis be favored over lower ones. The values constituting the *jus ad bellum*, having priority over those of the *jus in bello*, would on my reasoning have to be honored in such a case, even at some expense to the latter.

I have thus brought this discussion to the brink of morally admissible possibility so that we might look over and see what lies below. The view is not a pretty one. Having seen it, though, we may the more purposefully return to the other line of implication sketched before: the development of military capabilities suited to our moral commitments. We may still yearn—and work—for a world without war, for an end to the menace of catastrophic nuclear war, for an end to the arms race; yet with such military capabilities we would be the better prepared to meet morally the threats to value that may be expected to be inevitable so long as these ideals are not achieved.

Notes

1. Michael Walzer, *Just and Unjust Wars* (New York: Basic Books, 1977).

2. See Paul Ramsey, *War and the Christian Conscience* (Durham, N.C.: Duke University Press, 1961), and *The Just War* (New York: Charles Scribner's Sons, 1968); William V. O'Brien, *The Conduct of Just and Limited War* (New York: Praeger, 1981).

3. The term is O'Brien's and is meant by him to emphasize the difference in order of priority between the *jus ad bellum* and the *jus in bello*, which has to do with war-fighting once the initial decision to make war has been made. See O'Brien, *Just and Limited War*, esp. chaps. 1–3.

4. Cf. Stanley Hoffmann, *Duties beyond Borders* (Syracuse, N.Y.: Syracuse University Press, 1981), pp. 46–55, and James Douglass, *The Non-Violent Cross* (New York: Macmillan, 1968).

5. Cf. Ramsey's criticism in *The Just War*, pp. 259–278.

6. Hoffmann, *Duties*, p. 59ff.

7. For an example of such tracing in contemporary argument, see Ramsey, *War and the Christian Conscience*, pp. 34–37.

8. For discussion, see James Turner Johnson, *Just War Tradition and the Restraint of War* (Princeton, N.J.: Princeton University Press, 1981), pp. 131–150.

9. See Laurence Beilenson, *Survival and Peace in the Nuclear Age* (Chicago: Regnery and Company, 1980).

10. On the loss of community and its implications, see James Sellers, *Warming Fires* (New York: Seabury Press, 1975), and Thomas Luckmann, *The Invisible Religion* (New York: Macmillan, 1967).

11. This is a familiar theme in the thought of Reinhold Niebuhr. Cf. his *Christianity and Power Politics* (New York: Charles Scribner's Sons, 1940), and *The Structure of Nations and Empires* (New York: Charles Scribner's Sons, 1959).

12. Cf. Walzer, *Just and Unjust Wars*, pp. 133–135.

13. Cf. Ramsey, *The Just War*, pp. 141–147.

14. This concept, taken over from Roman law by Augustine and Isidore of Seville, was central to the definition of just war given in medieval canon law. See *Corpus Juris Canonici*, Pars Prior, *Decretum Magistri Gratiani*, Pars Secunda, Causa XXIII, Quaest. II, Can. II.

15. This is another *jus ad bellum* criterion that came from Roman law through Augustine into church law; see ibid. But it had a more central place in the thought of Thomas Aquinas, who connected it to the words of Paul in Romans 13:4: "[The prince] is the minister of God to execute his vengeance against the evildoer." See Thomas Aquinas, *Summa Theologica*, II/II, Quaest. XL, Art. 1.

16. I make this judgment cognizant of the minority tradition in Christian just war theory from Augustine forward that allowed some forms of war for religion; in Augustine's words, repeated for canon law by Gratian, "The enemies of the church are to be coerced even by war" (*Decretum Magistri Gratiani*, Quaest. VIII, Can. XLVIII). In fact, however, efforts to justify wars in Western cultural history, even those clearly involving some benefit or detriment to religion, have generally been justified by appeal to the other reasons already given: protection of the innocent, retaking of something lost, punishment of evil. For discussion of this issue of religious war—and by extension ideological war—see James Turner Johnson, *Ideology, Reason, and the Limitation of War* (Princeton, N.J.: Princeton University Press, 1975), chaps. I–III.

17. See ibid., pp. 266–270.

18. An early version of this kind of argument undergirded massive retaliation strategy, which Robert W. Tucker in *The Just War* (Baltimore, Md.: The Johns Hopkins Press, 1960) regards as an expression of a general American moral attitude justifying all-out responses to injustice received rather than limited uses of force proportionate to harm done to U.S. interests. But suppose that this opposition to limited warfare is retained while all-out retaliation is itself denied as immoral (although the use of deterrence as a *threat* continues to be accepted); then the argument changes shape, though its fundamentals remain. Such a new version of the moral argument for deterrence and against limited warfare can be found in the 1983 Pastoral Letter of the U.S. Catholic bishops. (See National Conference of Catholic Bishops, *The Challenge of Peace* (Washington, D.C.: United States Catholic Conference, 1983). The purpose of deterrence, as defined here, is "only to prevent the *use* of nuclear weapons by others" (par. 188, emphasis in original). "War-fighting strategies," including even *planning* for fighting nuclear war at a limited level over a protracted period, are explicitly rejected (pars. 184, 188, 189). The reason is the prudential judgment that limited nuclear warfare can be expected to escalate to "mass destruction" (pars. 151–61, 184). Although this suggests heavier reliance on conventional weapons (par. 155), even a conventional war "could escalate to the nuclear level" (par. 156). Although the resultant position is not *explicitly* a deterrence-only one, it is difficult to find in the pessimism toward limited war and war-fighting strategies expressed in the bishops' letter any room for limited

and proportionate responses to limited levels of harm done, such as the traditional *jus in bello* implies.

19. John Stuart Mill, "The Contest in America," in John Stuart Mill, *Dissertations and Discussions* (Boston: William V. Spencer, 1867), pp. 208–209. The full text of the passage in question, written to oppose England's siding with the Confederacy in the American Civil War, is as follows:

> War is an ugly thing, but not the ugliest of things: the decayed and degraded state of moral and patriotic feeling which thinks nothing *worth* a war, is worse. When a people are used as mere human instruments for firing cannon or thrusting bayonets, in the service and for the selfish purposes of a master, such war degrades a people. A war to protect other human beings against tyrannical injustice; a war to give victory to their own ideas of right and good, and which is their own war, carried on for an honest purpose by their own free choice—is often the means of their regeneration. A man who has nothing which he cares about more than he does about his personal safety is a miserable creature who has no chance of being free, unless made and kept so by the existing of better men than himself. As long as justice and injustice have not terminated their ever renewing fight for ascendancy in the affairs of mankind, human beings must be willing, when need is, to do battle for the one against the other.

20. Desiderius Erasmus, Letter to Antoon van Bergen, Abbot of St. Bertin, dated London, 14 March 1514; number 288 in *The Correspondence of Erasmus, Letters 142 to 297,* trans. R.A.B. Minors and D.F.S. Thomson, annotated by Wallace K. Ferguson (Toronto and Buffalo: University of Toronto Press, 1975), lines 47–63.

21. That is, for such pacifists the rejection of force has itself become a value, or it is necessarily implied by some other value (for example, Christian love in some forms of religious pacifism); in either case it is unassailable from outside the moral system in which this value is held. Other forms of pacifism, of course, reach their judgment against the use of force by argument based not on the evil of force as such but on the harm to some higher good that the use of force may entail. The contemporary position sometimes called *just-war pacifism,* which is based on a prudential calculation of proportionality, is such a form of pacifism.

22. See, further, James Turner Johnson "On Keeping Faith: The Uses of History for Religious Ethics," *Journal of Religious Ethics* 7, no. 1(Spring 1979):98–116.

23. Erasmus, Letter, 14 March 1514, lines 17–24.

24. See, further, Roland H. Bainton, *Christian Attitudes toward War and Peace* (New York and Nashville: Abingdon Press, 1960), p. 131, and Lester K. Born, *The Education of a Christian Prince by Desiderius Erasmus* (New York: Octagon Books, 1965), pp. 1–26.

25. See, for example, Richard A. Falk, *A Study of Future Worlds* (New York: Macmillan/The Free Press, 1975).

26. John Howard Yoder, *Nevertheless* (Scottdale, Penna., and Kitchener, Ont.: Herald Press, 1976), p. 33.

27. Condemnation of "militarism" has become a common feature of the public policy statements of many Protestant denominations. See, for example, the statements by The Christian Church (Disciples of Christ) and the Reformed Church in America in Robert Heyer, ed., *Nuclear Disarmament* (New York and Ramsey, N.J.: Paulist Press, 1982), pp. 245–246, 251–252, 267. A prominent example of condemnation of war-fighting strategic planning is the U.S. Catholic bishops' pastoral; see National Conference of Catholic Bishops, *The Challenge of Peace,* paragraphs 184–190. Such thinking is far more like the traditional pacifism represented by Yoder and Erasmus than it is like the reasoning of just war tradition.

28. Jonathan Schell, *The Fate of the Earth* (New York: Avon Books, 1982), p. 85.

29. Ibid., p. 78.

30. See, for example, the discussions of noncombatant immunity found in Walzer, chaps. 8–10. Despite the criticisms I have earlier directed at the U.S. Catholic bishops' letter, it clearly embodies an understanding that the values that might be endangered by an enemy are not trivial; they include "those key values of justice, freedom and independence which are necessary for personal dignity and national integrity" (National Conference of Catholic Bishops, *The Challenge of Peace,* paragraph 175).

31. See, for example, Louis Rene Beres, *Mimicking Sisyphus* (Lexington, Mass.: Lexington Books, D.C. Heath and Company, 1983), pp. 15–24; cf. the argument of the U.S. Catholic bishops, note 18.

32. O'Brien, *Just and Limited War,* chap. 1.

33. Cf. National Conference of Catholic Bishops, *The Challenge of Peace,* pars. 188, 190.

34. Philip Green, *Deadly Logic* (New York: Schocken Books, 1968), pp. 249–51.

35. Cf. National Conference of Catholic Bishops, *The Challenge of Peace,* pars. 175, 188. This document, on my reading, is only a whisker away from the deterrence-only position on nuclear weapons; that whisker is the ambiguity maintained in the threat of strategic nuclear retaliation, specifically in the possible difference between "declaratory policy" and "action policy" (par. 164). Paragraph 148 denies counterpopulation retaliation; paragraph 184 repeats this and also undercuts the possibility of counterforce strategic retaliation. These themes recur elsewhere in section II of the document as well. Is the "conditional acceptance of nuclear deterrence" (par. 198) in this Pastoral Letter then anything more than a "conditional acceptance" of the *possession* of such weapons (not making any distinctions among types, purposes, or relative destructive power, but treating all nuclear weapons the same), and does not the "no first use" position taken in the letter (par. 150 and *passim*) in practical terms collapse into a policy of "no use at all"?

36. See John Eppstein, *The Catholic Tradition of the Law of Nations* (Washington, D.C.: Catholic Association for International Peace, 1935), p. 132.

37. National Conference of Catholic Bishops, *The Challenge of Peace,* par. 134.

38. Heyer, *Nuclear Disarmament,* p. 266.

39. Cf. Walzer, *Just and Unjust Wars,* pp. 329–335.

40. Carl von Clausewitz, *On War,* ed. and trans. Michael Howard and Peter Paret (Princeton, N.J.: Princeton University Press, 1976), p. 370.

41. See, for example, Paul Fussell's argument in *The Great War and Modern Memory* (New York and London: Oxford University Press, 1975), passim, that modern war is inevitably totalistic, chaotic, beyond human control, and disproportionately destructive of values.

42. Cf. National Conference of Catholic Bishops, *The Challenge of Peace,* pars. 155, 215–16.

43. See, further, Sam Cohen, "Rethinking Strategic Defense," in Robert W. Poole, Jr., ed., *Defending a Free Society* (Lexington, Mass.: Lexington Books, D.C. Heath and Company, 1984), pp. 99–122.

44. Walzer, *Just and Unjust Wars,* chap. 16.

45. See, further, my discussion of Walzer on this matter in *Just War Tradition,* pp. 24–28.

46. Franciscus de Vitoria, *De Jure Belli,* section 37, in Franciscus de Vitoria, *De Indis et De Jure Belli Relectiones,* ed. Ernest Nys (Washington, D.C.: Carnegie Institute, 1917). Vitoria makes clear, however, that he thought few wars meet the test of an unambiguous conflict of justice against injustice.

4

Justice, War, and Politics: The Problem of Supreme Emergency

Gerald M. Mara
Georgetown University

Supreme Emergency and the Value of Politics

Current debates about the morality of nuclear deterrence address immediate moral and political problems whose significance can scarcely be overemphasized.[1] These discussions, however, also raise (for nonpacifists, at least) less overwhelming but still important *theoretical* questions about the possibility of justifying wars and the likelihood of setting binding moral limits on their conduct in the modern age. From one perspective, of course, these problems can be seen as direct consequences of the development of nuclear weapons. Michael Walzer, David Hollenbach, and others have suggested that nuclear arms represent a war-fighting technology whose use simply cannot be evaluated by currently available moral categories, certainly not by those supplied within the religious or secular variations of the just war tradition. Walzer explains the moral anguish that often accompanies the endorsement of nuclear deterrence "as resulting from the monstrous immorality that our policy contemplates, an immorality that we can never hope to square with our understanding of justice in war. Nuclear weapons explode the theory of just war. They are the first of mankind's technological innovations that are simply not encompassable within the familiar moral world."[2]

Despite the conceptual havoc wrought by nuclear weapons, however, Walzer has no difficulty deciding how the maintenance of a nuclear deterrent can be evaluated. It can be seen as responding to a permanent condition of "supreme emergency," under which actions, ordinarily blameworthy if not repulsive (for example, deliberately harming noncombatants or, in the case of nuclear deterrence, *threatening* harm to noncombatants) become, though not justifiable, *necessary* under conditions that threaten the life of the political community. "Utilitarian calculation can force us to violate the rules of war only when we are face-to-face not merely with defeat but with a defeat likely to bring disaster to a political community."[3] It should be recognized that this appeal to emergency could also justify the *use* of nuclear weapons. It is, to say the least, very difficult to show that the use of nuclear arms would respect the traditional limits of proportionality and discrimination set on the conduct of war by just war theory. Under certain conditions, however, their employment could be seen as a response to a contemporary supreme emergency—a nuclear attack by an enemy power or even an unprovoked conventional attack, for example on western Europe by Warsaw Pact forces. Thus even the first use of nuclear weapons might be defended as a supreme (though catastrophic) necessity. It is not precisely true, then, that nuclear weapons explode the *theory* of the just war. Rather, nuclear weapons expand the range of actions or intentions that can be defended *only* in terms that lie at the outskirts or, perhaps, beyond the borders of just war reasoning.

No one could deny that nuclear weapons have permanently altered the contours of the international landscape. Their incredibly destructive force poses unprecedented challenges to modern societies. Their use must be prevented and their expansion controlled within an international situation where tensions remain and *real* threats persist. Ultimately, nuclear weapons may make war between the superpowers unthinkable under any political circumstances that can be reasonably anticipated. But nuclear weapons damage the *structure* of our ethical reasoning, placing ethics itself in distress, in Hollenbach's phrase, only if they expose fundamental deficiencies in the ways we think about armed conflict, in the theoretical framework that accepts supreme emergency as a reasonable evaluative category.

This claim has been made by writers as different as Phillip Green and Jonathan Schell. For Walzer, accepting an appeal to supreme emergency requires us to invest the political community with a value that can justify the terror bombing of Germany in World War II or the threats to incinerate the populations of New York and Moscow under the deterrence strategy of mutually assured destruction. Walzer finds this conclusion to be highly problematic but nonetheless unavoidable within his own perspective on just war:

> [C]ommunities in emergencies seem to have different and larger prerogatives [than individuals]. I am not sure that I can account for the difference, without ascribing to communal life a kind of transcendence which I don't believe it to have. Perhaps it is only a matter of arithmetic: individuals cannot kill other individuals to save themselves, but to save a nation we can violate the rights of a determinate but smaller number of people.[4]

Green, however, denies that mere national interests can justify inflicting the agonies of total war on innocent civilians, even under conditions of supreme national emergency.[5] For him, supreme emergency would appear to require precisely the ascription of an unjustifiable transcendence to communal life. Thus Schell, who writes in a much more popular context, contends that we face a basic choice: pressing the arms race to its nightmarish finale or radically restructuring the community of nation-states whose competing interests have been revealed as dangerously immature by the march of weapons technologies.[6] For all their differences in substance and style, both Green and Schell claim that nuclear weapons explode just war theory in a much more radical sense than Walzer intends. From their perspective, nuclear weapons expose the poverty of any perspective that accepts the inevitability of competing, conflicting national communities. In reality, this structure of international relations and thus the concept of supreme national emergency are contingent. For Green, "[i]t would be easier to argue . . . that in the nuclear age the basic concept of national sovereignty must be partially or totally rejected."[7]

In a sense, then, it is supreme emergency itself that introduces Hollenbach's crisis in ethics and that forces Green to reveal the poverty of sovereignty. By accepting appeals to supreme emergency, we must, apparently, value states over people. But the rejection of supreme emergency would seem to require a very radical critique of politics. Thus the challenge advanced by Green, Schell, and others compels us to reconsider the *basic* assumptions underlying reflective evaluations of war. They demand no less than a reconsideration of the value of political communities, returning us to the fundamental questions that confront political philosophers. Thomas Pangle articulates the importance of these questions with extraordinary clarity:

> In discussing international relations, we are often heard to use the term "national interest." . . . The bellicose possibilities implied in this appeal have always raised questions in men's minds. Just what do we mean when we make such an appeal? What is the content of national interest? What content must it have to become morally preeminent, to justify resolute international competition and, if necessary, great bloodshed? What limits, if any, are there on what can be done for the national interest once it is so understood? What is the ground or source of such limits?[8]

In this chapter, I want to suggest that although the objections raised by Green, Schell, and others may have considerable merit when applied to some conceptions of politics, they do not have equal force against all possible justifications of political communities. I want to propose that a certain view of politics— one informed or stimulated by the reflections of Aristotle and Plato—is less vulnerable to Green's objections. This interpretation of political life can also provide us with a way of evaluating situations of national emergency that avoids some of the problems inherent in Walzer's position.

Interpreting Supreme Emergency

An acceptance of supreme emergency is not, of course, a rejection of our ability to make moral judgments about actions performed in wartime situations.

Supreme emergency is not equivalent to what Walzer calls the "war is hell doctrine," in which moral restraints crumble before the unalleviated horror of armed conflict. Indeed, the principle itself presupposes the validity of critical evaluations in "normal" wartime circumstances. It identifies conditions of last resort and thus illuminates, so to speak, an ordinarily *compelling* "moral reality" (in Walzer's phrase). Only a serious, immediate threat to the life of the polity where reasonable defensive alternatives are absent can justify ignoring the constraints normally in force. For similar reasons, the recognition of supreme emergency is not simply a redirection of ethics along lines supplied by a statist realism, for within such a perspective the state is under no obligation to distinguish those actions that are essential for its survival from those that are simply profitable or advantageous. Although the activities accepted within appeals to supreme emergency are by definition insupportable under any normal morality, the very recourse to this appeal implies the recognition of a coherent ethical framework capable of binding the ordinary activities of political communities.

Accordingly, those wishing to employ the category of supreme emergency are intensely concerned to prevent hypocritical or ideological misuses. Therefore, Walzer institutes a more or less objective test for the validity of such appeals; a community's existence, its "ultimate values," must be jeopardized by the imminent actions of a belligerent. Warlike actions that, however menacing, do not threaten these ultimate values fail to introduce a condition of emergency. Thus employed, the standard cannot be invoked to justify actions that are merely convenient or prudential. Moreover, this objective test avoids the difficult and often ideologically biased task of making comparative evaluations of regimes. Walzer's attempted objectivity is apparent in his paradigmatic case of a genuine supreme emergency. In 1940 the Nazi threat to the West was so imminent as to justify the terror bombing of German cities. By 1942, however, the danger had sufficiently lessened so that not even the rightness of the Allies' cause could justify the continuation of the saturation bombing policy.[9]

Despite its careful discriminations and moderate intentions, however, the principle of supreme emergency has been roundly criticized by a number of ethicists, generally for a kind of moral incoherence. According to these critics, such appeals portray the same act as right *and* wrong. Walzer himself lends considerable support to this conclusion when he claims that those who are forced to kill noncombatants in such circumstances are murderers, though in good causes.[10] Hollenbach sympathizes with the moral posture behind this tortured response but cannot avoid concluding that the response itself is absurd. "Murder, by definition, is unjustified killing. To declare it morally legitimate is to make a nonsensical statement: this act is both justified and unjustified at the same time."[11]

My own reaction is that such criticisms understate the tragic complexity of supreme emergency. Such appeals do not merely demand that particular moral prohibitions be overridden. On a deeper level they involve a recognition that the moral features of the world have, temporarily at least, changed in a decisive way. Moral actions and judgments *required* in one context are seen as naive, even dangerous, in another. A murderous act under the pressure of a genuine emergency ceases at that time to be unequivocally murderous. The designation *murder*, rather, is part of a perspective or a system of judgment that is being overridden. Only in retrospect, after the demands of necessity have lessened or disappeared, can judgments of murder and determinations of innocence and guilt according to normal morality be rendered. This interpretation of supreme emergency, however, would appear to reinforce the suspicion that, whatever its intentions, its result is to separate morality from politics. The extent of this disjunction is revealed by three related observations.

First, there *is* an important sense in which appeals to supreme emergency can be critically evaluated. However, that evaluation touches only the adequacy of the threat perception and the effectiveness of the chosen response. Supreme emergency can be wrongly invoked. Threats that are impending and serious but fall short of jeopardizing ultimate values do not justify the same response as those that pose a genuine menace to the life of the polity. Even a menace remote enough to be met by more temperate responses cannot justify a successful appeal to necessity. Likewise, supreme emergencies can be wrongly handled. The only acceptable response is one which is effective in countering the threat at hand. A misguided response is not condemned merely because of inefficiency but because normal moral categories (Walzer's "war convention") reemerge. Respecting the life of noncombatants becomes once again a binding limitation on all acts of war. However, the morality of the war convention exercises no force if the threat is *truly* serious and imminent and if the proposed response has a reasonable chance of diminishing immediate jeopardy. It is precisely in this situation where the doing of justice is prohibited if justice would let the heavens fall.

The significance of this dismissal of justice for the benefit of politics is intensified within a second observation. Supreme emergency may less often resemble a Homeric critical moment (*kairos*) than St. John's choice between damnation and salvation. Salvation is usually not the work of a moment but of a lifetime. In certain situations communities exist within ongoing, rather than discrete, conditions of emergency. For Walzer, Britain's supreme emergency in World War II extended from 1940 to 1942. Merleau-Ponty presents the Soviet Union as facing dire emergencies from its inception until virtually the end of the war against Hitler. Supreme emergencies can apparently become definitive features of political existences. Walzer himself supplies the most striking example of this when he notes that nuclear deterrence has tended to make supreme emergency itself a "permanent condition." Under these circumstances, however, it becomes increasingly questionable whether conditions of supreme emergency can simply illuminate, without materially affecting, the normal moral landscape—human psyches if not human practices—below. Accordingly, Britain's terror bombing of Germany, for Walzer necessary only until 1942, became an accepted policy (not without its own rationale) thereafter. Even if one agrees with Merleau-Ponty's assessment that Bukharin and Zinoviev represented real threats to the Soviet revolution in the 1930s, the same could hardly be said of Andrei Sakharov in the 1980s. Specifically with regard to nuclear deterrence, it is difficult to believe that the willingness to unleash thousands of nuclear warheads on an adversary's cities is without its permanent psychic effects on the way life is normally lived within the superpowers.[12]

The long-term effects of actions committed under the duress of necessity take on added significance within my final observation. It may be more difficult than it initially appears to separate authentic supreme emergencies from the characteristics of the particular regimes involved. In the *Politics,* Aristotle reminds us that a regime is defined less by its borders (a wall around the Peloponnesians does not make the Peloponnese a city) than by its goals, what it cherishes or despises.[13] According to this perspective, the preservation of a community is essentially tied to the continuance of its way of life. Values or ways of life that are central to communities can be strikingly different; truly devastating threats can vary accordingly. The West essentially depends not only for its prosperity but also for some portions of its identity and legitimation on its modern industrial base.[14] A vital Shi'ite religion is the heart of the Islamic Republic of Iran. Ancient Sparta flourished when spirited patriotism prevailed; indeed, Xenophon tells us that the regime itself changed when patriotism was supplanted by venality. The Soviet Union, self-defined by its revolutionary aspirations at least, relies on the collective organization of its resources and activities. Thus legitimate responses to supreme emergencies could include not only Britain's desperate counterattack but also the nuclear maintenance of Western access to the Persian Gulf, the crushing of religious dissidence in contemporary Iran, and the violent collectivization of the *kulaks* under Stalin. From this vantage point, an objective criterion of supreme emergency that avoids commentary, either critical or recognizant, on substantive community values may be chimerical. By consciously avoiding the comparative evaluation of competing regimes, Walzer's version of supreme emergency may implicitly embrace a theoretical recognition of all goals that are essential to the regime or dominant community.

Together, these observations suggest that appeals to supreme emergency create a gap between morality and politics that is more permanent and more serious than Walzer believes. An accurate image of this separation may be supplied by Max Weber's distinction between the ethics of faith and the ethics of responsibility. Taken to its extreme conclusions, this distinction consigns even the most politically astute moralist to political irrelevance at a time when moral judgments about politics (or moral restraints on politics) are most needed. Conversely, the cold recognition of political demands may mean a tortured but resolute acceptance of criminality, "a pact with the powers of hell" in Raymond Aron's (critical) phrase.[15]

Yet despite these stark consequences, it is not clear that the principle of supreme emergency can be jettisoned. I want to suggest that Walzer's conception of supreme emergency can only be understood and accepted within the context of his just war theory as a whole. That theory or perspective can be rejected only if it proves to be inferior to any obvious alternatives.

Individuals or Communities?

Conceptually, though certainly not historically, the contemporary just war framework can be seen as providing an alternative to two competing theoretical perspectives: that which focuses on the centrality of individuals and that which endorses the priority of the community.

The first of these alternatives is represented by the variety of liberal political theories: politics is justifiable or praiseworthy because it protects individual rights. In international affairs the business of the state is truly national *security*. Its war-making powers should be exercised primarily if not exclusively in support of the rights of its individual citizens. Walzer clearly accepts this justification of national defense:

> "The duties and rights of states are nothing more than the duties and rights of the men who compose them." This is the view of a conventional British lawyer for whom states are neither organic wholes nor mystical unions. And it is the correct view. When states are attacked it is their members who are challenged. . . . We recognize and explain this challenge by referring to their rights.[16]

Thus there is no civic or communal entity with an existence or body of rights beyond the existences and rights of its collected members. In Robert Nozick's phrase, politics can be "seen through."[17] Walzer's conclusions about politics' reducibility to its individual citizens are strikingly similar to Nozick's. "Individual rights (to life and liberty) underlie the most important judgments that we make about war. . . . States' rights are simply their collective form."[18] Although Walzer does not dwell on the theoretical grounding of this assessment ("How these rights are themselves founded I cannot try to explain here"), other writers have made clear that it depends on a view of individuals as individual*ists* who can without essential assistance define and secure their own best interests. Nozick describes this position with characteristic clarity when he praises his "minimal state" because of its respect for the dignity of individuals: "[I]t allows us, individually or with whom we choose, to choose our life and realize our ends and our conception of ourselves, insofar as we can."[19]

Liberal political theory thus casts a very critical glance at attempts to justify large-scale personal sacrifices for the good of the whole. Since the purpose of politics is the protection of individuals, any course of action threatening harm to large numbers of citizens for the common good is potentially as nonsensical as the simultaneous praise and blame of the same act. This perspective is clearly visible within Hobbes's political theory, expecially in his denial that individuals can be *blamed* for refusing to face certain death for the sake of the commonwealth. Only when dangerous actions prevent even greater personal dangers, when danger is consistent with "the end for which the sovereignty was ordained then there is no liberty to refuse."[20] Thus there is an important theoretical connection between the individualist principles that support the liberal state and the arguments of those critics of nuclear deterrence who condemn that policy as *absurdly* jeopardizing the lives it should protect.[21]

We do not need to be reminded, however, that individualism has its dark side. The liberal perspective may be hard pressed to explain or endorse acts whose continuance we might wish to preserve—for example, individual acts of self-sacrifice for the sake of the whole, or collective risks to protect the rights of others. Liberal morality can, of course, praise sacrifice as a supererogatory act. But such behavior is, by definition, beyond what is normal or expected. In Rawls's words, "[a]n act which would be very good for another, expecially one which protects him from great harm or injury, is a natural duty required by the principle of mutual aid, provided that the sacrifice and hazards to the agent are not very great. Thus a supererogatory act may be thought of as one which a person does for the sake of another's good even though the proviso that nullifies the natural duty is satisfied."[22] Moreover, it is not irrelevant that from the standpoint of the most radical but perhaps most consistent liberal theorist, Thomas Hobbes, acts of sacrifice or risk can be traced to a fatal ignorance or foolhardiness that blinds one to the supreme evil that is violent death.

The negative dimensions of individualism's self-centeredness, however, are not confined to callous isolationism. The individualist perspective may be unable to afford protection to those whose protection would oppose or jeopardize the perceived good of the liberal community. For example, the social contract variant of liberalism, at least as expressed by Hobbes and Locke, promises no justice to those outside the covenant.[23] Thus both see conflicts between states as occurring in the condition of nature, where the categories of justice and injustice do not apply.[24] Indeed, in the pursuit of the good of its citizens, it is impossible for Hobbes's commonwealth to violate the law of nature even in "the infliction of what evil soever, on an innocent man, that is not a subject, if it be for the benefit of the commonwealth, and without violation of any prior covenant."[25]

This problem cannot be completely avoided by dismissing contractarianism in the name of utility. Strictly applied, of course, utilitarianism's boundaries do not stop at national borders (Mill is concerned to maximize benefits to *mankind*). But it is not difficult to picture occasions where large populations would, on utilitarian premises, legitimately benefit from injustices to the few. Utility appears to be a particularly hazardous principle to apply in international affairs, where large nations often prosper at the expense of smaller ones] It is true that Mill (in "A Few Words on Intervention") echoes the respect for the sovereignty of nation-states recognized in international law. But this respect is confined to civilized or progressive states. "The only moral law for the relation between a civilized and a barbarous government are the universal rules of morality between man and man—that is, utility.[26] It is not unreasonable, moreover, to suppose that universal utilitarian morality should exercise its force most strongly in the gravest of human interactions, which often extend well beyond boundary-crossing interventions. Our experiences with modern war show that it is quite possible to excuse deliberate harm to noncombatants by pointing to its beneficial consequences for humanity. This was precisely the rationale used to support the decision to drop atomic bombs on Hiroshima and Nagasaki.[27]

Of course, both contract theory and utility place substantial reliance on the abilities of individuals to develop responsible moral sensibilities. Neither Locke's rational contractarians nor Mill's progressive individualists would be likely to impel their societies toward aggression or conquest. Neither contractarianism nor utility, however, can supply principles capable of restraining a liberal society's conduct in cases where its interests are perceived to be truly at stake. Consistent upholders of either of these two principles are likely to resemble Brian Barry's tough-minded utilitarians who insist on the necessity of subordinating intuitions or sentiments to calculation in cases where those demands conflict. Moreover, liberalism's reluctance to comment on ultimate goals means accepting the fact that individual development can extend in a variety of directions. That individuals or individualist societies will grow toward responsibility and benevolence rather than toward acquisitiveness and tyranny is a matter of hope or faith for liberal theorists rather than an essential requirement of liberal theory.[28]

Thus, although appeals to supreme emergency appear to be illegitimate or contradictory in circumstances where large degrees of civic sacrifice would result, they also appear to be unnecessary or superfluous in cases where the community's interests would be well served by destructive acts. As a result, the kinds of actions that can be defended on grounds of necessity cease to be moral exceptions, acceptable *only* in situations of moral last resort. Despite their best intentions, the principles of contractarianism and utility threaten to coopt actions committed under the duress of supreme emergency into the normal features of the moral world.

To avoid endorsing the abuses of either calculating individuals or committed champions of the general welfare, Walzer and Nozick recommend the adoption of binding side constraints that prohibit actions violative of basic human rights. Walzer and Nozick differ significantly about the possibility of overriding these constraints in times of national emergency.[29] Both, however, see these restrictions as being essential additions to the (basically sound) liberal perspective. This respect for human rights not only restrains abusive acts but also potentially allows for a certain kind of activism in defense of the rights of others, even at some risks to the agents.

It remains to be shown, however, how this kind of restraint, much less a risk-laden activism, can be consistent with the psychology of interest that underlies liberal political theory. From the standpoint of this psychology there would appear to be an implicit but fundamental tension between a politics protective and supportive of its citizens' interests and a politics sensitive to the basic rights of *all* members of the human community.[30] Consequently, a fundamental reassessment of the human psyche may be in order. John Langan's suggestion that "we must not make on the national level the mistakes which Kant so vehemently deplored on the individual level, the mistakes of identifying happiness and virtue, interest and morality" seems to be very good advice.[31] But Kant is able to maintain these distinctions only through a radical separation of our empirical or affective motivations from our purely rational, and therefore free, capabilities. Still, we must explain our capacity to resist affections in the name of rationality by a deeper but far more opaque *interest* in the moral life.[32] Thus Kant's speculations serve more to articulate than to resolve the moral dilemmas secreted by an acceptance of liberalism's empirical psychology.

Kant's radical separation of morality from interest has more immediately serious consequences for attempts to set moral limitations on the conduct of war. Since wars are always fought for the sake of interests, there can be no *just* war.[33] Supreme emergency is not, therefore, to be understood as a condition that escapes and therefore presupposes valid moral judgments, but as the extreme conclusion of the furtherance of interest. The only *rational* goal of international politics is, rather, a perpetual peace among republics that internally and externally respect the dignity of free and rational human beings, appreciated as ends in themselves. Because of the incongruity between empirical interests and moral imperatives, however, perpetual peace can only be achieved by the progress of increasingly violent wars, which inspire, if not pacifist rationality, then pacifist revulsion.[34] Not only is limited war indefensible on (purely) rational grounds, but also restraints on the intensity of war-fighting may actually retard the emergence of a lasting condition of peace.

Thus, although Hobbesian and Kantian theories of individuality are surely very different from one another, they both reject the validity of supreme emergency due to their prior rejection of the possibility of just wars. Whereas Kant might celebrate these rejections as unmasking chauvinistic hypocrisy, the consequence is that it becomes impossible to fix *moral* limitations on the conduct of war. The denial of supreme emergency within the strict individualist paradigm stems from its conception of war as an unrelieved moral wasteland devoid of moral distinctions, incapable of moral restraint.

Supreme emergency is likely to get a better reception among proponents of communitarianism. This position, which receives such divergent expressions as Hegel's idea of the state as ethical reality, Arendt's praise of the sublimity of political activity, and Gadamer's identification of language as the primordial phenomenon of humanity, expresses dissatisfaction with attempts to define individuals and individual rights apart from their cultural contexts. Social practices (to use MacIntyre's term) are constitutive of human life. Thus Hegel claims that even the possessor of Absolute Wisdom cannot escape the determinative influence of his time and culture any more than he can sever the intimate bond between his spirituality and his physical existence.[35] In its stronger version, expressed in the later philosophy of Hegel, this position invests society with a value that transcends and is only implicitly recognized by its citizens.[36] Hannah Arendt's more down-to-earth praise of politics suggests that individuals are truly fulfilled only in the pursuit of public principles.[37] In either case the community is to be treasured because the value that it opens to or confers on individuals is more ennobling than the private pursuit of material satisfaction.

This position, therefore, soundly rejects Green's contention that national interests, thus understood, are destructive of human interests. From this perspective, wars are to be evaluated in terms of their relation to *community* values. To be sure, many such wars are justified by their defensive intentions. But focusing on the defense of society can lead to regarding as a matter of course a degree of sacrifice that would shock individualists. Moreover, it is hardly unthinkable that an aggressive war could make a positive contribution to communal solidarity. Hegel presents an extreme version of this claim in the *Phenomenology*, in which war's capacity to break up "the form of fixed stability" allows Spirit to guard "the ethical order from shrinking into merely natural existence."[38] From a less speculative vantage, writers as different as Machiavelli, Rousseau, and Nietzsche have noted the dependence of patriotism on bellicosity. The bonds of strong communities may indeed *rely* on an aggressive posture toward outsiders.

Under these circumstances, the prospects for discovering a moral imperative for the restraint of war are not encouraging. Even those partisans of community who despise political violence argue that responsibility for the rational justification and restraint of war must rest with the community itself. Arendt locates the communal potential for self-restraint in the political capacities to promise and to forgive.[39] These capacities however, are beneficial only in communities disposed to use them well. Arendt's endorsement of the value of all principles that encourage the restraint of personal selfishness prevents her from commenting on the substantive differences among societal goals.[40] That a community's principles will incline more to moderation than to dominance is as much an act of faith as the liberal reliance on the good will of individualists. Rousseau highlights the contingency of this expectation in the *Discourse on Political Economy* when he observes that there is nothing in the nature of a virtuous republic that would prevent it from waging an unjust war.[41]

From the communitarian perspective, then, supreme emergency is not so much a situation in which normal moral rules must be overridden as a description of critical danger to the life of the commonwealth. Supreme emergencies differ from other cases of international hostility only in their intensity. Thus the communal paradigm resembles the liberal perspective in at least one respect. It tends to incorporate actions done under what Walzer calls supreme emergencies within its normal moral outlook.

For vastly different reasons, then, the communitarian and individualist paradigms threaten to place the wartime actions of states beyond moral criticism. Among the many virtues of contemporary just war theory is its concern to reestablish the possibility of critical evaluation through an avoidance of the extremes dictated by both of these positions.

Just and Unjust Wars

Current just war thinking, particularly as expressed by Walzer, recognizes, of course, the importance of those phenomena at the center of both the individualist and communitarian positions. It therefore attempts to incorporate the advantages of both without falling victim to the shortcomings of either. Walzer's strong individualist commitment precludes his investing the community with a transcendent value, but he also rejects the suspicion that communities are simply insidious fictions. His alternative begins with what he calls the "legalist paradigm," which establishes the rights of territorial integrity and political sovereignty as essential to nation-states. Although we cannot grant supervening status to community *values,* we can at least presume that all nations ought to be politically independent, capable of forging their own destinies and managing their own affairs. This treatment of the rights of communities is analogous to John Rawls's respect for the primary goods of individuals, things such as security and autonomy, which we presume all human beings desire regardless of the specifics of their fuller life plans. Just as Rawls's principles of societal justice are designed to protect the primary social goods of individuals, so Walzer's legalist paradigm protects the primary political goods of nations.

Adherence to the legalist paradigm has the consequence of virtually stipulating the injustice of nondefensive wars (although it is important to realize that Walzer's "defense" includes assistance rendered to a victim of aggression by nonthreatened states or subsequent punishment imposed on a repulsed attacker). In this respect Walzer diverges somewhat from other contemporary just war proponents—for example, James Johnson—as well as from selected representatives of the classical just war tradition. For Johnson, although defense against aggression is the primary and most unambiguous *casus belli,* the possibility of a justifiable *non*defensive war remains. At most, the claim that there can be no just war without prior or imminent aggression is, legalistically speaking, a rebuttable presumption that can be rejected in certain circumstances. Walzer's reliance on the legalist paradigm thus compels him to resist efforts to expand the justification of war beyond defense even in cases of interventions designed to protect human rights.[42]

Walzer's concern to restrict just wars to defense is in part a reflection of his discomfort with the status that must be accorded the political community within any coherent effort to defend the moral use of wartime force. The temptation to affix a transcendent value to community must be countered by severe individualist side constraints on decisions to fight and on methods of fighting wars. Thus the defensive boundary that circumscribes war decisions is paralleled by the human rights that restrain war conduct. "A legitimate act of war is one which does not violate the rights of the people against whom it is directed. . . . This fundamental principle underlies and shapes the judgments we make of wartime conduct."[43] Still, Walzer is not Kant. War conduct may remain just even when noncombatant lives are taken, as long as the fatal effects are unintentional (in the strong sense that positive efforts, even those requiring some risks, are made to avoid them) and part of an otherwise legitimate series of wartime activities. Moreover, lives of noncombatants become to a degree expendable when a nation faces the cold stare of supreme emergency.

Thus Walzer's version of just war theory respects both the value of politics and the rights of individuals. Although there are important differences among the major modern representatives of just war thinking, all seem similarly concerned to avoid both the approach that "sees through" politics and that which reifies or exalts the political community. Wars can be *just* only because there are morally defensible national interests, values for which we are (and should be) "willing to sacrifice and die," in William O'Brien's terms.[44] Wars can also be *unjust* if their aggressive motivation or bestial conduct jeopardizes the lives and welfare of innocent individuals. In Johnson's formulation, "[t]he response that says, yes, here are some conditions in which it is morally right to protect value goes on to set limits to what may rightly be done toward that end."[45]

This praiseworthy attempt at balance, however, necessarily incorporates a certain amount of imprecision. Although the just war framework can help us to avoid the extremes of the individualist and communitarian positions, it is less useful when called on to set priorities between the demands of community and the rights of individuals. Thus adherents to the just war framework may legitimately disagree about a variety of fundamental issues. This is apparent, for example, in the disputes of Rawls, Johnson, and O'Brien with Walzer over the relative priority of just cause in the restraint of war conduct. Rawls, Johnson, and O'Brien all suggest that the existence of a defensible *casus belli* allows considerable latitude in war conduct. At the very least, the burden of proof falls upon those who condemn acts of war which effectively support just causes. In Rawls's terms, "[a]cts permissible in a war of legitimate self-defense, when these are necessary, may be flatly excluded in a more doubtful situation."[46] For Walzer, however, this reasoning counsels the objectionable importation of a "sliding scale" into judgments about war conduct. "The greater the justice of my cause, the more rules I can violate for the sake of the cause."[47] A similar disagreement over basic priorities underlies Walzer's exchanges with Gerald Doppelt and David Luban over the permissibility of interventions to defend human rights.[48]

It does not appear that a position can be taken in either of these disputes without moving just war theory in the direction of one of the two polar positions it has intended to avoid. Walzer's concern to protect the war convention from absorption into the war decision represents a strong commitment to the rights of individuals. Johnson's and O'Brien's recommendations that a wider latitude in war conduct be allowed for the just defense of values is more communitarian in focus. That this ambiguity occurs within the *structure* of just war theory is suggested by Walzer's rich presentation, which at times inclines to individualism, at others to communitarianism. Walzer can, consistently within the parameters of his own position, both reduce collectivities to individuals and, in Luban's critical assessment, be romanced by the nation-state.

Walzer's reluctant acceptance of supreme emergency is, perhaps, his reaction to the dilemmas posed by just war's ambiguity in the darkest times—those situations in which the rights of innocents collide with community survival. No position grounded in a state's right to self-defense can coherently deny the force of that right when the state's very existence is threatened. But the nature of the acts required in response to an authentic national emergency often preclude their acceptance within the limits set by just war theory. Thus supreme emergency cannot be a component or dimension of just war reasoning, narrowly understood. However, supreme emergency serves to establish the limits within which just war theory can be consistently applied, while accepting the necessity of the frightening choices that lie byond its borders. Accordingly, it *is* a part of Walzer's just war reasoning, broadly understood. Its contribution is essential if Walzer is to avoid two equally unacceptable alternatives. The first is a rejection of the possibility of identifying just uses of force in international conflict, leading either to pacifism or to the adoption of the "war is hell" doctrine. The second is the expansion of the just war doctrine to cover even situations of national emergency by means of the principle of *proportionality:* the demand that harm to noncombatants be balanced against the goals such harm would further.

Walzer's distrust of proportionality stems in part from its resemblance to the sliding scale. Although its supporters assure that *dis*proportionate force is precluded, the difficulty is that the dimensions of the proportionate change with circumstances. As the stakes increase, levels of justifiable force intensify and the strictness of protection afforded to individual welfare relaxes. Thus O'Brien contends that the just defense of the West allows a high, though not limitless, degree of "collateral" (unintentional) damage to noncombatants.[49] Whereas supreme emergency identifies a strict departure from normal moral prohibitions, appeals to proportionality signal a gradual disappearance of moral restraints on war-making as community interests intensify.

Proportionality also tends to place greater reliance on estimations of the comparative values of different regimes. The worth of the values being defended is a crucial element of the proportion. Although this concern avoids the forced value-neutrality of the legalist paradigm, it is more open to serious abuse unless its supporters can provide acceptable criteria for comparative political judgments. Johnson suggests that our inclination to support values by affirmation is sufficient phenomenal evidence that we cherish a variety of human goods beyond survival. Although this observation communicates an important psychological truth, the absence of a critical mechanism for comparing different value complexes compels us to risk subordinating the legitimate protection of life and liberty to the most vehement affirmations. As Walzer wryly notes, everyone's troubles make a crisis.

Finally, proportionality's capacity to free those who act in its name from the burdens of guilt may not be completely beneficial. Langan addresses this problem indirectly but forcefully in his observations on certain Catholic discussions of nuclear deterrence. "[D]iscussions of these matters [include] a certain tendency to assume that once the morally correct choice of action has been discovered and chosen all will be well. This is accompanied by an understandable reluctance to be clear about the costs, the harms, and the negative implications of the positions that have been recommended."[50] Walzer's description of supreme emergency as *murder* in a good cause hardly glosses over the moral seriousness of the act in question.

Within Walzer's formulation, then, supreme emergency and the just war reasoning beneath it bridge the gap between individualists and communitarians by recognizing the continued relevance of human rights side constraints on actions in defense of community *except* in those instances where restraint is almost certain to bring disaster to the political body. One consequence of the position, of course, is that possibilities for critical evaluation by just war theory, strictly understood, disappear at the moment of their greatest necessity. By itself, this conclusion may be no more than an accurate reflection of a tragic reality. But supreme emergency is also compromised by its inability to supply the guidance that Walzer implies is most necessary. I have suggested that supreme emergencies cannot be understood without implicit or potential references to the characters of the regimes involved. The standard of supreme emergency cannot, then, be applied to a multitude of different societies on a purely objective or neutral basis. Moreover, it may not be the case that supreme emergency simply illuminates a normal moral reality that can be ignored only in extreme crises. Rather, our characterization of that reality may be significantly affected by an acceptance of the validity of supreme emergency.

There is an important theoretical connection between the recognition of supreme emergency and the endorsement of nonintervention, which protects even abusive regimes from external interference in their affairs. In both cases, the right of a political community to exercise and protect its capacity for self-determination is accorded dominant priority.

Nonetheless, despite its flaws, Walzer's version of the just war position appears to be more comprehensive and more critical than either individualism or communitarianism. It may represent the best opportunity available, apart from categorical pacifism, to set moral limits on armed conflict. And pacifism does not include among its many virtues the capacity for effective interaction with a truly hostile world. Are we, then, compelled to accept the validity of supreme emergency while seeing its ambiguities and shortcomings themselves as illuminations of the darkest side of human affairs?

Politics, Virtue, and Necessity

The just war perspective may not, however, represent the only means of avoiding the individualist reduction of politics and the collectivist sanctification of community. Another alternative seems implicit in the tradition of political thought developed by Plato and, especially, Aristotle. In their eyes, politics has a more important purpose than simply protecting the material interests of individuals. The classical alternative, however, is neither a Kantian rejection of interest as a viable moral standard nor a communitarian denial of individuality as a legitimate political concern.

In Aristotle's view, politics may be *necessary* to provide security for individual private activities, but politics is *praiseworthy* because of its potential for encouraging the "flourishing" (Anscombe's term) of individual moral virtue or excellence. The production of excellent citizens is the litmus test of a good society. "The lawgivers make their citizens good by their customs, and this is the aim of every lawgiver; however, if they do this poorly they fail; this separates a good regime from a bad one.[51] Assessing the differences among societies therefore presupposes our ability to compare the values of different interests or ways of life in a conclusive, binding fashion. It is not enough that values be affirmed. They should be capable of at least relative justification from the standpoint of someone wishing to make a rational choice about the best way of life. Plato and Aristole would dispute, then, John Stuart Mill's cornerstone principle that a good's desirability is shown by the mere fact that it is desired. This disputation, however, does not endorse a Kantian rejection of interest as the only path toward morality. It is not simply that there may be moral (or not immoral) interests, but rather that the categories of interest and morality ultimately converge. Justice or morality is the true human interest. The happiest way of life accessible to most human beings is that devoted to the performance of morally virtuous activities.

The elucidation of that practically virtuous life is the chief mission of Aristotle's *Ethics*. Although a full account of Aristotle's position (assuming it can be given) is out of place here, we can at least outline its most relevant features. The best way of life accessible for most people is the practice (insofar as possible) of the virtues of prudence, justice, and moderation.[52] This expression may sound platitudinous, but Aristotle believes he can show that these qualities have a precise content and that their presence or absence exerts a formative influence on the human personality. This perspective on the virtues does not so much require us to practice certain definite activities (statemanship, scholarship, philanthropy) or to occupy certain identifiable positions or social roles. What is important is that such roles or activities be compatible with excellence (or flourishing) and that they be capable of performance or completion in virtuous ways.[53] Statesmanship and philanthropy do not exhaust the range of desirable activities possible in the variety of cultural circumstances that can surround human beings. But the range is not so broad as to include under any circumstances swindling, drug dependency, or sadism. In this context it is particularly important to note that even this indefinite conception of the best life furnishes grounds for criticizing both the unlimited pursuit of material interests on the part of Hobbesian individualists and the spirited commitment to warlike excellence found in many strong communities.

Although there are important differences and qualifications, Plato and Aristotle both contend that advances toward moral virtue and happiness can only be made, for most human beings, within the boundaries of an association or partnership (*koinōnia*). The political partnership is the highest form of association because it makes this highest human good accessible.[54] The classical position, however, does not replicate either the strong communitarian assertion of the priority of the "state" to individuals or its weaker allegation that the most fulfilled life is that which most fully participates in socially defined practices. Aristotle praises the city precisely because of the benefits it provides to individuals. And given that there is a rationally based difference among the qualities of various individual goods, not all communities are equally praiseworthy. Constitutions (*politeiai*) are defined by the values or goals that they encourage. Different regimes can, therefore, be evaluated in terms of how well *their* particular values match the life that is most desirable for members of the human species.[55] On the basis of this comparison of goods, Aristotle is able both to assess the general nature of good politics (an isolated city whose members act justly toward one another is better than a tyrannical regime bent on domination)[56] and to make more precise evaluations of particular regimes (Sparta's pursuit of excellence is flawed because it fosters only a part—and not the most important part—of virtue: courage).[57]

Thus the Aristotelian perspective on political conflict is distinct from, yet potentially inclusive of, the positions espoused by individualists and communitarians. The provision of security is not an incidental or unimportant political good. But the basic importance of security should not blind us to the higher human status of those more complete activities whose furtherance gives politics its own appropriate function or dignity. Accordingly, security should not be awarded preeminence in all cases where collective safety conflicts with the protection of or a resistance to more encompassing or definitive common purposes. However, not all community values are of equal importance or merit. Thus societies that jeopardize the security of their own citizens or of others for the sake of furthering misguided or objectionable civic values can be legitimately criticized (if not condemned) and thus consciously avoided as desirable models for imitation. In a sense, then, the criticism of these communities' wartime practices is simply a continuation of a more general objection to their natures or purposes.

However, the course of human events does not guarantee that ugly choices will be faced exclusively by ugly communities. Thus some actions necessary for the defense of just societies may be very harsh indeed. For Aristotle such actions may not be unjust, but neither are they simply just or desirable:

> In the case of just actions, just retributions and punishments do stem from virtue, but they are necessary; thus they are only noble necessarily (because it is more desirable that neither men nor cities be in need of such things), whereas actions aiming at honors and resources are the noblest absolutely. The former actions remove something evil, but actions of the latter kind are the opposite—the foundation and generation of good things.[58]

Nonetheless, this recognition of necessity would appear to introduce the same problems that beset supreme emergency. Necessity confronts the just *and* the unjust. From this perspective, the politics of virtue seems as incapable as supreme emergency of making qualitative distinctions among the various regimes confronted by authentic crises. But perhaps not. Aristotle's acceptance of necessity is qualified by the insight that not all ways of life or all communities are equally desirable. All individuals and associations (human or otherwise) have intense needs for the security and resources which would allow them to achieve or continue their characteristic modes of activity. However, both the scope and quality of equally intense needs vary with the activities that require support. To build on one of Aristotle's key examples,[59] olympians need more nourishment than academics. Likewise, I suppose, alcoholics and devotees of *The Well Body Book* have vastly different dietary and life-style requirements if they are to continue *their* characteristic activities. The formally similar functions of these two sets of needs do not, however, prevent us from saying that one is better than the other.

It is much the same with regimes. Sparta's need to enslave the Helots in order to support the luxurious life-style of the courageous few is formally identical to but qualitatively distant from a good city's need for a broad, moderate middle class. Yet both these institutions or requirements may be jeopardized by emergencies that are truly regime threatening. Even in the cases of such emergencies, then, there are different *kinds* of necessities, corresponding to the relative gradation of regimes. A well-ordered, just society appeals to a different type of necessity in defense of *its* ultimate values than does a rapacious and tyrannical one. When evil regimes are placed (or place themselves) in situations where additional crimes are *truly* necessary to preserve their collective identities, they appeal to a kind of necessity that is nearly subhuman in nature. There is a difference between an appeal to necessity in the name of survival alone and an appeal in the name of survival and justice.[60]

However, this distinction among kinds of necessity is problematic in at least one important sense. It implies that just regimes may justly subvert justice—a prototypical version of the sliding scale. Indeed, the praise of politics as *the* essential medium for the achievement of the good life may appear to provide a far stronger excuse for individual crimes committed in the name of the common good. This assessment is supported by the fact that Aristotle does not categorically reject the possibility of a just *aggressive* war. A city may justly fight not only to defend itself but also to exercise rule over those who would benefit from it and even to master (*despozein*) those who deserve to be slaves.[61]

This threat can be mitigated, however, by recognizing that the connection between virtue and necessity is not unidirectional. Efforts dictated by necessity must also be judged in terms of their effects on the quality of life in a given society. Within Aristotle's perspective, means are not related to ends merely instrumentally. Rather, practical actions taken in pursuit of some good materially affect the actor's capacity to achieve or enjoy that good. Our characters (*hexeis*) are in a way constituted by our actions (*praxeis*).[62] In this sense, isolated vicious actions necessary for the pursuit of just ends threaten the very capacity to enjoy or practice justice.[63] Thus, even if classical political philosophy is, in its attitude toward war, compelled, in Leo Strauss's words, "to take its bearings by the practice of bad cities,"[64] it is not compelled to accept the conclusion that "where the very safety of the country depends upon the resolution to be taken, no considerations of justice or injustice, humanity or cruelty, nor of glory or shame, should be allowed to prevail."[65]

In the most extreme case imaginable, the preservation of the quality of life in a just community would be directly incompatible with actions necessary for communal survival. Life would be secured only under the condition of a community's surrendering its destiny to the despotism of a truly vicious regime or only at the cost of its committing atrocious crimes against innocents. Conversely, the defense or support of justice would require extreme risks of communal extinction. On an individual level, Plato's Socrates has no difficulty choosing between survival at the price of corruption and the fatal pursuit of goodness. But it would be extraordinarily simple-minded and inhumanly presumptuous to contend that this choice is as easily made or as clearly defensible in the case of communities (or those leading or speaking for communities).[66]

In less extreme circumstances, however, this complex relationship between justice and necessity offers a useful corrective to the sliding scale. Even if the defense of a just regime should allow more latitude in the means selected than the defense of an abusive or tyrannical one, that community's justice also places limitations on the ways in which the regime (in the Aristotelian sense) may be supported. The choice of unjust or vicious means, even as necessities, may ultimately corrupt the justice of what is to be preserved. This observatiion is not a hollow call for societies to sacrifice their lives for their virtues. Nor is it intended to condemn those that have awarded priority to communal survival. The relationship does, however, enable us to examine choices made under the duress of emergency according to a different perspective than simply the accuracy of the threat assessment or the effectiveness of the proposed response. Moreover, this part of the classical position may provide (leaving theological supports aside for the moment) the only plausible psychological grounds for respecting moral limitations on actions responding to conditions of necessity.

Thus the classical framework apparently supplies a conception of political necessity that is distinct from that employed within Walzer's formulation of supreme emergency. The Aristotelian view of necessity does not avoid reference to the qualitative differences among regimes. Moreover, by relating necessity to justice in a constitutive, rather than instrumental, way, the classical version calls our attention to the impacts of just causes on necessary actions. Taken together, these two features of the classical framework help to reduce the distance between politics and morality that seems unavoidable within the principle of supreme emergency. Just as important, however, this perspective on necessity can illuminate ongoing moral dilemmas about the use of force in a way that amplifies the insights supplied by the contemporary just war view. This can be suggested by briefly considering how the classical paradigm would address some of the issues raised within debates over nuclear deterrence.

According to the classical perspective, there is a significant difference between the pursuit of self-aggrandizing and competitive national interests and attempts to fulfill or approximate the praiseworthy human political interest in establishing communities that encourage the flourishing of an excellent quality of life. Thus, whatever the merits of Green's criticisms of the politics of superpower competition, the theoretical implications of his statement are vitiated by his failure to include alternative conceptions of political interests within his critical scope. According to Aristotle, not all political conflicts are self-indulgent or vainglorious competitions between collective material interests or value affirmations.[67] Thus we cannot determine before the fact that *no* political (in the best sense) interests can justify the physical dangers and moral uncertainties of deterrence. Indeed, given the potentially overwhelming influence of politics on the quality of human life, even the possible *use* of nuclear weapons to defend some political existences or, more important, to resist others cannot be condemned in advance as absolutely the worst possibility in the course of human events. Reflections on the prospects of humanity under a victorious Naziism are overused (and sometimes misused) by writers dealing with this subject. But in this case this example strikes me as an absolutely appropriate response.

But the classical position's complex inclusivity of both communitarian and individualist priorities suggests that the personal security of individuals is not simply overshadowed by dominant community values. The comparison of civic purposes that identifies those worthy of defense at great sacrifice or those requiring resistance at all costs must be more than ideological. For example, the classical view would without question reject the contention that all values that are central to contemporary Western society can truly justify defense by means of hideous weapons. Values that demand such great sacrifices also demand mature and critical justification. Thus, from the Aristotelian perspective, both liberal and conservative ideologies are superficial imitations of the careful evaluation of political alternatives that must be at the center of all practical political theory. Moreover, given the essential connection between the nature of regimes and the nature of threats, the model of politics that I have endorsed also demands that our assessment of threats be critical and discriminating. We must recognize and deal with the many relevant differences between the mortal threat posed to the future of the West by the Nazis and the more subtle dimensions of the complicated threat posed by the obnoxious Soviet regime.

Likewise, since the political community exerts such a critical influence on individual character, we are also compelled to inquire about the effects of the nuclear arms race on the psyches or personalities of individual citizens. This is not simply a matter of the sporadic uneasiness prompted by the realities of deterrence. It could be argued that the official willingness to destroy millions of innocent civilians under the deterrence strategy of mutual assured destruction both relies on and contributes to a contempt for life that threatens to pervade a broader public than the community of strategic planners. Walzer's incontestable conclusion that deterrence has become a permanent condition renders this problem especially acute.[68]

Finally, this deeper view of politics suggests that our current reliance on deterrence should, in the best of cases, encourage us to reexamine the theory and practice of those values that we deem central to our way of life. Such a reexamination would involve neither self-righteous polemics nor guilt-ridden rejection, but sincere efforts at self-improvement. No one believes such efforts would be easy or noncontroversial. But it is decidedly *not* true that the only possible alternative postures within debates over Western values are those that confidently proclaim the sublimity of our society on the one hand, and those that cynically deny the importance of any differences between the superpowers' political and social systems, on the other.

Objections and Responses

The classical position would appear, then, to avoid the problems posed by both individualists and communitarians without slipping into the difficulties that beset the modern just war position. But despite these putative advantages, a number of significant objections can be raised against the position I have sketched.

Potential critics surely will claim that attempts to subject real political communities to a standard of moral virtue (or the *quality* of life) are either laughably inappropriate or dangerously presumptive. But the plausibility of the Aristotelian model may be strengthened by noting its important similarities with Walzer's more down-to-earth morality. First, both positions are *demanding*. Walzer's strict standards of what we ought to do conflict as often as do Aristotle's with what it would be profitable or gratifying or safe to do. Walzer's normal moral reality in which people have the "duty to accept risks (and perhaps to die)" inclines much more to an Aristotelian or Socratic challenge to our instincts and self-assurance than to the Rawlsian characterization of a normal moral act as that which benefits another at minimal hazard or sacrifice to the agent.

Yet, for both Walzer *and* Aristotle, *ought* implies *can*. Although moral actions are difficult, even exemplary, they are not in any way superhuman. Aristotle's *Ethics* is not the glorification of a shining yet remote moral ideal, but the outline of the right things done in the right ways at the right times.[69] This mirrors Walzer's commitment to possibility, which is exhibited through the richness of his examples—pictures of real individuals choosing to undergo great risks or sacrifice rather than to violate the moral reality of the war convention. Indeed, at least some of Walzer's examples of respect for the rights of noncombatants could also be interpreted as efforts by moral agents to preserve a certain quality in their lives. Walzer notes that even during Britain's darkest hour some of her officers resisted the terror bombing strategy precisely to maintain their distance from the Nazi regime. A reminder of Socrates' argument in the *Gorgias* is appropriate here. It is better to suffer injustice than to do it. A respect for the "rights" or welfare of others, even at great personal risk, is one definitive or characteristic feature of the virtuous person's behavior.

The compatibility between the Aristotelian perspective and the best features of Walzer's just war framework prompts greater attention to the advantages of the classical view. Walzer intends to avoid, as much as possible, the difficult problem of making comparative evaluations among regimes. But I have suggested that the principle of supreme emergency cannot function without a recognition of the dominant community values that are in jeopardy. By focusing expressly on the relative merits of different regimes, the Aristotelian perspective deals explicitly and critically with issues that are implicit but unexamined within Walzer's treatment. It is certainly true, as Langan has noted, that evaluation comparisons of the justice of regimes are notoriously complex and perilously liable to ideological distortion.[70] Still, it is hard to dispute that a position that hypothesizes that these problems can be addressed by coherent discourse is more promising than one that, however reluctantly, accepts them as inescapably aporetic or relativist.

A deeper objection, of course, is that the rational evaluation of different ways of life or public values is simply impossible. The inadequacy of the conceptual framework is explicitly discussed with regard to questions of war and peace by

David Lewis. Lewis contends that the notion of a permanent or unified human character can be rejected once we recognize and expose its cornerstone: the (for him) highly questionable religious view of the soul.[71] I will not comment on Lewis's strategy of rejecting religious claims by counterassertion. However, it is far from clear that Aristotle's theoretical psychology depends on a theological perspective. The conception of a permanent human *hexis* is, for him, confirmed by a rational analysis of human passions, potentials, and characteristics.[72] Such a conception may, therefore, be implicit in the very structure of moral or political philosophy. Although I cannot do more than make my own assertions here, I believe that Salkever, among others, has shown that explicit attempts to deny the plausibility of a conception of human excellence are focused to rely on such a conception in making that very case.[73]

However, even commentators much more in sympathy with the classical tradition have wondered whether its conception of virtue is not historically outmoded. At least two particular observations predominate. The first is that the classical tradition seems to focus inordinately on a courageous virtue that can only be supported within an aristocratic or warrior society. Walzer, indeed, comes close to equating virtue with a kind of aristocratic courage.[74] A related critical observation, made by Pangle among others, is that the Aristotelian concept of virtue quite explicitly depends on small communities for its encouragement. Its appropriateness for judging actions of large industrial societies is, therefore, highly questionable.[75]

Yet both Aristotle and Plato seem acutely sensitive to the dangers of confusing courage (*andreia*) with virtue (*aretē*). Courage is one virtue or a part of virtue, but it is not the whole of virtue or virtue, simply. The Aristotelian or Platonic intent is to diminish the value of courage as compared with the other practical virtues of prudence, justice, and moderation.[76] Moreover, the equation of virtue with courage seems frustrated by successful attempts to substitute flourishing,[77] happiness,[78] satisfaction,[79] or rationality[80] for "virtue" within contemporary practical philosophies informed by Aristotelian principles.

These modern attempts to redefine the substance or content of classical virtue while preserving its formal centrality in moral theory also suggest that the prospects for identifying and pursuing an excellent quality of life in modern societies are not as dismal or hopeless as they might initially appear. At the very least, the hostility of modern society to virtuous practice—noted by MacIntyre, for example—appears as a conclusion to be firmly established rather than preemptively stated.[81] The difficulties of articulating contemporary accounts of the quality of life and the best regime, as well as relating those accounts to questions of domestic justice and international restraint are, of course, enormous. But it is as encouraging as it is intimidating to realize that adopting the classical perspective is a commitment to developing and asking certain questions rather than the process of applying principles that are foregone conclusions. In the nuclear age we are particularly well advised to be critically open to a variety of political possibilities and critically distrustful of the value of political abstractions.

Conclusion

I have suggested that an Aristotelian conception of politics provides a view of political necessity that is not liable to some of the drawbacks of the more modern conception of supreme emergency. This more complex view of necessity does not require us to sacrifice a critical posture toward the merits of different regimes or to despair of the possibility of fixing moral limits on reponses to crises even as we recognize the demands imposed on societies in supreme emergencies. I want to close, however, by noting one strong point of similarity between the Aristotelian version of necessity and modern appeals to supreme emergency. It is their sense of tragedy. Langan suspects that the tragic outlook of supreme emergency may accurately reflect the darkness and incoherence of the world we face.[82] The classical view helps to shed light and provide order. But neither illumination nor coherence can change the phenomenal reality of a world in turmoil. The classical view in no way suggests that the physical and moral agonies of war can be redeemed or transcended by conceptual clarity. At most, such a perspective can provide us with insights that allow a better response to a human, therefore moral, challenge whose enormous costs seem unable to deter its eternal return.

Notes

1. See, for example, William O'Brien, *The Conduct of Just and Limited War* (New York: Praeger, 1981); "The Peace Debate and American Catholics," *Washington Quarterly*, Summer, 1982, pp. 219–222; John Langan, "Between Religion and Politics: The Morality of Deterrence," chapter 6, this book; David Hollenbach, "Ethics in Distress: Can There be Just War in the Nuclear Age?" chapter 2, this book; James T. Johnson, "Threats, Values, and Defense: Does Defense of Values by Force Remain a Moral Possibility?" chapter 3, this book. Most of these authors consider questions whose outlines are broadly set by at least three seminal works: Michael Walzer, *Just and Unjust Wars* (New York: Basic Books, 1977); Paul Ramsey, *The Just War: Force and Political Responsibility* (New York: Scribner, 1968); Phillip Green, *Deadly Logic: The Theory of Nuclear Deterrence* (Columbus: Ohio State University Press, 1966). For revised or expanded versions of the Ramsey and Green positions, see also Morton Kaplan, ed., *Strategic Thinking and Its Moral Implications* (Chicago: The Center for Policy Study, University of Chicago, 1974).
2. Walzer, *Just and Unjust Wars*, p. 282.
3. Ibid., p. 268.
4. Ibid., p. 254.
5. Phillip Green, "Strategy, Politics and Social Scientists," in Kaplan, *Strategic Thinking*, pp. 44–46.
6. Jonathan Schell, *The Fate of the Earth* (New York: Knopf, 1982).

7. Green, *Deadly Logic*, p. 247. Both Green and (eventually) Schell admit that politics must be the vehicle by which outmoded and dangerous expressions of national interest are surpassed. This sort of human development requires that we see restrained politics as a transitional phase between ardent patriotism and a stable world without borders or that we distinguish, as Green does, between "statism" and good politics (see Kaplan, *Strategic Thinking*, p. 59). It does seem odd, however, to expect that politics can be the efficient cause of the disappearance of political associations. And Green's identification of a healthy democracy as the alternative to competitive nationalism seems to place inordinate faith in a process with highly uncertain outcomes. (Nationalistic ideologies are deficient because they offer partial versions of national interest. What would a full version look like?) Moreover, neither solution entertains the plausibility of a worthwhile discrete or appropriate political interest different from the immediate preferences of those individuals who make up a given society. Consequently, good politics can be found in those associations that are, in a sense, the most devoid of specifically public characteristics.

8. Thomas Pangle, "The Moral Basis of National Security: Four Historical Perspectives," in Klaus Knorr, ed., *Historical Dimensions of National Security Problems* (Lawrence: Kansas University Press, 1976), p. 387.

9. Walzer, *Just and Unjust Wars*, pp. 261–263.

10. Ibid. pp. 323, 334–335.

11. Cf. Hollenbach, "Ethics in Distress," chapter 2, this book.

12. There are, to be sure, significant differences between psychic effects, especially those spread over large populations through causes that are only dimly perceived, and practices. But psychic characteristics can certainly influence attitudes toward or the willingness to entertain or reject certain options for practical action. Moreover, for those who are persuaded by the Aristotelian insight that political or social structures inevitably exert enormous influence on individual character, those psychic effects themselves are hardly trivial or inconsequential. For a further discussion of the "duration" problems attending supreme emergency, see Stephen E. Lammers, "Area Bombing in World War II: The Argument of Michael Walzer," *Journal of Religious Ethics* 111(1983):96–113. Langan makes brief but suggestive remarks concerning the impact of deterrence postures on moral standards in "The American Hierarchy and Nuclear Weapons," *Theological Studies* 43(1982):447–467.

13. Cf. Aristotle, *Politics*, 1273a, 40–42.

14. The term legitimation is Jurgen Habermas's. See Habermas, *Legitimation Crisis*, Thomas McCarthy, trans. (Boston: Beacon Press, 1975). My use of it is similar to his in that I intend to refer not to legal or constitutional legitimacy but to a more general confidence in or dissatisfaction with the regime. In this sense, the inability to maintain or protect institutions or practices deemed essential to a particular society's way of life can threaten *delegitimation*, either for a particular government or administration or for basic assumptions or principles. Thus the failure of material progress to make human beings happy could, under certain conditions, delegitimize the consummate or overarching pursuit of material acquisition. In giving U.S. industry such a central role in our culture or society, I do not intend to sneer at some presumed American venality. Nor do I accept fully Habermas's diagnosis of or proposed solutions to the woes of Western capitalism. I am simply stating what I take to be a reasonably plausible conclusion based on empirical evidence.

15. Quoted by Maurice Merleau-Ponty, *Humanism and Terror*, John O'Neill trans. (Boston: Beacon Press, 1969), p. xli.

74 · Theory

16. Walzer, *Just and Unjust Wars*, p. 53.

17. Robert Nozick, *Anarchy, State and Utopia* (New York: Basic Books, 1974), p. x.

18. Walzer, *Just and Unjust Wars*, p. 54. Both Walzer and Nozick see individual or corporate aggression as crossing the "boundaries" that surround individual activity.

19. It is hard to read this without thinking of John Stuart Mills's paean to individuality in *On Liberty*. Mills's praise of individuality is, however, reliant on its contribution to utility rather than on any "abstract right." Nozick's respect for individual self-determination is *sui generis*. The lack of a cogent derivation of individual rights is viewed by Peter Singer ("Why Nozick Is Not So Easy to Refute," *Western Political Quarterly* 29[1976]: 191–192) and Stephen Salkever ("Freedom, Participation and Happiness," *Political Theory* 5[1977]:395–396), among others, as a serious deficiency in Nozick's political theory. Walzer's similar reluctance to ground individual rights is criticized by Pangle in his otherwise highly complimentary review of *Just and Unjust Wars* (*American Political Science Review* 72[1978]:1393–1395).

20. *Leviathan*, Chapter 21.

21. Green, "Strategy, Politics and Social Scientists," p. 52; Walzer, *Just and Unjust Wars*, pp. 276–277.

22. John Rawls, *A Theory of Justice* (Cambridge, Mass.: Harvard University Press, 1971), pp. 438–439.

23. This would also appear to be true of the contract theories of Rousseau and Kant in the sense that justice to noncontractors cannot be inferred from the provisions of the contracts themselves. Rawls's veil of ignorance would appear to avoid this consequence, but only at the price of stipulating the absence of all political interests or identities from the original position. Providing political grounds for justice is less a problem to be solved than a question to be reduced to its nonpolitical elements.

24. Locke's position is surely stated less baldly than Hobbes's. Locke *does* speak of unjust wars, principally referring to instances of blatant aggression (*Second Treatise*, 176). But the force of Locke's conclusion is weakened considerably by the impossibility of impartial judgments in the state of nature. Since every individual or association in nature is the sole judge of what is truly required for its preservation, aggressive acts deemed truly *necessary* cannot be condemned as unjust violations of the law of nature. Locke ultimately condemns those who trouble their neighbors *without cause* (*Second Treatise*, 176), virtually confining unjust aggression to the actions of international gangsters, if not paranoid psychopaths. But the aggressive actions of industrious mercantilists could not be condemned as unjust as long as they responded to situations perceived as affecting community welfare. In this area, my reading of Locke closely follows that of Richard Cox, *Locke on War and Peace* (New York: Oxford University Press, 1960).

25. *Leviathan*, Chapter 28. It can be argued that the same position is articulated much more boldly by Machiavelli. The absence of restraints on war-fighting when "the very safety of the country" is at stake is asserted within a philosophical context that proclaims the necessary and essential selfishness of human nature (Cf. *Discourses* I, iii, xxxvii; II, Introduction; III, xli). Just as for Hobbes, Machiavelli's conception of national emergency represents not a moral exception but an extreme case that can nonetheless be interpreted within a universally applicable moral framework.

26. John Stuart Mill, "A Few Words on Intervention" in *Dissertations and Discussions* (New York: Haskel House, 1973), pp. 238–263.

27. Cf. Walzer's account, *Just and Unjust Wars*, pp. 266–268. I should emphasize that this difficulty attends average as well as classical utility. The principle of average utility prevents us from choosing a policy that would increase the sum total of happiness by favoring the strong interests of a few (for example, Callicles' men of intense desires) over one that would increase the average satisfaction of representative men (even if the sum total of happiness turned out to be less than under the first option). As Rawls correctly notes, average utility threatens to subordinate the needs of the least favored to the majority instead of to the elite. President Truman's decision to drop atomic bombs on Japan could be justified as satisfying the demands of average utility.

28. This is true, I would suspect, even for those liberal theorists who supply a content to the best life encouraged or presupposed by liberal politics. For Brian Barry that life is a life of freedom that can, by definition, find expression in a number of very different directions. Cf. *The Liberal Theory of Justice* (Oxford: Clarendon Press, 1973). This same problem, incidentally, also attends the endorsement of political principles based on either personal or communicative autonomy. See Gerald Mara, "After Virtue, Autonomy: Jurgen Habermas and Greek Political Theory," *Journal of Politics* 47(1985):1036–1061.

29. Although Nozick does not confront this issue directly, his concern to avoid any semblance of statism suggests that he would view appeals to supreme emergency as unjustifiable boundary crossings in the name of a chimerical collective interest. Nozick's radical individualism also leads him to be much less sympathetic than Walzer to the conduct of soldiers forced to fight in an unjust war. For Nozick, "[I]t is the soldier's responsibility to determine if his side's cause is just; if he finds the issue tangled, unclear, or confusing, he may not shift the responsibility to his leaders, who will certainly tell him their cause is just. . . . Thus we return to the point that some bucks stop with each of us" (Nozick, *Anarchy, State and Utopia*, p. 100). Nozick's individualist reasoning on this issue may well be more internally consistent than Walzer's. But the price Nozick pays is to ignore the very real sense in which war is (from the individual's point of view) a kind of tyranny (Walzer, *Just and Unjust Wars*, pp. 29–32). The dismissal of this question (and similar ones) may prompt us to question the adequacy of Nozick's admittedly consistent judgments. Walzer, of course, also disputes that the tyranny of war necessarily prevents us from making moral judgments about the wartime conduct of statesmen and soldiers (cf. Walzer, *Just and Unjust Wars*, p. 40).

30. As noted earlier, Rawls intends to solve this problem in the original position by making politics irrelevant to the choice of principles of justice. Brian Barry denies, however, that Rawls escapes the influence of the industrialized nation state in his construction of the original position. For Barry, this causes Rawls virtually to ignore the problem of justice among developed and underdeveloped societies (cf. Barry, *Liberal Theory*, pp. 128–133).

31. John Langan, "National Interest, Morality and Intelligence," *Studies in Intelligence* 27(1983):57–69, at 61.

32. *Groundwork of the Metaphysic of Morals*, H.J. Paton, trans. (New York: Harper Torchbooks, 1958), Section III, pp. 128–129.

33. *Perpetual Peace*, Lewis White Beck, trans. (Indianapolis: Bobbs-Merrill, 1957), Section II, p. 18.

34. Ibid., First Supplement, pp. 24–32.

35. *Philosophy of Right*, T.M. Knox, trans. (New York: Oxford University Press, 1967), Preface, p. 11.

36. Ibid., section 261, p. 162.

37. Hannah Arendt, *On Revolution* (New York: Viking, 1965), p. 285; *Between Past and Future* (New York: Viking, 1968), pp. 152–153.

38. *Phenomenology of Mind*, J.B. Baillie, trans. (New York: Harper Torchbooks, 1967), section VI, A, p. 474.

39. *The Human Condition* (New York: Viking, 1953), pp. 236–247.

40. Cf. Salkever, "Freedom, Participation, and Happiness," p. 399.

41. *Discourse on Political Economy*, G.D.H. Cole, trans. (London: Everyman's Library, 1950), p. 291.

42. Walzer, *Just and Unjust Wars*, pp. 61–62. Walzer is willing to override the legalist paradigm's prohibition of interventions in cases of secession and counterintervention (both of which imply that there is no clearly self-determining community with rights to be violated) as well as in cases of humanitarian intervention "when the government turns savagely upon its own people" (*Just and Unjust Wars*, p. 101). Even in this case, Walzer feels he can respect the spirit of the legalist paradigm because such savagery causes us to "doubt the very existence of a political community to which the idea of self-determination might apply." Doppelt, particularly, remains skeptical concerning whether Walzer's strict noninterventionism is, in principle, consistent with his respect for human rights (Gerald Doppelt, "Walzer's Theory of Morality in International Relations," *Philosophy and Public Affairs* 8(1978):3–26). But it should be noted that Walzer is vulnerable to this criticism precisely because he is unwilling to commit himself to either of the two less useful polar positions that his just war theory tries to avoid.

43. Walzer, *Just and Unjust Wars*, p. 135.

44. "The Peace Debate and American Catholics," p. 222.

45. Johnson, "Threats, Values, and Defense," chapter 3, this book.

46. Rawls, *A Theory of Justice*, p. 379.

47. Walzer, *Just and Unjust Wars*, p. 229.

48. Gerald Doppelt, "Walzer's Theory of Morality"; David Luban, "Just War and Human Rights," *Philosophy and Public Affairs* 9(1980):160–181; Michael Walzer, "The Moral Standing of States: A Response to Four Critics," *Philosophy and Public Affairs* 9(1980):209–229. See also Doppelt's and Luban's replies to Walzer in *Philosophy and Public Affairs* 9(1980):398–403, 393–397.

49. *The Conduct of Just and Limited War*, pp. 28–30.

50. "Between Religion and Politics," chapter 6, this book.

51. *Nicomachean Ethics*, 1103b3–7.

52. Or, most appropriately in this context, the virtues that can be practiced especially in peace or at leisure. Cf. *Politics* 1334 a23–26.

53. This means that the activities in question must be able to make a positive contribution to the development of a morally excellent personality or character. This requirement prevents us from including frivolous or juvenile (though decidedly nonvicious) behavior within the scope of potentially virtuous activities. We can avoid supporting the activities of Rawls's notorious grass-counter (as well as those of people who devote their lives to collecting baseball cards or memorizing dialogue from Rosemary Rogers novels) without establishing one or more inflexible patterns to which all truly upstanding individuals should conform.

54. This account abstracts, of course, from the praise that Aristotle accords the life of philosophy. Insofar as philosophy represents the pinnacle of human existence, the best way of life in decidedly apart from the city. Cf. *Nicomachean Ethics*, 1177 b2–6.

55. Cf. *Politics* 1276 b31–34. This account clearly inclines to the more systematic differentiations between true goods and apparent goods found in *Nicomachean Ethics*, 1113a–b, and between the good man and the good citizen, found in the *Politics* 1276 b16–1277 b31.

56. *Politics*, 1325 a34–b27.

57. *Politics*, 1271 a42–b4.

58. *Politics*, 1332 a10–19.

59. *Nicomachean Ethics*, 1106 b1–5.

60. This distinction also helps us to separate those emergencies that may confront *any* society (for example, cases of aggression that are purely territorial) from those directly related to the nature of the regime (for example, the threat posed to the Republic of South Africa by the neighboring black states owing to South Africa's apartheid policy). For Aristotle, as for Walzer, I think, the latter kinds of emergencies are to be taken much more seriously because they are *truly* regime-threatening. It is also an interesting empirical or historical question as to how common *purely* territorial aggression has been.

61. *Politics*, 1334 a3.

62. *Nicomachean Ethics*, 1114 a4–11.

63. Cf. *Politics*, 1325 b2–6.

64. Leo Strauss, *Thoughts on Machiavelli* (St. Louis: University of Washington Press, 1969), p. 299.

65. Machiavelli, *Discourse on the First Ten Books of Titus Livius*, III, xli, in *The Prince and the Discourses*, Christian E. Detmold, trans. (New York: Modern Library, 1950), p. 528.

66. Again, this is especially so because the provision of security cannot simply be dismissed as incidental to the purpose of politics. Although security is a necessary though not sufficient benefit of political communities, it is *eminently* necessary. Cf. *Politics* 1278 b24–31.

67. For Green, of course, it is much better that such conflicts be expressed in terms of interests (which can be compromised or bartered) than in terms of ideals (which leave little room for accommodation). Indeed, Green traces the apparent reluctance of strategic theorists to challenge the overall policies that guide their analyses to the slavery of instrumental reason to the *passions* of the age ("Strategy, Politics and Social Scientists," p. 40). Thus a politics responsive to prudent and restrained interests is preferable to a passionate nationalism. In this regard, Green's observations parallel R.M. Hare's distinction between interest-satisfaction and fanaticism (in *Freedom and Reason* (London: Oxford University Press, 1963), chap. 9). Neither Green nor Hare envisages the possibility of a politics that avoids both the facilitation or refereeing of conflicts of interest *and* the consummate pursuit of ideals. David Norton, in "Can Fanaticism Be Distinguished from Moral Idealism?" *Review of Metaphysics* 3(1977):497–507, objects to Hare's separation of interests from ideals by noting that ideals can serve to channel or shape interests. It also seems to me that interests can play a crucial role in moderating or humanizing ideals. Indeed, this may be one (admittedly awkward) way to characterize Aristotle's ethics and politics, which escape both a slavery to particular interests and a subordination to overarching ideals.

68. I do not mean to suggest that arguments over the relative effectiveness of mutual assured destruction versus "flexible response" as deterrence strategies are unimportant or secondary. I am simply trying to identify one aspect of their more broadly political consequences that could easily be overlooked within more narrow contexts. Even it it

should be true that mutual assured destruction is the most effective deterrence strategy available, its effectiveness should not (obviously) lead us to overlook its adverse consequences in other areas. Plausible cases for MAD have been made by, among others, Robert Jervis, "Why Nuclear Superiority Doesn't Matter," *Political Science Quarterly* 94 (1979–1980):617–633 and George Quester, "Traditional and Soviet Military Doctrine: Tendencies and Dangers," in Douglas MacLean, ed., *The Security Gamble* (Totowa, N.J.: Rowman and Allenheld, 1984), pp. 28–49.

69. Cf. *Nicomachean Ethics*, 1106 b20–32. As noted earlier, Aristotle is concerned to distinguish his accessible practical morality from the remote intellectual virtue of the philosopher who is, in some sense, more divine than human (cf. *Nicomachean Ethics*, 1177 b26–27).

70. Langan, "Between Religion and Politics," chapter 6, this book.

71. David Lewis, "Devil's Bargains and the Real World," in MacLean, *The Security Gamble*, pp. 141–153, at 145–146.

72. I discuss this feature of Aristotelian teleology as an alternative to the more purposive or intentional model criticized by, for example, Spinoza. See "Liberal Politics and Moral Excellence in Spinoza's Political Philosophy," *Journal of the History of Philosophy* 20(1982):229–250.

73. Cf. Salkever, "Freedom, Participation and Happiness," pp. 405–407. Lewis himself lends support to this claim when he contends that patriotic "retaliators" who "intend to launch more of a counterattack than could possibly be right" are "wicked," even if sometimes for admirable reasons. In this case wickedness is our dominant evaluation of the characters or personalities of those in question, even if we recognize that there is "much good mixed in with their wickedness." Cf. Lewis, "Devil's Bargains," p. 150. My dissent from Lewis's psychology, however, should not obscure my concurrence with many of his (to me) very sensible observations on nuclear strategy and strategic thinking, especially on pp. 152–153.

74. *Just and Unjust Wars*, pp. 34–35, 277.

75. Pangle, "Moral Basis," pp. 310–311.

76. *Politics*, 1271 a42–b4; *Laws*, 631 c5–d3.

77. G.E.M. Anscombe, "Modern Moral Philosophy," reprinted in W.E. Hudson, *The Is-Ought Question* (London: Macmillan, 1969), pp. 175–195.

78. Salkever, "Freedom, Participation and Happiness," p. 405.

79. Henry B. Veatch, "The Rational Justification of Moral Principles: Can There be Such a Thing?" *Review of Metaphysics* 29(1975):217–238.

80. Stephen Salkever, "Who Knows Whether It's Rational to Vote?" *Ethics* 90 (1980):203–217.

81. Cf. Alasdair MacIntyre, *After Virtue* (Notre Dame: Notre Dame University Press, 1981), pp. 182, 237, 144–145.

82. Langan, "Between Religion and Politics," chapter 6, this book.

Part III
Technology

5
Technological Developments and the Evaluation of War

James E. Dougherty
St. Joseph's University

My purpose in this chapter is to examine certain questions concerning technological feasibility and probability in the nuclear age. I am not a technologist, but when it comes to passing practical judgments on issues regarding nuclear deterrence, weapons developments, and strategic doctrines, those of us in the so-called softer sciences—political scientists, philosophers, and moral theologians—as well as elected public officials must listen to what is being said by leading hardware experts, military commanders, and strategic analysts about the present state of the arts in defense technology. The evaluation of technologies apart from strategies for their use, whether threatened or actual, makes little political or military sense. We must also take into account the crucial factor of cost and the realities of the budgeting process, however difficult predictions in these areas may be.

The subject of innovation in military technology is a vast one. Even the most superficial survey of the entire spectrum would be impossible. The many new missiles and warheads, aircraft, precision-guided munitions (PGMs), radars, sensors, lasers, thermal imaging techniques, satellites, global positioning systems, and electronic warfare and antisubmarine warfare (ASW) measures now entering national inventories or still on the drawing board or in testing or development stage make up the technological determinants of the continued effectiveness of deterrence, of the degree to which nuclear can be replaced by conventional deterrence, of where the nuclear threshold will be, of whether new weapons systems and deployment patterns will be destabilizing or stabilizing, of whether nuclear war can be limited and controlled, and so on.

I shall focus on four issues:

1. What are the new conventional technologies? What kind of impact are they having on automated battlefield scenarios for NATO Europe? Is the conventional balance shifting from an offensive to a defensive advantage?

2. Is it likely that NATO will be able, in the next few years, to rely sufficiently on conventional defense capabilities as to subscribe to a policy of no first use of nuclear weapons under any circumstances, as urged by the U.S.

bishops and others including McGeorge Bundy, George F. Kennan, Robert S. McNamara, Gerard K. Smith, Fred Charles Iklé, Irving Kristol, Adam Roberts, Victor F. Weisskopf, Michael Carver, and Herbert F. York.[1] Advocates of no first use usually have felt compelled to recommend it primarily out of fear that escalation in a nuclear war could not be controlled, and secondarily out of an awareness that the deterrent credibility of a first-use threat in Europe has undergone serious erosion. Therefore, we must pose the following closely related question:

3. If deterrence should fail and nuclear war breaks out, can it be limited, controlled, and terminated before it escalates to the level of an all-out strategic exchange, which poses the specter not only of the mutual annihilation of the two superpowers and their allies, but also of potentially cataclysmic consequences for humankind and the planet as a whole?

4. What are the prospects of success for the concept of strategic missile defense as a substitute for deterrence based on the threat of a destructive nuclear exchange, whether countervalue or counterforce? This was the hopeful "vision of the future" that President Reagan held forth in his address of March 23, 1983, often referred to as his Star Wars speech. What is the likelihood of the implementation of such a program?

The Automated Battlefield

What are the new conventional technologies? What kind of impact are they having on automated battlefield scenarios for NATO Europe? Is the conventional balance shifting from an offensive to a defensive advantage?

At the outset, a few general observations should be made about the conduct of battle in the automated military environments that are emerging on the earth's surface, both land and sea, and in the adjacent atmosphere. First, no battlefield can ever be fully automated. Command, control, communications, and intelligence (C^3I) will always depend ultimately on human judgments, not on computer operations. The human element will remain much more important on earth—in minute-to-minute tactical decisions at very local levels—than in space, where some systems may be programmed to make automatic responses. An air-land battle in the NATO area will be a more complicated affair than a naval-air battle involving surface ships, submarines, aircraft, and missiles. Even a maritime encounter will be characterized by many imponderables that would make the outcome difficult to predict, but the problem is further compounded on land—further still if we try to envisage coordinated operations by a combination of ground, air, and naval forces.

Let us not underestimate the incredible confusion, chaos, and disarray that will confront military commanders even in a conventional war in Europe—one waged not with nuclear weapons but with tanks and antitank weapons; fighter-bombers equipped with stand-off air-to-surface missiles; air defenses based on AWACS and surface-to-air missiles; mortars, cannon, rockets, and conventional artillery; ship-launched, conventionally armed cruise missiles; and other precision-guided munitions not already mentioned. During the last ten years, NATO military analysts have derived some comfort from the thought that emerging conventional technologies (though not yet available in sufficient quantities) may be gradually tilting the European military balance, at least theoretically, toward the defense with regard to capabilities against advancing armor and against aircraft overflying hostile territory. The technological developments that have inspired the optimism include:

Antitank guided weapons (ATGW)

Thermal imaging (TI) techniques for night surveillance

New sensors (electrooptical, infrared, radar, and laser)

Sideways-looking airborne radar (SLAR)

Surface-to-air, air-to-surface, and surface-to-surface missiles

Electronic intelligence (ELINT), electronic countermeasures (ECM) and electronic counter-countermeasures (ECCM)[2]

Perhaps the most intractable factor of all pertains to C³I. In *War and Peace*, Tolstoy trenchantly describes the Battle of Borodino as a battle of information, command, control, and communication. Napoleon was constantly inundated by messengers reporting from the front, but the military situation had already changed by some minutes when he received the report, and had changed further by the time his new orders reached the front-line commanders. The speed of communication has increased greatly since 1812, but so has the speed of military movement and the dynamic of battle. The so-called fog of war has always been a problem, and the situation is growing worse on the automated battlefield. Although improvements are steadily being made in reconnaissance, surveillance, and target acquisition, the ability to destroy targets still runs ahead of the ability to locate them and identify them properly. Despite all our advances, the techniques of identification, friend or foe (IFF) are still far from perfect, and our own or allied forces or innocent civilians can become casualties from "friendly fire."[3] This raises a moral question concerning the degree to which a local commander or soldier-technician can rely exclusively on computerized equipment without human observation or confirmation to identify an acquisitioned target as military rather than noncombatant and hostile rather than friendly. As the time for decision to fire a weapon or not is reduced to a few seconds, human beings will feel increasingly compelled to depend on computerized information.

For several years it has been taken for granted that NATO forces have held the advantage in early warning and communications systems; quality of aircraft (range, payload, and all-weather capabilities); superior quality of the Leopard 2 and XM-1 tanks over Soviet models; a broader spectrum of naval capabilities; superior antitank weapons; and a range of precision-guided munitions. Weaknesses that have troubled NATO planners have included: dependence on trans-Atlantic resupply lines; inferior reserves and reinforcement capabilities (largely because of geographic disparities); a smaller number of airfields; a lack of protective shelter; a lack of rationalization and standardization and a limited degree of interoperability among national systems of weapons and equipment (for example, in fuel, ammunition, tank tracks, and radios); low or uneven on-hand spare parts inventories and resupply stocks; and the "maldeployment" of U.S. and British forces on the Central Front.[4]

Western military analysts have generally assumed for several years that the principal conventional strengths of Warsaw Pact forces derive from their quantitative margins of combat-ready troops, tanks, aircraft, artillery, and armored personnel carriers (especially on the Central Front, where the Pact holds a two and a half to one edge in armor); much greater Soviet manpower reserves and rapid reinforcement capabilities (thanks to geographical factors and a military transport capability that permits river-crossing without bridge-building); highly developed electronic warfare (EW) and chemical warfare (CW) capabilities; a very high degree of standardization in weapons and equipment; and large on-hand stocks of combat supplies. One of the greatest advantages is that which can accrue to an aggressor from surprise and freedom of choice as to the location, magnitude, direction, and strategy/tactics/weapons involved in the initial attack.

NATO planners have long assumed that the preferred Warsaw Pact attack strategy would be to concentrate overwhelming force (armor and armored infantry) at the point of least resistance; to pin down and annihilate NATO's forward defense units; to achieve theaterwide air superiority by carrying out lightning strikes against NATO airfields and air defenses, as well as nuclear storage sites and command-and-control installations; and to open a wide hole through which fresh second-echelon or "follow-on" forces moved up from the rear could pour for a deep penetration into NATO territory.[5]

A few years ago, there was considerable concern over the possibility that Warsaw Pact forces might be able to execute a surprise attack from a "standing start," depriving NATO of adequate warning time, which depends on the amount of perceptible preparatory mobilization and movements that must precede an attack. This does not at present appear to constitute a major concern of NATO planners, although there is some question about the ability to detect a partial mobilization.[6] NATO leaders are more worried about the quantitative imbalance. They know that NATO has long enjoyed qualitative superiority in certain dimensions of available technology. Realizing that both sides have access to new technologies, they must expect that eventually the Soviet Union will be able to narrow the qualitative gap in specific areas. Meanwhile, they are well aware that in a specific engagement, a qualitatively superior tank or plane that can handle two-to-one odds may be overcome by a three-to-one or four-to-one ratio. They occasionally derive some comfort from the larger political-strategic vulnerabilities that confront the Soviet Union, including the need to deploy forces against China, the potential unreliability of some Warsaw Pact armies,[7] and the problem of sabotage by underground resistance groups in eastern European countries.

Information can now be collected more rapidly and in greater abundance than ever before, but such collection is not helpful unless data processing systems permit timely responses. As combat units become smaller and faster-moving, the need for real-time and rapid data transmission increases, and the integrated command, control and information system (CCIS) including such software technologies as the networking of computers and tactical units, becomes more crucial.

Photograph reconnaissance by satellites and aircraft is highly developed for precombat and relatively static situations, but there will always be a troublesome time-lag problem in fast-changing circumstances of penetration, flanking, and enveloping maneuvers. Some local commanders will have difficulty in determining the direction of attack. Local commanders may think they are receiving too little or too much contradictory information and may complain that they are not getting clear and timely orders from higher echelons. Whereas an aggressor's forces can proceed "by the numbers" in the early stages of the war, perhaps for two or three days pushing ahead furiously to preordained objectives and destroying all military targets en route before consolidating and regrouping, defender forces depend more heavily on information about what is happening. The defense should enjoy an advantage in familiarity with the terrain, but modern reconnaissance technology has undoubtedly reduced its significance.

Weather may be a more important factor. Both terrain and weather may affect the operations of both sides more or less equally, or they may help or hinder one side more than the other. Additional imponderables that may prove more decisive include leadership, training, discipline, troop morale, force readiness, determination and toughness, strategy and tactics, and the technical skill levels of military personnel in utilizing sophisticated (or oversophisticated) equipment under the conditions of incredible stress that would prevail on an automated battlefield. Here we must heed the words of Mao: "In war it is not weapons that count, but the power of man."

No First Use and the Conventional Defense of Europe

Is it likely that NATO will be able, in the next few years, to rely on conventional deterrence capabilities and to subscribe to a policy of no first use of nuclear weapons?

In view of the foregoing considerations, the question arises whether NATO can put itself in a position where it could rely sufficiently on a conventional strategy to announce a policy of no first use of nuclear weapons against a Soviet conventional attack in Europe. Within recent years, many in the West have called for a rethinking of NATO strategy and a lessened reliance on a nuclear response in case of aggression. We cannot review here the history of the Lisbon conventional force goals; Eisenhower's so-called New Look; the doctrine of massive retaliation; the concept of the conventional pause; the shift to flexible response after the withdrawal of France from NATO's integrated military command; and all the debates since the 1960s about the tilting balance in Europe, the credibility of the U.S. nuclear guarantee, the danger that the security of western Europe might be decoupled from that of the United States, and NATO's perceived need to modernize its nuclear forces in Europe by deploying new longer-range missiles while withdrawing more than a third of the shorter-range tactical nuclear weapons deployed on land two decades ago.

Since President Eisenhower opted in 1953 for a reliance on nuclear deterrence for the defense of NATO Europe (because he believed that the requirements for a conventional strategy—estimated in 1952 at more than 90 divisions—would bankrupt the West, every U.S. president, every Supreme Allied Commander, Europe (SACEUR) and the overwhelming majority of pro-NATO strategic analysts on both sides of the Atlantic have concurred in the proposition that the extension of deterrence to Europe, and the preservation of peace in that region, depends on a credible pledge by the United States to resort to the use of nuclear weapons if necessary to halt a massive Soviet attack. In their Pastoral Letter, the U.S. bishops acknowledge the importance of nuclear deterrence in NATO strategy. But although they concede that the policy debate over the *real* versus the *theoretical* possibility of a limited nuclear exchange is inconclusive, strong doubts on this score led them to reject all strategies for initiating and fighting a nuclear war. Since these two questions—the policy of no first use and the ability to limit nuclear war—are so intimately connected in the thinking of moralists and strategists, before we can answer question 2 posed earlier, it is necessary to try to answer question 3.

The Controllability of Nuclear War

If deterrence fails and nuclear war breaks out, can it be limited, controlled, and terminated before it escalates to the level of an all-out strategic exchange, which poses the specter not only of the mutual annihilation of the two superpowers and their allies but also of potentially cataclysmic consequences for humankind and the planet as a whole?

The bishops, after receiving testimony from a dozen former and incumbent government officials, including three secretaries of defense and high-ranking figures in the Department of State and the Arms Control and Disarmament

Agency, concluded that nuclear war probably could not be kept limited because commanders operating under conditions of great stress and confusion accompanying nuclear hostilities—with the confusion perhaps compounded by computer errors—would probably not be able to exercise strict control and maintain a policy of discriminate targeting.[8] Anyone who has pondered the uncertainties of limited nuclear war and the controllability of escalation can well appreciate the bishops' concern. Prediction in the social sciences is very iffy, and the forecasting record of social scientists is not impressive. Broad aggregate trends may lend themselves to probability forecasting under carefully prescribed conditions and on the basis of a solid and comprehensive empirical data base extending with sufficient depth backward in time, plus an insightful knowledge of new factors and forces likely to exert influence on future events. Unique events, however, especially those that depend on the choices of individuals or small groups of decision makers, are virtually unpredictable.[9] Albert Wohlstetter writes:

> The bishops cite experts as authority for their judgment that any use whatever of nuclear weapons would with an overwhelming probability lead to unlimited destruction. And some of their experts do seem to say just that. But some they cite appear only to say that we cannot be quite sure . . . that any use of nuclear weapons would stay limited.[10]

No experts can judge with any reliable degree of accuracy or certitude the probability that nuclear war either will or will not occur, or can or cannot be limited. Donald M. Snow is correct when he says that

> . . . since nuclear weapons represent an unprecedented phenomenon in military experience, there is essentially no experiential, empirical base on which to build theory about nuclear consequences. For example, it is either true or false that nuclear war would inevitably escalate to general exchange, but since there has never been a nuclear war in which both combatants possessed these weapons, what would happen remains speculative.[11]

The experts disagree on this as they do more often than not on most matters. Twenty to twenty-five years ago, when the United States enjoyed nuclear superiority and was presumed capable of controlling escalation by imposing upper limits, a great many leading Western analysts—indeed, nearly all of them—wrote about the possibility and necessity of keeping nuclear war limited as an alternative to "massive retaliation." These included Henry Kissinger, Robert E. Osgood, Anthony Buzzard, Herman Kahn, Raymond Aron, Thomas C. Schelling, Klaus Knorr, Thornton Read,[12] and even Robert McNamara, who enunciated a no-cities doctrine in his Ann Arbor speech of June 1962:

> The United States has come to the conclusion that, to the extent feasible, basic military strategy in a possible general nuclear war should be approached in the

same way that more conventional military operations have been regarded in the past. That is to say, principal military objectives . . . should be the destruction of the enemy's military forces, not of his civilian population.[13]

McNamara subsequently shifted from a limited-counterforce doctrine to one of assured destruction that was deemed more stabilizing, but his Ann Arbor position was significant at the time. Schelling gave the following exegesis:

> Even a major attack on military installations need not, according to McNamara's declaration, have to be considered the final, ultimate step in warfare, bursting the floodgates to an indiscriminate contest in pure destruction. He was talking about a much larger and more violent "limited war" than had theretofore received official discussion, but the principle was the same. What he challenged was the notion that restraint could pertain only to small wars, with a gap or discontinuous jump to the largest of all possible wars, one fought without restraint. His proposal was that restraint could make sense in any war, of any size. . . .[14]

The global environment—technological, political, and strategic—has undergone a fundamental change since the late 1950s and early 1960s, when U.S. strategic nuclear superiority made the failure of deterrence seem to be such an infinitesimal possibility as to warrant no urgent concern. Defense Secretary James Schlesinger recognized the evolving situation in 1974 when he called for a strategy of selective targeting and limited nuclear options. This tendency led to a fundamental review of U.S. targeting policy by the Carter administration in 1977 and culminated in the announcement of a strategic doctrine known as *countervailing strategy,* embodied in Presidential Directive 59 in August 1980.[15]

Walter Slocombe, former deputy undersecretary of defense for policy planning, has argued in his explanation of countervailing strategy that the fundamental U.S. objective of deterring war has remained unchanged; that countervailing strategy is neither a new doctrine nor a radical departure from previous U.S. strategic doctrine, but only an evolutionary refinement and recodification of it; that it is not assumed that the United States can either win a nuclear war or keep it limited; and that the strategy's sole purpose is to broaden the spectrum of U.S. capabilities (vis-à-vis the Soviet military buildup) in order to restrain a wider range of threats than could be restrained previously, including Soviet nuclear attacks on sets of targets smaller than a massive strategic strike would entail. In a passage particularly relevant to a moral evaluation of the strategy, Slocombe wrote:

> The United States has never—at least since significant numbers of nuclear weapons became available—had a doctrine based simply and solely on reflexive massive attacks on Soviet cities and population. Much of the current debate over our strategic nuclear forces has been distorted by the misconception that we have, in the past, been following such a doctrine. Though it is true that strategic

forces programming was often discussed in terms of ability to destroy urban/ industrial targets, previous administrations, going back almost two decades, recognized the inadequacy of a strategic targeting doctrine—a plan for use of weapons if deterrence failed—that would give us too narrow a range of employment options. . . . The unquestioned attainment of strategic parity by the Soviet Union has underscored what was clear long before—that a policy based only on massive retaliation against Soviet cities is an inadequate deterrent for the full spectrum of potential Soviet aggressions.[16]

There can be little doubt that the increasingly strident public rhetoric concerning the possibility of fighting, limiting, and winning nuclear war, whether short or protracted, has definitely frightened our allies and the moral critics of U.S. deterrence policy—perhaps even more than it has frightened Soviet military and political leaders. That rhetoric began in the Carter administration and was developed to a higher pitch in the Reagan administration, contributing on both sides of the Atlantic to the growth of an emotional reaction to all nuclear deterrence strategies and defense buildups of any kind.

Recent years have witnessed a decline in the number of writers who are willing to argue explicitly that it is possible to keep a nuclear war limited. Colin S. Gray, Keith Payne, and Edward Luttwak are among the principal figures in this group, which encompasses many other analysts who think that nuclear war is wageable, winnable, and survivable, and that defensive damage-limiting efforts are worthwhile. These include Leon Gouré, Michael Deane, T.K. Jones, and the proponents of "protracted war."[17] Strategists in this school of thought seem logically compelled to hold that some kinds of limitation are possible and probable despite technological developments; that escalation can be controlled; and that the nuclear superpowers, acting from sheer self-interest, can and will stop far short of mutual annihilation if deterrence should break down.

The limitation of nuclear war would require on both sides a great deal of political self-restraint and a very highly developed system of C^3. Even if we assume a very strong mutual determination to prevent uncontrollable escalation, and a desire to avoid damaging the adversary's C^3 structure (despite powerful military incentives in some cases to destroy it), the performance of that structure may not prove adequate to the demands placed on it in time of crisis because of many factors—jamming, deception, infiltration, and sabotage; staffing by incompetent or poorly trained personnel who are indifferent or bored before the crisis and psychologically shocked once nuclear hostilities have been initiated; improper netting and coordination of communicating units; technical equipment failures; time lags; human operating errors under conditions of extreme stress; misinterpretation of information and/or orders; atmospheric and ionospheric disturbances; and the communications blackout effects (lasting several hours) of electromagnetic pulse (EMP) from the detonation of large thermonuclear weapons in the atmosphere; and other causes.[18]

Desmond Ball has analyzed these vulnerabilities of C^3 systems and their implications for the control of nuclear war. He points out that the National

Command Authority (NCA) is vulnerable to attack by submarine-launched ballistic missiles (SLBMs), for which the warning time would be minimal. The continuity of political leadership and its ability to rendezvous with the National Emergency Airborne Command Post could be gravely threatened in the early stages of a nuclear war, especially if Washington had just received a heavy snowfall. Ball describes similar and even technologically more complex difficulties and failures that could arise in the operation of airborne C^3 systems (for example, of SAC or the Navy, affecting the communications links between command centers and intercontinental ballistic missiles (ICBMs) or SLBMs or both); of satellite warning, reconnaissance, and communications systems (thereby degrading our intelligence concerning what is actually happening worldwide); of the Washington-Moscow hotline, on which continuous communication between superpower political leaders in a controlled war would vitally depend; and of the submarine command and control system, not because of the survivability of the submarine but rather because of the special problems of maintaining dependable communications with submerged submarines, properly functioning navigation systems, and the ability to use SLBMs selectively. It is not likely that Ball would be substantially reassured by the Reagan administration efforts, given high priority since late 1981, to increase the survivability of C^3 systems.[19]

Ball concludes that C^3 systems could support escalation control only for a relatively small portion of strategic nuclear forces, only for a brief period, and only in situations where the Soviet Union practices restraint. Several other analysts, including Michael Howard, Andrei Sakharov, Spurgeon M. Keeny, Jr., Wolfgang K.H. Panovsky, Ian Clark, and Robert McNamara, essentially agree with the thesis that nuclear war could not be controlled.[20] Soviet strategic theoreticians have always been extremely critical of U.S. notions concerning limited nuclear options, selective counterforce targeting, and countervailing strategy. Yet paradoxically, ever since the days of V.D. Sokolovskiy, they were for a long time convinced, or at least sounded convinced, that the best way to deter nuclear war is not by threatening assured destruction but rather by being fully prepared to carry out a preemptive nuclear strike if nuclear war should ever appear to be inevitable and imminent, and to wage nuclear war for the purpose of achieving complete military victory. Although they insist that the use of nuclear weapons must always be subject to political control and that some targets are of higher priority than others for defeating the enemy and limiting damage to the Soviet Union, Soviet commentators do not think of controlled or limited war as most Western writers do. For them, selectivity is to be understood in the context of simultaneous and massive blows, not sequential, restrained, discriminating "surgical" strikes.[21]

It is noteworthy that the foregoing discussion refers to the problems of C^3 in a high-level nuclear exchange in which strategic military, political, and administrative power, command and communications centers are all being destroyed at a rapid rate. Some Western arms control experts, though conceding that there is only the scantest evidence in Soviet literature of an interest in sparing the adversary's C³ facilities, nevertheless urge U.S. policymakers to announce a policy of avoiding "C³ decapitation"—that is, not targeting those installations in a nuclear war for the sake of preserving the means of control and limitation, in the hope that the Soviet Union will get the message and reciprocate.[22] It would be a step toward arms control maturity if both superpowers could credibly and symmetrically renounce the intention to "decapitate" the adversary in the event of deterrence failure. But a unilateral renunciative policy, if it should be taken seriously by the other side, might well have unintended—and disastrously destabilizing—consequences. Since targeting intentions are unverifiable by the adversary, changes in the declaratory policy may not be beneficially effective.[23]

Here we confront a profound intellectual challenge, one that cannot be satisfactorily met merely with a straightforward analysis of what constitutes moral or immoral policy and action. Rather, what is involved is a deep desire to do what is morally right, but where the policy judgment depends less on clear-cut moral principles than on a prudential political calculus of probability, of what will strengthen or weaken the deterrent to war, and that requires an empirical judgment derived from human experience, concerning the incentives and disincentives, the promises of rewards and the threats of costs and punishments, that influence the behavior of governments in this world. Judgments of political probability are much more difficult to make than judgments of morality, and it is unfortunate that persons of good will are often tempted to convert the former into the latter, and to assume that those who arrive at political-strategic assessments different from their own must somehow be morally deficient.

The world will probably be better off if the most influential policymakers in the United States and the Soviet Union (as well as other nuclear-weapons states) always assume in advance of the outbreak of war that a nuclear exchange could not be limited. Such a conviction, if shared on a widespread basis by both superpowers, would tend to strengthen deterrence against the outbreak of any war containing a built-in escalation potential. The logic of deterrence itself demands this type of rationality; all the imponderables and uncertainties involved should compel responsible policymakers to conduct themselves with consummate caution in time of crisis.

Responsible governments, however, unlike their critics, cannot be content with this. They must also be prepared for the possibility—however low the probability may be—that deterrence might fail. But since they know that any use of nuclear weapons might erupt uncontrollably, they are under a heavy moral obligation to be ready to do whatever they possibly can to compensate with rational decision making *after* the fact for a collapse of rational decision making *before* the fact. For this, discreet planning ahead of time is essential, even though it may be highly desirable to mute public rhetoric about strategies for fighting nuclear war. John Courtney Murray insisted on planning for limited nuclear war as a moral imperative of the highest order. Since it may be necessary, he said, it must be made possible.[24]

Just as Soviet theoreticians believe that their strategy of the preemptive strike (if nuclear war should appear inevitable and imminent) strengthens deterrence, a U.S. strategic doctrine of selective targeting and limited nuclear options in retaliation, rather than a spasmodic assured destruction strike, can if handled properly also be viewed as strengthening deterrence on the Western side, regardless of whether the Soviet leaders happen to like it or not. The fact that they and others contend that virtually every modification of U.S. strategic doctrine brings nuclear war closer does not necessarily make it so.[25] If deterrence should fail and if nuclear war should break out—either a war that begins as nuclear or a conventional war in which the nuclear firebreak is crossed—it will then be of the utmost urgency for the leading political and military officials on both sides to become convinced quickly that it can and must be limited, that city destruction must be avoided, that the command, control, and communications (C^3) networks of the adversary must be kept intact for the sake of controllability, and that the use of nuclear weapons against military targets must be as discriminating as possible, with minimal collateral damage inflicted on innocent populations, until both sides can terminate the conflict as quickly as possible on terms no more disadvantageous to each other than a continuation of nuclear war would be for each other and for the international community.

No thoughtful person can hesitate to agree that if nuclear deterrence should break down and if nuclear hostilities should begin (whether deliberately at the initial moment of the conflict, or from a conventional war that escalates, or even unintentionally), it must be kept limited. It cannot be allowed to escalate uncontrollably according to some politically and morally blind dynamic of military-technological capabilities that we must "use or lose." Popes, bishops, theologians, other religious and philosophical moralists and legal authorities who subscribe to a theory of just and limited warfare—because of faith or ethical imperatives based on the Gospel or other Scriptures; on the natural law of reason; or on concern for life, humanity, the biosphere, and civilization—have long condemned any deterrent strategy that operationally contemplates countercity, countervalue, or counterpopulation nuclear or conventional strikes in which large (though never quantitatively delineated) numbers of deaths of "innocents" result.[26] The bishops condemn a counterforce strategy the effects of which (in the form of "indirect deaths" and collateral damage) would be virtually indistinguishable from a countercity war.[27] (Decisions as to the numbers of justifiable deaths and the amount of justifiable destruction in a war is related to the values at stake, and the determination of "proportionality" is, in the final analysis, a function of political leadership.)

The subject of limited nuclear war can be evaluated only in the context of specific scenarios. At the lowest level of nuclear violence, one can imagine a demonstration explosion or the nuclear destruction of a single target (such as a satellite in space, a ship or group of ships at sea, or a remote air or naval base) with highly limited collateral effects if escalation does not go beyond a comparable retaliatory attack. Such targets could be destroyed by relatively low-yield weapons—say, 15 to 100 kilotons (kt)—with little delayed radiation effect from global fallout. If low-yield neutron warheads or atomic weapons were used against advancing Soviet armored units in sparsely inhabited areas, such as the desert approaches to the oilfields of the Persian Gulf–Saudi Arabian area or along the autobahn in the hilly forested sectors of the Fulda Gap, most of the casualties would be military; but collateral damage to civilians might run into the tens of thousands. (It has been estimated that each low-yield weapon used against army units in the field might produce an average of 1,000 civilian casualties in a densely populated rural region.) A nuclear attack on an air base could produce 100,000 civilian casualties in most of the more densely populated areas of eastern or western Europe. In such areas, if civil defense preparations and capabilities are low, a counterforce nuclear exchange between NATO and Warsaw Pact forces could result in a few million deaths, with civilian casualties running perhaps three to five times higher than the military.[28]

Counterforce strategic warfare cannot be equated with limited warfare. Military targets include nuclear forces (ICBMs, intermediate-range ballistic missiles (IRBMs), nuclear-weapons storage sites, command centers, airfields supporting nuclear-capable aircraft, nuclear missile-firing submarines and their bases); conventional military forces, airfields, ports, supply and storage depots, marshaling and transport centers, and so on; key C^3 facilities (military and political); and economic and industrial targets, beginning with those that immediately support the war effort and gradually encompassing, if the war is protracted, those industries that contribute war-fighting power. The use of limited nuclear options, with selective targeting of nuclear weapons against a small number of military units, bases, and marshaling points is at least theoretically conceivable, although it creates several problems. First, it provides the other side with both the incentive and the opportunity to execute an all-out strategic strike in retaliation. Second, it presupposes that the adversary must be able to see that it is a limited action, perhaps only against conventional forces, bases, and staging areas, with the major portion of strategic forces being withheld to threaten much greater damage unless satisfactory peace terms can be negotiated very quickly. This means that C^3 assets must be left intact in the initial stages of the war so that escalation can be controlled. Whether political and psychological pressures to terminate the conflict at a low-level nuclear exchange will outweigh the pressures to escalate on either or both sides cannot be predicted. Much would depend on the degree to which the political leadership on the two sides would intensify communications and carry on rational negotiations.

As soon as one tries to envisage a fairly large-scale nuclear counterforce exchange, the concept of limited collateral damage in any traditional sense is transcended. It has been reported that more than 40,000 Soviet target installations have been identified and included in the U.S. Single Integrated Operational Plan (SIOP) and National Strategic Target List (NSTL). Counterforce strategy does not mean that the United States would aim 40,000 nuclear warheads at those targets. That is not possible, simply because the United States at present possesses about 10,000 strategic nuclear warheads, of which from 4,000 to 7,000 could be expected to reach their targets. Since more than half of all U.S. strategic warheads are sea-based and are subject to communications, navigational, and operational problems (arising from the fact that they are less accurate than land-based ICBMs and bomber-launched cruise missiles), a U.S. first strike against Soviet strategic and Eurostrategic nuclear missiles designed to limit damage to the United States and its European allies would probably be carried out primarily by Minuteman III ICBMs, 550 of which carry three 170 or 335 kt warheads and 450 of which carry one 0.5 megaton (mt) warhead. Such a disarming first strike is, of course, disavowed by the United States in its official declaratory policy, and is cited here merely as the most extreme example of a purely counterforce strike that the United States could possibly attempt. Since most Soviet nuclear missiles, bases, and other assets are located in densely populated areas west of the Urals, the collateral casualties would probably run, at a minimum, into the tens of millions—with no intention of targeting cities as such. Moreover, the U.S. Minuteman force, even supplemented by currently planned MX deployments, could not assure destruction of all Soviet land-based nuclear forces; and the Soviet Union, even if less efficiently than the United States, would probably be able to launch a substantial portion of its approximately 10,000 strategic and Eurostrategic nuclear warheads on warning. Given the lower accuracies of Soviet weapons, the exchange might well produce casualties in the United States and western Europe numbering in the tens if not scores of millions. In other words, a strategic yet limited nuclear exchange beginning with a U.S. counterforce attack and kept at a low level because of the threat of escalation is a hypothetical possibility under certain assumptions of Soviet strategic conservatism and rational decision making under stress. Given the foreseeable difficulties, however, prudent political leadership cannot regard it as likely, even though no one can speak of its probability in any precise mathematical sense because there exists no empirical base for a judgment as to probability.[29]

Those who emphasize the uncontrollability of nuclear war usually describe conditions of C^3 chaos and confusion that would prevail at high levels of nuclear exchange. In this connection, it should be kept in mind that even a limited nuclear war could quickly reach a level of destructiveness productive of widespread disaster as a result of blast, heat, fire, radioactivity, and other effects. Recently there have been dire warnings of global climatic catastrophe from scientists concerned about a "dark nuclear winter." Carl Sagan has pointed out a discomfiting paradox: Whereas a "nominal" low-yield attack exclusively on cities might be carried out with as few as 100 megatons of nuclear power, a full-scale counterforce exchange could easily involve the detonation of 5,000 megatons—enough to initiate an ice age for at least a year. The effects, which would include smoke, dust, and radioactive fallout; the chemical ignition of nitrogen in the air; the destruction of gas ozone in the middle stratosphere; severe and prolonged low temperatures (40° to 80° F below normal for the Northern Hemisphere); and an increased flux of solar ultraviolet radiation harmful to nucleic acids and proteins, the fundamental molecules of living organisms.[30]

Granted that a high-level nuclear war may be uncontrollable, that need not hold true for *every* nuclear war, regardless of how it begins. It is conceivable that a low-level nuclear war in which C^3 remained intact on both sides could be terminated before the escalation went beyond control. It is possible to imagine an engagement at sea in which small numbers of nuclear weapons are used without igniting a nuclear conflagration on land, or a "nuclear shot across the bow" in Europe that would halt a conventional aggressor in his tracks and drive both sides to the table of serious negotiations. Could the superpowers exchange limited nuclear blows either in Europe or in another region (for example, the Persian Gulf area) without unleashing their strategic arsenals on each other's territory? Certainly the Europeans for many years have feared precisely that—a war limited to the in-between ground of Europe, with the homelands of the superpowers preserved as sanctuaries. Undoubtedly the pressures on both superpowers to escalate rather than suffer a defeat would always be great. Those pressures would be greater in Europe than in another region, because of the stakes involved, and they would weigh more heavily on the West than on the Soviet Union because if the Soviet Union attacked conventionally in Europe and its forces were stopped by a limited NATO use of nuclear weapons, the defeat for the Soviet Union would be much less serious than would the defeat suffered by the West if those forces were not stopped.

Deterrence is strongest before the outbreak of any war. It is weaker after the start of a conventional war between the superpowers and their allies. In a protracted conventional war with horizontal escalation, nuclear assets would undergo rapid degradation, being quickly overrun, destroyed, or otherwise rendered inoperative. It is difficult to imagine that a Soviet conventional attack in Europe would not involve the very high priority targeting, with nonnuclear weapons, of nuclear-weapons storage facilities and delivery systems. (Presumably NATO would hit similar Warsaw Pact targets, but their locations are probably less well known.) To what extent can either side afford to see its nuclear assets (warheads, missiles, aircraft, artillery, and so on) incinerated before the impulse to use them becomes irresistible? As a conventional war expands, the deterrent against initiating the use of nuclear weapons is bound to grow progressively weaker.

The bishops were obviously impressed by an article in *Foreign Affairs* written by four former government officials (who had played a key role in earlier administrations in the formulation of U.S. deterrence and arms control policies), warning against uncontrollable escalation and advocating a policy of no first use for NATO—policies that they had never been known to espouse during their period in office.[31] The bishops were apparently less moved by a response to that article written by four West German analysts—two from each of the major political parties—who cautioned against selective ideas that cater to current widespread anxieties in an environment in which there exists much confusion between a strategic, offensive first strike against the adversary's homeland and a purely defensive first use of nuclear weapons on the territory of the victim of aggression. "What matters most," said the West Germans, "is to concentrate not only on the prevention of nuclear war, but on how to prevent *any* war, conventional war as well" in Europe.[32]

It is the bishops' fear of human inability to keep nuclear war limited that leads them to the no-first-use position. In their judgment, even though the use of nuclear weapons might be theoretically justifiable in certain situations for self-defense, the risk of uncontrolled escalation is so great that the deliberate initiation of nuclear warfare against conventional aggression would not be morally justified. The final text, instead of categorically denouncing any first use as immoral, refers to the bishops' quest to reinforce the barrier against any use of nuclear weapons—especially any risk of quick and easy resort to nuclear weapons, as J. Bryan Hehir put it in an exchange of views with the writer.[33] The nuanced passages in the final text follow:

> At the same time we recognize the responsibility the United States has had and continues to have in assisting allied nations in their defense against either a conventional or a nuclear attack. Especially in the European theater, the deterrence of a *nuclear* attack may require nuclear weapons for a time, even though their possession and deployment must be subject to rigid restrictions.
>
> The need to defend against a conventional attack in Europe imposes the political and moral burden of developing adequate, alternative modes of defense to present reliance on nuclear weapons. Even with the best coordinated effort—hardly likely in view of contemporary political division on this question—development of an alternative defense position will still take time.
>
> In the interim, deterrence against a conventional attack relies upon two factors: the not inconsiderable conventional forces at the disposal of NATO and the recognition by a potential attacker that the outbreak of large-scale conventional war could escalate to the nuclear level through accident or miscalculation by either side. We are aware that NATO's refusal to adopt a "no first use" pledge is to some extent linked to the deterrent effect of this inherent ambiguity. Nonetheless, in light of the probable effects of initiating nuclear war, we urge NATO to move rapidly toward the adoption of a "no first use" policy, but doing so in tandem with development of an adequate alternative defense posture.[34]

The question of whether NATO will be able—politically, economically, and militarily—to reduce its reliance on nuclear deterrence and shift to a no-first-use conventional strategy will remain controversial. For some years, NATO governments have expressed a desire to reduce their reliance on nuclear weapons and to build up conventional capabilities in order to raise the nuclear threshold, but defense elites within NATO are still opposed to a declaratory policy of no first use for several reasons:

1. No one denies that a purely conventional deterrent would be much more costly, and probably less effective, than a mixed nuclear-conventional one. Some NATO officials fear that the debate over a no-first-use policy could split the alliance in two.[35]

2. For more than two decades, the United States has been urging the western Europeans to increase their conventional capabilities. These efforts have met with very limited success, partly because of popular constraints on defense spending in all democratic countries, but also because the Europeans are convinced that nuclear deterrence is more effective than conventional defense planning, which in their eyes is economically wasteful, politically undesirable, and militarily futile.

3. Western European publics and governing elites have depended so long on the U.S. nuclear guarantee that, regardless of how great a credibility problem may attach to it, they find continuing dependence on it less unpalatable than any of the alternatives being proposed. Politicians faced with growing demands for scarce budgetary resources are reluctant to incur the displeasure of electorates by calling for the substantial increases in defense spending that a conventional strategy requires.

4. To the extent that the western Europeans can increase their expenditures for conventional capabilities, this may be more than offset by U.S., British, and French preparations to meet out-of-area commitments in the Middle East, the Asia-Pacific region, Africa, and the Central America–Caribbean region.

5. Most NATO countries, particularly West Germany, face the prospect of declining military manpower recruitment pools, and a decrease in the willingness to perform military service.[36]

6. The new PGM and other technologies that are now emerging, most of them by no means cheap, hold promise for enhancing NATO's ability to give a good nonnuclear account of itself, but it will be several years before they become available in large operational quantities.

7. NATO strategists are not ready to renounce the first-use option at a time when the Soviet Union is known to be deploying additional intermediate-range nuclear missiles in East Germany and Czechoslovakia.[37]

8. Given their own usually xenophobic and paranoid reaction to every new development in NATO, Soviet political and military leaders cannot be expected to manifest keen enthusiasm for anything NATO does. If the Western alliance shifts emphasis, as many would have it do, from a nuclear to a conventional strategy, the Soviet leadership will probably fasten on such a trend as one more compelling proof that NATO is plotting war.

Indeed, if we have reason to fear that nuclear war-fighting strategies may increase the probability of nuclear war, then perhaps we need to give some thought to the possibility that a swelling chorus in favor of denuclearizing and conventionalizing NATO's strategy may eventually lead to results that are not entirely benign. Conventional strategies, to be credible, must be war-fighting strategies. Is there any reason to believe that these may increase the probability of the outbreak of a war that begins as a conventional one and escalates to the nuclear level?

Both bishops and other advocates of no first use insist that they do not wish to make the world or Europe "safe for conventional war" (whose horrors may well be indistinguishable from those of a limited war waged with low-yield nuclear weapons in a discriminating manner against adversary military formations).[38] Yet that may be the unintended consequence of advocating and eventually adopting an absolute and unconditional no-first-use policy, if it makes conventional attack the least bit more attractive to Soviet leaders and military planners (assuming they could take seriously a NATO policy of no first use, accompanied by previous and subsequent modifications of force postures to make such a policy meaningful, such as the withdrawal of shorter-range nuclear weapons that might be overrun before authorization to use them could be received—a process already under way for the last three years).[39]

A no-first-use policy would, of course, require a fundamental revision of what has been engraved in stone as NATO strategy for three decades. It is sometimes suggested that NATO could alter its declaratory policy without endangering the security of its members because, as long as nuclear weapons are available in western Europe, Soviet planners could never be sure that they would not be used first. The problem with this semantically clever solution is that it is too clever by half, for once the alliance's policy is changed there will be irresistible political pressures to modify the basic nuclear-weapons deployment pattern regardless of the degree to which there has been any compensating conventional buildup.

Western strategic analysts have been working overtime trying to substitute conventional for nuclear deterrence in Europe. Samuel P. Huntington, for example, contends that a forward defense strategy of pure denial is not sufficient to deter, for it makes it easier for an aggressor to weigh the costs and gains of an attack; he proposes a conventional strategy that combines defense with retaliatory punishment. NATO, in his view, should break out of its Maginot Line mentality, backed with a threat of nuclear incineration, and seek to deter a Soviet attack by threatening to carry out a counteroffensive thrust aimed at liberating eastern Europe.[40] Other strategists who prefer the traditional NATO strategy of attritional confrontation warn that maneuver-oriented defense, pulling back here and pushing forward there, could be "a formula for disaster," for it may enable the attack to penetrate deeply, envelop NATO forces, and sever their lines of communications.[41]

Actually, the alliance operates within fixed limits.[42] It dare not swing so far toward the nuclear side as to reduce its conventional forces; at present it cannot go so far in the opposite direction as to renounce its option of using nuclear weapons first, if necessary. Both conventional force improvement and nuclear modernization are necessary to preserve stable equilibrium. The more usual prescription is for a conventional force effort that will make it possible for NATO to adopt a policy of no early use or use only in extreme circumstances.[43]

NATO has a moral and political obligation to move in this direction, although it may not be easy to raise the nuclear threshold too much without at the same time raising the chance that conventional war will occur. Unfortunately, there are no simple solutions to the West's security dilemmas in the nuclear age. As long as the Soviet Union presents both a conventional and, increasingly, a nuclear threat to western Europe, NATO cannot renounce the first-use option. In the final analysis, the issue may be an exquisitely academic one. If the Soviet Union should ever decide to attack western Europe, it may well decide at the same time that it must go nuclear at the start, regionally and strategically, rather than leave the option of first activating the central strategic systems to the United States. Those Europeans who are strong proponents of nuclear deterrence hope that the Soviet leaders see and will continue to see it this way. The Europeans think that this would be the best guarantee of an indefinitely long period of successful and stable deterrence until the perceptions that nation-states harbor of their security problems undergo substantial change.

One can readily imagine that the president of the United States, after consulting with the leaders of the Atlantic Allies, might decide—on the basis of the dictum that "no war is just if it does more harm than good to the state"[44]— that it would be disproportionate, counterproductive, and unjustifiable to invoke nuclear weapons in a concrete war situation. Yet in the current international political-strategic real world, it could be irresponsible for NATO to announce in advance that it will renounce the initial use of nuclear weapons under all future contingencies. If this were not merely a sham but something that could be taken seriously by the other side, it would be bound to reduce in that other side's calculations what up to now has operated as an inhibiting element of uncertainty, which makes a westward thrust by the Warsaw Pact an unpredictable leap into the unknown.[45] The removal of that uncertainty would inevitably weaken deterrence more than can be compensated for by any shift to conventional emphasis within the realm of realistic expectation. It could spawn a very real danger that Soviet leaders might be emboldened to engage in imprudent risk-taking in a future critical confrontation in Europe on the expectation that the West, paralyzed by fear of a massive conventional attack, might feel compelled to back down. In that situation, however, the West, with its back to the wall, may very well conclude that it cannot retreat.

The Vision of a Star Wars Defense

What are the prospects of success for the concept of strategic missile defense as a substitute for deterrence based on the threat of a mutually destructive nuclear exchange, whether countervalue or counterforce?

Prior to the launching of the Soviet Sputnik in October 1957, talk about war in space was confined to science fiction writers. Developments in the 1960s, when increasing numbers of reconnaissance satellites and manned vehicles were placed in orbit, reached a climax in 1969 with a landing on the moon. The 1960s brought spectacular photographs of other planets within our solar system, the beginning of a long series of space shuttle flights, and the first test of an antisatellite capability by the Soviet Union.

The Outer Space Treaty of 1967 prohibits "the placing in orbit around the Earth of any objects carrying nuclear weapons or any other kinds of weapons of mass destruction."[46] The treaty emphasizes the use of outer space for peaceful purposes, and forbids the establishment of military bases, installations and fortifications, the testing of any kind of weapons, and the conduct of military maneuvers on celestial bodies. Nevertheless, the use of military personnel for scientific research or any other peaceful purposes is not prohibited. Since 1957 the superpowers have been responsible for more than 90 percent of the 2,500 satellites that have been placed in orbit for a variety of purposes—weather forecasting, commercial television, navigation, ocean surveillance, reconnaissance, military communications, early warning, nuclear test detection, scientific exploration and research, and so on. Two-thirds of all satellites have been military, as have been nearly all personnel in their space programs.[47] The military orientation of the Soviet space program has been more pronounced than that of the United States.[48]

Antisatellite Systems

Two decades ago, both superpowers developed marginally effective antisatellite systems, which aroused little interest. In February 1976, the Soviet Union resumed antisatellite system (ASAT) testing to which the outgoing Ford administration and its successor paid notice. Conservative security policymakers feared that a first strategic nuclear strike against the United States would be preceded by an attack on all U.S. intelligence-gathering satellites, which would leave the nation technologically deaf, dumb, and blind. The Carter administration entered into Geneva negotiations with Moscow on an ASAT weapons ban, but they led nowhere and were discontinued after the Soviet invasion of Afghanistan. The Carter administration had seemed interested in an ASAT Treaty that would ensure the continued survival of systems on which strategic deterrence and arms control verification depend and which would avoid a costly new round of high-tech arms competition in space.[49]

The Soviet Union has tested and deployed a somewhat cumbersome yet operational system capable of threatening low-orbit reconnaissance and navigation satellites but not of reaching U.S. Navstar satellites, which orbit at an altitude of 20,000 kilometers (km), or U.S. early warning and communications satellites deployed in geosynchronous orbit 36,000 km above the earth.[50] Launching the Soviet ASAT—a two-ton warhead on a liquid-fueled booster—could take up to twenty-four hours, until the earth's rotation brings the orbital track of the target to within a few hundred km of the launcher, and interception might take another revolution or two around the earth. Waiting time could be a serious problem if several satellites were to be targeted simultaneously, and might provide several hours notice that a strategic attack was imminent. The United States would probably have no choice but to regard an attack on its space-based communications as a direct attack on its territory and a *casus belli atomici.*[51]

During 1983 it was clear that the U.S. Air Force was preparing the first test of an ASAT system that would enable F-15 fighter planes to place missiles on target within an hour after takeoff. Reports that the U.S. ASAT would be technically superior to that of the Soviet Union led Premier Yuri Andropov, in his last public meeting before his death, to propose to nine Democratic senators a complete ban on ASAT weapons, as well as a moratorium on the deployment of "killer satellites."[52] Although House and Senate committees pressed for such a moratorium pending negotiation toward a mutual and verifiable ban, the Reagan administration initially displayed little interest in Andropov's offer, expressing serious doubts about the verifiability of a ban.[53] The U.S. Air Force actually tested its ASAT rocket from the F-15 in January 1984, not against an actual physical target but only against a defined point in space, because of a congressionally imposed restriction.[54]

In late June 1984, when the Soviet Union reiterated its proposal to undertake talks in Vienna in September on an ASAT ban, the Reagan administration somewhat unexpectedly expressed interest in doing so, while at the same time indicating a hope that such talks could be broadened to encompass the possible resumption of suspended negotiations in Geneva on strategic and intermediate-range nuclear missiles.[55] Proponents of an ASAT Treaty feared that superpower competition in this dimension would create strong pressures, at moments of serious crisis, for each side to "decapitate" by depriving the opponent of eyes, ears, and voice, thereby decreasing crisis stability and increasing the probability of war. Given the intimate connection between ASAT and ABM technologies, they also feared that stepped-up efforts in the former category would undermine the ABM Treaty and precipitate a dangerous race for space-based ballistic missile defense.[56]

Ballistic Missile Defense

The late 1970s and early 1980s produced a burgeoning literature on the feasibility of ballistic missile defense (BMD). Writers commonly spoke of the need for a layered defense—either two tiers or three. The two-tiered system involves an endoatmospheric terminal defense system of the types associated with SAFE-GUARD, Site or Hardpoint Defense and Low Altitude Defense (LoAD) and a less clearly defined exoatmospheric system intended to intercept incoming missiles in midcourse before reentry into the atmosphere. Terminal defense, the most highly developed phase, uses ground-based phased array radar, computers, and missile interceptors armed with nuclear warheads. The term usually used to describe this system, *conventional terminal defense,* though somewhat misleading, refers to the fact that this is the familiar type of ballistic missile defense that was regulated by the ABM Treaty of 1972, the type that both sides were deploying at that time. Up to now it has been assumed that a nuclear warhead is necessary to destroy an incoming warhead within the atmosphere, below 100,000 feet. It has also been taken for granted that conventional terminal defense can effectively protect ICBM sites, especially if deployed preferentially and with deceptive basing and mobility for both the ICBMs and the BMD, but that conventional terminal defense could not adequately protect cities.[57]

The three-tiered defense system included the two layers just described and added a third layer of so-called exotic systems, which usually involved directed energy weapons (DEW). These latter weapons are of two types: high-energy lasers or particle beam weapons. Both operate from space-based platforms and would be aimed at enemy missiles in the boost or postboost phase of their ballistic trajectory. If it can be developed, such a BMD system would constitute a defensive shield far out in space. One of the principal putative advantages of exoatmospheric systems, both boost-phase and midcourse BMD, is their nonnuclear kill capability.

Each of the three layers would have a "leakage" rate. Let us suppose the leakage rates for the boost phase, midcourse and terminal defense systems to be, respectively, 40, 25 and 20 percent.[58] If the Soviet Union were to launch a strategic first strike with 300 missiles and, say, 3,000 warheads, the number penetrating the first outer-space layer would be 120 missiles carrying 1,200 warheads (not yet separated). The number of individual warheads penetrating the second, mid-course layer would be 300, and 60 would penetrate the third layer. Sixty warheads in the megaton range, of course, could do a catastrophic amount of damage. But whereas 300 heavy missiles with 10 warheads each might conceivably knock out more than 90 percent of a U.S. ICBM force unprotected by BMD, they could not be relied on to destroy more than a small portion of a BMD-protected missile force. That is why BMD has often been suggested in recent years as a remedy for Minuteman vulnerability or as a supplement to MX deployment in fixed silos.

As early as 1981, the Defense Advanced Research Projects Agency (DARPA) was reported to be carrying out a series of development programs known as the Triad to produce a fully operational space-based battle station. Elements being developed were a high-power chemical laser, an optical system to expand the laser beam and send it on its way, a pointing-tracking system to spot a target and track it, and a sensor system to detect the heat exhaust of a missile in its launch phase. Working with DARPA on the program were Rockwell, TRW, Hughes Aircraft, Lockheed, and Boeing.[59]

In the early 1980s, speculation on the possibility of developing antimissile defense increased, as did controversy over its feasibility. Most of the discussion at that time was in the context of terminal defense for MX. Some of it related to General Daniel Graham's proposal for the development of so-called High Frontier technology—the emplacement of a few hundred vehicles in orbit to intercept and destroy Soviet missiles in the postboost phase with laser or nonnuclear projectile weaponry prior to MIRV dispersal. Graham argued somewhat optimistically that such a system could be deployed within three to five years largely from "off-the shelf" technology and at a reasonable cost compared to the projected costs of 200 mobile MXs, 100 new B-1 bombers, and other quick fixes to reduce ICBM vulnerability. Missile defense, he argued, did not have to be foolproof, merely effective enough to complicate Soviet calculations and substantially reduce confidence in the chances of success for a counterforce first strike.[60]

The pace of the national debate over space-based defense, however, did not really quicken until President Reagan offered his vision of a fundamentally new approach to the problem of security in the nuclear age, in his Star Wars speech of March 23, 1983, in which he asked whether it would not be better to apply our scientific ingenuity to the task of saving lives rather than avenging them, by building a stable system of defense that would no longer rest on the threat of retaliation to deter attack. The president asked whether it would be possible to intercept and destroy strategic ballistic missiles before they reached our soil or that of our allies.

> I know this is a formidable technical task, one that may not be accomplished before the end of this century. Yet, current technology has attained a level of sophistication where it is reasonable for us to begin this effort. It will take years, probably decades, of effort on many fronts. There will be failures and setbacks, just as there will be successes and breakthroughs. ... But is it not worth every investment necessary to free the world from the threat of nuclear war?

Reagan acknowledged that defensive systems pose certain problems and ambiguities, especially if paired with offensive systems, in which case they might arouse fear that aggression is being prepared. Despite all these difficulties, he called on the scientific community that gave us nuclear weapons to use its talents to render nuclear weapons impotent and obsolete. He announced that, consistent with national obligations under the ABM Treaty and for close consultation with allies, he was taking the first step by:

> directing a comprehensive and intensive effort to define a long-term research and development program to begin to achieve our ultimate goal of eliminating the threat posed by strategic nuclear missiles. This could pave the way for arms control measures to eliminate the weapons themselves. We seek neither military superiority nor political advantage. Our only purpose—one all people share—is to search for ways to reduce the danger of nuclear war.[61]

The president, it should be noted, was prudently vague in setting forth his vision. He did not commit himself to any specific technological approach. White House officials later said that the program might involve different types of directed energy weapons—lasers, microwave devices, charged and neutral particle beams, and projectile beams, which theoretically could be directed from satellites, aircraft, or land-based installations to knock out hostile missiles after they had been launched.[62]

Within a few weeks, the Star Wars speech came in for a good deal of criticism. Jeremy J. Stone, director of the Federation of American Scientists, along with Spurgeon M. Keeny, Jr.; Raymond L. Garthoff; and John Rhinelander (who all had been involved in the negotiations for the 1972 SALT I Accords), said that a space-based missile defense system would require a renegotiation and amendment of the ABM Treaty or else would lead to the collapse of what many advocates of arms control regard as the single most important U.S.-Soviet arms control agreement ever concluded.[63] Concern over the fate of that treaty was voiced frequently.[64] Realizing this, President Reagan and his advisers emphasized that his program calls for research, which is not prohibited by the treaty, and that new technologies resulting from it would perhaps become practical only "twenty years down the road," allowing plenty of time for discussions with the Soviet Union as required by the treaty.[65] Nevertheless, since Article V, Section 1 of the ABM Treaty commits the parties "not to develop, test or deploy ABM systems or components which are sea-based, air-based, space-based or mobile-land based,"[66] and since it is difficult to draw a clear line between research into the feasibility of a concept and the development or testing of a capability, concern over the fate of the treaty was not allayed.

Some commentators wondered whether the president's overture was a prelude to a new moon crusade designed to demonstrate U.S. high-tech prowess. They asked whether the shift from offensive to defensive weapons development would be likely to make people feel more secure by offering an alternative to a policy of launch on warning or to automatic and instant retaliation against a first strike.[67] Against the view of Defense Undersecretary Fred Iklé that space-based defense would move war "out there where the people aren't," Richard L. Garwin told a Senate committee (some months before the president's speech), "Space wars are not an alternative to war on earth . . . [but] a prelude to war on earth."[68]

Critics of the Reagan proposal included Senator Edward Kennedy, who branded it as a case of employing "misleading Red-scare tactics and reckless Star Wars schemes;"[69] Jan M. Lodal, who accused the president of creating false hopes and intensifying dangers by offering the "chimera of a perfect or safe defense" when there is no technological magic that can render nuclear weapons obsolete;[70] McGeorge Bundy, who deemed "astonishing" the president's "quick-trigger personal response to the frustrations of military advisers" anxious to defend "the increasingly implausible MX missile;"[71] the editor of the *New Republic,* who called the plan "pie in the sky . . . a shining-laser-on-a-hill idea" that Reagan the optimist could not resist trying out on the country;[72] and Anthony Lewis, who saw in the president's vision "a mixture of wishful technology and muddled strategy . . . a dangerous fantasy."[73] Bundy's principal complaint was that, unlike Franklin Roosevelt, who did not decide to proceed with the atomic bomb project until the question of scientific soundness and technological feasibility had been professionally reviewed before recommendations were presented to him, Reagan took the initiative by telling the scientific and defense engineering communities in which direction they should concentrate their research during the next two decades.[74] Many other scientists and former policymakers declared themselves opposed to weapons in space. Acting as a sort of shadow government through their influence with the Congress, they helped to stall the first test of a U.S. ASAT weapon. For years, such organizations as the Federation of American Scientists and the Union of Concerned Scientists have regarded themselves as a "scientific countervoice" on matters of U.S. strategic weapons policy.[75]

Virtually all those who are skeptical of or opposed to BMD in space employ a generally similar array of arguments:

1. Defense against strategic missiles will not work; a foolproof system is unattainable.[76]

2. Even if we could mount an overwhelming national effort to support an all-out BMD program, and achieved 95 percent impenetrability, there would still be enough "leakage" to destroy civilization.

3. As Jerome B. Weisner,[77] Jan Lodal and others have pointed out, ballistic missile defense would provide no protection against bombers or increasingly numerous terrain-hugging and terrain-matching cruise missiles, which could destroy the ground-based components of the BMD system.

4. A program of active and passive defense against all types of weapons would probably require at least a doubling of our present budget of $250 billion per year, with a commensurate increase in fiscally ruinous deficits—not a politically attractive prospect.

5. An all-out BMD program would not only cause the collapse of the ABM Treaty but would also fundamentally alter the strategic assumptions on which mutual nuclear deterrence has rested since the 1950s.[78] (Ironically, even some antinuclear protesters who regard deterrence as an insane policy have criticized the Star Wars approach on the grounds that it weakens mutual deterrence.)

6. Without adding to their sense of security, it will further arouse the fears of our European allies that the United States is abandoning its philosophy of stable mutual deterrence and arms control based on restrained parity; that it is triggering a new upward spiraling of the arms race; that it is bent on restoring its strategic superiority; that it is contemplating ways of waging, winning, and surviving nuclear war; and that it is increasing the probability of nuclear war.

7. Over the space of two decades, the Soviet Union would have ample time to develop countermeasures.

8. The greatest danger would be a radical destabilization of the nuclear balance. The *New Republic* put it this way:

> If one side appeared on the verge of being able to destroy the other's ballistic missiles in flight, the chances of war would increase dramatically. The side with the defensive system would be tempted to attack; the side without one would be even more tempted to launch an early firststrike before the other's defensive system became operational.[79]

I have reservations about or disagree with some of the foregoing arguments, but I set them forth here as fairly as possible to illustrate the reasons that many people have misgivings.

A number of scientists, engineers, military strategists (including currently active or retired officers), and government policymakers and administrators who are more inside than outside government and more directly connected with the space-defense research efforts of the past decade are understandably somewhat more favorably disposed to the Reagan proposal and more optimistic about its feasibility.[80] However, even within the government and among experts who continue to consult with the Pentagon on weapons programs, there is plenty of disagreement. Some who support research into space-based defense are not at all enthusiastic about General Graham's High Frontier approach. Edward Teller, for example, complains that some critics attack him for ideas that are not his, but belong to the High Frontier group. Teller is reported to favor nuclear-explosion-created X-ray lasers, whereas General Graham wants to put several hundred satellites in orbit, each equipped with forty to fifty nonnuclear rockets to intercept oncoming Soviet missiles. Graham says that the X-ray laser, based on a satellite platform, must destroy itself in order to operate even against a single Soviet missile aimed at it, and then would not be available to defend anything else.[81] Others who have been working within the missile defense research program are at odds over the switch of emphasis from long-wavelength chemical lasers to short-wavelength lasers created by electrical or nuclear sources.[82] They undoubtedly fear that the modest progress already made with the technology that was used to destroy a Sidewinder antiair missile in 1984 will be downgraded in favor of a more futuristic and untried technology.

Advocates of space-based defense admit that a perfectly leakproof system is certainly not, so to speak, in the stars at present, and may never be. Despite the president's optimistic rhetoric, they insist that the system can make a very significant difference without being 100 percent effective. A multilayered defense, they contend, would be able to blunt such a large proportion of a Soviet missile barrage that Soviet planners could never be certain how many targets would be destroyed. If BMD is deployed, it would compel the Soviets to abandon the simple arithmetic of aiming two warheads at each ICBM and face a much more difficult calculus of determining how many and which warheads would penetrate.[83] Even if this would reduce the hypothetical vulnerability of the U.S. land-based force from, say, 85 or 90 percent in a Soviet first strike (with no U.S. launch on warning) to 30 or 40 percent, this would greatly reduce Soviet confidence and thereby strengthen rather than undermine deterrence. Most advocates resent the Star Wars designation that has been attached to the concept (especially when used by opponents) because, they say, it is no longer a science fiction idea but is founded empirically on studies, research, and actual experiments over the course of several years.[84]

As one might expect, a number of commentators have been neither proponents of the system nor hostile to it. Former Defense Secretary Harold Brown admits that there have been some promising preliminary experiments, but he concludes that the systems proposed fall into the "category of the plausible but ineffective." He has misgivings because, realistically, both sides can be expected to deploy BMD systems, and this might increase the risk-taking propensity of one or the other in time of crisis, and because the cost of such systems might prove greater than the cost of countermeasures. He supports research and study in defense technologies, but not development, testing, or deployment at present. He warns against excessively building up public expectations, undermining deterrence, or distracting from arms control efforts, and sensibly notes that the "search for technological breakthroughs is no substitute for political and negotiating skill, nor for competent military planning and strategy."[85]

Zbigniew Brzezinski says that the president's effort "to move away from deterrence based on the mutuality of offensive capabilities . . . to a posture in which defensive systems more than compensate for the ability of offensive systems to dictate the outcome" of a war is a "truly significant change of priorities . . . not to be dismissed lightly." Though basically sympathetic to the president's concern over the scale and momentum of the Soviet buildup, he is nevertheless disturbed by the possible reactions of the European allies and by the possibility that his proposal may compound the current confusion in the defense debate over the MX and the B-1.[86]

Obviously, the scientists and engineers are not of a single mind on the subject. Not being a physicist, I cannot pass technical judgment. As a political scientist, I cannot help noticing that many, though not all, of the scientists who are against defense in space—and those in this category appear to be more numerous (or more articulate) and, generally speaking, better known in the policy community—have been inclined to oppose most proposals for new weapons systems advanced during the last thirty years or more on the grounds that they were prohibitive in cost, technologically infeasible, militarily useless, provocative of a wasteful arms race, adverse to prospects for arms control and disarmament, strategically destabilizing, and tending to increase the likelihood that nuclear war will occur. Conversely, most of the advocates of space-based defense have been favorably disposed in the past to new programs that offered any hope of strengthening the deterrent posture of the West. It is difficult to escape the conclusion that on both sides scientific judgments are strongly influenced by prior political and strategic preferences.

In October 1983 a senior interagency panel that included the secretary of defense and the national security adviser submitted to President Reagan a report recommending that the United States embark on stepped-up research on new space weapons, including lasers, for the purpose of demonstrating by the early 1990s or even earlier the feasibility of ballistic missile defense technologies. The proposed program was defined as having the limited aim of demonstrating the feasibility of BMD, not of deploying a full-fledged capability. The cost of demonstration was estimated at between $18 billion and $27 billion, whereas the cost of deploying a fully operational system would come closer to $100 billion.

The early technology demonstrations mentioned included the following:

1. Underground tests in Nevada to bring the Lawrence Livermore Laboratory's X-ray laser to full military power, to control the laser beam spread, and to drive multiple lasers from a single power source.

2. Acquisition and tracking of reentry vehicles using longwave infrared (LWIR) sensors and high-altitude aircraft.

3. Demonstration of endoatmospheric interception of warheads using nonnuclear kill devices.

4. Use of ground-based short-wavelength lasers in an ASAT role.

5. Capability for acquisition and tracking of ICBM targets in the boost phase.

6. Airborne optical system sensor and low-cost homing interceptor for terminal and midcourse tiers.[87]

A Defense Technology Studies Team headed by former NASA Director James C. Fletcher made an assessment of specific tasks and precise time frames (from 1985 to 1988) for feasibility demonstrations that made up an integral part of the interagency report to the president. The Fletcher commission decided that the existing triadic space laser program based on ALPHA, LODE, and TALON GOLD should be continued, but it also called for a change in emphasis from the experiments on chemical lasers that have received funding priority in the past to X-ray lasers, excimer and free electron lasers, neutral particle beams, and kinetic energy hit-to-kill devices (for example, pellets that could be discharged against an ICBM to destroy it on impact at very high speeds). The Fletcher group also saw the need for the development of a Saturn 5-Class booster to lift an orbital payload for the deployment of a manned space station.[88] This was a prelude to the president's announcement, in his State of the Union Message in January 1984, that he endorsed the development of a permanently manned station in space as the nation's next major goal in that environment.[89] The Study Team stressed the importance of using directed energy and/or kinetic energy means to destroy missiles within the first five minutes of boost-phase flight.[90]

Is a multilayered BMD system technologically feasible and achievable by the beginning of the next century? I am inclined to think that much of the skepticism that has been directed at the idea by critics and opponents has been politically motivated. We have ample evidence that scientific-technical judgment on feasibility can be influenced by political preference either for or against a specific weapons system or a specific arms control measure.[91] Those who do not want a space-based defense system doubt its feasibility; those who want one deem it feasible. The history of advanced weapons technology is on the side of those who say that it can be done, given the leadership, the determination, the goal definition, and the allocation of the resources needed to carry out the research, engineering, and development under intelligent, efficient management.[92] Granted, these are big ifs, each of which can lead to serious problems, uncertainties, and adverse tradeoff effects.

We should recall that scientists were not at all sure in 1939 that an atomic bomb could actually be built, and yet the Manhattan Project was successful by 1945. A few years later, some eminent physicists who were not keen about developing a thermonuclear weapon estimated that it would take thirty years to do so. We tested one in 1953. Nearly all of our early space launchings were miserable failures in the period 1958–1961, but once Kennedy set the national goal of placing a man on the moon, NASA accomplished it by 1969. Throughout the decade of the 1960s, opponents of the ABM argued, not with perfect logical consistency, that ABM on the one hand would be technically infeasible and prohibitive in cost, and on the other would be strategically destabilizing. Nevertheless, by 1969 Moscow was sufficiently concerned about U.S. prowess in defense technology to enter into serious negotiations. Some representatives of the Fourth Estate derived a certain amount of glee from the early test failures of cruise and Pershing II missiles, but the performance of those systems has gradually improved.

The demonstrations of space technology capabilities that are now being planned will consume a modest but not insignificant portion of the defense budget—a few percent over the next three or four years, rising toward 6–8 percent in the early 1990s if full deployment becomes the goal. With regard to negative implications, space programs will compete with other demands of the military services for a slice of the defense budget devoted to high technology at a time when nearly all weapons systems are becoming more complex and costlier. One should not, however, overlook the fact that the currently scheduled space efforts will probably produce spinoff effects for the operating capabilities of all three services—Army, Navy/Marines and Air Force. Those experimental programs will be fraught with implications for the automated battlefield and the air-land battle; for ocean surveillance and ship navigation; reconnaissance and monitoring missions of all types, including arms control verification, early warning, and other deterrence-strengthening activities; C^3; and data-processing systems throughout the military establishment.

This does not mean, however, that all the services are equally enthusiastic about the creation of an integrated command for space that would control all military satellites, military uses of the shuttle, and space-based defense programs. The Navy, for example, which depends on space assets for current operations more than the other branches do, has misgivings that it will lose the flexibility that goes with direct, immediate control of its own space programs, tailored to its own day-to-day needs. Naturally, there is some fear that the effort to create a single space command will be an extremely complex organizational task. Perhaps it is inevitable that subordinate commands in all services will come to look on it with suspicion as the largely computerized superbrain of a super-defense department. Nevertheless, President Reagan on March 27, 1984, named Air Force Lieutenant General James Abrahamson to head what had by then become known as the Space Defense Initiative (SDI).[93]

Possible Soviet Reactions to U.S. Space Programs

There is no way to predict reliably what will be the Soviet reaction to a serious BMD program by the United States. The Soviet leaders have already accused the United States of abandoning arms control and preparing recklessly for war.[94] Soviet defense planners could react in several different directions, perhaps simultaneously. First, they could continue emphasizing the accumulation of offensive capabilities by multiplying their MIRVs to saturate any defensive system the United States might deploy. Given their advantage in big missiles, this may be one of their easier and cheaper options. But such a result would foreclose the "restructuring of Soviet forces" envisaged in the Scowcroft report and in the U.S. negotiating position in START.[95]

Second, the Soviets could decide to place even greater emphasis on their own formidable BMD program. Historically, they have been much more interested than we in missile defense. Back in the early 1960s, when Robert McNamara was ridiculing the notion of missile defense and insisting that it would always be cheaper to saturate Soviet defenses with MIRVs, Soviet leaders showed interest in buying all the defense that rubles could buy—which was not much at that time. If Soviet BMD technology had been as good as that of the Americans, Moscow might not have been interested in negotiating the ABM Treaty. Under the circumstances, however, they were anxious to get the United States out of the missile defense business, and later they followed the U.S. lead by developing MIRVs for their much heavier missiles. If, as many analysts of the arms race are sure, the Soviet leaders sooner or later emulate U.S. technological developments, they may very well eventually decide that they possess enough offensive capabilities and that for the future, defensive efforts, even if only 50 percent or 60 percent effective, seem worthwhile to them.

Mention should be made here of Pentagon fears that the Soviet Union is now completing the research, development, and testing needed to start deploying an ABM system within three to five years—one that would give Moscow a substantial time lead over the United States.[96] Some observers have taken exception to the assessment that the United States has moved ahead of the Soviet Union in ASAT capabilities. A General Accounting Office (GAO) report has asserted that the ASAT now being tested (against points in space, not actual missiles) ". . . is not designed to meet the current Joint Chiefs of Staff ASAT requirements. As a result, it will not be able to negate 122 of the 175 threat satellites—70% of the projected threat."[97] The Soviet Union is close to launching a new large space booster from Turyatam.[98] Finally, the Soviet Union has been accused of committing a clear violation of the ABM Treaty, not by conducting research on missile defense, but by placing a large phased-array radar near Abalakova, deep in the interior of the country. The treaty permits such radars to be located along the periphery of the national territory, where they are usable for early warning of attack, but locating them in the interior is forbidden. A report from a U.S. interagency review concludes that since the face of the radar essentially points inward, it "could be used as part of a battle management system for a large-scale Soviet ABM system."[99]

In view of the already keen interest shown by the Soviet Union in missile defense, an observation by Robert M. Bowman, who directed "star wars" development for the Air Force from 1974 to 1978, merits careful attention. Whereas a defensive system would be

> . . . of little use against a massive first strike, it might be capable of destroying a few dozen missiles. Such a system might be able to protect an aggressor from the few retaliatory missiles missed by his first strike. Thus, we dare not let a potential enemy deploy a space-based defense of even limited effectiveness, which might make him believe he could launch a first strike and be safe from retaliation. . . .

Unfortunately, space-based beam weapons, even if relatively ineffective against ballistic missiles, would be very effective against satellites, including similar systems on the other side. Thus, if we both had such systems, the Soviet Union could use its system to destroy our defensive systems without warning, striking at the speed of light. We would be defenseless, while they would have a shield to protect against our retaliatory forces, making a first-strike threat against us more likely. The net effect of such systems on both sides is to give an enormous advantage to the one striking first.[100]

From this it can be deduced that the worst of all possible outcomes would be for the United States to demonstrate the feasibility of BMD and then not develop and deploy it. Successful demonstration may virtually commit the United States to go all the way in the absence of substantial cuts in Soviet strategic forces, as a result of START negotiations.

Third, the Soviet Union, rather than embarking on a protracted period of costly competition in space, may be motivated to improve the prospects for human life on earth by entering into meaningful negotiations for deep cuts in the missile forces that threaten each side. From our standpoint, this would be the most desirable of the three policy courses. Nevertheless—given the history of the rivalry between the two superpowers; the nature of their cultures, ideologies, national characters, and political systems; the depth of their differences over values, goals, and perspectives on how the world should be organized in the future; and the actual record to date of their policies regarding deterrence, defense, and arms control—we should not be too optimistic about the prospects of avoiding arms competition in space. Much has been written and spoken about the current miserable state of U.S.-Soviet relations, and how the Soviet leadership deems it futile to try to reach an understanding with the Reagan administration. Regardless of who heads the administration in the next two decades, however, and regardless of whether the United States decides to go all out for BMD, the Soviet Union will be more likely to choose a combination of the first and second courses than to choose the third—the strengthening of its military power over any fundamental shift of policy toward improving the quality of life. We are dealing here with probabilities, not certainties, and other possibilities do exist. Extrapolation of probabilities from the empirical record of what has been does not relieve us of the moral obligation to keep searching for realistic ways of bringing about a better situation.

Conclusions on Missile Defense

1. From a purely technological standpoint, the feasibility of a moderately effective BMD system based in space and on the earth's surface can probably be demonstrated before the end of the present decade at a cost of $25–$30 billion. Whether or not the Space Defense Initiative will actually lead to the deployment of a missile defense system, however, will depend on national and international

political-strategic developments, including the outcome of elections and the defense and arms control philosophy of future administrations, as well as programs in superpower arms negotiations.

2. Although President Reagan struck a very optimistic note in March 1983, suggesting that the fear of nuclear attack might be lifted from us, Secretary Weinberger admitted a few weeks later that we are not talking about a flawless system that could serve as a safety dome over civilian populations.[101] Even without being leakproof, a BMD system could nevertheless have a significant effect on the strategic situation, either by making deterrence more stable (that is, compounding the uncertainty of a would-be attacker's calculations) or by undermining deterrence (that is, arousing Soviet fears to the point where Moscow may be tempted to strike preemptively in a crisis).

3. Despite the charges of many that the SDI will violate the ABM Treaty, it should be possible with adequate care and legal advice to demonstrate technical feasibility without doing anything that contravenes the clear prohibitions of the treaty, which forbids the deployment of all ABM systems for the defense of national territory and the development, testing, or deployment of ABM systems or components that are sea-based, air-based, space-based, or mobile land-based. According to an agreed interpretation of the treaty:

> . . . in the event ABM systems based on other physical principles and including components capable of substituting for the ABM interceptor missiles, ABM launchers, or ABM radars are created in the future, specific limitations on such systems and their components would be subject to discussion in accordance with Article XIII and agreement in accordance with Article XIV of the Treaty.

Thus there could be no deployment without consultation or some change in the provisions of the treaty by amendment or in the legal status of the treaty as a result of either abrogation or permissible withdrawal.

4. President Reagan's SDI should be evaluated more in terms of its probable consequences than of its technical feasibility. The technical obstacles to be overcome are formidable and cannot be dismissed lightly. But its future seems likely to depend largely on political-strategic perceptions and assessments.

5. Space-based defense will be desirable if it would motivate the Soviet Union to shift emphasis in its weapons programs away from the further accumulation of offensive strategic weapons toward the acquisition of defensive capabilities and if it would produce an international climate conducive to the symmetrical growth of interest in genuine arms control and arms reduction by both superpowers.

6. The move toward BMD could have significantly negative consequences if it were to:

1. Drive the United States into defense bankruptcy, detract from other important and perhaps even more urgent defense programs, or arouse widespread public opposition to defense spending.

2. Frighten and alienate our European allies to such an extent that the Atlantic Alliance undergoes disintegration.

3. Provoke within the Soviet leadership a paranoid reaction that dooms meaningful arms control negotiations.

4. Provide the Soviets with a powerful incentive to undertake a crash BMD deployment program of their own in preparation for launching a preemptive strategic nuclear strike before the U.S. BMD system has become operational, on the assumption that they can destroy or render inoperable the bulk of the U.S. nuclear forces and use their BMD to blunt a retaliatory blow. This would be the worst possible consequence.

7. The Soviet Union can be expected to try to develop countermeasures to degrade the effectiveness of the U.S. BMD. In the past, Soviet leaders have always been more interested than ours in active and passive defense. Their military efforts in space are older than ours and much larger in volume. They have never abandoned interest in defense, as we did after the ABM Treaty. Even now, they are closer to deployment than we are, and the Reagan administration seems convinced that they have taken the lead in breaking out of the ABM Treaty with the radar at Abalakova. Most of our scientists, including some of the severest critics of the U.S. space effort, are confident that we are ahead of the Soviets qualitatively, especially with respect to electronic countermeasures (ECM) and counter-countermeasures (ECCM).[102] Opponents of BMD take this to mean that we can afford to lay back. Others take it to mean that we can afford to go ahead without fear of provoking a Soviet preemptive strike.

8. I am inclined to agree with those who think that BMD, even though it cannot provide absolute protection, would strengthen deterrence by creating additional uncertainty in the minds of those who might ever be tempted to carry out a strategic first strike. The Soviets (as both Russians and communists) are innately and consummately cautious. They are deterred, probably more than we are, by an inability to predict the outcome of a strategic nuclear exchange. BMD on the Western side would significantly compound that inability.

9. What about the cost? Our space-based defense program is budgeted at $1.7 billion in FY 1985. The five-year demonstration effort recommended by the interagency panel is estimated to cost $26 billion, only about 10 percent of one year's defense budget between now and 1989. If we decide to go for full deployment by the end of the decade, the whole program could cost a total of $250 billion to $500 billion over ten years. As Everett Dirksen used to say, we are now talking real money. We would have to figure carefully what that would mean in terms of unemployment, inflation, social welfare programs, deficits, interest rates, economic growth, and other real defense needs and human needs right down here on earth, at home and abroad. If the American people could be persuaded that the whole security situation can be radically changed and the

world made safe from the danger of nuclear war, they would probably be willing to devote an additional 5 percent of GNP to that objective for a decade or so. But there is a strong groundswell among opinion-shaping elites against the SDI as both technologically dubious and economically extravagant—a diversion from other defense programs and a potential strategic-moral disaster. With Pentagon bureaucrats reported as sabotaging SDI; 1984 Democratic candidate Walter F. Mondale on record as opposed; and administration advocates toning down their optimistic claims and favoring a cautious, low-key approach in an election year, congressional politicians were reluctant to make firm commitments on the $26 billion needed to demonstrate feasibility.[103]

10. The reactions of the European allies are very difficult to estimate because of their fluctuating character. Initially, they were quite cool. West European governments resented the fact that they had not been consulted in advance about the Star Wars proposal, which in their view was poorly timed, coming in the midst of the controversy over intermediate nuclear force (INF) deployment. There was a revival of the old fears of the 1960s—that the United States might throw up a shield around Fortress America, leaving Europe vulnerable to the Soviet SS-20s. Many were concerned about the cost of missile defense, the fate of the ABM Treaty, and the potential shift from arms control to a destabilizing escalation of the arms race that would increase the probability of nuclear war.[104]

By the time the NATO parliamentarians met in November, U.S. policymakers had managed to attenuate some of the Europeans' fears. There were no reasons, they said, that a BMD system effective against SS-18s and SS-19s could not be employed against SS-20s. On the subject of cost, Richard DeLauer, undersecretary of defense for research, argued that the president's call would not lead to spending much more than the Defense Department had already planned to budget for BMD in the next five years. U.S. officials pointed out that the ABM Treaty had been linked to an expectation that arms control negotiations would bring about a reduction in the threat posed by Soviet heavy missiles, an expectation that was never fulfilled, and that the Soviet Union was already more in violation of the ABM Treaty than a U.S. research program could possibly be. They also insisted that BMD would strengthen the credibility of the U.S. deterrent pledge and improve the prospects for arms control. Some European misgivings lingered: superpower BMD would degrade the British and French nuclear forces, and the Europeans would have to help pay for BMD in a one-way technological transfer that would benefit the United States. In the end, the NATO group was grudgingly supportive, conceding that however undesirable the move to space might be, a Soviet presence in that area would be less desirable. With the passage of time, however, the pendulum of European official attitudes swung back to skepticism and nervousness as fear grew that the SDI would leave Europe unprotected, destabilize deterrence, decouple the defense of Europe from that of the United States, doom the prospects of arms control, and increase the danger of war.[105]

11. What of the danger that our BMD might motivate the Soviet Union to carry out a preventive strike? Those who are confident of the effectiveness of deterrence find that scenario unrealistic. The United States enjoyed substantial superiority in strategic nuclear power for many years and never contemplated striking the Soviet Union, when the levels of damage that the Soviet Union could inflict in retaliation were far lower than they are today. Even now, when the United States is often accused of making preparations for nuclear war-fighting, the administration has not yet taken a single step toward that significant accompanying defense program that many strategic analysts regard as an essential ingredient of a war-fighting strategy—civil defense preparations.

The Soviet Union knows that, and knows that there is little reason to fear a future deliberate first strike by the United States, even after it has deployed BMD. Indeed, even assuming that the United States possessed a BMD system of 80 percent effectiveness—a high estimate—the Soviet Union would still be able to penetrate the U.S. defensive shield with more than a hundred times as much megatonnage as it could have thrown at the time of the Cuban missile crisis. Soviet strategic theorists undoubtedly realize that a BMD system would make the United States and its allies less vulnerable to political intimidation than they are today, and that is sufficient reason for leaders in Moscow to invoke their most fearful rhetoric against the idea. It is not, however, sufficient reason for them to abandon their historic strategic aversion to the cosmic gamble, the final roll of the dice.

During the SALT I period, there was much speculation in the West that the Soviet Union would take advantage of its tremendous margin of nuclear superiority over China to carry out a preventive strike against that country during years of maximum ideological hostility. Even in that one-sided situation, the Soviets were deterred by the unpredictability of the outcome. Any future confrontation with the United States would pose infinitely greater uncertainty and danger. One can fairly assume a high degree of rationality in the political decision-making processes of both capitalist and communist governments, and can also assume that each side recognizes the ultimate bottom-line rationality of the other side when it comes to avoiding nuclear war. It is difficult to take seriously any rhetoric to the contrary—rhetoric about fighting, limiting, winning, and surviving a nuclear war. One is entitled to conclude that such rhetoric is primarily political and irrelevant to the real strategic situation. If we cannot have confidence in the bureaucratic decision-making rationality on which the success of deterrence depends, then there is no other politically proposed solution to our human dilemma with a chance of succeeding, because every one of them presupposes a higher degree of human rationality. If the United States moves toward BMD over a fifteen- to twenty-year period, the Soviet Union is not likely to perceive the kind of dramatic increase in threat that would plunge it into an irrational, spasmodic response such as a preventive strike. It will have plenty of time to select from a variety of alternate and rational strategic reactions short of the cosmic roll of the dice.

12. The best possible outcome of the new U.S. commitment to demonstrating the feasibility of space-based missile defense would be to create a new international political climate more conducive to genuine arms control and substantial reductions in offensive nuclear arsenals, flowing from an increased awareness on the part of both superpowers that endless and ever more costly competition in advanced weapons technology is futile and detrimental to the quality of life on earth. That is certainly what the Europeans would like to see, and why they support the current U.S. program of research rather than watch the Soviet Union take the lead in space. But I am not terribly optimistic about such a denouement, however devoutly it may be wished. Hans Bethe, Victor Weisskopf, and others have suggested that the two superpowers might carry out the joint development of antimissile defense. Yuri Andropov called on scientists on both sides to discuss the implications of large-scale missile defenses. President Reagan, in an offhand comment, said it was "something to think about and look at."[106] The *New Republic* formulated the idea this way:

> One solution for the here-to-there problem is an American offer to share antiballistic missile technology, a new Baruch Plan. If each side knew where the other was in its research, and if both could be assured that they were at roughly equal levels of defensive capacity, we might be able in the next generation safely to enter an era in which the ballistic missile might indeed be rendered obsolete.[107]

These are hopeful thoughts on which to conclude, but they presuppose a radical turning around of the way the superpowers perceive their security problems. This would require not only political intelligence of the highest order, but also a symmetry of fundamental human trust, for which up to now there is little evidence.

Notes

1. For the bishops' view that it would not be morally justifiable to initiate the use of nuclear weapons against a Soviet conventional attack on Europe, see their Pastoral Letter on war and peace, *The Challenge of Peace: God's Promise and Our Response,* in *Origins* 13(May 19, 1983):par. 150. See also McGeorge Bundy, George F. Kennan, Robert S. McNamara, and Gerard K. Smith, "Nuclear Weapons and the Atlantic Alliance," *Foreign Affairs* 60(Spring 1982):752–768; Fred Charles Iklé, "NATO's 'First Nuclear Use': A Deepening Trap?" *Strategic Review* 8(Winter 1980):18–23; Irving Kristol, " 'No First Use' Requires a Conventional Build-up," *Wall Street Journal,* March 12, 1982; Adam Roberts, "The Critique of Nuclear Deterrence," in *Defense and Consensus: The Domestic*

Aspects of Western Security, Part II, Adelphi Paper No. 183 (London: International Institute for Strategic Studies [IISS], Summer 1983); Victor F. Weisskopf, "Nuclear War: Four Pressure Points," *Bulletin of the Atomic Scientists* 38(January 1982); Field Marshal Lord Michael Carver, "No First Use: A View from Europe," *Bulletin of the Atomic Scientists* 39(March 1983); Herbert F. York, "Beginning Nuclear Disarmament at the Bottom," *Survival* 25(September–October 1983):227–231.

2. Only a few samples of a voluminous body of literature can be cited: Johannes Steinhoff and Anthony Farrar-Hockley, "The Scope and Direction of New Conventional Weapons Technology," in *New Conventional Weapons and East-West Security: Part I,* Adelphi Paper No. 144 (London: IISS, 1978); Walter Pincus, "Budget is Full of Anti-Tank Weapons," *Washington Post,* December 1, 1982; Mark Hewish, "Thermal Imaging: The British Approach," *International Defense Review* 17, no. 1(1984):67–72; Philip E. Van, "Electric Warfare," *International Defense Review* 16, no. 9(1983):1273–1275; Ramon Lopez, "The Airland Battle 2000 Controversy," *International Defense Review* 16, no. 10(1983): 1551–1556; Phil Williams and William Wallace, "Emerging Technologies and European Security," *Survival* 26(March–April 1984):70–78.

3. Wing Commander Tony Le Hardy, "Communications in NATO: Establishing the Missing Links," *International Defense Review* 16, no. 12(1983):1733–1737; Wing Commander P.F.J. Burton, "The Royal Identification Problem," *RUSI* (Journal of the Royal United Services Institution for Defense Studies), December 1983, pp. 40–44.

4. "Maldeployment is a residue of wartime planning for the invasion of *Festung Europa,* which put the British on the left, to the north. Four decades later, they are still there, where they would have to bear the brunt of a Soviet thrust across the northern plains." The relative advantages and disadvantages of the two alliances have been discussed frequently in the annual publications of the International Institute for Strategic Studies (London), *The Military Balance* and *Strategic Survey.* Concerning the lack of interoperability, the NATO allies have not been able to resolve their disagreements over which radio frequency bands should be used. Gowri S. Sundarom, "NATO's Future IFF System," *International Defense Review* 16, no. 10(1983):1419–1422.

5. Boyd D. Sutton et al., "Deep Attack Concepts and the Defence of Central Europe, *Survival* 26(March–April 1984):51–52.

6. John J. Mearsheimer, "Why the Soviets Can't Win Quickly in Central Europe," *International Security* 7(Summer 1982):38–39.

7. Dale R. Herspring and Ivan Volgyes, "Political Reliability in the Eastern Europe Warsaw Pact Armies," *Armed Forces and Society* 6(Winter 1980):270–296.

8. *The Challenge of Peace,* pars. 158–159. Government officials who testified included Caspar Weinberger, secretary of defense; Lawrence Eagleberger, undersecretary of state for political affairs; Eugene Rostow, then director of the Arms Control and Disarmament Agency; Ambassador Edward Rowny, General USA (Ret.), chief of U.S. delegation to the Strategic Arms Reduction Talks (START); George Seignious, General USA (Ret.), former director of the Arms Control and Disarmament Agency; Harold Brown, former secretary of defense; James Schlesinger, former secretary of defense; Gerard Smith, former director of the Arms Control and Disarmament Agency and former chief of the U.S. delegation to the SALT I negotiations; Helmut Sonnenfeld, former counselor to the Department of State; and Herbert Scoville, former deputy director of the CIA.

9. James E. Dougherty, "The Study of the Global System" in James N. Rosenau, ed., *World Politics* (New York: Free Press-Macmillan, 1975), esp. pp. 618–622; and Nazli

Choucri and Thomas W. Robinson, eds., *Forecasting in International Relations: Theory, Methods, Problems and Prospects* (San Francisco: Freeman, 1978).

10. Albert Wohlstetter, "Bishops, Statesmen and Other Strategists," *Commentary,* June 1983, p. 17.

11. Donald M. Snow, *Nuclear Strategy in a Dynamic World* (University: University of Alabama Press, 1981), p. 7.

12. See Henry A. Kissinger, *Nuclear Weapons and Foreign Policy* (New York: Houghton Mifflin, 1957); Robert E. Osgood, *Limited War: The Challenge to American Strategy* (Chicago: University of Chicago Press, 1957); Sir Anthony Buzzard, "The H-Bomb: Massive Retaliation or Graduated Deterrence?" *International Affairs* 32(April 1956); Herman Kahn, *Thinking about the Unthinkable* (New York: Horizon Press, 1962); Raymond Aron, *The Great Debate: Theories of Nuclear Strategy,* trans. Ernst Pawel, (Garden City, N.Y.: Doubleday, 1963); Thomas C. Schelling, *Arms and Influence* (New Haven: Yale University Press, 1966); and Klaus Knorr and Thornton Read, eds., *Limited Strategic War* (New York: Praeger, 1962). None of these writers advocated limited nuclear war. They all agreed that the concept involved chilling uncertainties; that the West needed conventional arms in sufficient quantities that it would not have to resort to nuclear weapons except in extreme circumstances; that the distinction or firebreak between conventional and nuclear weapons was the most salient and readily perceptible difference in the quality of weapons available for combat and that the threshold for crossing over to nuclear weapons should be as high as possible without removing entirely from the aggressor's calculations the possibility of evoking a nuclear response at some point. But none of them wanted Western security to rest exclusively on the most frightful of all deterrent strategies—a policy of massive retaliation implicit in which was the concept of an all-out, spasmodic strike with thermonuclear weapons against the adversary's populations.

13. Robert S. McNamara, "National Security and NATO," Department of State *Bulletin* 47(July 9, 1962):67. The Ann Arbor strategy, as Russell F. Weigley has noted, "harbored an incongruity between the idea of a counterforce strike focused upon the enemy's nuclear force and the avowal that the United States would never launch a preemptive first strike." Either the U.S. force could not hit Soviet missiles after they had been launched, or else, if the U.S. surviving force went after the residual Soviet force (a concept not often discussed in those days), there might not be enough capability remaining to destroy the Soviet forces. *The American Way of War: A History of United States Military Strategy and Policy* (Bloomington: Indiana University Press, 1973), p. 444.

14. Thomas C. Schelling, *Arms and Influence* (New Haven: Yale University Press, 1966), p. 162.

15. *Report of the Secretary of Defense to the Congress on the FY 1975 Defense Budget* (Washington, D.C.: U.S. Government Printing Office, March 4, 1974), pp. 35–41; "Address by Defense Secretary Harold Brown, Naval War College, Newport, R.I.," *New York Times,* August 21, 1980.

16. Walter Slocombe, "The Countervailing Strategy," *International Security* 5 (Spring 1981):19.

17. See Colin S. Gray, "Nuclear Strategy: The Case for a Theory of Victory," *International Security* 4(Summer 1979):54–87; Colin S. Gray and Keith Payne, "Victory is Possible," *Foreign Policy* 39(Summer 1980):14–27; Edward Luttwak, "How to Think about Nuclear War," *Commentary* (August 1982):21–28. Gouré, Deane, and Jones have

long stressed the importance of active and passive defenses for survivability. Secretary Weinberger spoke of "protracted war" and "horizontal escalation" but did not use the term *protracted nuclear war,* although critics assumed that it was implicit in his thinking. He has officially expressed the belief that neither superpower could win a nuclear war. *Annual Report to the Congress,* FY 1984 (Washington, D.C.: U.S. Government Printing Office, February 1, 1983), p. 51.

18. Desmond Ball, *Can Nuclear War Be Controlled?* Adelphi Paper No. 169 (London: IISS, Autumn 1981), pp. 9–14. Cf. defense secretary's *Annual Report to Congress,* FY 1984, p. 272, on efforts to internet satellites, tactical units, command centers, and computer-based information centers into a "network virtually invulnerable to destruction."

19. Ball, *Can Nuclear War Be Controlled?,* pp. 14–26.

20. Michael Howard, "On Fighting a Nuclear War," *International Security* 5(Spring 1981):3–17; Andrei Sakharov, "The Danger of Nuclear War: An Open Letter to Dr. Sidney Drell," *Foreign Affairs* 61(Summer 1963): esp. 1009–1011; Spurgeon M. Keeny and Wolfgang K.H. Panovsky, "MAD vs. NUTS: The Mutual Hostage Relationship of the Superpowers," *Foreign Affairs* 60(Winter 1981–1982):287–304; Ian Clark, *Limited Nuclear War* (Princeton, N.J.: Princeton University Press, 1982); George F. Kennan, *The Nuclear Delusion* (New York: Pantheon Books, 1972), esp. p. 195; and Robert S. McNamara, "The Military Role of Nuclear Weapons," *Foreign Affairs* 62(Fall 1983):59–80. Ian Clark argues that there is no intrinsically antagonistic relationship between *jus ad bellum* and *jus in bello,* between the purpose of war and the means of war, but that limitations must derive from the nature and purpose of war itself. He insists that the theorists of limited nuclear war have failed to provide an adequate political theory persuasively relating the political ends with the nuclear means of war. See Clark, *Limited Nuclear War,* pp. 238–240.

21. V.D. Soklovskiy, *Soviet Military Strategy,* Harriet Fast Scott, trans. and ed. (New York: Crane, Russak, 1975). This very influential work was originally translated into English in 1963. Soviet military writings in a similar vein during the succeeding decade and a half led Richard Pipes to the conclusions he reached in "Why the Soviet Union Thinks It Could Fight and Win a Nuclear War," *Commentary,* July 1977. There ensued quite a debate on the differences between U.S. and Soviet approaches to deterrence and arms control. Cf. Stanley Sinkiewicz, "SALT and Soviet Doctrine," *International Security* 3(Spring 1978):84–100, and Fritz W. Ermarth, "Contrasts in American and Soviet Strategic Thought," *International Security* 3(Fall 1978). For additional perspectives on the Soviet attitude toward waging nuclear war, see Leon Gouré, Foy D. Kohler, and Mose L. Harvey, *The Role of Nuclear Forces in Current Soviet Strategy* (Coral Gables, Fla.: Center for Advanced International Studies, Miami University, 1974); Benjamin S. Lambeth, "The Sources of Soviet Military Doctrine," in F.B. Horton, Anthony C. Roberson, and Edward L. Warner III, eds., *Comparative Defense Policy* (Baltimore: The Johns Hopkins University Press, 1974), pp. 200–216; Joseph D. Douglass, Jr., *Soviet Military Strategy in Europe* (New York: Pergamon Press, 1980); *Can Nuclear War Be Controlled?* pp. 30–35; Raymond L. Garthoff, "Mutual Deterrence and Strategic Arms Limitation in Soviet Policy," *Strategic Review* 10(Fall 1982):36–51; Richard Pipes, "Soviet Strategic Doctrine: Another View," *Strategic Review* 10(Fall 1982):52–58; Gerhard Wettig, "The Garthoff-Pipes Debate on Soviet Strategic Doctrine: A European Perspective," *Strategic Review* 11(Spring 1983):68–78; and Jonathan S.

Lockwood, *The Soviet View of U.S. Strategic Doctrine* (New Brunswick, N.J.: Transaction Books, 1983), esp. chaps. 8 and 9.

22. Interview with Robert S. McNamara, *Newsweek,* December 5, 1983.

23. A group of governmental experts appointed by the secretary-general of the United Nations to study confidence-building measures concluded that mere declarations of intent and promises to behave in a certain way in the future in cases of armed conflict do not satisfy the exigencies of removing perceptions of threat and suspicion. Promises and declarations of intent are worthless unless accompanied by concrete measures and actions the results of which can be examined and assessed. Without such concrete actions, there is a risk that the whole confidence-building process will become illusory, if not counterproductive. Several of the study's authors clearly had no-first-use declarations in mind. *Comprehensive Study on Confidence-building Measures,* A/36/474, Report of the Secretary-General, United Nations, New York, 1982, pp. 9, 12. See also Falk Bomsdorf, "The Confidence-Building Offensive in the United Nations," *Aussenpolitik,* English edition, vol. 33, no. 4(1982):375–376.

24. John Courtney Murray, "Theology and Modern War," in William J. Nagle, ed., *Morality and Modern Warfare* (Baltimore: Helicon Press, 1960), p. 28.

25. Desmond Ball cites unnamed Western strategists who think that the Soviet Union would like to see the West condition itself in to such a self-paralyzing state of mind; see Ball, *Can Nuclear War Be Controlled?* p. 33. In an earlier and different strategic context, Bernard Brodie, often regarded as the grandfather of nuclear deterrence theory, argued that limited-war strategies do not necessarily increase the probability of total war as a result of escalation, so long as the parties sufficiently recognize the danger. *Strategy in the Missile Age* (Princeton, N.J.: Princeton University Press, 1959), p. 353. Brodie's view in this matter is interesting inasmuch as he was not at all friendly to the concept of limited nuclear war. He conceded that the United States had to be prepared for any contingency, but he was committed to a notion of deterrence effective enough to rule out any use of nuclear weapons. He was less worried about the uncontrollability of escalation than about cavalierly erasing the distinction between conventional and nuclear weapons. Ibid., pp. 321–327, 329–331, 348–357. A subtle analyst, he perceived disadvantages in each of the two mutually incompatible positions—that limited wars will inevitably erupt into total ones, and that, total wars having been "abolished," a nuclear war could easily be kept limited.

26. Address to the Peoples Assembled in St. Peter's Square, Easter, April 18, 1954, in Harry W. Flannery, ed., *Pattern for Peace* (Westminster, Md: Newman Press, 1962); Address to Delegates to the Eighth Congress of the World Medical Association, Rome, September 30, 1954, in ibid.; F.H. Drinkwater, "The Morality of Nuclear War," *Commonweal* 61(March 18, 1955); Francis M. Stratmann, O.P., *War & Christianity Today* (Westminster, Md: Newman Press, 1956); E.I. Watkin, "Unjustifiable War," in Charles S. Thompson, ed., *Morals and Missiles* (London: James Clark, 1959); Paul Ramsey, *War and the Christian Conscience* (Durham, N.C.: Duke University Press, 1961); Thomas Merton, "Nuclear War and the Christian Responsibility," *Commonweal* 75(February 9, 1962); John C. Bennett, ed., *Nuclear Weapons and the Conflict of Conscience* (New York: Charles Scribner's Sons, 1962); *Pacem in Terris,* Encyclical Letter of Pope John XXIII, April 11, 1963 (Washington, D.C.: National Catholic Welfare Conference, 1963); *Gaudium et Spes,* Pastoral Constitution on the Church in the Modern World, in Walter M. Abbott, ed., *Documents of Vatican II* (New York: American Press, 1966); William V. O'Brien, *War and/or Survival* (Garden City, N.Y.: Doubleday, 1969); James Turner

Johnson, *Just War Tradition and the Restraint of War: A Moral and Historical Inquiry* (Princeton, N.J.: Princeton University Press, 1981); William V. O'Brien, *The Conduct of Just and Limited War* (New York: Praeger, 1981); David Hollenbach, S.J., "Nuclear Weapons and Nuclear War: The Shape of the Catholic Debate," *Theological Studies* 43(December 1982); Robert F. Rizzo, "Nuclear War: The Moral Dilemma," *Cross Currents* 32(Spring 1982). In all these writings there is an implicit, if not explicit, condemnation of a counterforce strategy that would, even if urban populations were not intentionally targeted, result in the death of millions.

27. *The Challenge of Peace*, par. 145.

28. The estimates are based on a study made by the Swedish National Defense Research Institute. See *Comprehensive Study on Nuclear Weapons*, United Nations Center for Disarmament (New York: United Nations, 1981), pp. 62–64.

29. For analyses of U.S. nuclear targeting doctrine, see Victor Utgoff, "In Defense of Counterforce," *International Security* 6(Spring 1982); Desmond Ball, "U.S. Strategic Forces: How Would They Be Used?" *International Security* 7(Winter 1982–1983); Desmond Ball, *Targeting for Strategic Deterrence*, Adelphi Paper No. 185 (London: IISS, Summer 1983). Recent data on numbers and yields of U.S. and Soviet strategic nuclear forces can be found in *The Military Balance 1983–1984* (London: IISS, 1983), pp. 118–121.

30. See Carl Sagan, "Nuclear War and Climatic Catastrophe: Some Policy Implications," *Foreign Affairs* 62(Winter 1983–1984):257–292; Philip J. Hilts, "Scientists Say Nuclear War Could Cause Climate Disaster," *Washington Post*, November 1, 1983, and "'Nuclear Winter' Catastrophe Confirmed by Soviet Scientists," *Washington Post*, November 2, 1983; Constance Holden, "Scientists Describe Nuclear Winter," *Science* 222(November 18, 1983); R.P. Turco, O.B. Toon, T.P. Ackerman, J.B. Pollack, and Carl Sagan, "Nuclear Winter: Global Consequences of Multiple Nuclear Explosions," *Science* 222(December 23, 1983). For a dissenting view, see S. Fred Singer, "The Big Chill? Challenging a Nuclear Scenario," *Wall Street Journal*, February 3, 1984.

31. McGeorge Bundy, George F. Kennan, Robert S. McNamara, and Gerard Smith, "Nuclear Weapons and the Atlantic Alliance," *Foreign Affairs* 60(Spring 1982): 753–768.

32. Karl Kaiser, Georg Leber, Alois Mertes, and Franz-Joseph Schulze, "Nuclear Weapons and the Preservation of Peace: A Response to an American Proposal for Renouncing the First Use of Nuclear Weapons," *Foreign Affairs* 60(Summer 1982):1157–1170. Quoted at p. 1158.

33. Judy Freedman, "Centimeter of Doubt for Bishops on N-Ban," *Boston Globe*, March 1, 1983.

34. *The Challenge of Peace*, pars. 154–156.

35. On the economics and political prospects for a NATO conventional deterrent, see Michael Getler, "Atom Arms Debates Overlook Key Fact: They're Cheap," *Washington Post*, October 29, 1983; Charles W. Corddry, "Non-Atom Arms Asked for NATO," *Baltimore Sun*, May 17, 1983; John Tagliabue, "Bonn Balks at Weinberger's Arms Plans," *New York Times*, June 1, 1983; Fred Hiatt, "High-Tech Weapons Sharpen NATO Debate over Procurement," *Washington Post*, June 2, 1982; William Drozdiak, "NATO Allies Face Cost Dilemma," *Washington Post*, September 25, 1983; Elizabeth Pond, "Can NATO Lessen Its Nuclear Tilt?" *Christian Science Monitor*, October 14, 1983; "Battlefield Atom Weapons Here to Stay," *Suddetusche Zeitung*, October 25, 1983,

trans. in *German Tribune,* November 6, 1983; Gary Yearkey, "NATO Expected to OK Plan for More 'Smart' Nonnuclear Arms," *Christian Science Monitor,* May 14, 1984; Roger Thurow, "NATO's Economic Bind Restricts Its Defense Options," *Wall Street Journal,* June 5, 1984; "Supreme Commander Pessimistic on Defense Buildup," *Wall Street Journal,* June 5, 1984.

36. Wolfraam von Raven, "A Grim Perspective for the Bundeswehr," *German Comments: Review of Politics and Culture,* no. 1 (April 1983), pp. 25–31; John Vinocur, "Study by Bonn Foresees Trouble for the Military," *New York Times,* February 9, 1982.

37. "Soviet Said to Strengthen Battlefield Nuclear Forces," *Sun,* September 15, 1983; William Drozdiak, "Soviet Admits Missiles Already in Bloc States," *Washington Post,* October 18, 1983; Dusko Doder, "Moscow Says New Missiles Deployed in East Germany," *Washington Post,* May 15, 1984.

38. John Keegan, "The Specter of Conventional War," *Harper's* (July 1983), pp. 8, 10–11, 14; Elizabeth Pond, "Even Conventional War Is Unthinkable," *Christian Science Monitor,* October 13, 1983.

39. The United States, acting with full NATO approval, withdrew 1,000 nuclear weapons during the period 1980–1982 and in 1983 scheduled the withdrawal of an additional 1,400.

40. Samuel P. Huntington, "Conventional Deterrence and Conventional Retaliation in Europe," *International Security* 8(Winter 1983–1984).

41. John J. Mearsheimer, "Maneuver, Mobile Defense, and the NATO Central Front," *International Security* 6(Winter 1981):107.

42. Ibid., pp. 111–114.

43. General Bernard W. Rogers, SACEUR, though strongly in favor of a NATO conventional buildup, is opposed to a no-first-use declaration and wants NATO to develop by the end of the 1980s a conventional capability to defeat a nonnuclear attack "without necessarily resorting" to the use of nuclear weapons. "Greater Flexibility for NATO's Flexible Response," *Strategic Review* 11(Spring 1983):13, and "Conventional Punch That Might Avert a Nuclear Knock-out," *Manchester Guardian,* October 2, 1983.

44. The principle was enunciated by Vitoria in *Relectio de potestate civili,* 13, and by Suarez in *De Bello,* vol. IV. See E.B.F. Midgeley, *The Natural Law Tradition and the Theory of International Relations* (New York: Barnes and Noble, 1975), p. 65.

45. Richard Burt contended that "a conventional-emphasis strategy could actually provide the Soviet Union with incentives to escalate in time of war." "Reassessing the Strategic Balance," *International Security* 5(Summer 1980):50. See also Vincenza Tornetta, "The Nuclear Strategy of the Atlantic Alliance and the 'No First Use Debate'," *NATO Review* (September–October 1982); Barry Blechman, "Is There a Conventional Defense Option?" *Washington Quarterly,* Summer 1982, pp. 59–66; Fen Osler Hampson, "Grasping for Technical Panaceas: The European Conventional Balance and Nuclear Stability," *International Security* 8(Winter 1983–1984):57–82.

46. Treaty on Principles Governing the Activities of States in the Exploration and Use of Outer Space, Including the Moon and Other Celestial Bodies, Article IV. Text in *Arms Control and Disarmament Agreements: Texts and Histories of Negotiations* (Washington, D.C.: U.S. Arms Control and Disarmament Agency, 1982), p. 52.

47. Jean-Pierre Clerc, "The Militarization of Outer Space," *Le Monde,* August 2, 1983; and Norman R. Augustine; Lt. Col. Gunter H. Neubert, USA; Lt. Gen. Daniel O. Graham, USA (Ret.); and Dr. Barry J. Smernoff, "National Security Strategies for the

Use of Space," in Terry L. Heyns, ed., *Understanding U.S. Strategy: A Reader* (Washington, D.C.: National Defense University Press, 1983), pp. 85–133.

48. *International Security Dimensions of Space,* A Conference Report (The Eleventh Annual Conference, sponsored by the International Security Studies Program, The Fletcher School of Law and Diplomacy, Tufts University) (Cambridge, Mass.: Institute for Foreign Policy Analysis, 1982), pp. 4–6, 10–11.

49. Raymond L. Garthoff, "Banning the Bomb in Outer Space," *International Security* 5(Winter 1980–1981):25–40.

50. William J. Broad, "U.S. Advances System to Kill Satellites," *Sun,* September 11, 1983; Richard L. Garwin and John Pike, "Space Weapons: History and Current Debate," *Bulletin of the Atomic Scientists* 40(May 1984).

51. Richard L. Garwin, who strongly favors an agreement to ban ASATs, in a letter to Joseph D. Lehman, public affairs officer of the U.S. Arms Control and Disarmament Agency, on October 28, 1983, said that "an attack on the worldwide satellite system is an attack on the territory of the United States." *ACDA News,* November 8, 1983. See also Donald L. Hafner, "Outer Space Arms Control," *Survival* 25(November–December 1983):242–248.

52. Dusko Doder, "Andropov Urges Ban on Weapons to Attack Satellites: U.S. Senators Told of Space Moratorium," *Washington Post,* August 19, 1983; John F. Burns, "Andropov Issues a Promise on Antisatellite Weapons," *New York Times,* August 19, 1983.

53. R. Jeffrey Smith, "Administration Resists Demands for ASAT Ban," *Science* 222(October 28, 1983):394–396. For the problems of verifying a "no new types" ASAT ban, see Hafner, "Outer Space Arms Control," pp. 245–247. See also the administration's *Report to the Congress of U.S. Policy on ASAT Arms Control,* March 31, 1984; Francis X. Clines, "Reagan Satellite Arms Talks," *New York Times,* April 3, 1984.

54. Robert C. Toth, "Anti-Satellite Missile to be Tested by U.S.," *Los Angeles Times,* December 12, 1983; Fred Hiatt, "U.S. Tests Satellite Destroyer," *Washington Post,* January 21, 1984.

55. David Hoffman and Dusko Doder, "Soviets Oppose Link of Talks on Missiles, Antisatellite Weapons," *Washington Post,* July 2, 1984.

56. Garwin and Pike, "Space Weapons," p. 42; Peter A. Clausen, "Courting a New Arms Race," *New York Times,* April 10, 1984.

57. See, for example, Leon Gouré, William G. Hyland, and Colin S. Gray, *The Emerging Strategic Environment: Implications for Ballistic Missile Defense* (Cambridge, Mass.: Institute for Foreign Policy Analysis [IFPA], December 1979); Jacquelyn Davis, Uri Ra'anan, Robert L. Pfaltzgraff, Jr., Michael J. Deane, and John M. Collins, *The Soviet Union and Ballistic Missile Defense* (Cambridge, Mass.: IFPA, March 1980); William S. Schneider, Jr., Donald G. Brennan, William A. Davis, Jr., and Hans Ruhle, *U.S. Strategic Nuclear Policy and Ballistic Missile Defense: The 1980s and Beyond* (Cambridge, Mass.: IFPA, April 1980); Clarence Robinson, "Beam Weapons Technology Expanding," *Aviation Week and Space Technology,* May 25, 1981.

58. These leakage rates were suggested by William A. Davis, Jr., "Ballistic Missile Defense Will Work," *National Defense,* December 1981, p. 29. The final composite leakage in this model would be 2 percent.

59. David A. Andelman, "Space Wars," *Foreign Policy* 44(Fall 1981):95–96. The Defense Advanced Research Projects Agency (DARPA) has been working for several

years on high-efficiency infrared chemical lasers, large lightweight telescopes, and a precision pointing system for long-range military applications. See DARPA 1980 Research and Development Program, Summary Statement by Dr. Robert R. Fossum, director, before the Subcommittee for Research and Development of the House Armed Services Committee, 96th Congress, 1st Session, March 6, 1979, 1–5.

60. Lt. General Daniel O. Graham, U.S.A. (Ret.), "Toward a New U.S. Strategy: Bold Strokes Rather Than Increments," *Strategic Review* 9(Spring 1981):9–16.

61. "President's Speech on Military Spending and New Defense," *New York Times,* March 24, 1983.

62. Steven R. Weisman, "Reagan Says Plan on Missile Defense Will Prevent War," *New York Times,* March 26, 1983. For the wide variety of directed energy weapons under investigation in recent years, see William J. Beane, "The Navy and Directed Energy Weapons," *Proceedings* of the United States Naval Institute (November 1981); "DOD Weighs Laser vs. Neutron Beam for ASAT," *Aerospace Daily,* August 4, 1983; "Soviet Gains Spur U.S. to Boost Research on Microwave Weapons," *Sun,* August 13, 1983; Walter Pincus, "Panel Urges More Space-Defense Research," *Washington Post,* October 9, 1983; and William J. Broad, "X-Ray Laser Weapon Gains Favor," *New York Times,* November 15, 1983.

63. Charles W. Corddry, "Goal Seen as Threat to Treaty," *Sun,* April 5, 1983.

64. See, for example, William E. Jackson, Jr., "Shooting Down the ABM Treaty," *Christian Science Monitor,* April 11, 1983.

65. Steven R. Weisman, "Reagan Says"; Bernard Gwertzman, "Soviet Told by U.S. ABM Pact Stands," *New York Times,* March 27, 1983.

66. *Arms Control and Disarmament Agreements,* p. 140.

67. Lou Cannon, "President Seeks Futuristic Defense against Missiles," *Washington Post,* March 24, 1983, and "Defense Plans Could Bring Breakthrough, Revive Debate," *Washington Post,* March 24, 1983.

68. Flora Lewis, "Warning: Danger in Space," *New York Times,* April 11, 1983.

69. Hedrick Smith, "Would a Space-Age Defense Ease Tensions or Create Them?" *New York Times,* March 27, 1983.

70. Jan M. Lodal, "No, Mr. Reagan, It Won't Work," *Washington Post,* March 27, 1983, and "Can Reagan's 'Star Wars' Plan Really Work? No—This System Amounts to an Impossible Dream," *U.S. News and World Report,* April 4, 1983.

71. McGeorge Bundy, "A 'Quick-Trigger' Talk," *Washington Post,* March 28, 1983. Wolfgang K.H. Panvosky remarked that experts in these exotic technologies might be embarrassed by the president's optimistic tone. "The practitioners in the field are not anywhere near as gung-ho as the president's speech implies." Smith, "Space-Age Defense."

72. "Nuclear Fantasies," *New Republic,* April 18, 1983, pp. 7–10.

73. Anthony Lewis, "The President's Fantasy," *New York Times,* March 27, 1983.

74. Bundy, "A 'Quick-Trigger' Talk."

75. Opponents included Hans Bethe, John Steinbrunner, Paul Doty, Sidney Drell, Franklin A. Long, Robert S. McNamara, Philip Morrison, Wolfgang K.H. Panvosky, I.I. Rabi, George Rathjens, Jack Ruina, Carl Sagan, Glenn T. Seaborg, Kosta Tsipsis, James Van Allen, Victor R. Weisskopf, and Herbert F. York. Most of those listed signed a petition drafted by Richard L. Garwin and Carl Sagan, "Ban Space Weapons," *Bulletin of The Atomic Scientists* 39(November 1983):2–3. See also Robert Jastrow, "Reagan vs. the Scientists: Why the President is Right about Missile Defense," *Commentary,* January

1984, p. 23; John Noble Wilford, "Group of Top Scientists Close to Government Fighting Space Weapons Plan," *New York Times,* November 16, 1983; Charles Mohr, "Reagan is Urged to Increase Research on Exotic Defenses against Missiles," *New York Times,* November 5, 1983.

76. Speaking of such earlier systems as Nike-Zeus, Nike-X, and Sentinel/Safeguard, Jack Ruina of the Massachusetts Institute of Technology concluded that they could handle a few targets well but not large numbers of targets—decoys or warheads from MIRVed missiles. After being involved with ABM technology for more than two decades, he finds "a certain consistency in policy positions no matter what the new technology of the moment promises." *Washington Quarterly,* Autumn 1981, pp. 10–11.

77. Jerome B. Weisner's views are discussed in Lewis, "The President's Fantasy."

78. Peter A. Clausen, "Dooming Arms Control," *New York Times,* October 27, 1983.

79. "Nuclear Fantasies," *New Republic,* April 18, 1983, p. 8.

80. Advocates include David Andelman, John M. Bachkosky, Edward A. Brown, DARPA Director Richard S. Cooper, William A. Davis, Jr., James C. Fletcher, General Daniel Graham, Lieutenant Colonel Richard L. Gullickson of DARPA, Presidential Science Adviser George A. Keyworth, Edward Luttwak, Richard M. Roberds, James R. Schlesinger, Edward Teller, and Caspar W. Weinberger.

81. Daniel Southerland, "Top Scientist Defends Reagan 'Space Wars' Strategy," *Christian Science Monitor,* April 4, 1983.

82. Walter Pincus, "Anti-Missile Laser Plans Accelerated," *Washington Post,* October 9, 1983; Broad, "X-Ray Laser."

83. Gregory M. Lamb, "Anti-Missile Defense is Feasible Now, Says One Advocate," *Christian Science Monitor,* April 14, 1983.

84. See George Keyworth, "Can Reagan's 'Star Wars' Plan Really Work? Yes—Enormous Progress in Technologies Makes It Reasonable," *U.S. News and World Report,* April 4, 1983; Daniel O. Graham and Gregory Fossedal, "A Defense That Defends," *Wall Street Journal,* April 8, 1983; Richard M. Roberds, "Reagan's New Defense Weapons—Not Just a Dream," *Christian Science Monitor,* May 31, 1983.

85. Harold Brown, "It May Be Plausible—And It May Be Ineffective," *Washington Post,* March 27, 1983. William J. Perry, former undersecretary of defense for research and engineering in the Carter administration, was similarly ambiguous. He said that the new "technology could produce an operational system capable of degrading a nuclear attack, but not capable of protecting the nation from devastation in the event of a massive nuclear attack." Perry dwelt on the need for several hundred satellites to maintain enough laser beams to deal with a large-scale attack, the great pointing accuracy required, and the amount of energy it would take to burn a hole in the missile—ten times that already achieved for high-energy lasers. Since such a laser system would be too large to be launched from a space shuttle, assembly of each battle station might require four or five shuttle launches, and this would render the system vulnerable. "An Expensive Technological Risk," *Washington Post,* March 27, 1983.

86. Zbigniew Brzezinski, "Far Reaching and Risky," *Sun,* March 28, 1983.

87. *Report of the Future Security Strategy Study Group* (Hoffman Report). Summary in Clarence A. Robinson, Jr., "Panel Urges Defense Technology Advances," *Aviation Week and Space Technology,* October 17, 1983.

88. Clarence A. Robinson, Jr., "Study Urges Exploiting of Technologies," *Aviation Week and Space Technology*, October 24, 1983, p. 50.

89. Philip M. Boffey, "President Backs U.S. Space Station as Next Key Goal," *New York Times*, January 26, 1984.

90. Clarence Robinson, "Panel Urges Boost-Phase Intercepts," *Aviation Week and Space Technology*, December 5, 1983, pp. 50–61.

91. More than two decades ago, Robert C. Gilpin argued this point trenchantly in *American Scientists and Nuclear Weapons Policy* (Princeton, N.J.: Princeton University Press, 1962).

92. David A. Andelman, "Space Wars," p. 97.

93. Fred Hiatt, "Joint Space Command Sought," *Washington Post*, November 18, 1983; Charles Mohr, "General to Head Missile Programs," *New York Times*, March 28, 1984.

94. Andropov immediately called the Reagan program "a bid to disarm the Soviet Union" and an effort to sever the "interrelationship" established in SALT I between the ABM Treaty and stable deterrence, and to "open the floodgates to a runaway race of all types of strategic arms, both offensive and defensive." John F. Burns, "Andropov Says U.S. Is Spurring a Race for Nuclear Arms," *New York Times*, March 27, 1983.

95. Clausen, "Dooming Arms Control."

96. "Soviet Antimissile Lead Is Feared," *New York Times*, December 3, 1983; Michael Getler, "Soviets Seen Progressing toward a Missile Defense System," *Washington Post*, January 20, 1984; Walter Andrews, "Soviets Have at Least 2 Antisatellite Weapons," *Washington Times*, April 3, 1984.

97. Quoted in the editorial, "Handcuffed in Space," *Wall Street Journal*, February 3, 1984.

98. "Washington Roundup," *Aviation Week and Space Technology*, January 9, 1984, p. 15.

99. Paul Mann, "Interagency Review Lists Soviet Arms Violations," *Aviation Week and Space Technology*, p. 60; Henry Trewhitt, "President Says Soviets Violate Pact," *Sun*, January 24, 1968.

100. Robert M. Bowman, "Star Wars—Pie in the Sky," *New York Times*, December 14, 1983.

101. "Weinberger Softens Insistence on a Leak-Proof ABM System," *Washington Post*, April 12, 1983.

102. R. Jeffrey Smith, "The Search for a Nuclear Sanctuary (II)," *Science* 221(July 8, 1983).

103. Charles Mohr, "Study Assails Idea of Missile Defense," *New York Times*, March 22, 1984; Mohr, " 'Missile Defense' Now a Go-Slow Policy," *New York Times*, March 23, 1984; Fred Hiatt, "Reagan's 'Star Wars' Uncertain after Year," *Washington Post*, March 24, 1984; "What Star Wars 'Czar' Is Up Against," *U.S. News and World Report*, April 9, 1984; Bernard Weinraub, "Mondale Asks Ban on Arms in Space," *New York Times*, April 25, 1984; Walter Pincus, "Delay Urged in Space-Weapons Talks," *Washington Post*, April 26, 1984; Whitt Flora, "Research on ABM Meets Opposition from Senators," *Aviation Week and Space Technology*, April 30, 1984; Walter Andrews, "Bureaucrats Accused of Spiking Star Wars Plans," *Washington Times*, April 30, 1984; Walter Pincus, "Pentagon Wins Round in Bureaucratic 'StarWars,' "

Washington Post, June 17, 1984; Walter Andrews, " 'Star Wars' Misunderstood in Congress, Director Says," *Washington Times,* June 18, 1984; Fred Hiatt, "Low-Key Push Due 'Star Wars,' " *Washington Post,* June 19, 1984.

104. Peter Osnos, "Europe Finds ABM Ideas Disturbing," *Washington Post,* March 30, 1983, and "Europeans Challenging U.S. ABM System," *Aviation Week and Space Technology,* June 20, 1983.

105. Michael Feazel, "Europeans Support U.S. Space-Based Systems," *Aviation Week and Space Technology,* October 24, 1983, p. 59; Hiatt, "Weinberger to Reassure Allies on Star Wars Plan," *Washington Post,* December 2, 1983; Hiatt, "U.S. Antisatellite Plan Draws Fire," *Washington Post,* April 4, 1984; William Drozdiak, "Bonn Worried by U.S. Plans for Space Weaponry," *Washington Post,* April 4, 1984; " 'Star Wars' Plan Hit by W. German," *Washington Times,* April 10, 1984; James M. Markhorn, "Bonn Is Worried by U.S. Arms Research," *New York Times,* April 14, 1984; "NATO Challenges Cost, Practicality of U.S. 'Star Wars,' " *Sun,* April 24, 1984.

106. Bethe, Weisskopf, Andropov, and Reagan are cited in R. Jeffrey Smith, "The Search for a Nuclear Sanctuary (II)."

107. "Nuclear Fantasies," *New Republic,* April 18, 1983, p. 8.

Part IV
Practice

6

Between Religion and Politics: The Morality of Deterrence

John Langan, S.J.
Woodstock Theological Center
Georgetown University

Deterrence and the Perils of Moral Theory

Fortunately, many of the moral questions that arise in the source of our reflections on contemporary warfare are primarily hypothetical. Under what circumstances, if any, would it be right to use nuclear weapons? Can such use be controlled in the circumstances of modern warfare once hostilities begin? On the other hand, although the notion of deterrence is complex and elusive, there is an immediacy and urgency to the fundamental moral question about deterrence—namely, is it a morally justifiable policy? The immediacy of the question arises from the fact that deterrence is our current national policy. The question about the morality of deterrence is not what it might be right for us to do at some point in the future; rather, it challenges what we are doing now. A negative answer to the fundamental question would require sweeping changes in present policies and arrangements and would challenge established attitudes and values not merely in this country but around the world.

The close connection between judgment about the morality of deterrence and decisions with regard to U.S. policy can, of course, carry arguments in either direction. We may be moved by our concern over U.S. policy to question the rightness of deterrence, and vice versa. Further reflection makes it manifest, however, that we must distinguish particular twists and turns of U.S. policy from deterrence as a fundamental element in that policy, and must recognize that similar situations and policies can be found outside the current U.S.-Soviet relationship, so that there is need for a broader discussion of the moral perplexities to which deterrence gives rise, a discussion that reaches beyond the limits of current superpower confrontations. The close connection between moral evaluations of deterrence and policy decisions brings with it the continuing risk that our moral assessments may be corrupted or distorted and also makes it virtually impossible to conduct moral thought experiments without being influenced by our awareness of what for us is the paradigm case of deterrence. We do not have available to us for research on this topic a moral laboratory uncontaminated by concrete political and historical considerations.

In a complex, pluralistic, and innovative society, our confrontation with a problem as perplexing and controversial as nuclear deterrence cannot be resolved either by appeal to a commonly acknowledged moral authority or by reference to a common body of moral principles. An interesting illustration of this latter point can be found even where it is apparently being denied. The U.S. Catholic bishops in their recent Pastoral Letter affirm their desire to address their teaching on war and peace not merely to "the Catholic faithful," over whom they have religious authority, but also to the "wider civil community," which is "equally bound by certain key moral principles." The bishops are, as we would expect, approaching their topic from the tradition of natural law and the Western tradition of ethical monotheism. So they write:

> For all men and women find in the depth of their consciences a law written on the human heart by God. From this law reason draws moral norms. These norms do not exhaust the Gospel vision, but they speak to critical questions affecting the welfare of the human community, the role of states in international relations, and the limits of acceptable action by individuals and nations on issues of war and peace.[1]

This is probably as strong an affirmation of a natural law approach, with its characteristic concern for rational justification and the maintenance of social order, as one can expect to find today. For this very reason, however, it is particularly important to notice that the bishops do not expect to work out a detailed resolution of the specific moral problems that nuclear weapons present. Thus they acknowledge that "not every statement in this letter has the same moral authority" and that in the application of moral principles prudential judgments are involved based on specific circumstances which can change or which can be interpreted differently by people of good will (e.g., the treatment of "no first use").[2] The bishops do not believe that either the Scriptures or their own form of natural law methodology gives complete or intellectually compelling answers to the moral problems of the contemporary nuclear debate.

Furthermore, they have chosen to enter the arena of democratic debate in a society in which public opinion has an active role and in which divergent groups may be called to share in the task of "setting stringent limits on the kind of actions our own government and other governments will take on nuclear policy."[3] The U.S. bishops may set themselves to declare what the natural law that is binding on all of us requires with respect to contemporary warfare, but they have to recognize both that they do not have an a priori authority to teach the larger society beyond the church and that the theoretical framework they use in formulating and justifying their moral judgments does not command anything like universal assent. The bishops, along with assorted other religious and secular moralists, have to teach not from the proverbial ivory tower but from a contemporary tower of Babel, from which we can hear the voices not merely of Catholics and Presbyterians, Orthodox and Baptists, Muslims and Episcopalians, Methodists and Hasidim, but also of utilitarians and deontologists, emotivists and relativists, rationalists and voluntarists. They can in some measure earn an authority in the larger society by the care and candor of their approach and by a judicious combination of reasonable argument and respectful sensitivity to the values and interests under consideration. They can present themselves not merely as the guardians of a rich and distinctive heritage of moral teaching but also as the proponents of what Alan Donagan has spoken of as "the common morality," a body of principles that commands the general assent of thoughtful persons in our culture, despite the vagaries of the philosophers and social scientists.[4]

In my own view, the Catholic bishops have made both these moves in a fairly effective way. In doing this they are, of course, not alone. Any serious moral argument about policy in our society must find ways around or above or beneath the facts of our pluralism and our all too lively differences. In particular, no really interesting or informative argument about U.S. defense policy could be made without drawing on some rather large assumptions both in metaethics and in normative ethical theory. My point here is not to bring us back to the realm of ethical first principles and to hand over the debate to Aquinas and Kant and Hume and Mill, but to underline the fact that in our fragmented culture it is not possible to anchor controversial conclusions about practical morality by a straightforward appeal to theoretical first principles or to an accepted moral authority.

In debating the issues of nuclear morality, we are not simply dealing with what the followers of Thomas Aquinas spoke of as "tertiary principles" of the natural law, matters that could not be settled by a simple invocation of accepted moral norms but that required reflection by the wise;[5] we are doing so in an intellectual and social context in which those moral norms themselves may be subject to challenge or revision, to amendment or exception. In public discourse, we are dealing with a situation in which fundamental moral principles do not enjoy significantly more credibility or authority than conclusions about the moral status of deterrence, and in which such secondary principles as may be appealed to (the prohibition against taking innocent human life, the right and duty of national self-defense, the protection of the innocent against aggression, the prohibition of pointless retaliation) seem to point in opposite directions.

The consequence of this general situation is not that no correct judgment about the morality of deterrence can be reached, but that such judgments are vulnerable to fundamental challenges in public debate. We wind up in this area with a dramatic illustration of a point that was made in more general terms by Gilbert Harman in his recent book, *The Nature of Morality*—namely, that moral principles do not rely on observational evidence about cases and so cannot be established or overthrown by appeal to what is observed in the public realm.[6]

Two interesting illustrations of the inescapable inconclusiveness of the public moral argument about nuclear weapons and nuclear deterrence and of the imprecision and uncertainty that affect the theoretical bases of this argument can be drawn from recent writings of two active participants in the formation of the bishops' letter. In the current issue of *International Security*, Bruce Russett reflects on the conclusions of the letter in this area in the following terms: "There *is no* perfect practical solution to the problem of nuclear deterrence. Moral considerations further complicate the problem. The bishops' position in the final Letter is not so ambiguous as it is frankly torn between desirable ends."[7]

Father Bryan Hehir, in an instructive article on "The Just-War Ethic and Catholic Theology," has pointed to the inherent dilemmas that deterrence raises for ethical theory and has also underlined the way in which revisionist tendencies in Catholic moral theology of a broadly consequentialist sort broaden the range of ways in which moral principles are to be applied to particular cases. Hehir writes, "The revisionist position introduces a dimension of flexibility into the decision-making process precisely because of its teleological character." Teleological considerations are, as Hehir is quick to point out, fundamental to the just war criterion of proportionality, and are, of course, operative in classical formulations of just war theory by Aquinas and later Catholic theologians. But contemporary revisionism, if consistently applied, would require us to treat the rules of just war theory as no more than virtually exceptionless rules. This may be attractive or defensible on general theoretical grounds, but it clearly brings greater uncertainty and complexity into our arguments about the morality of nuclear weapons and nuclear deterrence than would be the case if we employed the approaches of a deontological pacifism that would treat the prohibitions against taking or threatening innocent human life as absolute, or of the antiutilitarian and quasi-deontological forms of natural law theory, which would permit such outcomes only as unintended and unavoidable results of actions undertaken for greater goods. Consequentialism —or the method of proportionate reason, as this revisionist tendency is often called—is often seen by its critics as being more complex and more liable to compromise and corruption than the more intransigent approaches favored in classical Catholic moral theology and in recent movements of an absolutist bent. Hehir observes:

> Flexibility, a broadly based moral calculus, and an ethic which tries to find its way through conflict situations by a process of negotiating the lesser evil are all inimical to the dike the pacifist would build against the threat to life posed by

modern war. The style of the revisionist case involves a willingness to re-examine even those principles within the double-effect calculus which provide the kind of absolute judgments the pacifist sees as necessary when dealing with human life. The two positions, therefore, are grounded in basically different conceptions of moral reasoning.[9]

In fact, the revisionist approach seems to be capable of endorsing both noncombatant immunity and nuclear deterrence.[10]

Proportionalism or consequentialism, whatever may be its difficulties in systematizing its procedures or in reaching definite conclusions, does at least encourage us to look reflectively at the complexity of the problem of national defense and to weigh carefully, without a premature closure, the diverse and conflicting values that constitute our contemporary nuclear predicament. The proportionalist approach may not resolve our theoretical problems, but it is a useful tool for exhibiting our difficulties. Even though the American bishops' document shied away from any overt acceptance of proportionalism or consequentialism, it can reasonably be argued that their central presentation of the problem of deterrence cries out for proportionalist treatment, for a judgment that endorses or accepts a course of action that in a given context protects and partially reconciles key values with each other, even though it falls far short of the ideal human response and even shows morally troubling features.[11] For this is how the bishops present the problem of deterrence after quoting John Paul II's judgment that deterrence is morally acceptable:

> In Pope John Paul II's assessment we perceive two dimensions of the contemporary dilemma of deterrence. One dimension is the danger of nuclear war, with its human and moral costs. The possession of nuclear weapons, the continuing quantitative growth of the arms race, and the danger of nuclear proliferation all point to the grave danger of basing "peace of a sort" on deterrence. The other dimension is the independence and freedom of nations and entire peoples, including the need to protect smaller nations from threats to their independence and integrity. Deterrence reflects the radical distrust which marks international politics. . . . Thus a balance of forces, preventing either side from achieving superiority, can be seen as a means of safeguarding both dimensions. The moral duty today is to prevent nuclear war from ever occurring and to protect and preserve those key values of justice, freedom and independence which are necessary for personal dignity and national integrity.[12]

It should be noticed that this dilemma is not put in terms of a simple conflict between self-interest and duty or between premoral values (survival, wealth) and moral values (justice, dignity). Rather, there are morally compelling considerations that urge us both to refrain from choosing to wage nuclear war and to defend ourselves and our allies against threats from unjust regimes. These are considerations that are present and powerful in a given historical context, and the decisions we have to make about them are not ultimately theoretical but concrete and historical. David Hollenbach has put the matter in concise terms: "Moral policy decisions are governed by the effort to pursue moral values in historically and politically effective ways."[13]

Deterrence and the Present Situation

In reflecting on the nuclear balance of terror between the superpowers, we are dealing with a situation that both continues and extends long-standing institutions and attitudes and at the same time transforms them into something new and different. Regrettably, however, unlike their stellar counterparts, moral *novae* do not produce added light. Rather, we are left with the elements of previous solutions to similar problems, along with a sense that they are no longer applicable and may well be misleading. A nice illustration of the contradictory impulses to which this combination of continuity and change gives rise can be found in the treatment of war in *Gaudium et Spes,* Vatican II's pastoral constitution on the church in the modern world.

This document is of particular interest since it is the foundation and point of departure for all the recent statements by various Catholic episcopal conferences and since it enjoys a higher religious authority.[14] It was issued in 1965, at a time when the central features of our present strategic situation were already clearly discernible: the mutual vulnerability of both superpowers, the drive to continuing technological innovation, the concern for careful management of superpower conflicts, the asymmetrical character of the two alliance systems around the superpowers. Crises in Berlin and Cuba, the dangers of atmospheric testing of nuclear weapons, and the Sino-Soviet split were already in the past, and the names of Brodie, Kahn, and Ramsey were already familiar to students of the nuclear mysteries when the fathers of the council turned to dealing with modern war. The council acknowledges the continuing place of war in human affairs and affirms the "permanent binding force of universal natural law and its all-embracing principles."[15] It explicitly reaffirms one of the key elements in previous just war resolutions of the problem when it says, "As long as the danger of war remains and there is no competent and sufficiently powerful authority at the international level, governments cannot be denied the right to legitimate defense once every means of peaceful settlement has been exhausted."[16] This affirmation of sovereignty and self-defense in a divided world points in the direction of an acceptance of deterrence as one instrument for protecting sovereignty, at least as long as the norms of *legitimate* defense are observed.

In the next paragraph, however, the council moves in the opposite direction:

> The horror and perversity of war are immensely magnified by the multiplication
> of scientific weapons. For acts of war involving these weapons can inflict

massive and indiscriminate destruction far exceeding the bounds of legitimate defense. Indeed, if the kind of instruments which can now be found in the armories of the great nations were to be employed to their fullest, an almost total and altogether reciprocal slaughter of each side by the other would follow, not to mention the widespread devastation which would take place in the world and the deadly afteraffects which would be spawned by the use of such weapons.

All these considerations compel us to undertake an evaluation of war with an entirely new attitude.[17]

Just what would count as an "entirely new attitude" and whether "nuclear pacifism" (the infelicitous name for the view that, by the moral criteria that make up just war theory, the production, possession, and use of nuclear weapons are not justifiable) was indeed the entirely new attitude that the council had in mind, or should have had in mind, became matters of controversy later on. But it is clear that the council was moving away from a routine endorsement of nuclear weapons as a simple corollary to its acceptance of national defense. What the council offers is not specific moral analysis of the legitimacy or illegitimacy of nuclear weapons. Rather, it combines an "unequivocal and unhesitating condemnation" of "any act of war aimed indiscriminately at the destruction of entire cities or of extensive areas along with their population," a condemnation that it explicitly links to earlier papal condemnations of "total war," with an underlining of the special responsibility of government officials and military leaders.[18] The prime objective of the council's concern is to prevent the use of nuclear weapons on a catastrophic scale. A clear recognition of the dangers of nuclear weapons joins national defense as a second fundamental element in the council's approach to deterrence. The warnings issued about the use of nuclear weapons do not, as we shall see, settle the question of deterrence, but they are not irrelevant to it. For the possession and deployment of nuclear weapons that are at the heart of deterrence policy can be conceived either as the foreshadowing of use (and thus worthy of condemnation) or as a means of preventing the use of nuclear weapons and even the outbreak of hostilities between the superpowers (and hence as a commendable means, the status of which is not altered by condemnation of use).

So in the next paragraph we can observe the council offering a generic description and tentative acceptance of deterrence, which is presented as a function independent of actual use but is not treated as a proven or fully reliable policy. Thus the council observes:

Scientific weapons, to be sure, are not amassed solely for use in war. The defensive strength of any nation is considered to be dependent upon its capacity for immediate retaliation against an adversary. Hence this accumulation of arms, which increases each year, also serves, in a way heretofore unknown, as a deterrent to possible enemy attack. Many regard this state of affairs as the most effective way by which peace of a sort can be maintained between nations at the present time.

Whatever be the case with this method of deterrence, men should be convinced that the arms race in which so many countries are engaged is not a safe way to preserve a steady peace. Nor is the so-called balance resulting from this race a sure and authentic peace. Rather than being eliminated thereby, the causes of war threaten to grow gradually stronger.[19]

The council here is more convinced of the moral unsatisfactoriness of the world order based on the balance of terror and of its eventual vulnerability than it is of a particular position on the legitimacy and effectiveness of deterrence. The council seems to have in mind three situations: one clearly worse than deterrence, namely the arms race; one clearly better, a "sure and authentic peace"; and deterrence itself. The council was particularly impressed by the cost of the arms race, which it described as a "treacherous trap for humanity and one which injures the poor to an intolerable degree."[20] It did not consider the comparative cost of reliance on conventional or nuclear weapons; and it did not explore the connections between deterrence in its various forms and arms races, connections that are likely to be closer and more apparent at times of technological innovation.

Why go back to the Vatican Council's treatment of deterrence, which seems rudimentary and dated in comparison with the more extended and more sophisticated treatments of these issues in the recent statements of the U.S. and the German bishops, not to mention a variety of ecumenical and secular statements? Without mentioning its special authority within the Catholic community and the merciful brevity of its discussion, we should note that Vatican II gives a particularly clear illustration of what is a standard pattern of reactions to the novelty of the world's nuclear predicament: affirmation of the right of national defense within the limits of just war theory; insistence on the horrors of nuclear warfare, with an accompanying recognition that the terms of the problem of warfare have now been drastically changed; and a final uneasy acceptance of deterrence, along with repeated warnings of dangers and abuses and exhortations to work for a mutual disarmament and a new world order. Here, as is often the case in church documents of this general type, there is a kind of averting of the eyes from what is being endorsed. The argument about just what it is right or wrong to do in the present order of things lacks the precision and specificity at which the Catholic casuistical tradition has usually aimed.

There are, I submit, three reasons for this moving out of focus. First, there is the common feeling among members of the clergy and church activists, a feeling I personally share, that in accepting deterrence we have done something terrible, we have endorsed a policy that is fraught with dangers and that may bring sinful humanity to the jaws of hell. Second, there is an underlying sense of the present as an interim, a time at the end of the age, which will yield to something either much better (a new world community aiming at the universal common good) or much worse (a nuclear holocaust perhaps followed by a regimented spartanism or a universal *gulag*). This brings the shape of the future into the center of our deliberations in a way that can divert our attention from the precise contours of the present policy dilemmas. The sense of the provisional character of the present world order combined with a sense of the urgency of action to distance ourselves from impending calamity and a sense of the limits of our ability to alter the terms of our predicament produces a sense of existential crisis, which inevitably in our culture has religious overtones and which may not be altogether dissimilar to the eschatological anxiety of the early Christians. Nuclear arms and the system of deterrence to which they have given rise are a *novum* drawing us into the future rather than focusing us on the present. A third reason, which is related to the second point, is the large element of factual uncertainty that the concern with the future introduces into the practical argument. Will deterrence work or not? What will happen if the West renounces deterrence or if nuclear proliferation produces a number of deterrence systems in different parts of the world? Reliable long-range judgments of what will happen as a result of either continued reliance on deterrence or its abandonment are notoriously hard to come by. The consensus of experts that deterrence if steadfastly maintained would only fail as a result of accident or irrationality falls far short of a guarantee that the worst will not happen. The hope of unilateralist critics of deterrence that unilateral renunciation of nuclear weapons will transform the character of our opponents remains a hope that is at variance with previous historical experience. The French bishops put the matter starkly in their recent letter:

> In a world where man is still a wolf to man, turning into a lamb can provoke the wolf . . . ill adjusted non-violence can provoke chain reactions of inexpiable violence.[21]

In any event, both positions on deterrence rely on important unverifiable and controversial predictive elements. This aspect of the dispute cannot be resolved by appeal to commonly held moral intuitions or to the principles of classical moral theory.

In reflecting on the perplexities that the present situation creates for moral theory, it is instructive to compare the parallel path that the distinguished contemporary U.S. moralist Michael Walzer traces from a different starting point, namely a secular contractarian understanding of political society in which the protection of human rights is accorded a fundamental importance, to very similar conclusions. In Walzer's view, nuclear deterrence rests on immoral threats against civilian populations. At least in 1977 it was his view that the superpowers were persisting in a policy of counterpopulation deterrence.[22] He rejects Ramsey's effort to salvage a form of deterrence that would stop short of the commitment to countercity strikes. Walzer concludes:

> Nuclear weapons explode the theory of just war. They are the first of mankind's technological innovations that are simply unencompassable within the familiar

moral world. Or rather, our familiar notions about *jus in bello* require us to condemn even the threat to use them. And yet there are other notions, also familiar, having to do with aggression and the right of self-defense, that seem to require exactly that threat. So we move uneasily beyond the limits of justice for the sake of justice and peace.[23]

Here, much as in Vatican II, we can see the stresses that deterrence as a *novum* puts on our system of moral judgment about politics and war and even on our moral language. We are at an impasse where the right and duty of national self-defense are perceived to be jeopardized by the obligation to respect the principle of discrimination and the norm of noncombatant immunity. This is a morally unsatisfactory situation, which can be extremely painful to those soldiers, policymakers, and citizens whose sensitivity to the evils of modern warfare is already high, or can produce a regrettable and potentially disastrous lessening of that sensitivity. What makes deterrence bearable for Walzer, and for many other theorists and observers, is that it serves to prevent the evil that it threatens. In fact, in our present condition, deterrence is a necessary means of preventing war. The necessity of deterrence is a conditional rather than an absolute necessity. This necessity arises from our will to preserve ourselves as an independent political community committed to its own values. Deterrence, in Walzer's view, "requires only that we see appeasement or surrender to involve a loss of values central to our existence as an independent nation-state."[24] It is the only practical course in "a world of sovereign and suspicious states."[25]

For Walzer, however, the necessity of deterrence does not establish its moral rightness, as it does, for instance, for the French bishops. He interprets it as a condition of supreme emergency—that is, a situation in which the imminence of danger and the seriousness of the threat make it justifiable to override the rules of war. Walzer's approach to justifying exceptions to the rules of war is, if I understand it correctly, akin to the views of those proportionalist moralists who wish to differentiate their method from straightforward utilitarian calculation. Walzer, while believing that situations in which it is justifiable to override the rules of war do arise, wishes to circumscribe the appeal to necessity. He is aware of the slippery slope and of the propensity of political and military actors to extend the notion of necessity and with it their freedom to use force. He writes:

> For the survival and freedom of political communities whose members share a way of life developed by their ancestors, to be passed on to their children are the highest values of international society. . . . The mere recognition of such a threat is not itself coercive; it neither compels nor permits attacks on the innocent so long as other means of fighting and winning are available.[26]

The situation must not allow for satisfactory or effective alternatives.

This last passage also serves to highlight the complex relationship between deterrence as a means and the goal that legitimates it—namely, the survival and freedom of the political community. For it is by preventing the use of nuclear weapons that deterrence can serve as a means to these higher political values, not by preparing the way for their use. Walzer's view of the prospects for limited nuclear war is remarkably close to the position of the U.S. bishops.

He says:

> It is not necessarily the case that every war would become a total war, but the danger of escalation is so great as to preclude the first use of nuclear weapons— except by someone willing to face their final use.[27]

He sees the possibilities of flexible response as minor variations, not fundamentally modifying the immoral threats inherent in a mutual assured destruction conception of deterrence. So his final judgment is that deterrence is both morally wrong and necessary and that we ought to move beyond it. He sums the matter up as follows:

> Nuclear war is and will remain morally unacceptable, and there is no case for its rehabilitation. Because it is unacceptable, we must seek out ways to prevent it, and because deterrence is a bad way, we must seek out others. . . . I have been more concerned to acknowledge that deterrence, for all its criminality, falls or may fall for the moment under the standard of necessity. But as with terror bombing, so here with the threat of terrorism: supreme emergency is never a stable position. The realm of necessity is subject to historical change. And, what is more important, we are under an obligation to seize upon opportunities of escape, even to take risks for the sake of such opportunities.[28]

There are four major points in Walzer's position that we need to observe. The first is the very close connection that he makes between the nation-state as a valuable form of political community and the practice of deterrence. As he acknowledges, this aggravates the problem of proliferation; it also, in contrast to some conservative presentations of international conflict, turns our attention away from the ideological aspects of the Western confrontation with the Soviets and from the complex problems of making comparative judgments about the justice of different regimes.

Second, Walzer's difficulties with the immoral and criminal character of deterrence can be alleviated if it is possible to devise a stable and credible deterrent that does not rest on the threat of mutual assured destruction and that does not violate the principle of discrimination. I say "alleviated" and not "eliminated" because even then the harm done to civilians could still be enormous.

Third, Walzer's conclusion that deterrence is both criminal and necessary has a very un-Catholic ring to it. In this regard, his language is more Protestant than Catholic. For Catholic moral theology has always resisted the view that it could be right, all things considered, to do what is morally wrong. My own conviction is that on the logic of this point the Catholic tradition (here joined by most contemporary moral philosophers) has it right, but that the darker and less coherent language of Walzer, Niebuhr, and the Protestant tradition is more faithful to the dark and incoherent reality of our choices in the international arena. Those of us working in the Catholic tradition have to remember that a clear and correct affirmation that it is morally right to choose in difficult circumstances the lesser of two evils should not blind us both to the real costs of such a choice (especially when these are borne by others) and to the responsibility that we may share for the way that the difficult circumstances have shaped the choice. In some Catholic discussions of these matters there can be a certain tendency to assume that once the morally correct course of action has been discovered and chosen, all will be well. This is accompanied by an understandable reluctance to be clear about the costs, the harms, and the negative implications of the positions that have been recommended. The Catholic stipulation that it can never be right to do what is morally wrong means that no group of bishops could accept the starkness of Walzer's characterization of deterrence and still treat deterrence as morally acceptable, even though they would agree with his judgments that deterrence is necessary and that we should seek an alternative to it.

Fourth, as Walzer himself senses, the invocation of the notion of supreme emergency to legitimate a semipermanent feature of the international landscape is highly paradoxical. This is especially true if we recall what he says in his general treatment of supreme emergency about the imminence of the threat if we are really to have a situation of supreme emergency. We need here to distinguish between deterrence as a social psychological system, which makes sense only if presented as an emergency measure for dealing with a crisis, and deterrence as a military political system that actually provides a familiar and stable, though admittedly imperfect, basis for relations between the superpowers. The state of contemporary military technology, however, makes it possible for the whole adversarial system of deterrence to pass from equilibrium through crisis to catastrophe in an astonishingly short period of time.

Deterrence: Interim, Crisis, and Utopia

The sense of deterrence as an interim regime deserves further reflection, for it figures prominently in such important recent assessments of deterrence as the 1979 testimony of Cardinal Krol in support of the SALT II Treaty and in the 1982 message of John Paul II to the United Nations Second Special Session on Disarmament. Cardinal Krol, in a text that shaped a great deal of the earlier part of the debate over the U.S. bishops' statement spoke of "the Catholic dissatisfaction with nuclear deterrence and the urgency of the Catholic demand that the nuclear arms race be reversed" and maintained that "it is of the utmost importance that negotiations proceed to meaningful and continuing reductions in nuclear stockpiles and eventually to the phasing out altogether of nuclear deterrence and the threat of mutual assured destruction."[29]

An important consequence of this assessment of deterrence is that ethical judgment is then made dependent on a reading of the historical situation, with its perils and possibilities. This is a move that may be taken for granted by political actors and most political commentators, but it is worth pointing out that it is a departure from the procedure of classical moral theology and philosophy. In assessing the morality of deterrence, we are not merely judging an ad hoc solution to a particularly difficult case of conscience, but are dealing with a complex of institutions, attitudes, practices, equipment, and personnel. Institutions or practices that are judged to be acceptable for a time are, I would argue, by that very token not to be regarded as institutions or practices that are required by human nature or by rational will as such. It can be argued that they are necessary evils or lesser evils, or that they are less incompatible with what human nature or rational will requires than alternatives within a given situation.

The treatment of deterrence in recent church pronouncements implies that this situation is more limited in scope than the general human situation, which is marked by conflict and division and has given rise to wars and the institutions of war-making. But it is broader in scope than individual episodes or cases such as the Cuban missile crisis. It is a situation that has developed within the memory of living people; both its origin and its outcome are thought of primarily as the result of human agency and decision. It is asserted that the situation in which deterrence is acceptable or justifiable is assumed to be limited; presumably, war might still be justifiable even after nuclear deterrence ceased to be justifiable. War between advanced industrial societies would then have to be limited; there would be no question of the total mobilization of one society's resources for the destruction of another society or political regime. We would move back to something like the "sovereigns' wars" of the eighteenth century, in which issues were serious enough to stimulate a resort to force but not so serious as to jeopardize the survival of the regime, much less of the contending societies. Whether the development of political life and conflict over the last century make this a plausible outcome is very doubtful, and whether either side would have confidence in the other's restraint once hostilities had begun is also very doubtful. It has, of course, been argued that the existence of nuclear weapons and of a system of deterrence would curb the level of violence in any conventional conflict between superpowers. As Walzer observes, "It is hard to imagine a repetition of Dresden or Tokyo in a conventional war between nuclear superpowers."[30]

Alternatively, one might expect that deterrence would yield to a new world authority, the presence of which would make war no longer legitimate. Both war and deterrence would then be seen as interim phenomena, with war merely having a longer run of legitimacy than deterrence. This would require what Jonathan Schell speaks of in the notorious final section of *The Fate of the Earth* as the task of "reinventing" politics and the world. It is certainly plausible to think that in a world in which there was general agreement to "lay down arms, relinquish sovereignty, and found a political system for the peaceful settlement of international disputes,"[31] neither war nor deterrence would be morally justifiable. The interim, as well as political history as we have known it, would be over. What moral obligations, if any, does the possibility of such a new situation create? On one side, we are tempted to say that morally ideal situations, or what we may refer to as utopian speculations or pious wishes, establish no obligations. Like other ideals, they are optional or supererogatory. They may tell us something about the yearnings of our hearts, but they do not establish the stern demands of duty. Goods, in this view, are objects of choice and are not to be imposed.[32]

On the other hand, the ideal situation is being offered as a means by which most grave evils are to be prevented.[33] If turning in the direction of Schell's new political world, or even to what Vatican II describes as a "family of nations" organized to promote "the universal common good," and creating "an order which corresponds to modern obligations,"[34] is a real and effective means to prevent the enormous evils of nuclear war, then such ideals have a moral urgency, an obligatory rather than optional character. But if one accepts the philosophical axiom that *ought* implies *can* and the corollary that we cannot be obligated to do what we cannot perform, then the obligatory character of such ideal situations obtains only if they are uniquely necessary to obtain obligatory goods or to prevent evils that it is morally necessary to prevent, and if they are attainable.

Proponents of a radically transformed world situation as a resolution of the problems of deterrence can easily make the points that nuclear war in all its forms is a great evil to be avoided and that deterrence may fail—points that all of us have to take seriously—but they commonly fail to show that what they propose is either uniquely necessary or actually available. The fundamental reason for this is that what we are offered by Schell and similar thinkers is not really a solution for a well-defined problem but, rather, a situation in which all the temptations and incentives to rely on nuclear weapons have been banished by stipulation. In the Garden of Eden or in the Kingdom of God, reliance on nuclear weapons would be both otiose and wicked. Juxtaposing an ideal situation with the realities of the present moment can serve to direct our attention to serious flaws in existing arrangements and can have an important motivating function. In the case of nuclear weapons and defense policies, such juxtaposition can be helpful in revealing the depth and shape of popular aspirations, which must be taken seriously in open and democratic societies. Thus, even if they are analytically misleading and conducive to overly broad moral condemnations of the status quo, they have some value and importance.

A further important feature of Schell's work and of the dreams of the more radical antinuclear protestors is their effective reduction of political life to a single issue. The clear priority accorded to the nuclear danger and the radical subordination of all other concerns to it that occurs, for instance, in Schell's description of the international political order and its institutions as "the debris of history," which has "become inimical to life and must be swept away,"[35] can be regarded either as a necessary clearing away of secondary distracting considerations or as an absurd and dangerous simplification. Both views are probably right at different times. To dismiss or even neglect the overriding importance of the question about nuclear weapons is to be guilty of unpardonable levity in the face of a very grave danger to our society, to civilization as we know it, and to the future of humanity. On the other hand, it goes against our historical experience and our sense of social reality to expect a rational reconstruction of the many different societies of the world and their diverse interests and policies around the single goal of preventing nuclear catastrophe.

Somewhat as in the case of the individual whose life is in jeopardy, in moments of crisis survival rightly and naturally becomes the dominant concern, the focus of attention, the value to be safeguarded through vigorous and concentrated action. But when the threat recedes, concentration on survival and the unilinear direction of personal energy that goes with it strike us as inappropriate, constricting, and even alarming. After the crisis is over, we expect people to return to the diversity of their pursuits and enjoyments; indeed, we regard this as healthy, as a sign of a return to normal conditions.

There is a strong propensity in the religious mind to welcome concentration of our energies on a unique dominant end.[36] "One thing alone is necessary." Often this end may be construed so as to allow the independent pursuit of a number of interests—for instance, if the end is taken as obeying the will of God or following nature or working for the glory of God. The end of practical activity, when conceived in religious terms, need not be a single policy objective; it may be a certain aspect of or relationship to things. Nonetheless, I would argue that the effort to focus political life around a single objective, such as the effort to direct all one's personal activities to a single goal, goes hand in hand with a certain sort of religious intensity, even though there is no strict logical relationship. So we find on the one side those who are seized by the gravity of the nuclear crisis moving to express their concern in religious categories. Thus the second chapter of Schell's book is largely an effort to fashion a theology of contemporary warfare for the nonbelievers and *bien pensants* who subscribe to the *New Yorker*.

On the other side we find those who yearn for a world situation that corresponds more closely with religious ideals resorting to the language of crises and to analyses that emphasize the imminence of catastrophe and imply the appropriateness of treating the issue in ways that transcend ordinary political conflict. Thus we find the U.S. Catholic bishops beginning their recent Pastoral Letter with a quotation from Vatican II: "The whole human race faces a moment of supreme crisis in its advance toward maturity."[37] After pointing to the "terror in the minds and hearts of our people" and offering a brief message of hope, the U.S. bishops go on to say: "The crisis of which we speak arises from this fact:

nuclear war threatens the existence of our planet; this is a more menacing threat than any the world has known. It is neither tolerable nor necessary that human beings live under this threat. But removing it will require a major effort of intelligence, courage, and faith."[38] This actually sounds rather mild when compared with some of the hysterical pronouncements about Armageddon that are routinely issued by peace activists. It can even be argued that the line of thought represented here does not play a significant part in the main argument of the bishops' letter. In one respect this would be correct, for it does not shape the final position on the legitimacy of nuclear deterrence. In another respect, however, it points to a fundamental reason for dissatisfaction with the bishops' conclusions, for the diagnosis of the situation that is offered here requires a more radical solution than the Pastoral Letter offers. Averting imminent catastrophe requires a single-minded concentration on what effectively leads to an outcome that is not merely desirable but also attainable. The elimination of the threat from nuclear weapons is surely desirable, but almost no serious political commentator regards it as attainable or likely. Very few would deny the potential for catastrophic outcomes for humanity that is present in any resort to nuclear weapons. As Chicken Little clearly saw, for the sky to fall would be a very bad thing for everyone.

What is needed but is not easily attainable is a perceptive estimate of the distance that separates us from the worst outcomes and a sense of our direction of movement toward or away from greater danger. Here it is helpful to recognize a distinction that must be drawn between immediate and general deterrence—that is, between those situations in which states are actively considering attacks and are to be dissuaded by retaliatory threats, and the continuing situation of hostility.[39] Once this distinction is drawn, the sense in which "nuclear war threatens," as the bishops put it, must be acknowledged to be different in temporary crises and in the long-term adversarial situation between the superpowers. The possibility of false crises and of misleading manipulation of public opinion creates the need just mentioned for a politically sophisticated and sensitive reading of the positions and policies of the adversaries. It must also be granted that, in our judgments as moral agents within a democratic system, the distinction between general and immediate deterrence is subject to two important qualifications. First, tendencies can develop within the adversarial situation that threaten the stability of the situation and make crises and explicit threats to use nuclear weapons more likely; it is a mistake to regard general deterrence as a static condition with no morally significant variations. Second, because of the time pressures that exist within crisis situations, the general lines of policy and the moral limits (if any) that are to be observed in declarations and actions involving nuclear weapons must be worked out beforehand. Moral judgments to shape national policy in crises have to be debated and decided under the conditions of general deterrence. The citizenry cannot count on having time to make its views known and effective under crisis conditions.

The rhetoric of nuclear crisis, though highly motivating over the short run, is more often misleading and unhelpful. A crisis can be defused; a definite short-term solution or agreement can be reached. But the nuclear threat, at least in the remote sense of there being people around with the expertise and the resources to make and to deliver nuclear weapons, will be a permanent element in humanity's future. The continuing possession of national arsenals and possibly of international arsenals under various arrangements is also likely to be permanent, although there remains the possibility that catastrophic nuclear exchange would produce a strongly pacifist revulsion. We can all agree that this represents a regrettable and imperfect situation, which bears the marks of human sinfulness; but we also have to undertake the task of devising the morally least unsatisfactory policies for working in the world as it is and is likely to be. Even if political leaders and the national communities they govern are unable to come out of this problem with clean hands, even if alternative political universes can be imagined that are logically possible and morally superior, we must bear in mind the task of protecting the well-being, the rights, and the communal existence of millions of people with divergent perceptions and priorities. This suggests that what we need is not so much an examination of the morality of deterrence that condemns or endorses deterrence as an abstract institution, but a morality of deterrence that examines and evaluates different policies and decisions that are made within a continuing international political context of which deterrence is a fundamental element.

We also have to recognize the profound difference between the crises in which options are restricted and obligations can be identified with relative clarity, and the long-standing situation of general deterrence, in which national security policy is a resultant of complex political factors, many of them worthy and legitimate on their own level. This complexity does not yield to either the single-minded pursuit of a single issue or solution, such as unilateral disarmament, or to a sharp dichotomy between the demands of a pure and altruistic morality and the self-centered desires of corrupt and oppressive states. For such a dichotomy overlooks the moral weight of national political communities.[40] Nations, even those under tyrannical regimes, are not bandits who can be simply commanded to drop their guns, whether this command comes from the sheriff of the West, the town clergy, or the people in the black hats.

Deterrence and the Turn to Politics

It is in this acceptance of political complexity and the realization of the genuinely perplexing character of our situation that the final positions adopted in the bishops' letter represent a growth in insight beyond the alarmist rhetoric of their exordium. The third section of their letter, on "The Promotion of Peace," is important not because it suggests a number of supererogatory things that peoples and nations might do after avoiding nuclear war; rather, work for disarmament and the improvement of relationships between the superpowers and their respective alliances are important precisely as means of avoiding nuclear catastrophes and increasing the acceptability of the general deterrence situation. Obviously, there can and will be disagreement about just what policies in this area are preferable to others; it will not normally be possible to point to a unique option that is morally obligatory. If we acknowledge the continuing presence of nuclear weapons and threats connected with them in our future, the moral task is not to abolish deterrence but to take those steps that, within the framework of deterrence, will contribute to the maintenance of peace and the avoidance of nuclear catastrophe. The important work of moral judgment, then, is done not in assessing deterrence in general but in looking, as David Hollenbach has urged, at the specific forms of deterrence, "the specific defense postures involving diverse weapons systems, targeting doctrines, procurement programs and master strategic concepts."[41] To this I would add that these specifics of the military and technical realm need to be interpreted in relation to broader diplomatic, political, and social tendencies: admittedly, this makes the task of evaluation more difficult and elusive. But it is necessary if certain problems are to be dealt with in straightforward terms. An example may illustrate this. Hollenbach proposes two criteria for the assessment of specific deterrence policies:

> First, any new policy proposal must make nuclear war less likely than the policies presently in effect rather than more likely.
>
> Second, any new policy proposal must increase the possibility of arms reduction rather than decrease this possibility. This second principle is really a corollary of the first, for a sustained, open-ended arms race can only have disastrous consequences in the long run (and perhaps in the short run).[42]

On the basis of these criteria, he opposes the deployment of Pershing II missiles in Europe because this would make general nuclear war more likely. The reason for this is that these missiles can strike Moscow within six minutes of launch and "their deployment may have the consequence of leading the Soviet Union to adopt a 'launch on warning' policy for their own missiles."[43] This in turn would, he believes, increase the chance of nuclear war.

There are three observations that I would like to point out in Hollenbach's procedure here that should not take away from my general sympathy with his position. The first has to do with the formulation of this second criterion, which wisely lays it down that new policy proposals (among which he clearly includes new weapons systems) must increase "the possibility of arms reduction." This, of course, is far less stringent than a requirement that they actually reduce the level of arms. The possibility requirement really directs our attention in the first place to certain properties and effects of weapons systems and policy proposals (for example, that they are very difficult to detect, are likely to be perceived as first-strike weapons, are more likely to provoke competing weapons systems on the other side), rather than to levels of arms possessed now or in the future. The possibility requirement, as contrasted with an actual reduction requirement, recognizes that arms reduction, if it is to be mutual, depends on the consent of the adversary. Decisions about new weapons systems are made in light of the declared policies and the suspected intentions of an adversary power with its own complex system of decision making. Actual reductions then depend on factors that are not within the power of one side in either the negotiating process or the "arms race." I take it that one of the points of Hollenbach's possibility requirement is to disallow moves by one side that impede the process of disarmament while not obligating one side to make reductions without reciprocity from the other. This seems to me to be both fair and correct.

Hollenbach's view also leaves room for the bargaining-chip argument often advanced in support of new weapons systems, since the function of the bargaining chip is to facilitate the working out of a satisfactory arms control or reduction agreement. The argument has been overused because it is a very general argument, which does not turn on the properties and effects of particular weapons systems but instead relies on the presumed desire of both sides to achieve parity at lower levels of cost. It also has the special charm of being an argument that can be used to endorse new weapons systems while paying at least lip service to the need for arms reduction. It is worth underlining the point that the bargaining-chip argument can be appropriately used only when the weapons system being argued for is *not* deemed essential to the national security. Whether or not Hollenbach wants to admit bargaining-chip arguments, it seems to me that they cannot and should not be excluded, even though there are many historical and political reasons to be skeptical of them. Another point that Hollenbach's presentation does not make explicit is that imposing an actual reduction requirement might well get in the way of his first criterion—namely, making war less likely. An actual reduction criterion, far from being a corollary of the first criterion, would actually be incompatible with it. For instance, we can conceive of cases in which a reduction in force levels could tempt the adversary to attack.[44]

The second main observation that I would like to make about Hollenbach's criteria is that they do not accord any clear place to the relevance of political considerations in assessing new weapons systems. To take a recent and controversial example of how this sort of consideration can be important and even decisive, it seems clear, at least to this observer, that one of the major purposes of the Soviet Union in orchestrating responses to the deployment of Pershing II and cruise missiles as it did was to create division between the NATO allies on whose territory the weapons are to be deployed, to show up the inability of these governments to convince their populations of the legitimacy of deploying the weapons, and to demonstrate that the new theater weapons would not have the reassuring effect on European regimes that was intended. The political stakes were very high, and it seems to me that these must be worked into a comprehensive approach to moral evaluation of these policy decisions. It is at least arguable, for instance, that the creation of a situation in which European governments were unable to ensure the deployment of the new missiles would have had destabilizing effects on the NATO alliance and on the world order of which it is a part, and might well have made war more likely in the long run. It is of course open to Hollenbach to reply that this point, even if true, does not show the wisdom or the moral rightness of the original decision to develop and deploy the missiles. I would agree, but the point would still stand that his criteria need complementing in a way that pays more regard to political factors in the adversarial relationship. It should also be observed that paying more attention to political factors in arriving at moral evaluations of new policy proposals and weapons systems need not incline us only in the direction of a more permissive position with regard to deployment of new weapons. It may, in fact, lead us to a more critical attitude with respect to decisions that are made largely as the result of technological impetus and opportunity, with insufficient regard for their impact on the political climate and for the occasional windows of negotiation that do open up.

My third main observation is a corollary of the second one—namely, that it is profoundly misleading to think that it is possible to make moral judgments on missile systems or other weapons without reference to the historical development and future prospects of the political conflict, the outcome of which the weapons are intended to influence. The arms race, no less than war, is the continuation of politics by other means. Neither development nor the denunciation of new weapons systems can substitute for political wisdom in dealing with the sources of conflict—sources that even in the unlikely event of general and complete disarmament would, if not properly dealt with, lead us back to armament. The yearning of many religious and secular moralists and activists for a world without nuclear weapons is an instructive indicator of dissatisfaction with deterrence in a divided, dangerous, and sinful world. But it should not lead us to a moral condemnation of deterrence as such; nor should it blind us to the decisive moral choices that must be made within deterrence.

Notes

1. National Conference of Catholic Bishops, *The Challenge of Peace: God's Promise and Our Response* (Washington, D.C.: United States Catholic Conference, 1983), par. 17.

2. Ibid., pars. 9, 10.

3. Ibid., par. 141.

4. Cf. Alan Donagan, *The Theory of Morality* (Chicago: University of Chicago Press, 1977), p. 6.

5. See the treatment of the derivation of precepts of natural law in Thomas Aquinas, *Summa Theologiae* I-II, 94 and 100.

6. Gilbert Harman, *The Nature of Morality: An Introduction to Ethics* (New York: Oxford University Press, 1977), pp. 3-9.

7. Bruce Russett, "Ethical Dilemmas of Nuclear Deterrence," *International Security* 8(1984):51.

8. J. Bryan Hehir, "The Just-War Ethic and Catholic Theology: Dynamics of Change and Continuity," in Thomas A. Shannon, ed., *War or Peace?* (Maryknoll, N.Y.: Orbis, 1980), p. 31.

9. Ibid., p. 32.

10. See Richard McCormick's arguments for noncombatant immunity as a virtually exceptionless moral norm in Paul Ramsey, ed., *Doing Evil to Achieve Good* (Chicago: Loyola University Press, 1978), pp. 42–44, and his interpretation of the use of the principle of the lesser evil in the European pastoral letters, in the March 1984 issue of *Theological Studies.*

11. For the bishops' reaction to the attack on consequentialism by Bishop Riley and Germain Grisez, see Jim Castelli, *The Bishops and the Bomb* (Garden City, N.Y.: Image Books, 1983), pp. 102–104.

12. *The Challenge of Peace,* pars. 174–175.

13. David Hollenbach, S.J., *Nuclear Ethics: A Christian Moral Argument* (New York: Paulist Press, 1983), p. 84.

14. See *The Challenge of Peace,* par. 7.

15. Vatican Council II, *Gaudium et Spes,* par. 79, in Walter J. Abbott, S.J., ed., *The Documents of Vatican II* (New York: Guild Press, 1966).

16. Ibid.

17. Ibid., par. 80.

18. Ibid.

19. Ibid., par. 81.

20. Ibid.

21. French Bishops' Conference, "Winning Peace," N.C. News Translation, in *Origins* 13(December 8, 1983):442.

22. Michael Walzer, *Just and Unjust Wars: A Moral Argument with Historical Illustrations* (New York: Basic Books, 1977), p. 278.

23. Ibid., p. 282.

24. Ibid., p. 273.

25. Ibid., p. 274.

26. Ibid., p. 255.

27. Ibid., p. 277.

28. Ibid., p. 283.

29. Key passages from these statements are cited in *The Challenge of Peace,* pars. 170–173. Krol's testimony is cited from *Origins* 9(1979):197.

30. Walzer, *Just and Unjust Wars,* p. 283.

31. Jonathan Schell, *The Fate of the Earth* (New York: Knopf, 1982), p. 226.

32. See the distinction of the place of ideals and visions in morality in P.F. Strawson, "Social Morality and Individual Ideal," in *Freedom and Resentment and Other Essays* (London: Methuen & Co., Ltd., 1974).

33. For the greater stringency of a principle of nonmaleficence see William K. Frankena, *Ethics,* 2nd ed. (Englewood Cliffs, N.J.: Prentice-Hall, 1973).

34. Vatican Council II, *Gaudium et Spes,* par. 84.

35. Schell, p. 219.

36. For a discussion of this notion as it applies to individual plans of life, see John Rawls, *A Theory of Justice* (Cambridge, Mass.: Harvard University Press, 1971).

37. National Conference of Catholic Bishops, *The Challenge of Peace,* par. 1, citing Vatican II, *Gaudium et Spes,* par. 77.

38. Ibid., par. 3.

39. See Patrick Morgan, *Deterrence: A Conceptual Analysis* (Beverly Hills, Calif.: Sage, 1977), pp. 31–43.

40. See Walzer, *Just and Unjust Wars,* pp. 53–55.

41. Hollenbach, *Nuclear Ethics,* p. 74.

42. Ibid., p. 75.

43. Ibid., p. 77.

44. See Sir Arthur Hockaday, "In Defense of Deterrence," in Geoffrey Goodwin, ed., *Ethics and Nuclear Deterrence* (New York: St. Martin's Press, 1982), pp. 75–79, for a lucid presentation of the necessity of minimum arms levels in order to maintain the stability of deterrence.

7

The Failure of Deterrence and the Conduct of War

William V. O'Brien
Georgetown University

T he most crucial single issue in the debate over the efficacy and morality of nuclear deterrence is whether it is possible to fight a limited nuclear war with morally permissible means if deterrence fails. No amount of emphasis on the subjective, or perception, dimensions of deterrence can erase the fundamental importance of the war-fighting contingency that is immanent in the deterrent posture. Since no deterrent posture can be assured of perfect success indefinitely, every deterrent must be based on credible war-fighting intentions and capabilities—unless it rests on a colossal bluff. There is no free lunch in nuclear deterrence. To profit from a credible nuclear deterrent, a nation must be willing to prepare for and face the serious contingency of nuclear war.

This hard truth is unpalatable to many strategic thinkers and unacceptable to most of those who have attempted to prescribe moral limits for the use of nuclear weapons. The practical possibility of limited nuclear war is widely discounted by strategists as well as moralists. Efforts to strengthen limited war capabilities are, moreover, generally discouraged by those who would escape nuclear dilemmas through arms control breakthroughs of unparalleled magnitude. The result is that the issues of the feasibility and morality of limited nuclear war are often brushed aside. Accordingly, participants in the present policy and moral debates over nuclear deterrence and defense go in two distinct directions. The majority assume that some kind of nuclear deterrence will continue to be effective for an indefinite future, that the less said about fighting nuclear war the better, and that the preferred policy and moral objectives are all tied up in the pursuit of drastic arms control measures. A small minority, myself included, consider limited nuclear war to be a prior question to arms control. Without the capability of waging a limited nuclear war if deterrence fails, deterrence ultimately may indeed fail. Arms control progress is widely believed to require stable deterrence. But stable deterrence cannot be based indefinitely on the threat to carry out nuclear war in forms that, by any criteria, would be suicidal and patently immoral. Thus we in the minority hold that the concept of limited nuclear war is not a dangerous heresy but, rather, the foundation for any realistic policy of nuclear deterrence and defense, which in turn can be the indispensable base for arms control progress.

In the current strategic policy debate there are many indications that mutual assured destruction (MAD) as a basic deterrence posture is discredited and that some kind of limited, counterforce, flexible response deterrence/defense posture is being progressively adopted.[1] There are many disclaimers stating that MAD never was, in fact, U.S. policy, that one must distinguish declaratory from operational policy, and that operational policy does not contemplate counter-value assured destruction as required by the MAD concept. Nevertheless, the fact remains that the nuclear balance of terror continues to rest on the credible threat of the United States and the Soviet Union to inflict unacceptable damage on each other's society in ways that defy the limits of traditional military science as well as the dictates of morality. Unless the nuclear antagonists move to strategies based more clearly on counterforce threats to military targets, accompanied by greatly increased efforts to limit collateral damage, the post-MAD era will differ from the MAD era more in degree than in kind.

This chapter will undertake to outline the requirements for a morally just and practically limited use of nuclear weapons for the contingency of nuclear war fighting when nuclear deterrence has failed and nuclear aggression has occurred. The U.S. Catholic bishops' 1983 Pastoral Letter, *The Challenge of Peace*, has assumed a central place in the debate and is prominent in the discussions in other chapters in this book. Accordingly, I will begin with a brief examination of what I take to be the major flaws in this document as they bear on the issues of efficacious nuclear deterrence and defense. I will then outline the moral analysis that the bishops failed to follow in its entirety when they applied just war principles to nuclear issues. Next, I will discuss some of the major objections to the concept of limited nuclear deterrence and defense. In my conclusions I will elaborate on the concept of a nuclear deterrence/defense posture based on just and limited war principles.

Observations on *The Challenge of Peace*

The 1983 U.S. Catholic bishops' Pastoral Letter, *The Challenge of Peace*, has served as a focal point for much of the emerging debate over justice and war in the nuclear age.[4] Unfortunately, the document is seriously flawed with respect to the two principal issues in question—namely, the ends for which nuclear deterrence and defense are maintained and the moral permissibility of these nuclear means.

The bishops' pastoral fails, first, to acknowledge sufficiently, much less define, a threat so grave to values so fundamental as to justify the risks and expense of the contemporary nuclear deterrence system so deplored by the bishops. The fact that the bishops reluctantly condone some sort of nuclear deterrent indicates that they perceive some kind of a threat to our fundamental values. Yet a reading of the pastoral leaves one wondering what threats the bishops perceive that warrant *any* form of nuclear deterrence, even a deterrent so nebulous as that which they accept provisionally, subject to major arms control efforts.[5] In just war terms, the just cause is never adequately established, with the result that the appropriateness of the means involved in nuclear deterrence and defense is assessed in an isolated ethics of means analysis.

The bishops hold themselves out as following just war doctrine in their analyses of nuclear deterrence and defense.[6] Normally, one would expect that a just war analysis would start with an estimate of the values at stake in a conflict and of the threats to those values posed by potential aggressors. In light of this estimate, a just cause might be posited. Then, and only then, would the means contemplated to counter the threat to the just cause be evaluated in just war terms. In the 1983 Pastoral Letter, the ethics of means analysis of nuclear deterrence is completed well before any discussions of the just cause, the values at stake, and the threats thereto are undertaken. Moreover, the discussion of the superpowers' relationship is brief, somewhat ambivalent, and certainly inadequate to serve as the basis for an end-means analysis with respect to a subject so awesome as nuclear war.[7] This is the first great flaw in *The Challenge of Peace.*

Underlying this first flaw in the Pastoral Letter is an overriding conviction that obviously dominates the document—namely, the belief that *no* just cause justifies recourse to nuclear war because of the unprecedented, open-ended destructive character of such a war.[8] This conviction is communicated throughout the pastoral. The result is that the bishops are manifestly placed in a dilemma. Their every instinct is, to use their favorite formulation, "to say 'no' to nuclear war."[9] However, they appear to be persuaded that the current international situation requires some kind of nuclear deterrence, preferably for as short a time as possible, in order that humanity can, as Vatican II put it, escape the "treacherous trap" of the arms race,[10] and to find deliverance in arms control progress leading ultimately to the complete elimination of nuclear weapons.[11] The problem for the bishops, then, is to reconcile the apparent unfortunate necessity of continued reliance on nuclear deterrence (for however brief a time) with the moral imperative "to say 'no' to nuclear war."

The bishops do not meet this problem by an invocation of the ethics of distress as described by Father Hollenbach.[12] They do not, in fact, attempt to justify any concrete form of nuclear deterrence. Rather, they condone a nominal, disembodied "deterrence" that cannot be based on *any* known form of nuclear war, since the bishops cannot think of any permissible form of nuclear war. Moreover, they strongly discourage efforts to define and make possible just and limited nuclear deterrence and defense.[13] From first to last the bishops want to "say 'no' to nuclear war," even though they purport to condone some form of nuclear deterrence that logically would imply that they are not saying "no" to nuclear war.

Authoritative interpreters of the Pastoral Letter have attempted to remedy this flaw by hinting that the pastoral should not be interpreted as excluding any and all forms of nuclear war. The frequently repeated formulation of the most authoritative interpreter of *The Challenge of Peace*, Father J. Bryan Hehir, the principal staff contributor to the document, is that the bishops come "within a centimeter" of condemning nuclear weapons outright but that they leave "a centimeter of ambiguity."[14] Indeed, in debates with Father Hehir I have gained the impression that the centimeter of ambiguity has widened to several centimeters. This is perhaps an inevitable effort to remedy the flaw inherent in a position that condones nuclear deterrence without seeming to accept any form of actual nuclear warfare as permissible for a just belligerent to employ in the face of nuclear aggression.

Notwithstanding these authoritative glosses, it is uncommonly difficult to find any centimeters of ambiguity with respect to use of nuclear weapons in the text of the pastoral itself. The document seems to reflect the deterrence-only concepts of many secular strategic experts.[15] Deterrence-only strategies, based on the proposition that the only rational purpose of nuclear weapons is to prevent the use of nuclear weapons, can be misleading. Although it is true that the preferred function of nuclear weapons is to prevent the aggressive use of nuclear weapons, that function must include the inherent function of their use in nuclear defense if deterrence fails. Taken literally, however, deterrence-only postures can produce a mind set that does not acknowledge the possibility that deterrence may fail and nuclear weapons actually be used. Part of this mind set may be traced to fascination with the psychological, subjective dynamics of deterrence. But part of it also arises from a failure, similar to that of the bishops, to accept as clear and present the Soviet threat to the United States and its allies. Absent a conviction that there is a clear and present threat of nuclear aggression or intimidation, it becomes possible to reduce "the threat" to a somewhat abstract phantom, handily disposed of by an equally abstract "deterrent."

To be sure, the deterrent is known to be based on real weapons systems, but somehow the conviction that their only purpose is (ideally) their nonuse in war, coupled with the conviction that there is no clear and present danger of nuclear aggression anyway, reduces the concepts of the threat and the deterrent to such subjective dimensions that the contingency of a serious threat, leading to failed deterrence, leading to nuclear war is dismissed as war-mongering and eroding confidence in "the deterrent." Typically, those with a deterrence-only mind set prefer some kind of minimal deterrence based on countervalue threats that, it is believed, will never have to be carried out.[16] When it is objected that this minimal countervalue deterrent, if ever transformed into a war-fighting operation, would be the most destructive and immoral of war-fighting options, it is answered that there will be no war-fighting and that it is subversive to deterrence stability even to talk about it.

Thus bishops, moralists, and peace activists are not unique in their varying degrees of reliance on deterrence-only concepts. A substantial body of strategic thought implicitly or explicitly tends toward deterrence-only approaches and eschews the subject of nuclear war-fighting. This is left to the so-called deterrence-plus advocates, who insist that deterrence postures must be twofold, embracing nuclear defense as well as nuclear deterrence.[17]

In this chapter I will not attempt to address the first deficiency in the U.S. Catholic bishops' 1983 Pastoral Letter, the estimate of the threat to the just cause of the United States and the Free World. I do assume the following:

1. There is a substantial threat of aggression and intimidation from the Soviet Union, and possibly from other powers possessed of nuclear weapons. The ultimate threat is either the physical destruction of the United States and its allies or their defeat leading to the forcible imposition of *gulag* regimes in which the fundamental freedoms and values that constitute our just cause would be lost.[18]

2. This threat is so manifest that there is a wide consensus among many, including the bishops who oppose nuclear war, that there must be some kind of nuclear deterrent posture to protect the West from aggression.

3. Threats to the allies of the United States are perceived by them to be sufficiently grave to warrant continuing reliance on the U.S. nuclear strategic umbrella, as well as theater and local mixed nuclear/conventional deterrence/defense forces, notwithstanding strong domestic criticism of U.S. deterrence/defense policies within those countries.[19]

4. For the present, the issue of deterring and defending against communist or other nuclear and conventional aggression and conquest is presented to the United States primarily in terms of threats to its friends and allies, not to itself, since there appears to be no major *casus belli* between the United States and the Soviet Union directly.

5. Accordingly, the issue of just cause underlying U.S. deterrence/defense policies is twofold. First, does deterrence/defense with nuclear weapons on behalf of the friends and allies of the United States meet just war requirements? Second, would a succession of Munich-like retreats from the threat and/or actuality of aggression based on nuclear weapons eventually leave the United States in a position wherein its own freedom and values would be endangered by a triumphant communist power enjoying the assets of many regions now friendly to the United States?

6. With respect to threats both to the friends and allies of the United States and to the United States itself, it is contended that these societies should be defended against communist subjugation by aggression or intimidation by all means permitted by just war doctrine—but *only* by the means permitted by just war doctrine.

7. Trends in U.S. deterrence/defense policies have been moving toward more counterforce and less countervalue strategies, but neither doctrine nor

practical arrangements have yet reached a point where U.S. policies can be said to satisfy the requirements of just war doctrine.

I want to emphasize the last two points. Although I would extract every possible justification for means used in defense against aggression on behalf of the essentially just cause of preserving the substance and values of the U.S. and other Free World polities, I would not violate the limits of just war doctrine, even for such a just cause. Specifically, I would not answer immoral countervalue nuclear attacks against U.S. population centers with retaliatory attacks against Soviet population centers. Accordingly, although I am encouraged by trends in U.S. strategic doctrine and deployments since the time of Schlesinger's initiatives in 1974, I remain dissatisfied with the present U.S. strategic nuclear posture, which still threatens collateral damage beyond the limits of just war. The purpose of this chapter is to explore the moral parameters of a deterrence/defense posture that would conform to just war limits.[20]

I further reject the solution of Michael Walzer in invoking a supreme-emergency justification for nuclear deterrence.[21] The dangers of such an open-ended concept, demonstrated by the German abuse of the so-called *Kriegsraison* doctrine that "necessity knows no law,"[22] are too great to risk. Moreover, it is my conviction that the answer to efficacious and morally acceptable deterrence and defense can be found within just war doctrine without recourse to the exceptional plea of supreme emergency.

In the subsequent discussion I will follow a deterrence-plus approach, assuming that no practical and morally responsible position on nuclear deterrence and defense can fail to face the contingency of failed deterrence and just defense.

Requirements for a Just and Limited Nuclear Deterrence and Defense Posture

The elements of just war doctrine are traditionally divided into a war-decision law, the *jus ad bellum*, and a war-conduct law, the *jus in bello*. The war-decision part of just war doctrine includes a number of categories. They are variously formulated and arranged, tending to produce a somewhat lengthy and disjointed agenda of issues. I prefer to retain the threefold breakdown of St. Thomas Aquinas—namely, competent authority, just cause, and right intention. Within these three basic war-decision categories I subsume other categories within an integrated just cause component.

However one arranges the elements in a just war analysis, it seems clear that a comprehensive treatment requires that all of the just war conditions be addressed. It is also clear that the logic of the just war doctrine derives from an exercise in weighing ends and means. As observed earlier, a complete just war analysis must start with the ends and then move to the contemplated means, rather than proceed, as the bishops did in their 1983 Pastoral Letter, to an independent ethic of means analysis without an adequate antecedent examination of the ends for which the means in question are intended to serve. It is always possible, of course, to conduct an independent moral analysis of a particular category of means, but in order to make the kind of practical judgments that the bishops make in *The Challenge of Peace,* one must undertake the full just war analysis, war-decision as well as war-conduct. In such an analysis of nuclear deterrence, the application of just war *jus ad bellum* would unfold as follows:

Competent Authority

In the case of nuclear war, the decision to use nuclear weapons may be synonymous with the decision to go to war. There are well-established constitutional requirements in the United States governing the commitment of the nation to war. These requirements have been difficult to apply in undeclared military interventions such as the Vietnam War. In such cases the issue has been the power of the executive branch to commit the United States to a course of action leading predictably to the engagement of U.S. forces in combat.[23] In the case of hostilities involving nuclear war, either immediately or in the foreseeable future, the decision to go to war becomes markedly more momentous. It may well have to be taken in circumstances different from those prescribed by the Constitution, involving a formal declaration of war by the Congress. Whereas competent authority raises constitutional issues in a modern constitutional polity insofar as conventional war or military interventions are concerned, the requirement of competent authority with respect to nuclear war enjoins practical capabilities on the part of the national authority committing the nation to the enormous risks of such a war.

The core issue of competent authority as it applies to nuclear war is whether the National Command Authority (NCA) has a reasonable prospect for controlling the use of nuclear weapons. Although the destructive effects of nuclear war generally are sufficiently damaging to raise presumptions against any use of nuclear weapons, the crucial issue in the debate over limited nuclear war is whether there is any reasonable hope of actually keeping a nuclear war limited. If there is not, then theoretical limited war concepts are insufficient to warrant engagement in nuclear hostilities even though the intent is to keep them limited.

The crucial technical issue that emerges with respect to the exercise of competent authority in preparations for and in the conduct of nuclear war is the present and probable future prospects for maintaining effective and survivable C^3I (command, control, communications and intelligence) systems. In order to meet the just war requirement of competent authority, as well as to have some prospect for complying with the other conditions of just war, a belligerent must have C^3I capabilities adequate to ensure control of its nuclear weapons systems so that actions initiating, escalating or reducing, discontinuing for pauses, or terminating nuclear war are at all times within its competence. Put negatively, as it often is in moral condemnations of nuclear war, there must be C³I sufficient to prevent nuclear weapons "escaping control."[24]

This requirement has the highest priority among the tasks facing any government that continues to prepare for the contingency of nuclear war. This priority was emphasized within the Carter administration and has been repeatedly acknowledged by the Reagan administration. It involves C³I requirements to provide: early warning of Soviet attack; timely information from the North American Air Defense Command (NORAD); suvivability for the NCA; constant communication with U.S. strategic forces and other forces worldwide; the ability to monitor the execution of national decisions, to monitor strike information in real time, and to assess damage to both sides; the capacity to reconstruct and redirect the strategic forces as the war proceeds; and continuous communication links with the Soviet Union.[25]

Writers such as Ball and Steinbruner have concluded that the odds are very much against the United States or the Soviet Union developing a C³I system that could survive a nuclear war beyond a very limited nuclear exchange. Accordingly, the theoretically plausible concept of an extended limited nuclear war controlled by the adversaries so that civilian damage was minimal is an illusion. If this is the case, the U.S. Catholic bishops are right in discouraging further efforts on behalf of limited nuclear war, the deterrence-only strategists are right in putting all their faith in deterrence, and the pursuit of just and limited nuclear deterrence/defense postures is wrong and dangerous. This judgment may be made without consideration of other important obstacles to the realization of just and limited nuclear war capabilities to be discussed later.[26] Just and limited war is, above all, controlled use of military force. Without control there is no just and limited war.

If the option of conducting some kind of nuclear defense in response to a nuclear attack by an aggressor were dispensable, the technical presumption against the feasibility of achieving the survivable C³I capabilities requisite to conduct controlled, limited nuclear war would suffice to discourage further pursuit of this goal. However, the alternatives to developing a limited nuclear war capability are, broadly, to rely entirely on the perpetual efficacy of nuclear deterrence based on the threat to wage essentially uncontrolled nuclear war if deterrence fails; to rely on a bluff deterrent, the failure of which would in fact lead to no nuclear response to nuclear aggression but simply to catastrophic defeat; or the abandonment of nuclear deterrence altogether, with predictable consequences for freedom and fundamental rights in a world where other powers would possess nuclear weapons and be willing both to threaten their use and to use them.

The other alternative, of course, is for the problem to be solved by massive arms control progress leading to the total elimination of nuclear weapons. Surely, if the odds against achievement of adequate survivable C³I capabilities are great, then the odds against total nuclear disarmament in the contemporary and foreseeable international system are staggering. For this reason, it is not enough to accept the judgment that prospects for survivable C³I are too poor to warrant continued efforts to improve them to the point where controlled limited nuclear war is conceivable. On the contrary, since the possibility of such improvement is not and cannot be proved to be beyond our capabilities, every effort to develop survivable C³I is called for.

No one can guarantee, either, that the efforts to develop adequate C³I will succeed or fail. Moreover, no verdict will be final in this regard, since science and technology will continue to unfold possibilities either to facilitate or to frustrate efforts to control nuclear war. We face an open-ended technical issue on which political, military, and moral estimates and decisions must be made.

As we review the prospects for C³I, it should be borne in mind that the requirements for conducting limited nuclear war are obviously vastly different from those for engaging in a general nuclear exchange. Apparently, until relatively recently the C³I requirements were viewed in terms of massive retaliation functions based on some version of mutual assured destruction strategies. Emphasis on limited, selective use of nuclear weapons has been prominent for only a decade or so, and thinking about C³I often seems to confuse the issues of limited use of nuclear weapons with those of a general strategic nuclear exchange. This is not to depreciate the grave problems of any kind of control of nuclear warfare but, rather, to suggest that sometimes discussions of these issues are blurred by the overriding specter of general nuclear war.

Existing analyses tend to emphasize the difficulties, if not the impossibility, of maintaining acceptable C³I throughout the course of an extended strategic nuclear exchange between the superpowers. However, if a nuclear deterrence/defense policy were grounded in a limited counterforce strategy, the problem might be more manageable, albeit formidable. Even a less total strategic exchange would damage C³I critically, if not fatally. Moreover, to the extent that counterforce strikes were directed at the enemy's C³I, the negative effects insofar as control is concerned might be as bad as or worse than those resulting from a general strategic exchange that included numerous countervalue strikes. To destroy or critically cripple an enemy's C³I would be contrary to the intention to wage limited nuclear war and to terminate nuclear exchanges as soon as possible.[27]

What emerges from an inquiry that assumes the necessity of limited nuclear war as an option for effective nuclear deterrence and refuses to accept the verdict that survivable C³I is possible in *any* nuclear war is this: the need to develop C³I capabilities sufficient to serve a nuclear war in which nuclear weapons were used only against military targets, permitting significant limitation of collateral damage, and in which the use of nuclear weapons was discontinued as soon as possible, once the advantage gained by the aggressor's employing them had been thwarted.

A recurring issue with respect to competent authority in nuclear war is the danger that C³I failures are likely to lead to unauthorized and uncontrolled use of nuclear weapons by subordinate commanders.[28] This is a serious issue, but it is important to note that there is an equally broad concern within the U.S. military that it will be inordinately difficult to get authority to use nuclear weapons and that they might not be used when their use was warranted. It should be observed that the kind of C³I failure that is feared would almost certainly result from the destruction and disruption caused by an aggressor's nuclear attack. If, in retaliatory nuclear strikes, the victim of aggression was not always able to control its nuclear forces, some of the burden of responsibility would have to be placed on the aggressor for the damage done by strikes initiated by subordinate commanders. However, the more positive point should be that the subordinate commanders' standing orders should emphasize the counterforce character of any nuclear strikes they may feel justifiable in launching. Finally, the effort to develop survivable C³I means must be pressed as a continuing top priority.

Moreover, even if C³I capabilities are greatly improved, there will have to be a marked improvement in the U.S. National Command Authority and general command processes to meet the requirements of competent authority. The poor performance in the abortive rescue effort in Iran,[29] and in recent deployments of U.S. forces in Lebanon,[30] do not encourage confidence in the ability of the NCA to conduct a tightly controlled, highly efficient limited nuclear war.

Underlying these technical and organizational issues is a fundamental political problem. There is a distinct lack of national consensus supporting the president of the United States in the use of force. The presumptions are mostly against rather than for him at every level, from minor involvement in counterinsurgency, to deployment of conventional forces in fight and negotiate situations, to debates over the defense budget and national strategy. Important elites and constituencies (religious, academic, journalistic) consider deterrence and defense something between a necessary and an unnecessary evil and project the view that one would be right most of the time if one systematically opposed any action that was taken to improve U.S. military power and to use it. Perhaps these elite biases are not shared by the public at large; in the post–Vietnam War era this is unclear. If these trends resisting recourse to force persist, however, it will be increasingly difficult to claim that the president of the United States has competent authority to commit the nation to nuclear war. But in a nuclear age wherein war is a constant possibility, a nation such as the United States must have that power entrusted to some authority, or it will not long be free. Given the necessity for extremely rapid and decisive decision making inherent in nuclear deterrence and defense operations, it must be assumed that the election of a president is sufficient to endow him or her with the authority to commit the nation to nuclear war unless specifically prohibited in particular circumstances by law.[31]

In summary, just war doctrine requires competent authority for the commitment of a polity to war. In the case of the United States and the possibility of nuclear war, competent authority means that the United States must possess the technical and organizational C³I capabilities requisite for the initiation, limitation, and termination of nuclear war operations. It also requires that there be a constitutional warrant for engaging in nuclear war. It is believed that, given the nature of nuclear war, this warrant must come from the constitutional powers of the president as chief executive and commander-in-chief and that the role of the Congress is significant primarily in its actions prior to any nuclear war resulting in guidelines and/or limitations affecting the president's exercise of his war powers and responsibilities.

Just Cause

Just war doctrine has developed a number of conditions to be met by the just belligerent. Rather than addressing each independently, I prefer to subsume a number of them under the category of just cause. The conditions to be discussed are: comparative justice, the *casus belli*, the calculus of proportion between the benefits of defending the just cause and the cost or damage of the just defense, and the exhaustion of peaceful alternatives to just war.

The *comparative justice* of the adversaries in the nuclear balance of power is an issue that is touched briefly by the 1983 U.S. Catholic bishops' Pastoral Letter but that needs more serious and prolonged study and debate. A generation of Soviet specialists in the West has been split between reassuring views of the Soviet regime that tend to place equal or greater blame on the United States for the Cold War and the nuclear balance of terror and hard-line views of the Soviets that tend to be discounted as exaggerated.[32] A balance held by nuclear weapons is too dangerous and tenuous to be maintained unless there is good reason to believe that there is a clear and present threat of Soviet and/or other aggression or intimidation leading to the reduction of additional areas of the world to some form of the *gulag* society. There needs to be a greater residual consensus, resistant to ephemeral surges of popular opinions and emotions, both in the United States and among its allies on the threat that warrants the maintenance of a nuclear deterrence/defense posture. If such a consensus is not forthcoming, the posture should be changed so as to address only the threats that are believed to be real.

In addition to consensus on threats to what we continue to call the Free World, there must be a greater agreement on polities and values worth defending against these threats. If one does not believe that it would be intolerable for South Koreans to live under the kind of regime that rules North Korea, or for West Germans to have to live under an East German regime, then threats to those polities might not warrant the dangers of nuclear deterrence and defense or even the costly and escalation-prone forms of available conventional defense.

It should be observed that a high consciousness of the character of opposing regimes prone to engage in war is discouraged by the value-neutral cast of modern international law, which looks only to the identification of aggressors, irrespective of their character and the probable consequences of their victories. Walzer, likewise, eschews the issue of comparative justice of opposing regimes.[33] It should be apparent, however, that it is not possible to complete the task of judging the proportionality of recourse to war with the just cause without examination of the values defended under the just cause and the probable injuries to those values that would result from defeat or submission.

In any event, contemplation of the nations presently protected from aggression and intimidation by the U.S. nuclear deterrent might lead to the conclusion that none of them were sufficiently important to warrant the risks involved in their defense by the United States with either nuclear or conventional means, bearing in mind always the risks of escalation in conventional defense. This was a conclusion suggested baldly by Charles De Gaulle in the early 1960s, when he justified his own independent nuclear *force de frappe*.[34] This issue has been buried under the artificial optimism of deterrence-only postures that discouraged contemplation of any actual nuclear war and, accordingly, any scrutiny of the probable occasions wherein such a war might occur. To the extent that one takes a deterrence-plus position and insists on confronting the possibility of deterrence failing and nuclear war being fought in defense of particular victims of aggression, it is impossible to avoid the question: What is worth the risk and the grim reality of nuclear war? Ironically, it was the failure of the French and the British to face the question of what was worth defending against aggression that brought them to grief in the 1930s. Now they and many other nations must depend on the United States' sense of what is worth defending for indispensable protection against intimidation and aggression.

The *casus belli* for nuclear war must be grounded on commitment to the defense of certain polities and values but must also include the practical circumstances in which a just cause is proclaimed and defended. One seldom has the luxury of going to war in reaction to a clear and present threat to or actual attack against the most highly valued, meritorious ally in circumstances where there is no question about the obligation to resist aggression. Modern wars often occur as a result of escalating threats, challenges, and minor aggressions that reach a point where the just defender or ally feels that there is no alternative to armed resistance—for example, the British and French response to Germany's 1939 invasion of Poland. Moreover, the victim of aggression may very well not be the ally with the highest ratings in the reports on domestic values and good government of Amnesty International or Freedom House—for example, South Korea in 1950, South Vietnam in 1965.[35]

Sometimes the need for collective defense, the need to stop and reverse an aggressor's political-military momentum, accidents in the course of quasi-belligerent competitive intervention, may lead to a war that may be in the right place at the right time in terms of political-military necessity but will be at an awkward place and time and in awkward circumstances from the moral perspectives of just war. In the world of political-military decision, it is necessary to seek the legitimate links between the underlying just cause and the underlying threat to that cause, on the one hand, and the immediate *casus belli* of a particular war, on the other. Thus defense of the struggling South Vietnamese polity might seem insufficient, viewed independently of other factors, to warrant U.S. military intervention. Defense of South Vietnam as part of a broader response to a spectrum of threats of communist aggression in South East Asia, grounded in a principled resistance to the spread of communist dictatorships by armed force and exported revolution, might well be considered a legitimate just war *casus belli*.

The *calculus of proportion* between the values of the polities defended and their just causes and the costs of such just defense, in light of the probability of success, is the central moral exercise in just war analysis. This analysis must begin with a realistic view of the probability of success. A just war in defense of fundamental freedoms and rights is warranted even if the probability of success is small in traditional terms but sufficient to make the price of aggression and conquest disproportionate and unacceptable to an aggressor.

In the case of nuclear war, the calculus of proportion is triangular. The anticipated costs must include: damage to all belligerents, damage to neutrals, and damage to the world generally. Clearly the estimate of damage must include future damage that may result from the pernicious effects of nuclear radiation as well as other long-term consequences of nuclear war.[36] Moreover, if it is thought that a nuclear war can be kept limited, the dangers of escalation are a central element in the calculus.

The prospects for concluding that recourse to nuclear war will be proportionate in all of these respects—between the belligerents, as concerns neutrals, and in global consequences—are clearly problematic. Nevertheless, confronted with nuclear aggression, a nation may have to engage in nuclear war. In reaching the decision to do so, it must have some working concept of success, if not victory, as a referent in the calculus of proportionality. A good deal of partisan debate has confused the issue of victory or prevailing in nuclear war. It should be emphasized that support for some kind of limited war in pursuit of a morally acceptable end does not mean endorsement of any particular formulation of nuclear victory. Critics of those who claim that nuclear "victory" is possible and worth pursuing often conclude that no victory, in the sense of no sufficient positive outcome, can result from any nuclear war. This may well be an unwarranted and overgeneralized view. Prescinding, therefore, from any extant versions of nuclear victory, it may be said that *success* in a nuclear war would be defined by attainment of the following objectives:

1. Successful resistance to intimidation and aggression.

2. Restriction of recourse to nuclear war means to a very low level, qualitatively and quantitatively.

3. Avoidance of enlargement of the area and scope of the nuclear war.

4. Early termination of use of nuclear weapons and of the war consonant with successful resistance to aggression.[37]

It should be observed that a limited nuclear war might result in political consequences that could be termed victory. Surely, if a state were drawn into a nuclear war by an aggressor's attack, there would be nothing immoral about trying to obtain the best political-military result possible while making every effort to limit the use of nuclear weapons as enjoined by items 2 through 4 of the preceding list. The legitimate objection to prospects held out for nuclear victory is, presumably, that they underestimate the risks and dangers of any recourse to nuclear weapons and encourage such recourse irresponsibly. Having acknowledged this point, however, there is no reason that nuclear planning should not seek to combine severe limitation of any nuclear war with substantial political-military advantages from such a war if it were initiated by an aggressor. It is clear, however, that in balancing limitation efforts with attempts to secure political-military advantage, the former should prevail far beyond the extent to which this might be the case in forming nonnuclear strategies.

Finally, it cannot be sufficiently emphasized that the calculation of proportionality is a continuous process, not something that is done only at the beginning of a war and then again at some critical juncture in the conflict. In the case of nuclear war, assessment of damage and monitoring of escalatory trends must be constant, and decision makers must be prepared to make rapid decisions designed always to limit the use of nuclear weapons. Such decisions would presumably be facilitated by prewar planning that identified key options and thresholds. Ironically, such planning, if made public, is usually enough to cause vehement accusations that the government is "planning a nuclear war." If nuclear war is a possibility, however, contingency plans for such wars must be made.

Although war may break out in unexpected places, there are a number of areas where the possibility of conflict possibly leading to nuclear war is enduring—the NATO–Warsaw Pact frontier, the Middle East, Korea. It may be assumed that contingency plans in considerable detail exist for the defense of U.S. allies in these areas. It should be possible to predetermine with some accuracy the probable effects of various levels of nuclear combat with known weapons systems, strategies, and tactics, and the probable effects of such a war on the belligerent states, on the neighboring neutrals, and on the rest of the globe. If such estimates indicate a priori an unacceptable level and scope of damage, thresholds should be set limiting the extent of recourse to nuclear weapons. It is a hard saying, but such limits must be enforced irrespective of enemy behavior or successes. As one willing to consider limited nuclear war options, I must emphasize that those options appear prima facie to be *very* limited.

I include the just war condition that the potential belligerent must *exhaust peaceful alternatives* for defending the just cause before recourse to war under the broad *just cause* category, because this requirement is integral to the determination that a just cause for war exists. It should hardly be necessary to state that every reasonable peaceful alternative to nuclear war should be exhausted before recourse to so hazardous a means of defending just causes is adopted. However, a realistic and fair acknowledgment of the practice of the United States with respect to recourse to force should oblige recognition that the United States is an unlikely aggressor. The likelihood of the United States being engaged in a nuclear war is overwhelmingly to be found in scenarios either of an aggressor's nuclear attack on the United States and/or some of its allies or of a conventional aggression against a U.S. ally leading to an escalation by either side to nuclear war. In none of these scenarios is there an opportunity for the United States to be the determining party insofar as the decision to go to war is concerned. What remains a major issue is whether the United States, in response to a conventional aggression against an ally, would initiate nuclear war.

Properly speaking, however, the decision to initiate nuclear responses to conventional aggression is concerned with the calculus of proportionality of ends and means discussed earlier rather than with the issue of exhaustion of peaceful alternatives to war. What, then, remains of the just war condition that war be a last resort insofar as U.S. nuclear deterrence/defense policies are concerned? It would seem that the requirement must be related to the behavior of a state prior to the crisis that might precipitate a nuclear war.

To have standing as a just belligerent in a nuclear war, a state must, first, have maintained a record of reasonableness with respect to peaceful alternatives to recourse to war as a means of settling whatever particular differences are likely to provide the specific *casus belli* for war. This does not mean that appeasement is required but simply that a state have a reasonable and forthcoming attitude toward serious differences that threaten to lead to war. Second, a state must have established a responsible record with respect to arms control, maximizing efforts to limit the consequences of nuclear war should it ever occur and to avoid it by means such as hot line agreements designed to prevent wars resulting from misperceptions and misunderstandings. Moreover, to the extent that the very process of arms control negotiations may in itself tend to discourage nuclear war, a record of honest involvement in arms control efforts will meet the just war requirement that the peaceful alternatives to nuclear war have been exhausted. Terms such as *exhausted* and *last resort*, of course, must be interpreted reasonably in the context of the situation, not literally.

Right Intention

Right intention has two connotations, utilitarian and moral. In utilitarian terms, the belligerent is bound to confine the pursuit of the war to what is truly necessary in order to achieve the objectives grounded in the just cause. Nothing beyond that is justified. Pursuit of the just cause should not be an open-ended warrant for gaining whatever advantages may become possible by reason of the fortunes of war.

In moral terms, the belligerent must never succumb to hatred and a lust for vengeance, no matter how cruel the war may be. The force used in a just war is used reluctantly, as a rare exception to the general presumption against war and killing that informs all just war doctrine.[38] Right intention means that the enemy must always be viewed and treated as human beings, not abstract aggressors on whom any retribution may be inflicted.

In both its aspects, right intention is a just war condition highly relevant to the possibility of just and limited nuclear war. The utilitarian component of right intention, which recommends itself in any war as a counsel of prudence, is especially relevant to the very idea of limited nuclear war as a very exceptional means for very exceptional circumstances. The moral injunction to be conscious of the common humanity of the belligerents is greatly needed when the possibility of vengeful retaliation by victims of nuclear aggression is all too evident. In our conference it was the distinguished military historian Michael Howard who reiterated the classic right intention requirement that the conduct of a just war ought not to be such as to jeopardize unnecessarily the possibility for a just and lasting peace. This concept of right intention is at once very difficult to follow in the heat of war, particularly in the horror of a nuclear war, and yet the only hope for consequences from a war commensurate with its costs.[39]

The just war doctrine's war-conduct law, the *jus in bello*, forms a separate part of the doctrine but is integrally related to the war-decision law, *jus ad bellum*, in a number of ways. The most important interrelationships of the two parts are: anticipation of the degree to which adherence to the war-conduct law will be probable in the war-decision calculus of proportionality and the same estimate of probable conformity with the *jus in bello* in the commitment to right intention. Clearly the interrelationship of the moral guidelines for going to war and for conducting war is singularly evident in the case of nuclear war, where the very possibility of engaging in such a war is contingent on the expectation that war-conduct limits of just war can be met.

The war-conduct law consists of two basic principles, proportion and discrimination, and in the detailed laws of war to the extent that just war supports rules of positive international law. The prohibition against genocide is also raised in connection with nuclear war and will be discussed later.

Proportion

The war-decision principle of proportion requiring that the overall costs of the war be proportionate to the good accomplished by defending the just cause has its counterpart in the war-conduct principle of proportion limiting the damage resulting from individual military operations to true military necessity. "Military necessity" can be an excuse for all manner of excesses in war but legitimate military necessity means that the measures taken by a belligerent are limited to what is reasonably necessary to accomplish the permissible objectives of war. Thus neither disproportionate overkill measures to achieve a permissible goal or measures to achieve an objective that is prohibited or disproportionate in itself are justified by legitimate military necessity.[40] The core, but not the entirety, of legitimate military necessity is the principle of proportion, grounded in turn in true military utility. The normative concept of proportionality is closely related to the political-military principle of economy of force.[41]

Thus the principle of proportion is the indispensable basis, but not the entirety, of the war-conduct law. The principle of legitimate military necessity requires that, in addition to proportionality, a military measure be consonant with the international law of war and relevant principles of natural law.[42]

The relation between the war-conduct and war-decision principles of proportion is integral and constant. As observed, the decision to go to war must anticipate the modes and methods to be employed, and they must provide the expectation that they can be used proportionally. This calculus of proportionality is twofold. First, it must be reasonably anticipated that the usual employment of the proposed means will be proportionate to the particular military ends of each operation. In other words, there must be an expectation of tactical proportionality in the use of the means contemplated. Second, it must be deemed probable that the cumulative employment of the means contemplated will result in costs proportionate to the strategic or overall objectives of the war. Such a calculation is often difficult, but it is particularly vital and perhaps more readily made in the case of nuclear war.

If, for example, one assumes a limited nuclear defense of Europe with small kiloton nuclear weapons at the tactical, battlefield level, it is readily evident that individual instances of recourse to such means might well be proportionate. Use of three battlefield nuclear devices to halt an aggressor armored column in comparatively open country would certainly seem to be proportionate. The use over time of 300 tactical nuclear devices, however, might be disproportionate because of their cumulative effects and their encouragement of escalation, even though each individual use was as proportionate in the tactical sense as was the case of the three nuclear devices. Moreover, even the use of three nuclear devices in clearly proportionate ways might be deemed disproportionate if the circumstances of their use raised the expectation of escalation to a disproportionate level.

The interrelationship of strategic, war-decision proportionality to tactical, war-conduct proportionality underscores the critical importance of the command, control, and communication (C^3) requirements for just and limited war discussed under the just war issue of competent authority. The tactical commander cannot be expected to judge whether his decisions to employ tactical nuclear weapons will lead to disproportionate cumulative results. He should be well aware of the problem and conservative in his disposition to employ nuclear weapons, but it is the responsibility of higher authority to evaluate overall trends and decide whether the clear necessities of particular tactical situations justify the use of nuclear weapons, thereby contributing to a total pattern of use that must be reconciled with the strategic, war-decision principle of proportion.

Critics of the principle of proportion at both the war-decision and war-conduct levels decry its propensity toward permissiveness. Obviously one can adjust one's justification of proportionality by adjusting one's ends and slipping into an end-justifies-the-means abdication of restraint. Although the danger is real, it does not and cannot remove the principle of proportion from its central place in the moral calculus of war decision and war conduct. Conscientious decision makers will attempt to make honest appraisals of prospective and current proportionality of means to ends. No ethical or legal prescription will salvage much from the conduct of dishonest, hypocritical, or cynical decision makers.[43]

Discrimination

The principle of discrimination or noncombatant immunity prohibits the direct intentional attacking of noncombatants and nonmilitary targets. Often held out as a clear, stark prescription that sharply limits the use of modern weapons, conventional as well as nuclear, the principle of discrimination is more complex and elusive than it may seem.[44] The scholarly literature on the subject is marked by debates over all aspects of the rule, including the definitions of *direct, intentional, noncombatants,* and *nonmilitary targets.*[45] It must be observed that this debate has not been clarified by church pronouncements, which, in modern times until very recently, did not conspicuously use the terminology and logic of the principle of discrimination in their analyses of nuclear war.[46] The upshot is that the principle of discrimination is a less clear and decisive source for limitation of modern means of war than it is often held out to be. Nevertheless, it is established both in just war doctrine and in contemporary international law as a basic principle, along with the principle of proportion.[47]

My own understanding of the principle of discrimination is that it prohibits disproportionate collateral damage in addition to prohibiting attacks on population centers, noncombatants, and nonmilitary targets as such. As the Pastoral Constitution on the Church in the Modern World of Vatican II proclaimed, countervalue attacks on cities violate the principle of discrimination.[48] The problem has been, of course, that the nuclear balance of terror has been thought to rest precisely on the threat of such attacks in retaliation for like attacks on one's own cities. Thus, by definition, strategic nuclear deterrence, to the extent that it has been based on some version of mutual assured destruction, has been based on the credible threat to execute countervalue, countercity attacks that, by any interpretation, violate the principle of discrimination.

The growing literature on U.S. deterrence strategies tends to argue that the operational, as opposed to the declaratory, policies never actually rested on this extreme threat of indiscriminate nuclear warfare.[49] Moreover, the United States has for some time distinguished targeting of cities *as such*, which it disavows, from targeting those elements of Soviet military power that are seen to be more relevant to the concept of *unacceptable damage* to the Soviets than are cities. This point is made in Judge Clark's letter to the U.S. Catholic bishops, cited in their 1983 Pastoral Letter.[50]

The bishops, however, rightly raise the question of colocation of legitimate military targets with population centers. There are many military targets in the Soviet Union that could be legitimately attacked under the principle of discrimination were it not for the fact that their location—for example, in Moscow—means that the collateral damage of nuclear attacks on them would surely be unacceptable. Some just war theorists would argue this point in terms of intention and the meaning of *direct* attack. I prefer to emphasize the disproportion between the permissible military destruction of military targets and the concomitant civilian damage.

However one attacks the problem, it seems clear that the disavowal by the U.S. government of the intention to attack cities *as such*, though welcome, does not adequately meet the requirements of just war for discriminatory conduct (or, for that matter, for proportionate conduct). What is needed is to construct a deterrence/defense policy that will threaten retaliation following a nuclear attack with means that are counterforce, proportionate, and discriminate. This means, in the first place, that no massive retaliation in kind would ever be contemplated even as a response to countervalue attacks on U.S. or allied cities. What just war doctrine might permit would be counterforce retaliation against military targets with means and in circumstances permitting the limitation of collateral damage to proportionate levels. Thus, if the Soviets have deliberately colocated a vital military installation in a populated area, but not squarely in the center of that area, it is conceivable that highly accurate nuclear strikes designed to produce only local and ephemeral fallout might be employed against the installation. It would be known that substantial civilian damage would ensue, but if the military importance of destroying the installation were sufficient, there might well be a plausible argument for attacking this military target even though the collateral damage was contemplated.

The practical issue is whether there are enough targets in the Soviet Union and allied countries that could be attacked in a counterforce manner with proportionate collateral damage so that the threat to do so would deter the Soviet Union from attacking the United States and its allies with nuclear weapons in either countervalue or counterforce strikes. Are there sufficient targets in the Soviet Union and its allies, the destruction of which would constitute unacceptable damage to the Soviets, to serve as the *only* targets threatened in a U.S. nuclear deterrence/defense posture? At present there does not appear to be an authoritative answer to that question, possibly because it may not have been posed in a sufficiently imperative manner. The United States seems to have settled into a no-cities-as-such strategy of threatening unacceptable damage to those targets most cherished by the Soviet leadership and to have accepted the manifest prospects for high collateral damage should nuclear retaliation ever occur.

The current U.S. strategic nuclear deterrent, then, is an improvement over that of the MAD era but does not meet the requirements of just war doctrine. It threatens measures that, if taken, would still be too indiscriminate and probably disproportionate as well. A limited nuclear deterrent/defense posture would strive to limit threatened retaliation to patently military targets that could be destroyed without disproportionate collateral damage. The United States could then threaten to destroy targets whose loss would constitute unacceptable damage to the Soviet leadership with means consonant with just war requirements. Such a deterrent might be effective because of its high credibility compared to the increasingly dubious threat of more radical nuclear retaliation. Moreover, in the event of failure of the deterrent, the measures threatened would make eminently more military sense than the destruction of population centers.

The capability to engage in such counterforce strikes and to threaten them as the basis for a deterrent posture must obviously be based on control—hence on solution of C^3I problems,[51] as well as accurate and strongly penetrating weapons capable of hitting and destroying well-protected military targets.[52] Having acknowledged all these difficult requirements for a strategic counterforce deterrence/defense posture, it should be observed that readiness to engage in extremely limited nuclear exchanges, involving only a few military targets, may well be sufficient to deter some forms of nuclear aggression and intimidation that may be more likely than the threat of a large strategic exchange. Granting that a nuclear deterrence posture must be sufficient to meet the worst-case threat, demonstration of the difficulty of attaining such a posture does not rule out the feasibility of a more limited posture sufficient to lower-level nuclear challenges.

Just war recognizes, in addition to the principles of proportion and discrimination, many of the detailed provisions of the international law of war, including those protecting prisoners of war and civilian populations. It should be noted that the international law of war is singularly lacking in effective limitations on means and methods of warfare. The greatest success of the law of war has been in the limitation of chemical warfare (CW), but even that success remains precarious.[53] Efforts to "solve" the nuclear problem by deriving bans on nuclear weapons by analogy or extrapolation from limitations on chemical or biological weapons, poison, and weapons or means that cause "unnecessary suffering" remain sterile. International law is the product of the practice of states. The practice of the states possessing nuclear weapons is to deploy them in a deterrent mode and to threaten their use. No accumulation of scholarly texts and paper resolutions can change that practice. There is no significant source of limitation on nuclear weapons beyond the principles of proportion and discrimination, shared with just war doctrine, to be found in the international law of war.[54]

Genocide—the systematic denigration and extinction of a class of people as such—is a crime against morality and international law.[55] Allusions to genocide sometimes find their way into discussions of nuclear war because of the horrendous power of nuclear weapons that might be used to destroy a whole people or class of people. The concept of genocide, however, adds nothing to the analysis of nuclear war. The concept was developed to deal with crimes against humanity such as the Holocaust. One of the most repugnant features of genocide is precisely that it is not seriously alleged to be based on any military necessity but is, rather, a completely gratuitous atrocity based on perverted ideology and inhuman hatred. It is not helpful to the moral analysis of nuclear war issues to introduce the concept of genocide, the more so since the concept has been badly misused and diluted in the years since the Nuremberg Trial.[56]

The just war *jus in bello*, then, requires that nuclear weapons conform to the limits of proportion and discrimination. Manifestly this is not easily done, but it is not impossible to conceive of proportionate and discriminate use of nuclear weapons. What is more difficult is to imagine a comprehensive nuclear deterrence/defense posture that will be effective while still conforming to the limits of proportionality and discrimination. It is appropriate at this point to discuss some of the recurring objections to the concept of just and limited nuclear war as a basis for a nuclear deterrence/defense posture.

Some Objections to Limited Nuclear Deterrence and Defense

The *first*, most critical objection to the concept of limited nuclear deterrence and defense is that it is technically and humanly impossible to control nuclear war. This contention has been made by a number of former defense officials—for example, Robert McNamara and Harold Brown—and former high military officers, in the form of the proposition that they have no confidence that nuclear war may be controlled.[57] They cite both technical properties of nuclear war and the C³I difficulties, as well as the likely inability of human beings to operate effectively in the environment of a nuclear war.[58]

If there were not a manifest and compelling need for a limited nuclear war capability to give credibility and sanctioning substance to a deterrent posture, it would be prudent to accept this opinion and abandon efforts to make limited nuclear war possible. That need, however, has remained manifest and compelling. It is significant that the officials quoted never stopped trying to control nuclear weapons as an instrument both of deterrence and of defense when they were in office. Secretary Brown, in particular, is noteworthy for his contributions to the development of strategies emphasizing counterforce, flexible response strategies.[59]

Moreover, statements by former and incumbent high defense officials should be read with an awareness of their natural propensity to support the credibility of the existing nuclear deterrence posture by discounting the possibility that it will ever fail to deter. As remarked earlier, this propensity has led to the deterrence-only mind set that resists any suggestion that the deterrent might fail as subversive to the credibility of the deterrent. However, unless by an act of faith it is assumed that deterrence could never fail, there is no alternative to preparing for that contingency and attempting to develop a limited nuclear defense capability. The fact that the effort is one that no one wants to undertake, in which experienced officials and military commanders have little or no confidence, still does not alter the necessity for a war-fighting capability under a deterrence-plus posture.

A *second* recurring objection to the promotion of limited nuclear deterrence/defense strategies is that efforts to make limited nuclear war possible make it more likely. Such efforts, it is held, are provocative, may tempt decision makers to try limited nuclear war options, and are destabilizing to the strategic nuclear balance, thereby increasing the dangers of nuclear war.[60] These predictions and assumptions are, however, speculative. There is little evidence to indicate that the availability of limited nuclear war options would generate a desire to use them in any case except reaction to nuclear aggression. On the contrary, there is reason to believe that the top decision makers and military commanders who are most familiar with nuclear options are among the most conservative in their contemplation of the actual exercise of those options.

It is probably the case that familiarity with nuclear weapons has made top Soviet decison makers and military commanders as cautious about possible use of nuclear weapons as has been the case with U.S. and other Western leaders. Although Soviet leaders have in the past demonstrated great callousness regarding human life, including the lives of their own military personnel and civilian population,[61] the tremendous destructive power of nuclear weapons surely is respected by elites who want, above all, to retain their powers and privileges. Nevertheless, a major problem for the stability-above-all school of nuclear thinkers and policymakers has been the consistent refusal of Soviet policymakers and theoreticians to accept Western theories about the primacy of the value of stable deterrence, with its corollary that one side should eschew advantages since such initiatives would be "destabilizing."[62] Soviet behavior in the years following conclusion of the SALT I agreements gives ample evidence that the Soviets are not content to rest in equilibrium in a putative nuclear balance but are determined to achieve any superiority that appears to be possible.[63]

It is true that evidence of an improved Western capability to wage limited nuclear war, if necessary, would certainly motivate the Soviet leadership to match and, if possible, excel this capability. This could be attempted notwithstanding disclaimers that the concept of limited nuclear war is acceptable to them—their standard position so far.[64] But it is certainly the case that the Soviet

Union will, in any event, whether the West takes initiatives to improve its nuclear options or not, move on all fronts to obtain military superiority wherever it appears to be possible. In these circumstances, the argument that Western efforts to develop a limited nuclear war deterrent/defense posture would be destabilizing loses force. Nothing will be destabilizing to the Soviets unless they consider it to be a concrete, specific threat resulting from an aggressive Western initiative. Yet, granting all reasonable possibilities for misperceptions and mis-understandings, it is very difficult to imagine the Soviet Union's leadership really concluding that the United States or any of its principal allies intends to attack the Soviet Union. On the contrary, the Soviets have ample reason to doubt the ability of a U.S. administration to consider seriously any kind of nuclear confrontation, given the constant and powerful elements in the U.S. political system that resist any suggestion of preparation for, much less engagement in, nuclear war. The doctrinaire concept of nuclear stability that has become a virtually unchallenged value in the West, the violation of which is seen as self-evident grounds for extreme counterreaction, is not shared in the Soviet Union. Soviet behavior has already demonstrated that the Soviet leadership is willing to risk violation of this Western norm of superpower behavior by provoc-ative arms programs. If the West undertakes remedial programs—not in the form of competing with Soviet strategic countervalue systems, but in the form of developing flexible response counterforce systems that could conceivably be used in a just and limited defense of the West—it is hard to see in such initiatives a dangerous act of destabilization. To be sure, the Soviets might doubt the long-term continuity and consistency of U.S. security policy. It should be a primary goal of U.S. and allied governments to convey a sense of continuity and consistency based on a lasting consensus about the Soviet threat and the policies necessary to meet it.

Likewise, with respect to arms control, there is little evidence to indicate that the Soviet leadership share the Western assumption that the basis for all arms control must be stable deterrence that is more or less frozen to prevent either side gaining some new advantage. That assumption, which has guided Western arms control thinking since the late 1950s, must be replaced by a different kind of assumption about stable deterrence. A Western deterrent that is practically and morally unusable as a war-fighting instrument if deterrence fails is not stable. A deterrent posture based on the credible willingness and capability to fight a limited nuclear war against a nuclear aggressor would presumably provide better deterrence and a firmer foundation for arms control negotiations.

A *third* recurring objection to limited nuclear deterrence/defense concepts is that they are rejected by the Soviet Union and, accordingly, are impractical. It is certainly the case that the Soviet leadership has a long and consistent record of rejecting and, indeed, condemning any suggestion of "rules of conflict" for nuclear war.[65] Although occasional indications may be found of recognition within Soviet military doctrine of the need for what might be called a flexible response spectrum of nuclear options,[66] the overwhelming trend of official Soviet doctrine and reactions to Western limited nuclear war concepts has been to hold out the threat of total war with all means, nuclear included, leading to a communist victory.[67]

Two basic responses are in order. First, no matter what the Soviet Union threatens by way of total war, the United States and its allies are morally constrained to prepare to respond to aggression with just war and limited-war means. If this means defeat and/or annihilation, that is the price for a principled adherence to the conditions of just war. Speculation that the Soviets might not conform to our just war and limited-war standards is no basis for abandoning our commitment to those standards.

Second, no amount of bellicose Soviet rhetoric and posturing can obscure the manifest risks of unlimited nuclear war, even to a side that prides itself on having acquired superiority and is willing to launch the first attack. Implementation of Soviet total war doctrine would require a degree of assured superiority that neither great nuclear power has achieved in the missile age and a measure of Western unilateral disarmament that is difficult to imagine. If nuclear weapons are ever used, it is as much in the Soviets' interest to develop rules of conflict to limit the damage as it is in the West's. Beneath the harsh rhetoric of Soviet doctrine, there is a hard core of cold-blooded, Clausewitzan military common sense that views the military instrument as a servant of political policy.[68] In the unfortunate event of nuclear confrontation or war, it could be expected that this core of political-military realism would prevail over the blustering threats of nuclear total war.

A *fourth* recurring objection to limited nuclear deterrence/defense approaches is that they threaten to contribute to perpetuation and worsening of the arms race. This is not the place to question at length the uncritical usage "arms race." Church pronouncements, in particular, are replete with condemnations of "the arms race," with few efforts to define the phrase. The term carries the connotation of a mindless spiral of competing developments of weapons systems that takes on its own logic and momentum and eventually leads to catastrophic war. Such a loss of control over means of deterrence and defense is certainly to be prevented. But little is said to permit us to distinguish mindless and self-perpetuating arms races from the normal upgrading of security systems that each nation is obliged to engage in as a prudent, necessary act of self-defense.[69]

In any event, efforts to achieve C^3I capabilities that could operate in a nuclear war environment; to develop accurate, hard-hitting weapons systems capable of carrying out discriminate counterforce attacks on military targets with minimal collateral damage; and to find defensive systems that could, in the future, reduce the vulnerability of civilian populations to nuclear blackmail and the threat of indiscriminate attack would not be mindless. Rather, they would be intelligent, principled efforts to escape the dilemma of relying on suicidal and immoral MAD and neo-MAD retaliatory systems as the sole basis for reaction to intimidation and aggression by a nuclear power.

It is not my intention to discuss at length the last category of just and limited war initiatives just mentioned, the so-called Star Wars approach of defense against nuclear attack. At best, the approach is something to pursue seriously for the future; it does not, in my judgment, alter the arguments justifying the need for a limited nuclear deterrence/defense posture. Certainly in the long run, however, efforts to escape reliance on the mutual hostage approach to super-power civilian populations must be considered enlightened. To argue against it on the grounds that such initiatives fuel the arms race is to accept in perpetuity some kind of mutual assured destruction balance of terror as the foundation of arms control and world peace.[70]

To be sure, advocates of halting the arms race and putting all hopes on arms control progress presumably expect to escape from the nuclear balance of terror by eliminating nuclear weapons. It remains a crucial and awesome question which is the more realistic hope—the elimination of nuclear weapons in a world in which they cannot be uninvented, or the achievement of a significant measure of defense against them.

A *fifth* objection to efforts to develop just and limited nuclear means—the last to be considered here—is that they would add to the already excessive costs of the defense budget at the cost of lessened resources for economic and social justice programs. This objection appears to rely on two assumptions that are questionable. First, it assumes, in effect, that no operational nuclear capability of any sort should be sought (for reasons mentioned in the previous four objections here discussed) and that, therefore, efforts to develop a limited nuclear war capability are not only dangerously wrongheaded but also a waste of money. However, if it is recognized that effective nuclear deterrence requires some kind of war-fighting nuclear capability, then the resources spent in developing one may be devoted to a risky venture, but they are a necessary and not an unjustified expenditure.

Second, this objection is part of a broader proposition that defense expenditures are doubly evil because, in addition to producing the means for immoral and catastrophic wars, they "rob the poor—shorthand for depriving the domestic budget of resources necessary to improve welfare and economic and social justice. This broader proposition also stresses the negative effect of arms expenditures by advanced powers on their policies with respect to the poor nations of the Third World.[71]

The superficial form of this argument would seem to be that, given finite resources, every dollar that is given to defense is denied domestic and international programs designed to promote social and economic justice. But, as both the pro-defense and pro-economic and social justice protagonists in this debate point out about the other side, resources allocated to a purpose are not automatically translated into practical results. The point is not so much how much is spent on these two great areas of public policy, but what is necessary to achieve agreed-on goals and whether the resources allocated are effectively employed. Each side in the debate can prove waste and corruption in the other side's programs. Each side can point to policy failures wherein well-intentioned programs simply did not work—weapons systems that repeatedly failed to function, social programs that did not achieve what they were designed to achieve.

Thus the superficial argument that rests on the gross allocation of resources to defense or to economic and social programs is inadequate. What is needed is a functional division of resources according to the legitimate needs of each function—namely, securing deterrence and defense and maximizing efforts to promote economic and social justice effectively. It is probably the case that many on both sides of the debate simply underestimate or even dismiss the legitimate demands of the other side. If, however, one approaches the problem from the perspectives of a balanced recognition of the requirements of both defense and economic and social justice, a quite different cast is placed on the subject.

A proper analysis will attempt to determine the reasonable requirements of defense first. Defense must come first because, without defense of the polity in a world marked by aggressive threats, no enlightened economic and social justice programs will long survive. Defense, however, should not be maximized without regard to the consequences for economic and social justice programs that relate to the very values that are being defended.

The problem is rendered particularly complex by the evidence that the more one attempts to conform defense policies to the requirements of just and limited war, the more costly they become. We began to learn this over thirty years ago in the era of the Eisenhower-Dulles-Wilson "more bang for the buck" policies based on countervalue massive retaliation.[72] Two broad trends are necessary to bring U.S. and Western deterrence/defense policies closer to the standards of just war doctrine. One is to develop credible counterforce nuclear strategies and capabilities founded on effective and survivable C^3I. The other is to reduce markedly reliance on nuclear weapons and to develop conventional strategies and capabilities sufficient to warrant diminution of the role of nuclear weapons as a kind of great equalizer covering up all conventional deficiencies. The first, conversion to a counterforce nuclear posture, may well cost more than continuation of strategies and systems still somewhat reflective of the mutual assured destruction concept. It is very likely, however, that the second desired trend, toward greater reliance on conventional defense, will involve substantial new costs to the point that overall defense expenditures will increase in proportion to the declining reliance on nuclear weapons, particularly strategic countervalue nuclear weapons. The U.S. Catholic bishops recognize this in their 1983 Pastoral Letter even as they continue to inveigh against the effect of defense expenditures on resources for economic and social justice.[73]

Defense expenditures are not inherently suspect and expenditures on programs designed to promote economic and social justice are not above reproach. Defense costs what it costs and must be provided for, or there will be no polities in which economic and social justice programs can flourish. Defense expenditures should be justified by policy decisions as to what is warranted, given threat assessments and the choice of deterrence/defense options. Just and limited defense programs, it may be presumed, cost more than defense programs that ignore moral restraints. If ever Star Wars defense programs appear to be feasible, the cost of defense may increase even more.[74] The prospects of high expenditures for just and limited deterrence and defense can be mitigated only by convincing demonstrations of a decline of those threats that warrant deterrence and defense. The position of this chapter has been that evidence of such a decline does not now exist.

The foregoing discussions are not intended to imply that the several objections to the concept of limited nuclear deterrence/defense are not serious and do not warrant continued consideration. The point is that, in my view, none of these objections is sufficient to induce abandonment of efforts to move from a deterrence/defense posture that is still unsatisfactory in both practical or moral terms to one that might meet the standards of just and limited deterrence and defense. It remains the case that the presumptions in the policy and moral debate have tended to be reversed from their proper formulation. It is not admissible to take the position that all presumptions are against limited nuclear deterrence and defense until it can be overwhelmingly demonstrated that such a posture is feasible. On the contrary, the presumption is against abandoning all hopes of developing an effective and morally permissible nuclear deterrence/defense posture, given the difficulties of the enterprise, and relying entirely on hopes that arms control progress will have solved all problems before the present nuclear deterrence system, based on immoral and potentially suicidal means, faces one challenge too many and collapses in catastrophe.

Conclusions

A useful guide in drawing conclusions for this effort to argue the case for a just and limited nuclear war fighting strategy and capability is provided by Father David Hollenbach's dual prescriptions that no nuclear strategies and weapons systems should be developed that increase the likelihood of the use of nuclear weapons and/or frustrate arms control efforts.[75] Superficially, efforts to develop just and limited nuclear deterrence/defense strategies and capabilities might seem to violate both criteria. As observed, it is widely assumed that such strategies increase the possibility of the use of nuclear weapons and undermine arms control efforts.

I have argued that these assumptions are not unchallengeable. A morally usable deterrence/defense strategy may be more effective than one based on threats to carry out attacks that are patently immoral, if an aggressor places some credence in the defender's adhesion to his own moral standards. To be sure, there is great *deterrent* force in the threat to retaliate against aggression with means so outrageously disproportionate to any reasonable military and political wartime end and so horrendously indiscriminate that the aggressor does not dare chance the possibility of the threat's being carried out. If, however, for whatever reasons, the aggressor does attack, the defender who has relied on the threat of "unthinkable" retaliation is confronted with the choices of: (1) carrying it out in a monstrous, immoral, countervalue attack with little expectation that more than vengeance will be served thereby; (2) carrying out a lesser retaliatory strategy that has, however, not been prepared with the necessary doctrine and capabilities; and (3) surrendering.[76]

It is possible that reliance on a deliberately outrageous and immoral deterrent posture will for some time deter the use of nuclear weapons better than reliance on a deliberately limited and morally permissible nuclear deterrence/defense posture. But this is an all-or-nothing proposition. If the immoral threat that deters so well ever fails, the reckoning will be horrendous. The argument in this chapter is that reliance on such a deterrent should not be perpetuated and that, since there must be some kind of deterrent, limited nuclear deterrence is enjoined by exclusion as well as by the moral imperatives of the just war doctrine. In my view, a just and limited nuclear deterrence/defense policy is required irrespective of its putative effectiveness, because that is the only policy that is permitted to those who would conform to just war doctrine. Additionally, it is my position that, if we assume that we are morally committed to the standards of just war, then we must build our nuclear deterrence/defense posture on the basis of means that are morally permissible.

For decades the United States and its allies profited from the so-called strategic nuclear deterrent umbrella without questioning the morality of the war-fighting strategies implicit in the deterrent posture. In recent years the moral as well as the strategic debate over the future of nuclear weapons has rendered impossible a continued reliance on policies that have been repeatedly condemned as immoral and criticized as being strategically inadequate. Something must replace the various versions of massive retaliation on which the West has relied for so long. To assert that arms control will remove the problem is to beg the question. Even given the most optimistic expectations for arms control, there is a substantial period ahead in which nuclear deterrence will be necessary. The contention of this chapter is that a just and limited nuclear deterrent posture is a moral and practical necessity for the indefinite future.

With respect to Father Hollenbach's second point, will the development of limited nuclear capabilities, C³I, and perhaps antimissile defense systems frustrate arms control efforts? To answer in the affirmative is to assume that the arms control approaches that have dominated the last twenty-five years are self-evidently valid and unchallengeable. This is hardly the case. Surely the foundation of contemporary arms control has been the concept of stable deterrence based on strategies of mutual assured destruction. Newhouse has rightly referred to the "theology" of stable deterrence in his analysis of SALT I.[77] Where do we stand on stable deterrence today?

In the first place, the "theology" (that is, doctrines held to be immutable and determinative of all issues of nuclear deterrence, defense, and arms control) of stable deterrence has been based on variations of mutual assured destruction. Whatever perpetuates the mutual population-as-hostage situation is stabilizing; whatever puts this relationship in question is destabilizing. This is the logic of the ABM Treaty of SALT I.[78] To be sure, the United States has attempted to mitigate the starkness of deterrence by shifting the definition of *unacceptable damage* to the Soviets away from destruction of cities *as such*, as discussed earlier, but the basic logic of the nuclear balance still reflects the long-established MAD concept.

As the moral and strategic debates continue in the West, it will simply be impossible to perpetuate this MAD concept or any close variations thereof as the very basis not only for avoidance of nuclear war but for arms control as well. Some new basis for nuclear equilibrium must be found. To profess support of nuclear disarmament, as the U.S. Catholic bishops and others do,[79] does not suffice. Any kind of arms control or disarmament will have to rest on the assurance that all parties are and will remain secure, and that will require some kind of mutual deterrence system. It has been argued in this chapter that such a system must provide both for the deterrence and the defense functions if it is to be credible. This, then, brings us back to the ultimate question: "What kind of nuclear defense would be possible and morally permissible if deterrence failed?"

Second, not everyone who cries "arms control, arms control," will enter into the desired better world to which arms control aspires. Arms control is not negotiation or conclusion of treaties for their own sakes. Arms control is simply an instrument of policy that may permit mitigation and ultimate improvement of the current state of affairs with respect to armaments. It is, indeed, quite likely that some of the just and limited nuclear war initiatives supported here would, in the short run, render more difficult the conclusion of arms control agreements. The objective, however, is not simply to negotiate more and to produce more arms control agreements. The objective is to provide the foundation for an effective and morally acceptable deterrence/defense posture from which it may be possible to negotiate limitations on modern weapons systems beneficial to all parties and to humankind. Further negotiations based on the assumptions of the MAD period will be either futile or dangerous. Arms control needs a new beginning, and that beginning is the establishment of a deterrence/defense posture capable of keeping the peace and worthy of the just war tradition.

This just and limited nuclear deterrence/defense policy must be based on nuclear war fighting strategies and capabilities that could carry out morally permissible counterforce nuclear operations without escalating to levels that would be both immoral and self-defeating. Such strategies and capabilities will be difficult to develop, but they are by no means impossible of achievement, and the effort must be made to make them available to those entrusted with defending freedom and fundamental values against the threats of totalitarian aggressors.

The quest for just and limited nuclear deterrence and defense, however, is such a difficult one that nuclear weapons must be reserved exclusively for countering threats and attacks with nuclear weapons. No first use of nuclear weapons should be both the prehostilities declaratory policy and the operational wartime policy of the United States and its allies. Given the risks of nuclear war, it is long overdue to sacrifice the "creative ambiguity" of a mixed nuclear/conventional deterrence posture in NATO and elsewhere.[80] In the first place, given the greater public consciousness of the practical and moral issues of nuclear war, we can no longer afford ambiguity on this subject for our political leaders, our military commanders and troops, and the public at large in the West. Second, we must force ourselves to develop adequate conventional deterrence and defense strategies and capabilities. It appears that this will not occur while the West continues to hide behind the possibility of nuclear response to conventional aggression. To be sure, a no-first-use policy may simplify both the strategic and the tactical calculations of aggressors, but that is the price that must be paid for responsible development of limited nuclear capabilities for the purpose of deterring and defending against nuclear attacks.

There is a distinct cost involved in increased defense expenditures and in wider and longer military service involved in relinquishing nuclear weapons as a means of deterring conventional aggression. This price must be paid and, if it avoids nuclear war, can hardly be considered excessive.

There is no certainty that just and limited nuclear war can be made possible, that a deterrence posture based on it will be effective, or that it will ultimately serve as a firm foundation for arms control progress. Feasibility remains the core issue of just and limited nuclear war, and it is incumbent on those of us who propose it as an objective to record honestly the prospects as strategic doctrine, military technology, and international and domestic politics combine to make it seem more or less realistic.

The most critical issue in question appears to be that of survivable C^3I. Strategically, the issue is whether U.S. targeting can be limited to military targets whose destruction would not cause disproportionate collateral damage. Admittedly this is a judgment call, but there is some reason to believe that current targeting of admitted military targets still assures excessive collateral damage. Development of ever-more-accurate weapons systems that can survive an aggressor's first strike is essential. Belated acceptance of the need for a greatly strengthened conventional deterrence/defense posture by the United States and its allies, involving in all likelihood revival of the draft in the United States, is another necessity. But the overrriding issue of just and limited nuclear deterrence and defense is whether or not such a posture should be made a national objective. Unless the kind of objections discussed briefly in this chapter can be overcome sufficiently to permit a national consensus in favor of developing and relying on a just and limited nuclear posture, the necessary components of such a posture will certainly not become a reality.

Notes

1. On the evolution of U.S. strategic nuclear doctrine, see, for example, Donald M. Snow, *Nuclear Deterrence in a Dynamic World* (University: University of Alabama Press, 1981), pp. 69–85; Aaron L. Friedberg, "A History of the U.S. Strategic 'Doctrine'—1945 to 1980," *Journal of Strategic Studies* 3(December 1980):37–71; Thomas Powers, "Choosing a Strategy for World War III," *Atlantic* 250(1982):82–100; Richard Smoke, *National Security and the Nuclear Dilemma* (Reading, Mass.: Addison-Wesley, 1984), chaps. 10–12, pp. 175–250; Lawrence Freedman, *The Evolution of Nuclear Strategy* (New York: St. Martin's Press, 1981); William H. Baugh, *The Politics of Nuclear Balance* (New York: Longman, 1984); Harold Brown, *Thinking about National Security: Defense and Foreign Policy in a Dangerous World* (Boulder, Colo.: Westview, 1983), chap. 5, pp. 49–85.

2. On the proposition that the declaratory policy of mutual assured destruction (MAD) has long been misleading and that the United States has targeted Soviet military forces and developed a strategy for conducting nuclear war, see Friedberg, "A History of the U.S. Strategic 'Doctrine'."

3. Judge William Clark, then the national security adviser, wrote to the U.S. Catholic bishops' Ad Hoc Committee on War and Peace as it was drafting the Pastoral Letter adopted by the bishops in May 1983: "For moral, political and military reasons, the United States does not target the Soviet civilian population as such. There is no deliberately opaque meaning conveyed in the last two words. We do not threaten the existence of Soviet civilization by threatening Soviet cities. Rather, we hold at risk the war-making capability of the Soviet Union—its armed forces and the industrial capacity to sustain war. . . ." National Conference of Catholic Bishops, *The Challenge of Peace: God's Promise and Our Response, A Pastoral Letter on War and Peace,* May 3, 1983 (Washington, D.C.: United States Catholic Conference, 1983) (hereinafter cited as *Challenge of Peace*).

As noted in the 1983 U.S. bishops' Pastoral Letter, Judge Clark's letter is reaffirmed in Secretary of Defense Weinberger's 1984 *Annual Report,* citing Caspar W. Weinberger, secretary of defense, *Annual Report to the Congress, Fiscal Year 1984* (Washington, D.C.: U.S. Government Printing Office, 1983) p. 55. However, the bishops observe:

> These statements do not address or resolve another very troublesome moral problem, namely, that an attack on military targets or militarily significant industrial targets could involve "indirect" (i.e., unintended) but massive civilian casualties. We are advised, for example, that the United States strategic nuclear targeting plan (SIOP—Single Integrated Operational Plan) has identified 60 "military" targets within the city of Moscow alone, and that 40,000 "military" targets for nuclear weapons have been identified in the whole of the Soviet Union. . . .

Challenge of Peace, par. 180, citing in note 82: S. Zuckerman, *Nuclear Illusion and Reality* (New York: Vintage Books, 1982); Desmond Ball, "Can Nuclear War Be Controlled?" *Adelphi Paper* no. 169 (London: International Institute for Strategic Studies [IISS], 1981); Powers, "Choosing a Strategy," pp. 82–110.

4. The official edition of *The Challenge of Peace* is cited in note 3. Commentaries and critiques of the Pastoral Letter include Judith A. Dwyer, S.S.J., ed., *The Catholic Bishops and Nuclear War* (Washington, D.C.: Georgetown University Press, 1984); James E. Dougherty, *The Bishops and Nuclear Weapons* (Hamden, Conn.: Archon Books, 1984); Michael Novak, *Moral Clarity in the Nuclear Age* (Nashville, Tenn.: Thomas Nelson, 1983); Philip J. Murnion, ed., *Catholics and Nuclear War* (New York: Crossroads, 1983); Philip F. Lawler, ed., for the American Catholic Committee, *Justice and War in the Nuclear*

Age (Lanham, Md.: University Press of America, 1983); Albert Wohlstetter, "Bishops, Statesmen, and Other Strategists on the Bombing of Innocents," *Commentary* 75(June 1983):15–35; Bruce Russett, "Ethical Dilemmas of Nuclear Deterrence," *International Security* 8(Spring 1984):36–54; Russett, "What the Bishops Did and Did Not Say," in "Correspondence," *Orbis*, Summer 1984, pp. 401–403; responding to: Keith Payne, "The Bishops and Nuclear Weapons," *Orbis*, Fall 1983, pp. 535–543; and Manfred Hamm, "The European Church and Arms Control," *Orbis*, Fall 1983, pp. 543–554.

5. See, in particular, *Challenge of Peace*, pars. 188–199.

6. Ibid., pars. 71–110.

7. Ibid., pars. 245–258.

8. Ibid., Introduction, pars. 1–4; part I, pars. 5–6; 13; 55; 101–110; part II, pars. 122–141. All these sections precede part II, section C, "The Use of Nuclear Weapons." By the time one reaches the analysis of morality and nuclear weapons, there is less than no doubt about the direction the analysis will go—namely, the injunction "to say 'no' to nuclear war"—for example in par. 132.

9. *To say "no" to nuclear war is both a necessary and a complex task.* We are moral teachers in a tradition which has always been prepared to relate moral principles to concrete problems. Particularly in this letter we could not be content with simply restating general moral principles or repeating well-known requirements about the ethics of war. We have had to examine, with the assistance of a broad spectrum of advisors of varying persuasions, the nature of existing and proposed weapons systems, the doctrines which govern their use, and the consequences of using them. . . . *In light of the evidence which witnesses presented and in light of our study, reflection, and consultation, we must reject nuclear war.* But we feel obliged to relate our judgment to the specific elements which comprise the nuclear problem.

Ibid., emphasis added.

In the words of our Holy Father, we need a "moral about-face." *The whole world must summon the moral courage and technical means to say "no" to nuclear conflict; "no" to weapons of mass destruction; "no" to an arms race which robs the poor and the vulnerable; and "no" to the moral danger of a nuclear age which places before mankind indefensible choices of constant terror or surrender.* Peacemaking is not an optional commitment. It is a requirement of our faith. We are called to be peacemakers, not by some movement of the moment, but by our Lord Jesus. The content and context of our peacemaking is set not by some political agenda or ideological program, but by the teaching of his Church.

Ibid., par. 333, emphasis added.

10. "Therefore, it must be said again, the arms race is an utterly treacherous trap for humanity, and one which injures the poor to an intolerable degree. . . ." Vatican II, *Pastoral Constitution on the Church in the Modern World (Gaudium et Spes)*, in Walter M. Abbott, S.J., ed., *The Documents of Vatican II* (New York: Guild/America/Association, 1966), no. 81, p. 295.

11. The U.S. Catholic bishops state:

185. While we welcome any effort to protect civilian populations, we do not want to legitimize or encourage moves which extend deterrence beyond the specific objective of preventing the use of nuclear weapons or other actions which could lead directly to a nuclear exchange.

186. These considerations of concrete elements of nuclear deterrence policy, made in the light of John Paul's evaluation, but applying it through our own prudential judgments, lead us to a *strictly conditioned moral acceptance of nuclear deterrence. We cannot consider it adequate as a long-term basis for peace.*

188. *On the basis of these criteria we wish now to make some specific evaluations:*
(1) If nuclear deterrence exists only to prevent the *use* of nuclear weapons by others, then proposals to go beyond this to planning for prolonged periods of repeated

nuclear strikes and counter-strikes or "prevailing" in nuclear war, are not acceptable. They encourage notions that nuclear war can be engaged in with tolerable human and moral consequences. Rather, we must continually say "no" to the idea of a nuclear war [emphasis in original].

(2) If nuclear deterrence is our goal, "sufficiency" to deter is an adequate strategy; the quest for nuclear superiority must be rejected.

(3) Nuclear deterrence should be used as a step on the way toward progressive disarmament. Each proposed addition to our strategic system or change in strategic doctrine must be assessed precisely in light of whether it will render steps toward "progressive disarmament" more or less likely.

Challenge of Peace.

12. David Hollenbach, S.J., "Ethics in Distress: Can There be Just Wars in the Nuclear Age?" chapter 2, this book.

13. The bishops discuss "Limited Nuclear War," pars. 157–161, and conclude that the risks "of crossing the boundary from the conventional to the nuclear arena in any form" are excessive (par. 161). They conclude: "We therefore express our view that the first imperative is to prevent any use of nuclear weapons and our hope that leaders will resist the notion that nuclear conflict can be limited, contained, or won in any traditional sense." *Challenge of Peace,* par. 161.

In the section preceding the conditioned toleration of deterrence (only) in pars. 185–186, quoted in note 11, the bishops reiterate their "severe doubts" about the concept of counterforce war-fighting strategies. Ibid., par. 184.

The bishops provide a clear example of their deterrence-only position when they specifically oppose, among other things: "The willingness to foster strategic planning which seeks a nuclear war-fighting capability that goes beyond the limited function of deterrence outlined in this letter." Ibid., par. 190. In other words, the bishops do not want the United States to plan for the contingency of the deterrent failing. They only want planning for an infallible deterrent. Deterrence-only deterrence strategies, are discussed later.

14. Father J. Bryan Hehir, principal staff person for the bishops' ad hoc committee that drafted the 1983 Pastoral Letter, has been quoted as follows: "If you ask me does it rule out any use of nuclear weaponry under any circumstances, the Letter never says that. There is a centimeter of ambiguity. And on that centimeter of ambiguity . . . [the deterrent rests]." Tom Bethell, "The Bishops' Brain," *American Spectator,* July 1983, p. 3. See Judy Foreman, "'Centimeter of Doubt' on N-Ban," *Boston Globe,* March 1, 1983.

Bishop John J. O'Connor of New York, the member of the bishops' ad hoc committee most conversant with national security issues, states:

> In applying Just War teaching rigorously, one finds it extremely difficult—not necessarily impossible—but extremely difficult to justify a nation's going to war today. Indeed, it is precisely in accordance with Just War teaching that the bishops take such a dim view of even the defensive use of nuclear weapons under *any* circumstances, although there is no outright condemnation of such use in the Pastoral Letter. Without prejudging every conceivable set of circumstances, or determining in advance whether it might or might not be morally lawful to use nuclear weapons defensively in a given situation, the bishops want to voice their very strongest opposition to the notion of nuclear war, and particularly, again, to the notion that nuclear war is winnable, in any traditional sense of the term.

Bishop John J. O'Connor, *The Challenge of Peace: An Introduction to the Bishops' Pastoral Letter* (Scranton, Pa.: The Guild, 1984), p. 19, emphasis in original.

15. Snow explains:

> The deterrence-only position emphasizes the enormous qualitative change that nuclear weapons have introduced and implies that any nuclear usage would be extremely difficult

to control short of a cataclysmic exchange in which the Soviet and American homelands would be largely decimated. Given that possibility, the purpose of deterrence (and thus nuclear weapons) is strictly deterrent—to keep the potential cost of initial weapons usage as high as possible. The method for doing this is mutual assured destruction: the threat that a nuclear attack will be met by a massive counterattack guaranteeing the effective destruction of the attacking state. Implicit in this analysis, according to Klaus Knorr, is the assumption that the usefulness of nuclear weapons "is narrow and specific, for it rests primarily on the ability to deter nuclear attack." (Citing Klaus Knorr, *On The Uses of Military Power in The Nuclear Age* (Princeton, N.J.: Princeton University Press, 1966), p. 89).

Snow, *Nuclear Strategy*, p. 5. See Snow's further discussion of deterrence-only approaches and authorities therein cited in ibid., pp. 44, 69–73. In his glossary Snow defines *deterrence-only* as "the strategic school of thought that believes that the only utility of nuclear weapons is their deterrent effect." Ibid., p. 244. See the discussion of the deterrence-only approach and its opposition to contemporary "limited nuclear options" strategies in Smoke, *National Security*. Albert Wohlstetter provides an authoritative and insightful critique of deterrence-only strategies in "Bishops, Statesmen, and Other Strategists," pp. 30–33.

16. On the countervalue emphasis in deterrence-only see Snow, *Nuclear Strategy*, pp. 5–6, 44, 72; Smoke, *National Security*, p. 222.

17. Snow describes the deterrence-plus school's disagreement with deterrence-only approaches as follows:

Deterrence-plus theorists disagree. They feel that, in a world of massive nuclear arsenals, the threat to destroy another society is an inadequate definition of nuclear purpose. Their critique rests on two basic points. First, the MAD threat is too inflexible. As Richard Rosencrance says, "If the choice was solely between inaction and Armageddon, there had to be another alternative.

Introduction to Richard Rosencrance, ed., *The Future of the International Strategic System* (San Francisco: Chandler, 1972), p. 6.

Since a nuclear attack could come in a wide variety of ways, carefully planned and proportionate means are needed to meet that attack (the "plus" in deterrence-plus). This logic leads to a second criticism of MAD: that it is not believable. Deterrence-plus theorists argue that nuclear war is not necessarily a general exchange between homelands destroying both, because both sides know the awful consequences of such attacks. As a result, general nuclear attack is the least likely form of nuclear aggression (because it is obviously suicidal), and thus the assured destruction threat is primarily a deterrent against the least likely form of nuclear war.

Snow, *Nuclear Strategy*, pp. 5–6. Snow analyzes the deterrence-plus initiatives of Robert McNamara in his 1962 Ann Arbor speech and of James Schlesinger in his 1974 strategic initiatives that have led to the present trend toward counterforce deterrence-plus policies and away from countervalue (in the sense of targeting cities as such) deterrence-only policies. Ibid., pp. 44–45, 69–73, 78–85. On this subject, see Smoke, *National Security*, pp. 220–223.

Jordan and Taylor use the terms "prewar deterrence" (deterrence-only) and "war-fighting deterrence" (deterrence plus). Amos A. Jordan and William J. Taylor, Jr., and associates, *American National Security: Policy and Process* (Baltimore, Md.: The Johns Hopkins University Press, 1981), pp. 224–225. They emphasize that whereas prewar deterrence requires survivability of a second-strike retaliatory capability, war-fighting deterrence requires "the *endurance* necessary to fight a war that could extend over a period of time and include a series of nuclear exchanges." Ibid., p. 245. They observe: "Of the two schools of thought . . . the second school [war-fighting deterrence] appeared to be gaining ascendance at the turn of the decade. The countervailing strategy, although evolutionary, appeared to be another step toward the position of the second school which advocates adoption of a U.S. nuclear war-fighting strategy." Ibid. [emphasis in original].

18. My estimate of the aggressive intentions of the Soviet Union is based on its historic record, particularly since World War II. It is clear to me that Soviet aggression and intimidation have been checked almost wholly by evidence of resistance by the United States and its allies. I consider the term *gulag* society to be fairly applied to the Soviet Union and other similar communist states. I take my inspiration from Aleksandr I. Solzhenitsyn, *The Gulag Archipelago, 1918–1956*, Thomas P. Whitney, trans. (New York: Harper and Row, 1973).

19. The perseverance of the NATO members in proceeding with the deployment of Pershing II and cruise missiles despite the massive propaganda efforts of the Soviet Union, coordinated with the European peace movement, and the Soviet walkout from the arms control talks, demonstrated a fundamental belief in Europe that Soviet aggression was a real possibility and that Soviet arms policies both with respect to strategic and theater nuclear weapons were destabilizing and dangerous.

20. In *The Conduct of Just and Limited War* (New York: Praeger, 1981), p. 135, I grappled with the question of deterring attacks on U.S. and allied population centers while conforming to just war standards. I concluded that the victim of a general counter-value attack on its population centers would not be justified in retaliating in kind against the aggressor's population centers, since the war would already be lost and the only purpose of the retaliation would be vengeance. I argued, however, that the victim of selective countervalue attacks on its population centers would be justified in retaliating with selective attacks on the aggressor's population centers as an intrawar deterrent against further countervalue attacks. I then viewed such retaliation as proportionate, although it would obviously be indiscriminate.

I no longer justify countervalue attacks on population centers, even to deter attacks on our own population centers. I would depend on counterforce retaliation to inflict such unacceptable damage as to deter the aggressor from continuation of his countervalue attacks. This position, however, is not easily reconciled with the natural instinct to protect population centers from attack or blackmail. If counterforce deterrence and, if necessary, retaliation would suffice to protect our population centers, military necessity and morality might be reconciled. If not, military necessity would have to bow to morality, and defeat would follow. Clearly this position depends on the realization of deterrence/defense strategies and capabilities that make possible effective counterforce action within the limits of just war.

21. Michael Walzer explains the concept of "supreme emergency" as consisting of two elements: (1) a threat of "danger" of "an unusual and horrifying kind," such as that posed by Nazi aggression and domination—"an ultimate threat to everything decent in our lives, an ideology and a practice of domination so murderous, so degrading even to those who might survive, that the consequences of its final victory were literally beyond calculation, immeasurably awful"; (2) the imminence of that danger warranting exceptional measures under plea of necessity in violation of the usual moral and legal norms for war—in Walzer's term, "the war convention." *Just and Unjust Wars* (New York: Basic Books, 1977), pp. 252–253. See, generally, ibid., chap. 16, pp. 251–268.

Walzer contends:

Nuclear weapons explode the theory of just war. They are the first of mankind's technological innovations that are simply not encompassable within the familiar moral world. Or rather, our familiar notions about *jus in bello* require us to condemn even the threat to use them. And yet there are other notions, also familiar, having to do with aggression and the right of self-defense, that seem to require exactly that threat. So, we move uneasily beyond the limits of justice for the sake of justice (and of peace)."

Ibid., p. 282.

Walzer concludes:

Nuclear war is and will remain morally unacceptable, and there is no case for its rehabilitation. Because it is unacceptable, we must seek out ways to prevent it, and because deterrence is a bad way, we must seek out others. It is not my purpose here to suggest what the alternatives might look like. I have been more concerned to acknowledge that deterrence itself, for all its criminality, falls or may fall for the moment under *the standard of necessity*. But as with terror bombing, so here with the threat of terrorism: *supreme emergency is never a stable position*. The realm of necessity is subject to historical change. And, what is more important, we are under an obligation to seize upon opportunities to escape, even to take risks for the sake of such opportunities. So, the readiness to murder is balanced, or should be, by the readiness not to murder, not to threaten murder, as soon as alternative ways to peace can be found.

Ibid., p. 283 [emphasis added].

The practical extent of this categorization of nuclear deterrence as a form of supreme emergency action is unclear in Walzer's discussion. He seems to be saying that the actual execution of the nuclear deterrent threat is totally beyond moral justification and that the threat itself, being immoral, is tolerable only under an argument of necessity or supreme emergency. If this is the case, his normative tolerance is limited to a deterrence-only perspective, and he is reduced to trusting that the deterrent will never fail before a better way to deal with the threat encompassed in the supreme emergency justification can be discovered—or the imminent threat recedes.

22. On the *Kriegsraison* doctrine that necessity knows no law, see: E. Ullman, *Voelkerrecht* (Freiburg: Verlag von M.C.B. Mohr, 1898), pp. 316–318; Dr. Franz von Liszt, *Das Voelkerrecht systematisch dargestellt* (Berlin: Verlag von O. Haring, Fuenfte Durchgearbeite Auflag, 1907), p. 320; Josef Kohler, *Not kennt kein Gebot* (Berlin and Leipzig: Verlags Buch Handlug Doctor Walter Rothschild, 1915); Kohler, "Notwehr und Neutralitat," *Zeitschrift fuer Voelkerrecht und Bundesstaatsrecht* 8(1914):576–578.

Among the critiques of the *Kriegsraison* doctrine see: John Westlake, *International Law*, Part II: *War* (Cambridge: The University Press, 1913), vol. 2, pp. 126–128; Charles de Visscher, "Les lois de la guerre et la theorie de necessite," *Revue générale de droit international public* 24(1917):74–108; Paul Weiden, "Necessity in International Law," *Transactions of the Grotius Society* 24(1939):113 ff.; N.C.H. Dunbar, "Military Necessity in War Crimes Trials," *British Yearbook of International Law* 29(1952):442; Dunbar, "The Significance of Military Necessity in the Law of War," *Juridical Review* 67(1955): 201.

A singularly good analysis of concepts of necessity ranging from *raison d'état* to *raison de guerre* (military necessity) to individual necessity is to be found in Max Huber, "Die kriegsrechtlichen Vertrage und die Kriegsraison," *Zeitschrift fuer Voelkerrecht und Bundesstaatsrecht* 7(1913):351–374. I review the literature and issues and relate them to the contemporary problems of the law of war in William V. O'Brien, "The Meaning of 'Military Necessity' in International Law," *World Polity* 1(1957):118–128.

23. I discuss the constitutional issues of competent authority in the United States in *Conduct of Just and Limited War*, pp. 17–18, 91–92.

24. On the propensity, if not the probability, of nuclear weapons to escape control, see, for example, *Challenge of Peace*, particularly pars. 152–156, 160–161. Walzer, *Just and Unjust Wars*, pp. 277–278.

25. C³I issues and current programs are discussed in Paul Bracken, *The Command and Control of Nuclear Forces* (New Haven: Yale University Press, 1983); Jonathan B. Tucker, "Strategic Command-and-Control Vulnerabilities: Dangers and Remedies," *Orbis*, Winter 1983, pp. 941–964; Kenneth L. Moll, *Strategic Command and Control* (Washington, D.C.: Congressional Research Service, 1980); *Strategic Command, Control and Communications: Alternative Approaches for Modernization*, A Congressional Budget Study (Washington, D.C.: U.S. Government Printing Office, 1981); *The World Wide Military Command and Control Information System—Problems in Information Resource Management*, Report by the Comptroller General to the U.S. Congress (Washington, D.C.: General Accounting Office, 1981).

See Organization of the Joint Chiefs of Staff, *United States Military Posture for FY 1983* (Washington, D.C.: U.S. Government Printing Office, 1982), pp. 24, 81–83; Caspar W. Weinberger, Secretary of Defense, *Annual Report to the Congress, Fiscal Year 1984* (Washington, D.C.: U.S. Government Printing Office, 1983), pp. 241–259.

26. On the inadequacies of C³I and the consequent objections to the concept of limited nuclear war, see John D. Steinbruner, "Nuclear Decapitation," *Foreign Policy* 45(Winter 1981–1982):16–28; Ball, "Can Nuclear War Be Controlled?"

27. Soviet strategic doctrine emphasizes early destruction of U.S. C³I. See V.D. Sokolovsky, *Soviet Military Strategy*, 3rd ed., Harriet Fast Scott, trans. (New York: Crane Russak, 1975), p. 78; Joseph Douglass and Amorreta M. Hoeber, *Soviet Strategy for Nuclear War* (Stanford, Calif.: Hoover Institution Press, 1979), p. 78. This doctrine, however, was developed when U.S. C³I was manifestly incapable of surviving beyond a very short nuclear war. U.S. C³I improvements might alter that doctrine.

The U.S. relies on three C³I approaches: fixed communication centers that can be improved by hardening; airborne systems such as the Air Force's Alternative Airborne National Command Post (AABNCP) and Post Attack Command and Control Systems (PACCS) and the Navy's Take Charge and Move Out (TACMO) system; and space-based orbiting communication centers, which are expected to become even more important in the future. The key to C³I survivability is redundancy of systems. That takes commitment, planning, and heavy allocations of budget priority.

28. On the danger of loss of control over elements of the nuclear forces, see Steinbruner, "Nuclear Decapitation" and Ball, "Can Nuclear War be Controlled?"

29. On the misadventures of the abortive U.S. rescue mission in Iran, see Paul B. Ryan, *The Iranian Rescue Mission: Why It Failed* (Annapolis, Md.: Naval Institute Press, 1985).

30. For a concise summary of U.S. involvement in Lebanon, 1982–1984, see Fred J. Khouri, *The Arab-Israeli Dilemma*, 3rd ed. (Syracuse, N.Y.: Syracuse University Press, 1985), pp. 444–445. The October 23, 1983, suicide bombing attack on U.S. Marines in Lebanon led to extended inquiries into the deployment and security of the Marine peace-keeping force. See, for example, Michael Getler, "Marine Commandant Says Beirut Bombing Toll Could Reach 239," *Washington Post*, November 3, 1983, A31, cols. 1–6.

31. The War Powers Resolution of 1973, Pub. 1, no. 93-148, 87 Stat. 555 (1973), is the principal legal constraint on the president's exercise of his powers as commander-in-chief. The resolution appears to have been intended primarily to limit the president's discretion in initiating military interventions in the manner of the Vietnam War, rather than his discretion to make the rapid decisions that could be expected in a nuclear confrontation. See President Nixon's veto message of October 24, 1973, "War Powers Veto Text," *Congressional Quarterly* 31(October 27, 1973):2855–2856; Statutory Comments, "The War Powers Resolution: Statutory Limitation on the Commander-in-Chief," *Harvard Law Journal on Legislation* 11(1974):181–204.

32. For a cross-section of contemporary views of U.S.-Soviet relations and the nature of the Soviet polity, see Adam Ulam, *Expansion and Coexistence: Soviet Foreign Policy, 1917-1973* (New York: Praeger, 1974); Ulam, "U.S.-Soviet Relations: Unhappy Coexistence," *America and the World, 1978, Foreign Affairs* 47(1979):556-571; Seweryn Bialer, *Stalin's Successors* (New York: Cambridge University Press, 1980); Bialer, "The Harsh Decade: Soviet Policies in the 1980s," *Foreign Affairs* 59(1981):999-1020; Thomas Wolfe, *Soviet Power and Europe, 1945-1970* (Baltimore, Md.: The Johns Hopkins University Press, 1970); George F. Kennan, *American Diplomacy* (Chicago, Il.: University of Chicago Press, 1984); Richard Pipes, *Survival Is Not Enough: Soviet Relations and America's Future* (New York: Simon and Schuster, 1984); Pipes, "Why the Soviet Union Thinks It Could Fight and Win a Nuclear War," *Commentary* 64(July 1977):21-34; Charles Tyroler, II, ed., *Altering America: The Papers of the Committee on the Present Danger*, introduction by Max M. Kampelman (New York: Pergamon-Brasseys, 1984); Raymond Garthoff, *Detente and Confrontation: American Soviet Relations from Nixon to Reagan* (Washington, D.C.: Brookings Institution, 1985).

33. Walzer raises the "better dead than red" issue briefly, discounting it largely on the grounds that nuclear deterrence has thought to assure avoidance of both stark alternatives. *Just and Unjust Wars*, pp. 273-274.

34. On the minimal deterrence concept of the French *force de frappe*, see Snow, *Nuclear Deterrence*, p. 37; Alexander Werth, *De Gaulle* (New York: Simon and Schuster, 1965), pp. 343-346.

35. See *Freedom in the World: Political Rights and Civil Liberties*, a series of annual volumes published by Freedom House (Boston and New York: G.K. Hall), published annually; Amnesty International, *Amnesty International Handbook* (London: Amnesty International Publications), published annually.

36. On the effects of nuclear war see Samuel Glasstone and Philip J. Donlan, eds., *The Effects of Nuclear Weapons* (Washington, D.C.: Department of Defense, 1977); *The Effects of Nuclear War* (Washington, D.C.: Office of Technology Assessment, 1979).

37. Harold Brown's explanation of the objectives of less-than-all-out nuclear war is grim and cautious:

> The countervailing strategy is less of a departure from previous doctrine than is often claimed. It keeps deterrence at the core of U.S. policy. And it implies no illusion that nuclear war once begun would be likely to stop short of an all-out exchange. But it does acknowledge that such a limited war *could* happen, and it seeks to convince the Soviets that if a limited attack by them somehow failed to escalate into an all-out nuclear exchange, they would not have gained from aggression. [emphasis in original]

Operationally, the countervailing strategy requires that plans and capabilities be structured to emphasize U.S. ability to employ strategic nuclear forces selectively as well as in all-out retaliation for massive attacks. This means having the necessary forces and evolving the detailed plans to ensure that Soviet leaders know that if they choose some intermediate level of nuclear aggression, the United States will exact an unacceptably high price in things that the Soviet leaders appear to value most, using large and selective but still less than maximal nuclear responses. The targets of such an attack could be military forces, both nuclear and conventional; the industrial capability to sustain a war; political and military leadership and control structures; and industrial capacity. Brown, *Thinking about National Security*, pp. 81-82.

In his last report to Congress, Secretary Brown stated: "Finally, in the event deterrence fails, our forces must be capable . . . of preventing Soviet victory and securing the most favorable possible outcome for U.S. interests." Harold Brown, secretary of defense, *Annual Report to the Congress, Fiscal Year 1981* (Washington, D.C.: U.S. Government Printing Office, 1980), p. 68.

Jordan and Taylor state:

> Precluding any prospect of Soviet "victory" in a nuclear exchange entails our having a war-fighting strategy and forces in order to "prevail" once hostilities break out. Prevailing means that, after waging a strategic nuclear war, the nation with the superior war-fighting capability is significantly better off (i.e., with less destruction of economic and social fiber, fewer casualties) than its opponent. Having a war-fighting capability thus implies having a damage-limiting ability. Ideally, a *true* damage-limiting force would possess a first-strike capability. *War-fighting capability*, however, is not quite that clear cut a concept, since the term contains several additional strategic and psychological elements. . . .

American National Security, p. 223 [emphasis in original].

38. On the presumption against killing in war and war itself, see St. Thomas Aquinas, *Summa Theologica, Secunda Secundae* 40(Art. 1); Francisco de Vitoria, *De Jure Belli,* in Alfred Vanderpol, ed., *La doctrine scolastique du droit de guerre* (Paris: Pedone, 1919), pp. 308–312; 326–329; James F. Childress, "Just-War Criteria," in Thomas A. Shannon, ed., *War or Peace: The Search for New Answers* (Maryknoll, N.Y.: Orbis, 1980).

39. On right intention, see O'Brien, *Conduct of Just and Limited War,* pp. 33–35.

40. I have developed the proportionality element of legitimate military necessity in "Legitimate Military Necessity in Nuclear War," *World Polity* 2(1960):48–57.

41. On the relation of the normative principle of proportion and the political-military principle of economy of force see O'Brien, *Conduct of Just and Limited War,* pp. 225–228, and authorities cited therein. Note in particular the emphasis on the correlation between normative proportionality and economy of force in U.S. Department of the Air Force, *International Law—The Conduct of Armed Conflict and Air Operations, 19 November 1976* AFP 110-31 (Washington, D.C.: Department of the Air Force, 1976), 1–6, 5–8, 5–10, 5–11.

42. I elaborate on the limiting force of international law and natural law on military utility justified as proportionate means in, "Legitimate Military Necessity," pp. 48, 58–63.

43. On the hazards of reliance on the normative restraining force of the principle of proportion, see Tucker's analysis in Robert E. Osgood and Robert W. Tucker, *Force, Order, and Justice* (Baltimore: The Johns Hopkins University Press, 1967), pp. 198, 202–203, 233–234, 237–240, 300–301, 314.

In the thought of Paul Ramsey, the principle of discrimination always takes precedence over the principle of proportion. Unless an act passes the test of discrimination, there is no question of going on to assess its proportionality. See, for example, Paul Ramsey, *The Just War: Force and Political Responsibility* (New York: Charles Scribner's Sons, 1968), pp. 429–431.

44. An authoritative definition of the principle of discrimination is given by Father Richard McCormick:

> It is a fundamental moral principle (unanimously accepted by Catholic moralists) that it is immoral directly to take innocent human life except with divine authorization. "Direct" taking of human life implies that one performs a lethal action with the intention that death should result for himself or another. Death therefore is deliberately willed as the effect of one's action. "Indirect" killing refers to an action or omission that is designed and intended solely to achieve some other purpose(s) even though death is foreseen as a

concomitant effect. Death therefore is not positively willed, but is reluctantly permitted as an unavoidable by-product.

R.A. McCormick, "Morality of War," *New Catholic Encyclopedia*, 14 vols. (New York: McGraw-Hill, 1967), vol. 14, p. 805.

45. Some of the principal contemporary sources on the principle of discrimination in just war doctrine are: John C. Ford, "The Morality of Obliteration Bombing," *Theological Studies* 5(1944):261–309; Ford, "The Hydrogen Bombing of Cities, in William J. Nagle, ed., *Morality and Modern Warfare* (Baltimore, Md.: Helicon Press, 1960), pp. 98–103; Ramsey, *Just War*, passim; James Turner Johnson, *Ideology, Reason, and the Limitation of War* (Princeton, N.J.: Princeton University Press, 1975), pp. 3, 26, 42–46, 69–73, 196–203, 227–239, 244, 246–252, 263; Johnson, *Just War Tradition and the Restraint of War* (Princeton, N.J.: Princeton University Press, 1981), pp. 26, 60, 66–69, 87, 131–150, 166, 170–171, 188–189, 197–198, 299–303, 312–320, 353–357; Tucker, in Osgood and Tucker, *Force, Order and Justice*, pp. 290–322.

My analysis is accompanied by a comparison of interpretations of the principle of discrimination or noncombatant immunity by international law scholars and by moralists. O'Brien, *Conduct of Just and Limited War*, pp. 52–56.

46. The following papal and conciliar pronouncements managed to discuss and broadly condemn nuclear war without explicit reference to the principle of discrimination or noncombatant immunity: Pope Pius XII, "Address to Delegates of the Eighth Congress of the World Medical Association," Rome, September 30, 1954, in Harry W. Flannery, ed., *Pattern for Peace: Catholic Statements on International Order* (Westminster, Md.: Newman, 1962), pp. 236–237; Pope John XXIII, "Peace on Earth (Pacem in Terris)," arts. 111, 126–129, in *Encyclical Letter* (Washington, D.C.: National Catholic Welfare Conference 1963, pp. 26–27, 29–30; Pope Paul VI, "Remarks before Recitation of the Angelus," August 8, 1965, in *The Pope Speaks* 10(1965):358, 406; *Gaudium et Spes*, nos. 80–81, pp. 293–295. These pronouncements are typical and include some of the most widely quoted official church statements on nuclear war.

47. See my discussion of the principle of discrimination in just war doctrine and the international law of war, as well as authorities cited therein, in *Conduct of Just and Limited War*, pp. 52–56.

48. "Any act of war aimed indiscriminately at the destruction of entire cities or of extensive areas along with their population is a crime against God and man himself. It merits unequivocal and unhesitating condemnation." *Gaudium et Spes*, no. 80, p. 294. Note that the Pastoral Constitution uses the adverb "indiscriminately" but that the principle of discrimination as such is never articulated in the document. This condemnation could equally be based on the principle of proportion.

49. On the difference between U.S. declaratory and operational strategies, see Friedberg, "A History of the U.S. Strategic 'Doctrine'—1945 to 1980."

50. See Clark's letter to the bishops, quoted in note 3, and Harold Brown's discussion of "unacceptable damage" to the Soviets in Brown, *Thinking about National Security*, pp. 81–82, quoted in note 37.

51. Jordan and Taylor give a brief, clear explanation of the relation of C³I to targeting, counterforce, and countervalue, in *American National Security*, pp. 231–240. See Harold Brown's discussion of C³I and its importance to the Carter countervailing strategy, in *Thinking about National Security*, pp. 78–83.

52. On the requirements for weapons system accuracy and penetrative capacities, see Brown's comments in ibid., pp. 81–83. On the accuracy of modern and future

weapons, see Wohlstetter, "Bishops, Statesmen, and Other Strategists," pp. 22–23, 31, and Snow, *Nuclear Strategy,* pp. 69, 91–92.

53. The basic international agreement limiting recourse to chemical and biological warfare is the Geneva Protocol for the Prohibition of the Use in War of Asphyxiating, Poisonous, or Other Gases, and of Bacteriological Methods of Warfare, 17 June 1925, 26 UST 571, T.I.A.S. 8061, 94 LNTS 65. See Ann Van Wynnen Thomas and A. J. Thomas, Jr., *Legal Limits on the Use of Chemical and Biological Weapons* (Dallas, Tex.: Southern Methodist University Press, 1970); O'Brien, *Conduct of Just and Limited War,* pp. 59–61; and authorities cited therein.

54. Numerous international agreements and declarations proclaim the elimination of nuclear weapons to be their ultimate goal—for example, the "1973 Agreement Between the United States of America and the Union of Soviet Socialist Republics on the Prevention of Nuclear War," T.I.A.S. 7186; "Non-use of Force in International Relations and Permanent Prohibition of the Use of Nuclear Weapons," Resolution 2936 (XXVIII) of the U.N. General Assembly, November 29, 1972, reproduced in Dietrich Schindler and Jiri Toman, eds., *The Law of Armed Conflict: A Collection of Conventions and Other Documents,* 2nd rev. ed. (Alphen aan den Rijn, Netherlands, and Rockville, Md.: Sijthoff and Noordhoff/Geneva: Henry Durant Institute, 1981), pp. 129–130.

However, the 1963 Test Ban Treaty (21 UST 483; T.I.A.S. 5433); the 1967 Treaty for the Prohibition of Nuclear Weapons in Latin America (22 UST 754; T.I.A.S. 7137); the 1972 ABM Treaty (23 UST 3435; T.I.A.S. 7503); the 1972 Interim Agreement on Certain Measures with Respect to the Limitation of Strategic Offensive Arms (23 UST 3462; T.I.A.S. 7504); and the unratified 1979 Treaty on the Limitation of Strategic Offensive Arms (SALT II) (see text and attached agreements in United States Arms Control and Disarmament Agency, *Arms Control and Disarmament Agreements,* 1982 ed. [Washington, D.C.: ACDA, 1982], pp. 246–277) all assume the existence and legality of nuclear weapons and the continuation of a stable nuclear deterrence balance as the highest norm of superpower relations.

55. See the definition and application of "crimes against humanity," the most heinous of which was genocide, Nuremberg International Military Tribunal, *Trial of Major War Criminals, Judgment,* 42 vols. (Nuremberg: Nuremberg International Military Tribunals, 1947–1949), vol. 22, p. 414; The Genocide Convention, Resolution no. 260 (III) A, U.N. GAOR, 3rd sess. (I), Resolutions, p. 174; U.N. Doc. no. A/810; U.S. Department of State Bulletin no. 3416 (1946).

56. I discuss the place of the concept of genocide in contemporary international law and politics in *Conduct of Just and Limited War,* pp. 56–58.

57. Four former U.S. officials, one of whom (McNamara) was the secretary of defense in the formative years of U.S. nuclear strategic doctrine, have stated:

> It is time to recognize that no one has ever succeeded in advancing any persuasive reason to believe that any use of nuclear weapons, even on the smallest scale, could reliably be expected to remain limited. Every serious analysis and every military exercise, for over twenty-five years, has demonstrated that even the most restrained battlefield use would be enormously destructive to civilian life and property. There is no way for anyone to have any confidence that such a nuclear action will not lead to further and more devastating exchanges. Any use of nuclear weapons in Europe, by the Alliance or against it, carries with it a high and inescapable risk of escalation into the general nuclear war which would bring ruin to all and victory to none.
>
> The one clearly definable firebreak against the worldwide disaster of general nuclear war is the one that stands between all other kinds of conflict and any use whatsoever of nuclear weapons. ... So it seems timely to consider the possibilities, the requirements, the difficulties, and the advantages of a policy of no-first-use.

McGeorge Bundy, George F. Kennan, Robert S. McNamara, and Gerard K. Smith, "Nuclear Weapons and the Atlantic Alliance," *Foreign Affairs*, Spring 1982.

Note that this so-called Gang of Four do not address the issue of responding to a nuclear attack, only that of first use, mainly in Europe, against conventional aggression. Former Secretary of Defense Harold Brown has written:

> There is no way of judging with any confidence what the process of fighting a nuclear war would be like. The magnitude of the destruction, the confusion, the psychological pressures on decision makers, the difficulty of making judgments about what was actually happening, and the problems in reestablishing any sort of civil or military order would all be incomparably greater than any that have ever been experienced by political and military leaders in past conflicts.

Brown, *Thinking about National Security*, pp. 79–80.

58. See Ball, "Can Nuclear War be Controlled? and Steinbruner, "Nuclear Decapitation."

59. Harold Brown's presentation of nuclear dilemmas is particularly striking. Having expressed his lack of confidence in any prospect of controlling nuclear war, Brown goes on to explain how he was obliged to lead an effort to develop the countervailing strategy as a practical alternative to what he perceived to be an excessive reliance on a nuclear deterrent based on mutual assured destruction of population centers:

> A strategic war that involved a massive attack on urban industrial areas would be unimaginably catastrophic. Many serious thinkers about the subject have concluded, partly because they believe that talking about any gradations in such a catastrophe increases the likelihood that it will happen, that the United States should have no plans for anything less than a total use of its strategic force against all kinds of Soviet targets. Some of this school maintain that the United States should have only one plan if a nuclear attack of any magnitude is launched against the United States by the Soviet Union under any circumstances—to retaliate by an all-out attack on Soviet urban and industrial areas.
>
> There is a good chance that any U.S.-Soviet nuclear exchange would escalate out of control. The possibility of such a total disaster is a significant element in overall deterrence. But it would be highly irresponsible to say that, because we cannot predict how such a war would happen, the United States should make no plans for how it will be fought. . . .
>
> It is hard to believe that serious thinkers would really want the United States to respond massively and indiscriminately without considering the nature of the attack being responded to. . . .

Brown, *Thinking about National Security*, p. 80. Brown then explains the Carter 1980 P.D. 59 countervailing strategy. Ibid., pp. 80–83.

60. On the proposition that efforts to develop credible limited-war strategies and capabilities will be provocative and destabilizing and tend to make nuclear war more likely, see Snow, *Nuclear Strategy*, p. 72; Smoke, *National Security*, pp. 222–223; Freedman, *Evolution of Nuclear Strategy*, pp. 374, 379–380, 393–394; Baugh, *Politics of Nuclear Balance*, p. 69.

61. The classic story of Soviet callousness for the lives of their own troops is told by Eisenhower, relating a conversation with Soviet Marshal Georgi K. Zhukov:

> Highly illuminating to me was his description of the Russian method of attacking through mine fields. The German mine fields, covered by defensive fire, were tactical obstacles that caused us many casualties and delays. It was always a laborious business to break through them, even though our technicians invented every conceivable kind of mechanical appliance to destroy mines safely. Marshal Zhukov gave me a matter-of-fact statement of his practice, which was roughly, "There are two kinds of mines; one is the personnel mine and the other is the vehicular mine. When we come to a mine field our infantry attacks exactly as if it were not there. The losses we get from personnel mines we

consider only equal to those we would have gotten from machine guns and artillery if the Germans had chosen to defend that particular area with strong bodies of troops instead of mine fields. The attacking infantry does not set off vehicular mines, so after they have penetrated to the far side of the field they form a bridgehead, after which the engineers come up and dig out channels through which our vehicles can go."

Dwight D. Eisenhower, *Crusade in Europe* (Garden City, N.Y.: Doubleday, 1952, p. 514.

62. On the Soviet view that a nuclear balance based on mutual assured destruction is unacceptable and that, "the success of deterrence requires a Soviet capability to defeat the United States in a nuclear war, a position arising from the communist precept of 'capitalist encirclement'" see Snow, *Nuclear Strategy in a Dynamic World*, p. 135. See Snow's overview of Soviet attitudes on nuclear issues, ibid., pp. 130–160 and authorities therein cited. See Freedman's chapter on the Soviet approach to deterrence, in *Evolution of Nuclear Strategy*, pp. 257–272.

63. Soviet rejection of the Western idea of sufficiency or equivalence, keyed to the goal of maintaining stable nuclear balances, is well demonstrated by Talbott's account of post–SALT I Soviet arms policies. Strobe Talbott, *Deadly Gambits: The Reagan Administration and the Stalemate in Nuclear Arms Control* (New York: Knopf, 1984), pp. 27–31. Talbott observes:

> The SS-20 was a classic example of the Soviet penchant for playing as close as possible to the edge of what is permissible under existing or prospective arms-control agreements, stopping just short of violating the letter of those agreements but nonetheless upsetting the stability and predictability that arms control is meant to help achieve.

Ibid., p. 30.

64. On the Soviet rejection of limited nuclear war, see Snow, *Nuclear Strategy*, pp. 138–143; Freedman, *Evolution of Nuclear Strategy*, pp. 110–112; and authorities cited in these two works.

65. Freedman traces the evolution and decline of McNamara's counterforce, "city-avoidance" strategy advocated in his 1962 Ann Arbor speech. Ibid., pp. 234–244. He points out the practical situation at that time—namely, "at the time the doctrine was being enunciated, the Soviet Union had no capability at all for mounting any sort of serious counterforce attack on the United States." Ibid., p. 241. He says:

> It is not surprising that the Kremlin rejected McNamara's ideas, preferring to concentrate propaganda on the terrible consequences of any war. The notion of "Marquis of Queensbury rules for the conduct of nuclear war" was treated with derision, with emphasis on the inevitability of mass destruction if nuclear war should break out.
>
> Nor was it clear to what purpose the Soviet Union might launch a counterforce attack of the type implied by McNamara's doctrine. In terms of the conventional military operations of the past, which the Russians could readily accept as a frame of reference, the only serious purpose would be a disarming preemptive strike. Otherwise one had to delve into concepts of signalling and bargaining which might make for interesting diplomacy but was not the stuff of traditional military doctrine.

Ibid., p. 241.

66. On the possibilities for greater Soviet interest in less-than-total-war approaches to nuclear issues, see Snow, *Nuclear Strategy*, pp. 142–143, and Baugh, *Politics of Nuclear Balance*, p. 63.

67. On the Soviet concept of total war for victory, see Snow, *Nuclear Strategy*, pp. 139–143, and Freedman, *Evolution of Nuclear Strategy*, pp. 269–272.

68. "'As applied to war,' wrote Lenin, 'the main thesis of dialectics . . . consists of the fact that *"war is simply the continuation of politics by other* [namely, violent] means. . . ."'" Sokolovskiy, *Soviet Military Strategy*, p. 173 [emphasis in the original].

69. On the use of the term *arms race* in church pronouncements, see, for example, *Challenge of Peace*, pars. 1, 126–138, 333; *Gaudium et Spes*, no. 81, pp. 294–295.

70. See President Reagan's "Star Wars" speech, "Peace and National Security," March 23, 1983 (Washington, D.C.: U.S. Department of State, Bureau of Public Affairs, Current Policy no. 472, 1983); *Weekly Compilation of Presidential Documents* 19, no. 12, March 28, 1983, pp. 442–448; Keith B. Payne, *Nuclear Deterrence in U.S.-Soviet Relations* (Boulder, Colo.: Westview, 1982), pp. 206–208.

71. Some typical expressions of the theme that resources allocated to defense are unjustly diverted from programs to increase economic and social justice are the following:

> While extravagant sums are being spent for the furnishing of ever new weapons, an adequate remedy cannot be provided for the multiple miseries afflicting the whole modern world. Disagreements between nations are not really radically healed. On the contrary other parts of the world are infected with them. New approaches initiated by reformed attitudes must be adopted to remove this trap and to restore genuine peace by emancipating the world from its crushing anxiety.

Therefore, it must be said again, the arms race is an utterly treacherous trap for humanity, and one which injures the poor to an intolerable degree. . . . *Gaudium et Spes,* no. 81, p. 295.

In *The Challenge of Peace*, the U.S. Catholic bishops lament "billions readily spent for destructive instruments while pitched battles are waged daily in our legislatures over much smaller amounts for the homeless, the hungry, and the helpless here and abroad." Par. 134. Global interdependence of the "single family" that inhabits the globe is invoked as providing the proper perspective for viewing the responsibilities of arms control. In par. 202, the bishops state:

> It is in the context of the United Nations that the impact of the arms race on the prospects for economic development is highlighted. The numerous U.N. studies on the relationship of development and disarmament support the judgment of Vatican II cited earlier in this letter: "The arms race is one of the greatest curses on the human race and the harm it inflicts upon the poor is more than can be endured."

Ibid., par. 269. This theme is pursued in pars. 270–273.

72. On Eisenhower's "more bang for the buck" massive retaliation policies, see Snow, *Nuclear Strategy*, p. 55.

73. The U.S. Catholic bishops mention the possibility that "Rejection of some forms of nuclear deterrence could therefore conceivably require a willingness to pay higher costs to develop conventional forces." They "acknowledge this reluctantly, aware as we are of the vast amount of scarce resources expended annually on instruments of defense in a world filled with other urgent, unmet human needs." *Challenge of Peace*, par. 216.

74. Opponents of Reagan's Star Wars program charge that all the proposed technologies have "staggering technical problems" and are all likely "to cost on the order of a trillion dollars." John Noble Wilford, "Group of Top Scientists Close to Government Fighting Space Weapons Plan," *New York Times*, November 16, 1983, A8, cols. 1–6.

Since Mr. Reagan's March 23, 1983, Star Wars speech, his administration has increased the budget for research on a defensive missile by $250 million, to a total of $1.17 billion in FY 1985. Lou Cannon, "Reagan Defends 'Star Wars' Proposal," *Washington Post,* September 5, 1984, A1, cols. 4–6; A6, cols. 1–6.

75. David Hollenbach, S.J., *Nuclear Ethics: A Christian Moral Argument* (New York: Paulist Press, 1983).

76. Herman Kahn expressed the essence of the concept of a threatening retaliation so extreme as to deter any rational actor in the title of his book, *Thinking about the Unthinkable* (London: Weidenfeld and Nicolson, 1962).

77. John Newhouse refers to the "theology of stability" in *Cold Dawn: The Story of SALT* (New York: Holt, Rinehart and Winston, 1973).

78. The opposition to Reagan's Strategic Defense Initiative is not only grounded in arguments that it involves violations of the ABM and space treaties but that, more fundamentally, it is profoundly destabilizing in that it challenges the mutual assured destruction balance of terror.

79. *Challenge of Peace*, pars. 203–208.

80. I borrow the term *creative ambiguity* from the English defense scholar Laurence Martin, who, writing of the role of nuclear weapons in NATO's deterrence/defense posture, says:

> By not insisting on too many clear definitions, a creative ambiguity was preserved. In this way tactical nuclear weapons could simultaneously offer a prospect of escalation sufficiently limited for the United States to contemplate, and sufficiently fraught with escalatory dangers to deter the Soviet Union and thereby reassure the Europeans against the risk of actually having to implement the strategy.

"Limited Nuclear War," in Michael Howard, ed., *Restraints on War* (Oxford: Oxford University Press, 1979), p. 106.

8
Nuclear Shadows on Conventional Conflicts

John Keegan
Royal Military Academy at Sandhurst

nyone who has read Dino Buzzati's strange and beautiful novel *Il Deserto dei Tartari*, usually known in English as *The Tartar Steppe*, will probably agree with me that it is one of the most powerful, if mysterious, literary creations of modern times.[1] Published in 1945, it is the story of a newly commissioned lieutenant, Italian in name, as are all his brother officers, though none belong to any identifiable army, whose first posting is to a remote border fortress, Fort Bastiani. His journey to his posting takes him into an increasingly bleak and deserted landscape, and his arrival introduces him into equally desiccated company. The fort, it quickly dawns on him, is not a normal military posting. It is a sort of life sentence.

Stranger still, it is a life sentence without a point. The fort deters a threat that will never materialize. This great desert plateau that stretches away through the surrounding mountains in front of its outposts and ramparts was once an invasion route. But no hostile forces had crossed it in living memory—or, indeed, in the lifetimes of generations long dead. Sentries are changed meticulously, old and new guards are relieved, the flag is raised and lowered at dawn and sunset. But the enemy that justifies these precautions never materializes—indeed, does not really exist.

That is the newcomer's instant impression. It is also the unspoken truth that underlies the life of the fort, sapping the will and energy of all who serve there. Yet there is another undercurrent: a half-terrifying, half-intoxicating belief that one day the enemy *will* appear again. It is that buried fear-and-hope that compels the officers sent to the fort—not all of them, but in the fort's value system the best of them—to decline postings away and to make their careers within its walls. Buzzati's hero is at first determined to leave at the earliest opportunity. Gradually, however, he, too, is bitten by the fear-and-hope of the forgotten enemy's reappearance. He, too, declines a transfer when one is due him. He settles into the fort's routine, undergoes a progressive detachment from the life of the normal world behind the frontier zone, passes from youth and lieutenancy to middle age and majority. Eventually, as retirement approaches, he sickens with a wasting illness. The fort commander urges him to leave, but he refuses. Only when signs appear of the fear-and-hope's materialization—the return of the unnamed enemy to the desert of the Tartars below the fort's walls—does the colonel insist. Buzzati's hero is borne away on a litter to the normal world below the mountains, amid the clatter of the garrison's preparations for war. But whether the enemy has really come to attack the fortress, and whether the hero survives his illness or succumbs, we do not learn.

Now, at one level *The Tartar Steppe* is clearly an allegory of life—of the ordeal of the individual bound to an existence whose point he cannot understand, but escape from which seems an act of cowardice and may be a denial of life's hidden purpose. Catholic theologians would say that *Il Deserto dei Tartari* is a profoundly eschatological novel. And so it is.

But it is also an allegory of a different kind—if I can coin a phrase, an essay in strategic teleology. It may have been entirely coincidental that the novel was published in 1945. If so, however, it was strikingly apt, with that intuition perhaps only great novelists have for the unperceived transformation of the world about them. For if forts and garrisons were symbolic of the way states had defended themselves against external threats from the beginning of time, then that particular year had an extraordinary symbolic importance. It was the year in which forts and garrisons lost their value as a means of ultimate defense—in which, indeed, the concept of ultimate defense—always a chimera—evaporated like morning mist under the heat of the desert sun.

As a result, *The Tartar Steppe* may be read, by the strategically minded, in two different ways, each autonomous, together highly complementary. In one way, Fort Bastiani and its garrison may be held to represent the institutions and personnel who manage the central strategic system, as we have come to call the superpowers' major nuclear forces. They, like Buzzati's hero, are chained to the service of a military system that will never be used—so, at least, their rational mind tells them. Buried beneath their reason, however, is the nagging fear that it might. And buried deeper still—at a level shared not only by them but by all citizens who belong to states that are nuclear powers—is the seductive, wicked flicker of hope that perhaps it might. To suggest that such a flicker never surfaces in the consciousness of the nuclear warriors is to assert that they are not human beings.

Let us not dwell on that feature of human psychology. The second way that *The Tartar Steppe* allegorizes the condition of the contemporary military establishment is in the ethos of the conventional forces of nuclear powers. They, like the garrison of Fort Bastiani, are men denied a clear and apparent purpose in life. The existence of nuclear weapons has robbed them of their age-old role as the ultimate guarantors of life and liberty to their civilian fellows. The ultimate threat has changed, and they are even less equipped than the nuclear warriors to oppose it. And when the threat presents itself in some diluted form—as a local war, or a peacekeeping mission—the ambient risk that their whole-hearted engagement might elevate a minor into a major conflict exerts a comparably limiting effect on their role. Deny it though they may, even to themselves, nuclear weapons have reduced the status of conventional warriors to that of the *gendarme*—an armed policeman whose freedom to deal in violence will always be constrained either by the doctrine of minimum necessary force or by the judgment of his political superiors that politics makes necessary an even less forceful response than that.

Hence—in part, at least—the distortions imposed on the strategy and tactics of limited wars fought by the nuclear powers since 1945. *Limited war* is a concept which has suffered heavily at the hands of scholars.[2] They have succeeded in demonstrating that the deliberate limitations apparently imposed on warfare in the past are usually explicable in terms that have little to do with human decision; incapacity operated far more often than judgments of inutility. But the military affluence enjoyed by the great powers during the 1950s and 1960s did endow them with the ability to choose how they would fight—when and if they did so. Thus we can objectively perceive, in Vietnam for example, conscious and chosen limitation of means and targeting at work. The result—the first shadow thrown by nuclear weapons on conventional warfare that I would identify—was, paradoxically, to intensify the cruelty of a war by its prolongation in time. No doubt it will be disputed that there was any quick means to settle the Vietnam War. The early mobilization of its reserves by the United States, the immediate extension of the bombing campaign to Hanoi and Haiphong, the invasion of the north by ground or amphibious forces might have had results quite other than victory. It will probably not be disputed, however, that such measures would have produced climactic results. In their absence, the war dragged on, permeating the physical and social environment of the Vietnamese with its effects: to mention but two, much of the countryside was depopulated and the rural population deracinated, while enormous areas of forest were ruined by cratering, metal fragmentation, and defoliation.[3]

War, as Clausewitz proposes to us, has its own grammar but not its own logic.[4] A second and reciprocal effect of military affluence in the nuclear world is that when states do impose limitations of time on the use they make of force, the level of violence exerted may be far greater than that intended. The intensity of the fighting in the strictly limited Falklands campaign surprised everyone, not least the immediate participants. Both sides were severely constrained by time— the Argentinians by the need to defeat the British task force before it was firmly lodged ashore, the British by the approach of the sub-Antarctic winter. The outcome was a frighteningly bitter and destructive series of small battles that destroyed life and material on a prodigal scale. British ship losses in San Carlos Water, Argentinian casualties at Goose Green, were far higher than had been expected or than experience predicated. One explanation of these unanticipated phenomena is that the two elite fighting forces engaged—the Argentinian air force and the British parachutists—adopted a virtual kamikaze approach to their missions, in an apparent and conscious attempt to escape a political or diplomatic restriction of their efforts, which they knew impended.[5]

If we include Israel within the nuclear power orbit—which, given its ambiguous client relationship with the United States, it is not inappropriate to do—we see the same "race against time" intensification of effect at work in its style of warfare. Israel, a beneficiary of modern military affluence par excellence, fights, of course, wars of national survival. But since its national survival is being measured in terms of the preservation of life as much as of retention of territory or *post bellum* advantage, Israel allows its Defense Force to expend firepower and material with a prodigality limited only by supply—of which, as yet, there has been no shortage. Because Israel's opponents, notably Syria, have recently come to share the fruits of military affluence—donated in Syria's case by the Soviet Union—a conjunction of military styles results; its effect is to produce wars of fleeting duration and quite unparalleled destructiveness. Until 1982, accidents of geography determined that such destructiveness had little collateral effect on the region's civilian populations or productive areas, but that alienation may in future not be counted on.[6]

Still, it would be perverse to argue that the shadow cast on the conventional warfare strategy of the nuclear powers, via their possession of such weapons, is black with malfeasance. So far no nuclear power has waged war directly with another, and I am naive enough to think that the prudence induced by the possession of nuclear arms imposes a fairly long periodicity on such wars as they do fight: if we exclude the Korean war, responsibility for the precipitation of which remains obscure (though it was certainly not that of the United States), the United States and the Soviet Union have each risked only one external military expedition in the last forty years. It is difficult to think of any other period of history in which the world's leading military powers committed their military forces to foreign war with such little frequency. Small campaigns of imperial conquest by Britain, France, and Russia dotted even the long peace between Waterloo and the Crimea; and in the succeeding hundred years, of course, during which the United States also rose to world power, all were at war, for colonial or great power purposes, at quite short intervals.[7]

Nuclear weapons cast their shadow, however, in many directions, and not merely whither the interests of the great powers run. The postwar world has been a world of many wars. Some have been the proxy wars of the great powers, waged against each other, or for some unilateral and local purpose, through the campaigns of third parties. Third parties also have done a great deal of fighting on their own account, and for a variety of reasons that can only with the greatest difficulty—if at all—be shown to fit within the strategy of East-West confrontation. Perhaps the simplest way to characterize many of these wars is in terms of local imperialisms coming to life again after the long ice age of European colonialism. In the Indian subcontinent, in Southeast Asia, in the Horn of Africa, in the Gulf, local hierarchies of race and religion, subordinated by the superimposition of white rule, are being thrashed out once more, in pursuit of claims or pretensions, and often in battlefields, familiar to the combatants before the Europeans arrived.[8]

It would be naive to expect that decolonization would have had a different outcome, but it can certainly be contended that it might not have had the outcome the successor states have undergone had the shadow of nuclear weapons not fallen over their world as well as ours. In the first place, the climate of strategic suspicion that the nuclear factor heightens (*induces* would be the wrong word) between the superpowers has made the arbitration of third-party disputes, particularly where the provision of peacekeeping forces would assist arbitration, a problem-fraught business. Peacekeeping in the heyday of great power management of the world was never easy to arrange and was always heavily motivated by self-interest and mutual distrust. It was, nevertheless, occasionally possible—as in the Lebanon in 1860 or in China in 1900—to arrange interventions in which all the powers were represented.[9] No intervention including contingents from the United States and the Soviet Union has ever been staged. One consequence of the indirectness of superpower involvement has been the delegation of peacekeeping functions to the armed forces of countries lacking the stature or firmness of purpose to see a mission through a crisis. An excellent example of such infirmity is yielded by the Middle East crisis of May–June 1967, when the supervisory units of the U.N. Force were withdrawn by their governments as soon as Egypt made it known that they were no longer welcome in Sinai.[10]

Moreover, even when a force from a superpower *is* committed to a peacekeeping mission—we are, in effect, discussing the United States—its freedom to execute its role is severely hampered by the nuclear factor, as we have just seen in Lebanon. The limitation on its effectiveness seems to operate as follows: concern for the sensitivities of its nuclear antagonist prevents the sponsoring power from securing the peace by a disarmament of the local contestants (since that would be to replace local military power with its own); but domestic opinion will not accept casualties suffered in the course of what appears to be half-hearted and ineffective pacification. Peacekeeping thereby is made merely palliative, securing at best a remission, not a cure, of the situation it was intended to settle.

None of that might matter were the local forces engaged in third-party conflicts still, as they used to be, equipped with fourth- or fifth-class arms and materiel. But that is no longer the case—a function of the prevailing state of military affluence, already mentioned, which ought now to be described. Nuclear weapons systems, it is accepted, are exceptionally expensive to procure and require expensive and continuous modernization. The budgetary climate thus generated has allowed the manufacturers of conventional weapons—the cost inflation of which has not until recently been as steep and has certainly not attracted as much public attention—to collude with the conventional forces in reequipment at steadily shortening intervals—a compensation, no doubt, for the decline of conventional forces from the place they held until 1945. The product of this process has been an enormous and ever-growing stock of second-hand arms of high quality, available for gifts, loan, or sale at bargain prices to states outside the East and West blocs. It is an important feature of this development that certain standard items, particularly ammunition, are less subject to the modernization process and so remain in production over several generations of reequipment, meanwhile cheapening by the familiar economy-of-scale effect.[11]

Local forces engaged in third-party conflicts are thereby enabled to inflict damage of an unparalleled and literally almost indescribable quality on each other and their environment. Nothing seen in newspaper photographs or on the television screen, for example, prepares a visitor for the extent of the devastation wrought in Beirut since 1975. Newsreels may suggest that the extent and degree of destruction equates to that in Belfast or in one of the blighted and abandoned districts of New York, but such an equation dissipates in the first minutes of a visit to the city. Along the Green Line separating Christian from Moslem Beirut, the city is laid waste for block upon block. Indeed, in an area equivalent to that filled in New York by Madison, Lexington, and Park Avenues from Grand Central Station to fifteen blocks northward, there are no inhabited buildings at all. The roads have been bulldozed clear of rubble and the walls of the buildings stand, but the floors and roofs have collapsed inward, leaving them open to the sky. This is the result not of shelling but of fires started in street-fighting. The truly extraordinary feature of the damage is that almost all of it is the result of small-arms and infantry weapon exchanges. Every building in the devastated zone is pockmarked with bullet strikes, only a few inches apart; those buildings that have been the focus of particularly intense gun battles have actually had their silhouettes altered by the weight of metal that has struck them. The Holiday Inn, Phoenicia, and Murr Tower hotels have each been struck by *millions* of rounds of small-caliber ammunition, which in Beirut is as easy to come by as confetti at a wedding and is dispersed quite as casually.[12]

Given the amounts of ammunition that have been sprayed about so prodigally, it is astonishing that civilian—and indeed military—casualties have not been higher. But they have been high enough—a widely accepted estimate is that thirty thousand Lebanese, from among a population of about three million, have died since 1975. The majority have been killed by their fellow citizens; in the process, Lebanon has become totally and perhaps irreversibly militarized. Every Lebanese male of military age appears to possess a gun; most have done service in the communal militias formed to substantiate the communities' political claims and defend their zones of residence. None of this, of course, goes to make an argument that military affluence has *caused* the Lebanese problem. But military affluence has both helped to make the problem what it is today and ensured that it is almost wholly resistant to solution.

Military affluence, though particularly apparent in its effects in Lebanon, has also marked the conflicts of states elsewhere in the Middle East, in Asia, and in Africa. The war currently raging in the Gulf between Iraq and Iran, shrouded though its conduct is in secrecy, appears to be one of the costliest of the last forty years. It is commonly estimated that between one hundred thousand and three hundred thousand lives have already been lost in its course. What is so extraordinary about this effect is that neither combatant produces heavy military materiel of any sort and each has been or is in severe financial straits. So plentiful and cheap, however, have primary military goods become in today's world that neither has the least difficulty in acquiring all it needs. Even if Iraq is the beneficiary of Soviet largesse in this respect, the Soviet Union is able to supply the want only because ammunition and everyday munitions are now commodities of overproduction.[13]

We may expect this strange and deplorable trend to continue. One consequence of decolonization has been not merely the emergence of large numbers of new sovereignties—over a hundred since 1945—but also of sovereign armed forces, all more or less well equipped to fight each other and likely to become better equipped as time passes. This trend will diverge further from the path taken by the conventional armed forces of the superpower world, which, as we have seen, find it increasingly difficult to sustain their credibility and self-image now that they are denied their historic role of acting as ultimate protectors of the nation.

Almost the last of the shadows cast by nuclear weapons that ought to be mentioned, however, connects with recent attempts to return a decisive role to the conventional armed forces of nuclear powers. The origins of that attempt were entirely admirable. It had long been a cause of concern, both in western Europe and Washington, that the effective defense of NATO's Central Front, in Germany, derived too much of its force from the threat to employ nuclear weapons, should the front ever be broken by conventional attack. Yet means to improve the defense that matched the menace offered—large Warsaw Pact numbers—carried too high a political and financial price. It was with interest, even excitement, therefore, that in the late 1970s politicians and commanders began to listen to reports from defense technologists and analysts that a new array of equipment would allow the Central Front to be defended without either an unbearable increase in financial cost or a heavier manpower commitment.[14]

The equipment promised—some of it already existed in prototype—performed three main functions:

1. It very much improved surveillance, target acquisition, and accuracy of weapon delivery over both long and short distances.
2. It extended the range at which enemy targets could be engaged.
3. It sharply increased the damage that could be inflicted by conventional warheads and other munitions.

As a result, it was possible to glimpse a scenario in which, were a Warsaw Pact tank army to attempt the penetration of the Central Front, its echelons would be identified and engaged at great distances from the point of attack, while the leading waves were deflected or halted by accurate point defense. These measures, together with the concomitant destruction of the hostile infrastructure—airfields, depots, pipelines, and communication chokepoints—promised to make conventional defense autonomous, and to free the NATO command structure of its fears that halting a Warsaw Pact break-in must entail recourse to nuclear weapons—or, alternatively, surrender.

The new equipment array was therefore to be welcomed—or was it entirely? Doubts about the desirability of strengthening so dramatically NATO's conventional capabilities arose quite quickly and from two separate and opposed sources. Europeans, particularly the Germans, who had always opposed recourse to nuclear weapons as a means of defending their soil, now decided that they feared the dissociation of nuclear weapons from European defense perhaps as much; equally, they disliked the prospect of a highly destructive war being fought on their soil with conventional weapons. At the same time, moderates among strategic analysts began to be alarmed by what looked like a revival of bellicosity among some of the strongest supporters of the new so-called defensive weapons. One of the attractions, it appeared, of conventional weapons with high accuracy and payload was that they might actually replicate in their effects those of low-yield nuclear weapons. The prospect therefore presented itself, to some at least, of waging a war in central Europe that NATO might actually *win*, without having recourse to nuclear weapons at any stage.

Needless to say, such a prospect could not be concealed from the Warsaw Pact, which, it might be expected, would naturally respond by modernizing its own conventional equipment array along similar lines. An undesired outcome of NATO's improved defensive strategy might therefore be to give another twist to the screw of escalation, threatening the continent with a large-scale conventional war between East and West that might result in destruction equivalent to that caused by a small-scale nuclear war.

From the contradictions of modern weapons policy it might thus appear that there is no escape, particularly as improvements in conventional arms threaten to transform them into the equivalents of some forms of nuclear weapons. To say that, however, is to be too pessimistic. The objection to many of the new forms of conventional weapons is that they are too *offensive* in character—designed to seek enemy targets deep within his territory and destroy them by so-called area effect. One unexploited feature of the climate of military affluence is that purely *defensive* weapons might now be designed and procured quite cheaply. This is not the place to argue at length the case for field fortifications. It is certainly true, however, that—without consolidating the boundary between East and West (a strong and understandable German concern), without dedicating much productive land to military use, without interfering with free communications in any direction, without preemplacing mines or other volatile munitions—it should now be possible so to engineer and landscape the eastern border region of West Germany as to make it impossible to penetrate by military attack.

To adopt such a strategic policy, desirable as I think it, would not be to solve all the world's military problems. The great scandal of arms supply to the Third World would remain—in the view of many, a real scandal crying to heaven for a just solution far louder than the potential scandal of nuclear war. To settle the long instability which has gripped Europe since 1945, however, would be to clear the decks between the two sides for a genuine effort at arms control. It would be odd if, after all, Dino Buzzati's vision were incorrect, and border fortifications still have their role to play in regulating peace between nations.

Notes

1. Dino Buzzati, *Il Deserto dei Tartari* (Milan: A. Mondadori, 1945).

2. See, among others, Robert O. Osgood, *Limited War Revisited* (Boulder, Colo.: Westview Press, 1979); Morton H. Halperin, *Limited War in the Nuclear Age* (New York: Wiley, 1963).

3. Guenter Levy, *America in Vietnam* (Oxford: Oxford University Press, 1978), pp. 258–266.

4. Carl von Clausewitz, *On War,* trans. M. Howard and P. Paret (Princeton, N.J.: Princeton University Press, 1976), vol. II, chap. 2.

5. Max Hastings and Simon Jenkins, *The Battle for the Falklands* (New York: Norton, 1983), esp. chaps. 9 and 13.

6. Chaim Herzog, *The Arab-Israeli Wars* (New York: Random House, 1982), pp. 315–323.

7. Cyril Falls, *A Hundred Years of War* (New York: Collier, 1962), remains a useful scholarly compendium.

8. Michael Carver, *War Since 1945* (New York: Putnam, 1981), is the most complete survey.

9. Antony Preston and John Mayor, *Send a Gunboat* (New York: Longmans, 1967), pp. 182–187.

10. Randolph S. Churchill and Winston S. Churchill, *The Six Day War* (London: Heinemann, 1967), pp. 30–32.

11. Mary Kaldor, *The Baroque Arsenal* (New York: Hill and Wang, 1981), passim.

12. John Keegan, "Shedding Light on Lebanon," *Atlantic Monthly,* April 1984.

13. Shirin Tahir Kheli and Shaheen Ayubi, eds., *The Iran-Iraq War* (New York: Praeger, 1983), pp. 180–181; M.S. El Azhary, *The Iran-Iraq War* (London: Croom Helm, 1984), pp. 18–19.

14. *Strengthening Conventional Deterrence in Europe*, Report of the European Study (New York: Macmillan, 1983), parts III and IV.

9

Nuclear Deterrence and Democratic Politics

Michael Walzer
Princeton University

here are many things worrisome and wrong in the nuclear policies of the
U.S. government (and in the policies of other governments too), and the
particular worries and wrongs on which I shall focus here are not the
most important. They are not entirely unimportant either, however, for they
have to do with democratic politics, one of the values that the strategy of
deterrence is meant to defend. Does deterrence defend democracy? It is now a
common argument on the left that the two stand, in fact, in sharp contradiction.
Richard Falk sums up the argument:

> Being constantly ready to commit the nation (and the planet!) to a devastating
> war of annihilation in a matter of minutes on the basis of possibly incorrect
> computer-processed information or pathological traits among leaders creates a
> variety of structural necessities that contradict the spirit and substance of
> democratic governance: secrecy, lack of accountability, permanent emergency,
> concentration of authority, peacetime militarism, extensive apparatus of state
> intelligence and police.[1]

The "structural necessities" of deterrence militate against public debate and
democratic choice, both among the people at large and among their representatives. We live in what might be called a nuclear autocracy. Again, this isn't the
worst charge that could be leveled, or that is leveled, against deterrence. Nevertheless, it's worth asking: Is it true?

Certainly, it wasn't democratic decision making that brought us to our
present state. The original decision to develop and produce nuclear weapons was
not publicly debated in any of the democratic states that have taken it (nor,
obviously, in any of the nondemocratic states). Not in the United States, where
the decision was made under conditions of wartime secrecy; and although the
later decision to build a hydrogen bomb was preceded by congressional hearings,

Reprinted by permission of *The New Republic*, ©1984, The New Republic, Inc.

neither the character of the debate nor the public humiliation of Robert Oppenheimer that terminated the debate are exemplary for democratic politics. Not in Great Britain, where the crucial decision to develop an independent deterrent was made in 1946 by the prime minister and five members of his cabinet—"the others," as Solly Zuckerman writes, "being kept in the dark."[2] Not in France, where the essential work was well begun before De Gaulle made it a matter of public policy that France should be a nuclear power. Not in India, where an underground test was the first announcement of the government's policy. Not in Israel, where some development has obviously been undertaken, though it is not clear, even to the citizens, whether the country actually has a bomb or not.

In all these cases, of course, the crucial decisions were made by elected leaders, and if elections are not the only constitutional requirement of democratic choice, they are the most basic requirement. We might be even more worried, then, about a great variety of lesser decisions that shape the way in which nuclear weapons are deployed (and hence the way they might be used) and that are made by men and women who hold no elected office at all. Consider the following example from Zuckerman's *Nuclear Illusion and Reality:*

> . . . long before any decision had been taken by the British Government to replace Polaris with Trident, long before the need for any such decision had been put to the Ministers, the men in the British nuclear weapons laboratory had preempted the situation. They had not only started to design a warhead for a MIRVed Trident missile; they had also, with American help, conducted underground tests of their designs.[3]

Theorists of nuclear autocracy are frightened by the prospect—or, better, the reality—of an "imperial president" with his finger on the nuclear button. But even an imperial president is likely to be ignorant of the scientific design of the weapons that his button would activate, unable by himself to choose among different designs with different short- and long-term effects. The tyranny of the weapons lab may well be more dangerous than the imperial presidency.

And if the president is ignorant, so are all, or almost all, the rest of us. The sense of technical incomprehension, which is both widespread and deep, undermines the self-confidence of ordinary citizens and generates a kind of apathetic trust in the experts—more apathetic than genuinely trustful. Of course, we don't understand, or most of us don't understand, the economy either. But we experience the effects of different economic policies, and these effects—the rate of inflation, say, or the rate of unemployment—are subject to continuous public measurement. So we feel ourselves competent to judge the managers of the economy, even if we aren't certain what it is that managers of the economy actually do. It's not clear, by contrast, how we are to understand our own experience of the effects of deterrence. The effect that we hope for is the avoidance of war, but the actual effect is this or that degree of risk of war, and one of the things we don't understand is what the risk is. There are no continuous or reliable measurements. How dangerous is the world we live in? And to what extent are those dangers caused by, to what extent are they controlled by, our nuclear strategies? If ordinary citizens can't give reasonably knowledgeable answers to questions like these, democratic choice is not a plausible option. But we can't, or many of us think that we can't—because of the "structural necessities" of a deterrent posture, secrecy above all, and then because of our inability to understand whatever technical data are made available to us.

So the policy of deterrence has been worked out and implemented by small groups of politically powerful or scientifically expert men and women. The most important arguments have been unpublicized; the key decisions have been taken in secret or on the basis of information fully available, or fully comprehensible, only to an inner circle of scientists, soldiers, and political leaders. And what is true of past choices about policies must be true a fortiori of future choices about the execution of policies. If a crisis comes, there won't be time for congressional hearings, editorials in newspapers and journals of opinion, the organization of parties and movements. Even in the inner circle, disagreements will be brief; and awareness may well come to the rest of us only in a blinding flash.

The charge seems, then, to be true: "One of the hidden costs of nuclearism," as Falk says, "has been an impairment of the quality of democratic political life."[4] But *impairment* is a relative term, and so we still need to ask how democracies have functioned in the past with regard to defense policy. We need to think, for example, about the major innovations in weaponry before the atomic bomb—the machine gun, the tank, the submarine, the airplane, poison gas, the blockbuster, the incendiary bomb, napalm. Did any of these come into the arsenal of the modern army as the result of a democratic decision (a public debate, a vote in the assembly)? The answer, of course, is no, and that answer suggests that contemporary nuclear politics is not so much an impairment of democracy as it is a sign of continuing inadequacy or failure.

I don't mean to argue that defense policy has never been an issue in democratic politics. Obviously, it has been. The size of the navy was hotly debated in the British Parliament in the early twentieth century. Billy Mitchell's campaign in the 1920s for an independent and greatly strengthened U.S. air force led to prolonged congressional hearings, a public demonstration of what bombers could do to battleships (covered with great excitement by the press), and finally a spectacular court martial. André Maginot waged a long battle, sometimes within the defense establishment, sometimes in the political arena, for his famous Line—and De Gaulle, later on, waged a similar battle, though less successfully, against the spirit of the Line. Winston Churchill in the 1930s staked his political career on a fierce critique of the military weakness of the National Union and Conservative governments. The defense budget is regularly subject to parliamentary or congressional scrutiny, and its total size, and sometimes also its specific allocations, are commonly questioned and debated. But these sorts of issues have mostly been the concern of the few; the most crucial debates have taken place (as with nuclear weapons and strategies) in committees and behind the scenes. They are rarely brought into the center of a political campaign, not by parties, not by candidates for office. Even a jingoist campaign is more likely to focus on attitude and posture than on actual military policy. By and large, there has been little sustained public interest in, and little democratic control over, the selection and deployment of weapons or the choice of strategies. The planning of wars, like the fighting of wars, has never been the focus of democratic attention.

At least this is true of modern and mass democracy. But perhaps the notion of impairment looks further back: I suppose that the Athenian assembly debated defense budgets and military plans, and although the debates are difficult to reconstruct, they were probably carried on with an intensity and a degree of publicity unknown since. It's not because of nuclear weapons, however, that we don't find ourselves sitting in anything like the Athenian assembly. Or perhaps Falk means us to look sideways, as it were, to smaller and more intimate democracies like Israel, where foreign policy is always at the center of a lively political debate. But with regard to the selection and deployment of weapons, there has never been much room for argument in Israel: each successive government has been committed to deploy the most advanced military technology it could develop or procure. And specific strategic decisions, like the decision to build the Bar-Lev Line, have been debated largely within the defense establishment and have not become (except, perhaps, after the fact) political issues—any more than nuclear policy has become a political issue. In any case, we can't choose smallness and intimacy.

II

Against this background, we might well be tempted to reverse the nuclear autocracy argument. For things do look different in the United States today; and from a democratic point of view, they look better. Needless to say, they don't look better in any other way. We might with good reason prefer a nondemocratic nondebate over the deployment of tanks to a very lively debate over the deployment of intercontinental ballistic missiles. Still, there *is* a lively debate going on right now—and a debate that seems to me without precedent in the history of democratic politics. I will try to describe its dimensions and then to assess its value.

Since I am a professor, I will begin with books. The point is obvious. An incredible number of books on nuclear deterrence and the dangers of nuclear war have been published in the last four or five years, some of them simple-minded and melodramatic, but many of them technically sophisticated, complex, and sober in their arguments. And not only published: these books have been widely reviewed and discussed, reprinted in cheap editions, sold in drug stores and suburban shopping centers. Books about war and weaponry have always been popular, but not books like these, which set out to disturb their readers and which criticize or defend government policies that most citizens, most of the time, prefer to ignore. Immediately after Hiroshima, thousands of Americans read John Hersey's account of the effects of the bomb. In the years since, however, the issue has been repressed; or it has been kept alive only by small groups of citizens or by marginal political movements. Now the debate seems general, participation widespread. The flood of books is only one sign of this; I could add descriptions of university courses, magazine articles, television programs, town forums; but the books seem to me most surprising, an unexpected sign of seriousness.

Even more surprising, and more serious, is the recent statement of the Catholic bishops. The church has been committed for many centuries to the doctrine of the just war, but the application of this doctrine to the planning of wars (and even, I think, its application to the conduct of wars) has been left to individual Catholics. Certainly the tradition of Catholic protest has had a "protestant" character—so it looks, at least, to an outsider; it has been a matter of private conscience and not of corporate decision. Father Ford's courageous opposition to terror bombing in World War II was the opposition of a single person, virtually unnoticed at the time; the same can be said of Miss Anscombe's opposition to "Mr. Truman's Degree" (granted by Oxford University in 1957), and also of the arguments against nuclear deterrence worked out by the English Catholic Walter Stein and his associates in 1961.[5] But now the U.S. bishops have spoken with a single voice and with the moral authority of their office, and their statement has been widely publicized and debated. Theirs is a new presence in U.S. political life (it is interesting that no one responding to it has raised the old specter of Romanism): it suggests a shift in the internal character, and also an enlargement of the scope, of democratic argument.

And many citizens have done what the bishops have done: joined together, taken a stand. There have been movements in the past against a war in progress— among the British at the time of the Boer War, for example, or in this country during the long years of Vietnam. There have even been movements against a war in prospect—the campaign of isolationists and America Firsters against U.S. involvement in World War II. But a campaign like today's Campaign for Nuclear Disarmament (CND) in Britain or the nuclear freeze movement in the United States, aimed at preventing the deployment or further development of a particular set of weapons, seems, again, without precedent. Was there ever a political movement, involving large numbers of citizens, against the battleship or the submarine or the bomber? I don't mean to sound naively amazed; there are obvious reasons for the shift in popular attitudes. But I do want to notice the shift.

The same shift has occurred at the level of electoral politics. Candidates for president in the United States today commit themselves for and against the nuclear freeze. They debate the merits of the B-1 bomber and the MX missile. Once again, I can't think of similarly specific debates in the past. Candidates have discussed the size of the naval budget or the need for military preparedness, but not the costs and benefits of particular weapons. In the course of the 1930s, the British and U.S. defense establishments made enormously important (and significantly different) decisions about the kinds of airplane they would build—decisions that effectively determined the kind of war they fought in the 1940s. But these decisions never became the subject of an electoral campaign, never became political issues; and it is difficult to imagine the circumstances under which they might have been turned into political issues. Who would have been the agents of such a turning? What would have been its causes?

What are the causes today? Two facts lie behind our current political arguments: that the risks involved in nuclear deterrence are very great, and that the risks are widely known. The risks of aerial bombardment were understood only in an abstract and impersonal way in the 1930s. People talked about them, wrote about them, sometimes in graphic terms; but the message did not sink in—perhaps because there had been no demonstration at the end of World War I comparable to Hiroshima and Nagasaki in 1945. Or perhaps there wasn't time enough between the two world wars to recover from the first and confront the specific dangers of the second. A general opposition to war, a dislike of conscription, a reluctance to pay for military preparedness, an uneasiness with patriotic speeches: all these were present in the 1930s, but not a close attention to weapons and strategies. The CND of the early 1960s may provide a rough analogy, for it too was marked by a generalized and not a specific opposition to nuclear weapons. Today both sorts of opposition are commonly expressed: advocates of disarmament have learned a great deal about first- and second-strike capacities, delivery systems, throw-weights, and so on. There is still a certain strident simple-mindedness in the public debate (on both sides), but there is also, by now, considerable sophistication and, given the technical difficulties, a surprising number of knowledgeable participants.

The firebombing of cities was never debated because it was never vividly imagined: it was not a popular nightmare. But a nuclear holocaust is vivid and frightening for millions of people. And democratic politics is responsive to risk, to the popular sense of vulnerability and danger, whenever that sense is sufficiently concrete. The sense of nuclear danger doesn't, in fact, work all that differently from the sense of economic danger, although concreteness is harder to come by. We know people who have been hurt by unemployment or inflation, not by atomic bombs. And concreteness is important, as the agitation for a test ban in the late 1950s suggests. What fueled popular concern and made a (limited) mobilization possible was in part the danger of war but, more important, the more immediate and comprehensible danger of contamination, cancer, birth defects, and so on. Today the danger of war, even without the experience, seems to have taken on a similar immediacy; and the current debate, the bishops' statement, the movement for a nuclear freeze, the rush of candidates to take positions—all this is the democratic response.

III

The test of a democracy is not that the right side wins the political battle, but that there is a political battle. Not just a random encounter or an intermittent campaign but a sustained and serious engagement of forces, with a well-informed public, a wide mobilization of citizens, coherently committed parties and movements. So we are beginning, though only just beginning, to meet the democratic test. In this case, however, more than in any other, we may well be less interested in democracy than we are in rationality. We want, we desperately need, the right side to win. A democratic decision to destroy the world would not be a satisfactory outcome; nor would a democratic decision that permits the world to be destroyed. Democracies, I have said, respond to risk, but they don't always respond in time or in the best possible way. Given the awesome choices that we face, do we really want a democratic response? How should the present debate be conducted? How should decisions be made?

Normal democratic politics seems somehow inadequate, designed to cope with different issues, different kinds of danger. Interest group organization, temporary and unstable coalitions, bargaining in the corridors, short-term compromise—this sort of thing is useful enough in all sorts of cases, but it seems of only dubious use in this case, incongruent with the risks involved and with the seriousness of the decisions required. Imagine one member of Congress saying to another (what any member of Congress could easily say): I'll vote to build the MX missile if you vote to ban the import of specialized steels. . . . The pairing is inappropriate; the negotiation is comic (but grimly comic). Perhaps this kind of politics is inappropriate to foreign policy generally. The point is often made, and even ordinary politicians are aware of its force; different mechanisms come into play, sometimes, when foreign policy is being debated. But if we think about the character of senatorial decision making during, say, the debate over the Panama Canal Treaty, the difference doesn't seem all that great. Presidential pressure, with its usual threats and promises, and the nervous sounding out of campaign contributors back home, seem to have played too large a role; the costs and benefits, justice or injustice of the treaty, too small a role. It may be the case that in the arguments over SALT II, senators drew more deeply on their own understanding and deepest convictions; even so, they were hardly unaware of more immediate political considerations. How can such considerations be avoided, when the men and women who vote yes or no are short-term officeholders who must themselves seek reelection?

But if normal politics is problematic, abnormal politics seems hardly less so. The excitement of mass movements that suddenly appear and as suddenly disappear; the mobilization of fear; marches, demonstrations, civil and uncivil disobedience: all this fits our sense of danger, but it is in its own way incongruent with serious decision making, with the complexity of the issues and the need for cool appraisal and study. Decisions about deterrence policy cannot be made in the streets. Nor, if they were, would the decisions be democratic, for the number of people in the streets, even when it looks very large (the streets are very narrow), is only a minority of the citizen body. The banners carried and the slogans chanted by the marchers don't make, aren't intended to make, coherent arguments. They make simple and striking arguments. Perhaps the leaders of the march have simple views; perhaps they have views that they are concealing from their followers. In any case, we need to consider their views in some other forum, and that brings us back to the committee rooms and corridors of normal politics.

It may be the case, however, that politics itself is a mistake—whether it takes the form of a deal or a demonstration, whether it brings interests or passions into play. Maybe we should leave nuclear decision making to an elite of experts, to scientists and strategists. That is more or less what we have done until now. I suppose political leaders in fact do something more than ratify decisions taken elsewhere; sometimes they negotiate or arbitrate the decisions; and commonly they front for their less visible colleagues, taking responsibility even when they aren't in fact responsible. And the decision actually to use the weapons, or not, remains their own, just as it was Truman's in 1945; that has not changed. Development and deployment, however, have pretty much slipped out of their hands. Technical competence dominates political authority, though it does so with the consent of the authorities; only recently has that dominance been called into question.

So it is the elite of experts, not democratic politics, that has brought us to our present state. That speaks well for the experts, it might be said; deterrence as they designed it has "worked," and we have avoided the catastrophe of nuclear war. On the other hand, the risks of catastrophe have probably increased over the years, along with the increase in the number of weapons and in their destructive capability. Deterrence has not been a steady state but a race, and every movement forward in the race, so we are told, jeopardizes the balance on which our safety depends. More accurately, our forward movement jeopardizes the safety of our adversaries, and theirs jeopardizes ours, and we are both driven to keep moving forward. Perhaps, then, the experts have not done well, or not well enough: we need to call their competence into question. I shall make only a few unsurprising points, adapted from the standard stock of democratic arguments.

First of all, the experts disagree among themselves. In the current public debate, all sides have their resident experts. But the disagreements obviously precede the public debate; they have surfaced briefly in the past, as in the Oppenheimer-Teller controversy or during the negotiation of the test ban treaty. Nor are the disagreements only technical in character—of the sort that might plausibly be settled within the community of technically knowledgeable people. Decisions about deterrence also raise moral and political issues, and scientists and strategists have moral and political commitments, even when they conceal these commitments and speak only the language of their trades. Shop talk is sometimes a necessity, sometimes an obsession; but it is also, sometimes, a way of concealing from lay people the ordinary character of disagreements in the shop. Some years ago, I had occasion to study the debate among British scientists over strategic bombing policy in the early 1940s. The most striking feature of the debate is that it was carried on entirely in technical terms. And yet a glance into the future suggested strongly that the real disagreement was political: the same men were to line up on the same sides again and again, although the technical issues were entirely different each time. In the event, Churchill made the crucial decision, and that was probably proper (though I think he made the wrong decision). A political choice is what was required then, and that is most often what is required now.

But political choice requires in turn what might best be called common sense, and of common sense the experts are often entirely bereft. Hence the second point: it is useful to have scientists and strategists who are narrow and deep, immersed in their data, committed to the beauty of their speculations, ready to follow the logic of their arguments and to accept the risks of absurdity (or what looks to the rest of us like absurdity). Not all scientists are like that, but it is good to have some that are. We need to hear what they have to say; we don't need to follow their advice. McGeorge Bundy has made this point very nicely in an article in *Foreign Affairs* in 1969:

> There is an enormous gulf between what political leaders really think about nuclear weapons and what is assumed in complex calculations of relative "advantage" in simulated strategic warfare. Think-tank analysts can set levels of "acceptable" damage well up in the tens of millions of lives. They can assume that the loss of dozens of great cities is somehow a real choice for sane men. They are in an unreal world. In the real world of real political leaders—whether here or in the Soviet Union—a decision that would bring even one hydrogen bomb on one city of one's own country would be recognized in advance as a catastrophic blunder. . . .

And yet, Bundy goes on, the spell of expertise is such that "the internal politics of the arms race has remained the prisoner of its technology . . ."—and hence of its technologists.[6] The unreal world is important to science because it is a world where the imagination is free. But politics is the art of negotiating constraints, and a free imagination is not always what one wants in a political leader.

My third point stands in partial contradiction to the second. If some scientists and strategists live in other worlds, others are all too committed to this world—that is, to their own research, their labs, their work groups, and so on. They have particular interests, just like all the rest of us. The adoption of *this* strategy or *that* weapons system enfranchises a particular group of strategists and scientists and disenfranchises others; large-scale disarmament would be a general disenfranchisement. This is undoubtedly one reason for the appeal of what is called worst-case analysis: it serves as an effective bar even to limited disarmament. "The worst cases that have bureaucratic power," as Hal Feiveson argued recently in *Dissent*, "appear to be those that can be ameliorated only by new and expanded weapons systems. . . ."[7] Which systems are better is always a hard question, but the crucial point here is that when they try to answer this question, the experts are by no means detached and impartial. They constitute a highly politicized elite. Given the "structural necessities" of nuclear deterrence, theirs is often the scientific equivalent of court politics—all whispering and intrigue. True science, by contrast, is democratic, a world of colleagues who talk out loud about what they are doing. The experts talk only to people with the same security clearance as their own. They produce, writes Feiveson,

> technical reports that often are not read at all, in which the authors remain anonymous, and where there is, in striking contrast to serious scientific work, little survival value in being right, little stigma in being wrong. There is often no effective peer review in the bowels of the great technical bureaucracies. . . .[8]

The experts would do better if their private politics was relocated, if it found its place within a genuinely democratic debate. That requires some reappraisal of the "structural necessities" of deterrence, but those necessities don't in fact extend very far back from the positioning and programming of the actual weapons; they don't extend to the choice of weapons or of strategic plans. These choices don't have to be secret; they are not made under emergency conditions; and they don't require, except when they come to be implemented, a concentration of political authority. No one has argued that the current, relatively open, debate about weapons and strategies undermines the effectiveness of our nuclear deterrent. This or that outcome might do so, but not the debate itself. It is a good thing, then, that all sides have their experts, so that what the experts say is subject to peer review—and so that the peer reviews are subject in turn to lay review.

IV

We are back, then, with democratic decision making. The Soviets and the Chinese may have no alternative to court politics, but we do. Is our alternative better? I want to argue, briefly, that the choice I have already canvassed between normal and abnormal politics does not exhaust the possibilities of democracy—for the combination of the two produces something different from either one alone. The practical opposite of nuclear autocracy is not interest group bargaining, nor is it a "green" revolution. Let me suggest an analogy that may be helpful here even though it is by no means exact. The practical opposite of capitalist oligarchy in the democratic societies of western Europe and North America was neither so-called bourgeois parliamentarism nor revolutionary radicalism. It involved important features of both. The combination is not well understood or even widely studied because its concrete forms, the labor movement and social democracy, are disdained among intellectuals on the left and right alike. Nor did the labor movement or the social-democratic parties ever achieve a decisive success. The inequalities they meant to abolish are still with us, though they are far less disastrous than they once were for everyday social life. A similar politics aimed at ridding the world of nuclear weapons is similarly unlikely to achieve a decisive success, but it may well reduce the prospect of disaster.

No other success is at all probable. There isn't going to be a revolutionary replacement of the present nuclear regimes: the streets will not take over the corridors. And there is no reason to expect the men and women who inhabit the corridors to transcend their normal politics and negotiate a nuclear break-through. SALT II+n won't be the final and definitive treaty. Indeed, there won't be a SALT II, let alone a succession of SALTs, unless the hand of the corridor people is pushed by the passions of the street people. At the same time, marchers and demonstrators can't by themselves produce a treaty; their demands must be mediated through a political and then through a negotiating process. The political process is necessary so that the treaty meets the needs of, and actually reassures, ordinary citizens, who may or may not be marching. The negotiating process is necessary so that the treaty constrains our adversaries, in whose countries no one is marching. Abnormal politics without mediation would be very dangerous, for it isn't isomorphic across the lines of the Cold War. This is an important point, commonly emphasized by opponents of contemporary peace movements. But normal politics without popular mobilization and the drama of the movements is also very dangerous, for it poses no serious obstacle to the forward pressure of the arms race.

The combination of normal and abnormal politics is not easy. The two are often sharply opposed, and it is only from some distance that one can endorse both. In practice, up close, one can't endorse both, or one can do so only serially, not simultaneously. Sometimes it is necessary to march; sometimes to campaign and vote; sometimes to lobby (sometimes, maybe, to stay home and write articles). Because the nuclear danger requires us to be anxious and impatient, and because democratic politics requires a canny and persistent patience, we will often disagree about where and how to focus our energies. Such disagreements have been common in the history of the labor movement. I can see no way to avoid them or to resolve them; we will often divide our labors. Perhaps it is worth recommending mutual tolerance among the advocates of normal and abnormal politics, but the recommendation is probably a waste of time—a certain intoler-ance is one of the things that keeps us all going. Still, there is a significant sense in which both sides are right, for it is only in combination that we can find the appropriate form of political action and struggle to bring common sense to bear on nuclear policy. Although neither set of political strategists is likely to state it clearly, the goal is simply this: to achieve a minimal and so a relatively decent deterrent policy (there is no such thing as a deterrent policy decent *tout court*) and a controlled and limited nuclear regime.

I must confess at the end of this chapter to a faith in common sense—a democratic extension, I suppose, of McGeorge Bundy's faith in the wisdom of "real political leaders." Men and women with common sense won't fight nuclear wars. I mean, *our* common sense, a twentieth-century artifact, trained by catastrophe. It requires an esoteric strategic doctrine or one or another kind of religious or political fanaticism to contemplate using the weapons we now possess. But common sense still leaves a lot of room for argument. So it is important that the arguments be carried on in the open and that ordinary citizens listen and join in. None of us, however, can listen all the time; the issues are too hard and too painful. That's why the intermittent but passionate outbursts of abnormal politics are both unavoidable and necessary. The day-to-day drift is always toward specialized, secret, technically complex, and esoteric doctrine. But real political leaders, *if they hear the clamor of their constituents,* can stop the drift. Nuclear deterrence will defend democracy only if it is democratically constrained. The last few years give us some reason to hope that the risks of deterrence will eventually generate a democratic politics capable of limiting those risks. But the most difficult work remains to be done.

Notes

1. Robert Jay Lifton and Richard Falk, *Indefensible Weapons: The Political and Psychological Case Against Nuclearism* (New York: Basic Books, 1982), p. 262.

2. Solly Zuckerman, *Nuclear Illusion and Reality* (New York: Vintage Books, 1982), p. 83.

3. Ibid., p. 107.

4. Lifton and Falk, *Indefensible Weapons,* p. 139.

5. See Ford's "The Morality of Obliteration Bombing" in Richard Wasserstrom, *War and Morality* (Belmont, Calif.: Wadsworth, 1970), pp. 15–41; G.E.M. Anscombe, "Mr. Truman's Degree," in *Collected Philosophical Papers,* vol. III: *Ethics, Religion and Politics* (Minneapolis: University of Minnesota Press, 1981), pp. 62–71; and Walter Stein, ed., *Nuclear Weapons and Christian Conscience* (London: Merlin Press, 1961).

6. Bundy, "To Cap the Volcano," *Foreign Affairs,* October 1969, pp. 9–10, 13.

7. H.A. Feiveson, "Thinking about Nuclear Weapons," *Dissent,* Spring 1982, p. 187.

8. Ibid.

Part V
Conclusion

10
The Future of the Nuclear Debate

William V. O'Brien
Georgetown University

T he contributors to this book agree that there is a historic debate in progress on nuclear deterrence, defense, and arms control policies. They also agree that there is a concomitant normative debate, not only about the moral permissibility of various strategies and approaches to nuclear questions but also about the relative merits of the moral theories and approaches employed in analyses of nuclear issues. There is every prospect for a lengthy and profound continuation of these complementary debates. That being the case, no effort to analyze the empirical and moral issues of nuclear deterrence, defense, and arms control can avoid being, to some extent, ephemeral and tentative.

The interaction of strategic doctrine and technological developments is open-ended. The response of ethics to this open-ended process must necessarily involve frequent adjustments to confront issues not known heretofore and/or issues that have not been adequately treated in the past. Moreover, ethical doctrines and approaches are themselves subject to change, independent of the influence of nuclear issues.

Awareness of these facts enjoins modesty in those who would undertake analysis and prescription with respect to the moral dilemmas of the nuclear predicament. On the other hand, the ever-present danger of disaster inherent in the nuclear balance of terror requires that our modesty not serve as an excuse for avoiding participation in debates on our nuclear policies. The task of the moralist in addressing nuclear issues is, therefore, twofold: First, he or she must attempt to analyze the present state of the great issues of nuclear deterrence, defense and arms control and to make recommendations regarding those strategies or approaches that seem most consonant with moral principles. Second, the moralist must project trends in contemporary strategic and technological developments so as to reconcile, if possible, his or her analyses and prescriptions for the present with the expected realities of the future.

It is not enough for the moralist to prescribe maximum efforts to achieve arms control "progress" in the near term. He or she must attempt to foresee the long-term implications of such progress in the light not only of known technological trends but also of future political-strategic possibilities. Necessarily, these efforts become increasingly speculative as future projection is extended. Nevertheless, the need for review and revision of estimates of both present and future situations is a continuing one. The moralist's responsibility for keeping up with the changing empirical situation is unavoidable.

Acceptance of the responsibility for following changing trends in strategic and technological realities also serves another important purpose. It may tend to discourage facile or utopian approaches to nuclear issues. Apocalyptic appeals for the elimination of nuclear weapons, if not the elimination of war itself, imply the possibility of solving the problems of nuclear deterrence and war and of human conflict. Yet there is no reasonable prospect of such revolutionary solutions in sight. Even the most optimistic estimates of prospects for solving these problems are subject to the challenges of ongoing political-strategic and technological changes. In any event, none of the contributors to this book encouraged hopes for revolutionary solutions to nuclear dilemmas. The implication of all of the chapters is that the practical and moral task of the strategic thinker and the moralist is one of containing and ameliorating our nuclear predicament as part of a very long term effort that may produce a safer and better world.

The contributors to this book leave us with an agenda for the continuing nuclear debate. Though by no means definitive, this agenda identifies the core issues that must be addressed as the debate continues. This agenda raises questions, first, with respect to the ethical approaches employed so far in dealing with nuclear issues and their sufficiency for the future. Second, the agenda suggested by our contributors involves the further reconsideration of basic strategic doctrines of deterrence and defense as well as the empirical assumptions on which they rest.

The agenda resulting from this book, then, raises two questions:

1. What ethical doctrine or approaches are most appropriate for the analysis of moral issues of nuclear deterrence, defense, and arms control?

2. What strategic doctrines, based on what empirical assumptions, are most likely to produce policies that provide effective deterrence and defense against aggression, are conducive to significant arms control progress, and still conform to the constraints of morality?

Moral Doctrine and Nuclear Dilemmas

In the preceding chapters, three principal doctrines or approaches to nuclear deterrence, defense, and arms control have been considered: pacifism, just war, and the ethics of distress or supreme emergency. Pacifist approaches have been referred to but not discussed at length, since the book is oriented toward a just war perspective. The two basic moral positions explored have been just war and the ethics of distress. Mara's critique of these two positions in the light of the Platonic-Aristotelian approach to political theory gives some indication of the availability of alternative approaches. The position he outlines, however, has not, to our knowledge, been taken prominently in the literature on morality and nuclear deterrence and war. It should be observed, however, that there is a historic connection between the Aristotelian concepts of man as a political animal and the state as a natural and indispensable social necessity and the Thomistic-Suarezian political thought that underlies just war doctrine. It would be interesting to pursue this connection with respect to the emphasis in just war doctrine, as understood by Johnson, Langan, Dougherty, and myself, on the value of the state and the right to defend it with just means.

In the present debate, however, the alternative moral frameworks being employed have been just war and supreme emergency (or ethics of distress)—two very different kinds of moral approaches. Just war is generally seen as the normal approach to the morality of war. The very formulation of concepts such as *ethics of distress* and *supreme emergency* denotes the need for abnormal approaches for abnormal situations. The two concepts cannot be compared in terms of their comparative appropriateness to the same situation. Rather, their appropriateness turns on our estimate of the nuclear situation. Is it essentially normal or abnormal?

The key proposition in question is that of Michael Walzer: "Nuclear weapons explode the theory of just war."[1] But this proposition and Walzer's supporting analysis in *Just and Unjust Wars* turn on assumptions that nuclear war will inevitably escalate to levels that violate all just war criteria. This assumption is widely shared. Former U.S. secretaries of defense, eminent military commanders, prominent scientists, and bishops have come to the same conclusion.[2]

Among the contributors to this book, however, Johnson, Langan, Dougherty, and I have refused to accept this conclusion as unchallengeable. It is, first, a speculative conclusion, not at present amenable to proof. Second, it is necessarily based on perceptions of developments in nuclear deterrence and defense throughout an era dominated by deterrence-only policies that placed total reliance on the efficacy of deterrence and eschewed discussion of nuclear war fighting if deterrence failed. Serious, sustained efforts to make possible limited nuclear deterrence and defense through deterrence-plus strategies are comparatively recent and incomplete. Nevertheless, a conservatism warranted by the awesome subject matter could well engender a presumption against the feasability of limited nuclear war and, accordingly, against the sufficiency of just war doctrine to deal with nuclear issues. This would leave a normative vacuum into which some concept of ethics of distress or supreme emergency might properly be introduced.

The choice of an appropriate and sufficient basis for moral analysis, however, is further complicated by the distinction between deterrence and defense, between threat and use. Theorists such as Walzer and Hollenbach, who start with the assumption that nuclear weapons cannot be used within just war limits, fall naturally into a deterrence-only approach to the utility of nuclear weapons. They accept the necessity of nuclear deterrence but not the legitimacy of nuclear defense against aggression should deterrence fail. To the extent that this is the case, the ethics of distress/supreme emergency arguments are advanced only to justify or explain the maintenance of a deterrent posture, not the actual conduct of nuclear war if that posture fails to deter. I fail to find in any of the discussions of ethics of distress, as set forth in the chapters of Fathers Hollenbach and Langan, reporting on the positions of the French and German bishops and Walzer, any hint that these "abnormal" ethical approaches have been invoked with a view to justifying the actual conduct of nuclear war. They have been raised in defense of the threat of nuclear war as a necessary deterrent.

If one takes the deterrence-plus position, as I do, together with Johnson and Dougherty, an ethics of distress/supreme emergency approach appears to be neither necessary nor helpful.[3] It is not necessary, in our view, because the assumption that nuclear war is uncontrollable is unproved and unhelpful and because it provides little or no guidance with respect to the contingency of nuclear war fighting, a contingency we believe must be faced if there is to be credible deterrence.

Here we find an example of the need for reconsidering normative positions in the light of changing empirical circumstances and possibilities. Walzer confines his inquiry into the possibility of limited nuclear war to a short section mainly focused on Paul Ramsey's efforts to reconcile just war doctrine with the strategic concepts of the time at which he wrote (1960s).[4] This effort, however, is already almost twenty years old. Neither Ramsey, nor Walzer, writing more recently, had before them the emerging possibilities of effective counterforce nuclear war and antimissile defense that might drastically alter the variables in nuclear deterrence and defense.[5] Were Walzer to produce a second edition of *Just and Unjust Wars*, he would surely have to revise this section. He might well, of course, come to the same conclusion, as more recent authoritative treatments have. Nevertheless, the case for Walzer's supreme-emergency, deterrence-only position is subject to review both on empirical and normative grounds. One has the impression that the ethics of distress concepts advanced by the French and German bishops, as reported by Father Hollenbach, have not been sufficiently thought through or elaborated to warrant speculation about their position with respect to the actual conduct of nuclear defense.

In any case, it is worthwhile to examine the concepts of ethics of distress or supreme emergency on grounds other than their sufficiency for the case of defense rather than deterrence. Father Langan rightly raises the question of the nature and duration of "emergency" ethics.[6] Walzer indicates that the supreme-emergency doctrine justifies the threat to commit murder. He wants to emphasize both the normative determination that the act threatened is criminal and the empirical determination that it is necessary to make this criminal threat in order to protect the most fundamental values of a threatened society. As to duration, Walzer indicates that the condition of supreme emergency necessitating reliance on a deterrent threat to commit criminal acts is open-ended. He says that a state of necessity is never stable and is subject to historic change. Walzer concludes that "we are under an obligation to seize upon opportunities of escape, even to take risks for the sake of such opportunities."[7]

The extremity of the moral predicament to which Walzer applies the concept of supreme emergency is summarized in his concluding sentence: "So, the readiness to murder is balanced, or should be, by the readiness not to murder, not to threaten murder, as soon as alternative ways to peace can be found." This sentence is written by one who believes that "Nuclear war is and will remain morally unacceptable, and there is no case for its rehabilitation."[8] Since nuclear weapons cannot be uninvented and the prospects for substantial nuclear proliferation are all too threatening, the duration of Walzer's supreme emergency might well be permanent.

If there is a serious prospect that we will face a period of protracted balance of terror, morally explicable in the concept of supreme emergency, it may be useful to compare Walzer's concept of supreme emergency with other normative doctrines of necessity. There are a number of these doctrines in domestic and international law. Domestic law in the Western legal systems recognizes abnormal states of necessity with respect to both individual and state actions. With respect to individual actions, the law of necessity takes the form of excusing the commission of criminal acts when they are done in circumstances of extreme necessity. In the continental European legal systems, terms such as *titre justificatif exceptionel* or *cause de justification* are employed to explain situations in which the state of necessity produces the effect of individual "irresponsibility."[9] Classic cases involved, for example, theft by a poor woman of food for her starving children.[10] English common law has occasionally dealt with cases of murder and even cannibalism by persons struggling to survive a shipwreck.[11]

These examples suffice to make the point that, in domestic legal systems, exceptions of necessity are *very* exceptional. The usual rationale for the exceptions of necessity is that the acts committed remain objectively criminal notwithstanding the law's lenience in excusing the guilty party from the normal legal consequences of his act. This rationale might resemble somewhat Walzer's concept of supreme emergency, in which the threat of murder is condoned because of necessity—but note that Walzer's case involves only threat, not act. The similarity is further limited by the fact that the domestic-law concept of necessity operates within an advanced legal system wherein authoritative legal decision makers are entitled to excuse criminal acts done in circumstances of extreme emergency, as they are also competent to excuse acts done under duress or by persons lacking mental competence. Walzer is dealing with actions governed much more loosely by the decentralized, primitive system of positive international law and by the moral doctrine of just war. There is no higher authority to authorize exceptions of necessity in international relations. Absent the rare case of enforcement of international law by war crimes proceedings or otherwise, the supreme-emergency argument is one advanced to one's own public and the world at large, not a legal plea decided on and sanctioned by an effective legal system.[12]

With regard to actions by states, an ethics of distress or supreme emergency is known to most systems of public law in the form of state of siege or martial law.[13] President Lincoln's invocations of emergency powers in the Civil War involved serious deviations from the normal rule of law and were of extended duration. Lincoln's measures were not checked by the operation of judicial review during the war.[14] Other U.S. presidents have exercised extraordinary wartime powers, which, likewise, were not checked either by the courts or by Congress during the war. Although there has always been a day of reckoning when at least some major wartime measures were condemned as unconstitutional by the courts, the U.S. experience has been that a president may go quite far in claiming supreme-emergency powers. However, no lasting injury has been done to the U.S. constitutional system by these exceptional presidential actions. (I would not consider the cumulative increase in presidential powers in the fields of foreign affairs and defense to be injurious, though this is perhaps debatable.)[15]

Other nations have not been so fortunate. Adolph Hitler's exploitation of emergency powers provided in the Weimar Constitution made possible many of his abuses that were technically legal.[16] Dictators frequently follow similar courses in expanding their power under color of emergency provisions that are either vaguely recognized in the law or simply alleged to be inherent in the ruler's office and responsibilities. Such abuses of supreme emergency powers often continue indefinitely, sometimes camouflaged by spurious legislation passed once control is in the hands of the usurping elements. Prolonged rule under a state of siege or martial law is usually considered evidence of a profound failure of government that is widely deplored by both domestic and international public opinion—for example, the state of siege regime of General Augusto Pinochet in Chile.[17]

The international law of war recognizes military necessity as a basic principle. That principle, however, limits conduct not only to that which is proportionate to a lawful end but also to measures that are permitted by the law of war. In my view, legitimate military necessity is also constrained by natural law principles such as those characterized as the principle of humanity in international conventions and the judgments of war crimes tribunals. Military necessity is not a warrant for the *exceptional* but a guideline for the permissible in war. The prevailing view of publicists, as of the U.S. government, is that the positive principle of military necessity permits all measures to which a belligerent is lawfully entitled. Claims for more are rejected. Thus, the concept of legitimate military necessity denotes normal, not exceptional, behavior and is related to the just war doctrine's war-conduct law *(jus in bello)* rather than to an ethics of distress or supreme emergency.[18]

The only international law doctrine resembling Walzer's supreme-emergency doctrine is the German *Kriegsraison* theory. In the years between the Franco-Prussian War and World War I, German philosophers, political and legal theorists, international lawyers, and military writers developed the *Kriegsraison* (military necessity) doctrine. Under this doctrine, the international law of war was considered to be an imperfect source of limitations on belligerent behavior. The doctrine held that "necessity knows no law" *(Not kennt kein Gebot)*. Therefore, legal limitations ought never to prevent a state from gaining victory in war, thereby protecting its fundamental values and vital interests. If victory could be achieved while generally obeying the law, so much the better. If, however, defeat might result from adherence to the limits of the law, then the law must be ignored.[19]

In the years before 1899, when the *Kriegsraison* doctrine was being developed, the international law of war consisted mainly of basic principles and customary rules. The *Kriegsraison* theorists took advantage of this state of the law to deprecate it as something less than fully binding on belligerents. Their maxim, *"Kriegsraison geht vor Kriegsmanier"* ("Military necessity takes precedence over the customary manner of conducting war") implied that the law of war was more a matter of comity or recommended behavior than of binding law.[20] This was unjustified, but the gap between open-ended military necessity and the law of war became crucial after the appearance of detailed conventional law in the 1899 Hague Conventions, to which Germany was a party. Reiterated and supplemented in the 1907 Hague Conventions, which were to be the principal sources of the international law of war on land throughout most of the twentieth century, these conventions were clearly intended to be legally binding on the parties. Yet up to and during World War I, German publicists, officials, and military commanders claimed that military necessity, reflecting fundamental *raison d'état,* should always prevail over the law of war.[21]

The sources of the *Kriegsraison* doctrine included some of the most influential political, legal, and military theorists.[22] At the heart of the doctrine is a Hegelian notion of the state as the highest source of values and, accordingly, of the inadmissibility of permitting the state's defeat and the subordination of its values to those of a conqueror. In this sense, the *Kriegsraison* doctrine tends to be more an argument that necessity (of state) *is* the law than that necessity (of state) knows no law. At the level of military thought, the influence of von Clausewitz prevailed. From Clausewitzian perspectives, adherence to marginal, would-be rules of international law must not be permitted to interfere with the conduct of war in accordance with the principles inherent in the nature of war.[23] These and other related concepts hardened in the development of a vision of Germany as being *sui generis,* a nation above all nations, divinely destined to prevail. The whole doctrine was then applied by strategists and geopoliticians who argued that Germany was encircled by treacherous enemies and that, in this state of *protracted emergency,* all measures necessary to the salvation and advancement of Germany were justified. Chancellor Bethmann-Hollweg's famous speech to the Reichstag, on August 4, 1914, justified the violation of Belgian neutrality, to which Germany was pledged together with the other principal European states, as follows:

> We are in a state of legitimate defense *(wir sind jetz in der Notwehr).* Necessity knows no law. Our troops have occupied Luxembourg and have perhaps already penetrated into Belgium. This is against the law of nations *(das widerspricht, den Gebeten des Voelkerrechts).* France, it is true, has declared to Brussels that it is determined to respect the neutrality of Belgium as long as its adversary respects it, but we know that France was ready to invade Belgium. France can afford to wait; we cannot. It is for that reason that we have been compelled to ignore the just protests of the governments of Luxembourg and Belgium. The injustices which we thus commit we will repair as soon as our military object has been attained. Anybody who is threatened as we are threatened and is fighting for its highest possessions can only have one thought—how he is to hack his way through *(wie er sich durchhaut).*[24]

Bethmann-Hollweg never produced any evidence that France was preparing to invade Belgium. On the other hand, the famous von Schlieffen Plan to outflank and crush the French armies west of Paris notoriously required that a large part of the German attacking force march through Belgium. This plan had been the basis of German strategy for over ten years. It was the operative source of Germany's necessity, not any developments at the beginning of the war. To be sure, the von Schlieffen Plan was intended to deal with the problem of a two-front war and to solve it by making possible a quick knockout blow in the west while holding in the east. The von Schlieffen Plan was based on the assumption that Germany's geopolitical-military predicament warranted whatever action might be necessary to ensure victory. This all made sense in terms of the German contention that Germany was in an extended state of supreme emergency or necessity that justified all measures taken to ensure its victorious survival.

It may very well be the case that other nations and statesmen have violated international law as egregiously as did Germany and the Kaiser's government, but they were not as brazenly candid about their rationales. In any event, this and other German proclamations of the *Kriegsraison* doctrine provided the allies with a rich source of propaganda. The "Huns" were painted as war criminals who deliberately violated international law in the course of their imperialistic and aggressive wars. The *Kriegsraison* doctrine was condemned by all leading non-German international law publicists.[25] Reflections of this condemnation have continued as late as the 1956 U.S. Army Field Manual 27-10, *The Law of Land Warfare.*[26]

It is not necessary to review all allied practices in World War I to state that, particularly with respect to the law of neutral rights at sea, the allies were guilty of their own violations of international law. They had, however, the good sense not to invoke *Kriegsraison* arguments. Rather, most of their questionable behavior was justified as reprisals for antecedent German violations of the law. Some dubious reflections of the reprisal justification appeared in the early phases of World War II, notably with respect to aerial bombing of cities.[27] But these end runs around the law remain modest beside the supreme-emergency claims of Winston Churchill on which Walzer relies for his supreme-emergency doctrine.[28]

To the extent that we accept the Churchillian supreme-emergency justification, everything that was considered necessary to the defeat of the Axis powers in World War II was justified. For example, the strategic bombing of Germany and Japan was deliberately waged in a countervalue, "city-busting" manner in order to break the will of the enemy civilian populations as well as to inflict military damage.[29] Virtually no criticism was leveled against these policies within the United Nations countries. The U.S. Army Air Force at times argued for a more counterforce bombing strategy, partly as a matter of military preference in consonance with the principle of economy of force and partly for moral reasons. Technical limitations, however, obliged the United States to cooperate in essentially countervalue, countercity "area raids" throughout most of the war.[30] On the home fronts these raids were generally greeted with almost biblical savagery and satisfaction. They were part of "total war" against "the Nazis." How did those policies and attitudes differ from those of the Germans who invoked the *Kriegsraison* doctrine?

The essential difference would seem to be that the values at stake and the plausible threat to them appear to us to be bona fide in the case of the United Nations in World War II but not in the case of the Germans in World War I. I take it that it is unnecessary to discuss justifications for the conduct of the Third Reich in World War II. As indicated, the *Kriegsraison* doctrine was based on the assumption that the German state possessed superior worth and had the right to greater latitude in self-preservation and self-advancement than other states. Few would accept this claim. Germany would be eligible for a supreme-emergency claim if its very existence and its fundamental values were at stake, but no more eligible than any other state. (I here eschew, since Walzer does, the issue of the comparative justice of states.) Moreover, to turn to Walzer's second criterion, the threat to Germany's survival and even to its vital interests was never so great as to warrant a supreme-emergency argument. One has but to look to the fate of Germany after a resounding (but not total) defeat to see that its existence and values really were not in question in World War I.

The question still remains whether Churchill was right in claiming supreme emergency for Britain and its allies in World War II. To answer that question, it is important to distinguish two threats, and the distinction is one that is extremely important to our current debates over nuclear deterrence and defense. Britain claimed supreme emergency for itself but also for a number of other states that had been or would soon be victims of Nazi (later Japanese) aggression. So one must consider whether Churchill's supreme-emergency claims were valid for the case of Britain standing alone, or whether they required the additional dimension of Britain standing for all states threatened by Hitler.

Walzer concludes that the existence of Great Britain as a free society was a sufficient cause to warrant the invocation of supreme-emergency powers, given the Nazi threat in terms of its nature, imminence, and probable consequences if successful. He reluctantly concedes that his "war convention" might have to bow before the exigencies of saving Britain from the Nazis.[31] That for him is the harder case. It is less difficult for Walzer to concede extraordinary powers to Britain as the leader of nations fighting the broader, open-ended Nazi threat. So there is a particular threat to Britain and a collective threat to a large number of other states. Supreme emergency applies, in Walzer's view, to both.[32] In this analysis he defines the character of the Nazi regime, the reality and imminence of the threat it posed, as the very definition, by example, of the kind of threat that warrants, if anything does, invocation of supreme emergency.[33]

It is instructive to note that whereas Walzer's general approach to aggression eschews the issue of the comparative justice of the belligerents, it is crucial in his theory of supreme emergency. Here the comparison with Germany in World War I is apposite. Despite their wartime propaganda, Germany and its enemies (except perhaps tsarist Russia, which did not survive the war) were not different in kind as polities. It was very unpleasant for Germany to be occupied in part by the Western allies after 1918, but there was no true threat to Germany's existence as a nation or to its fundamental values. To be sure, World War I did threaten and result in the extinction of Austria-Hungary, for better or worse in terms of the character of the regime. It was arguments of a supreme emergency for Germany, however, that dominated the conduct and the atmosphere of World War I. Austria-Hungary's predicament was not as central, in part because its military contribution and influence were decidedly inferior to Germany's. The stakes in World War II were quite different. Defeat by Hitler's Germany and its allies meant the end of freedom and fundamental human rights.

At this point one might pause and ask why, given this clear evidence of a United Nations just cause, it is necessary to invoke supreme emergency. Why not simply operate on the basis of just war doctrine? The reason this is difficult is that the United Nations proceeded to wage total war against the Axis in a manner that severely violated the war-conduct part of just war doctrine.[34] Walzer apparently feels that both the intention and the behavior of Britain and its allies were so violative of just war standards, notably with respect to strategic bombing of Axis cities, that a supreme-emergency justification is necessary to defend these policies. In pursuing this point, he concludes that the United Nations exceeded the limits not only of just war doctrine but also of supreme emergency.[35] In this respect the United Nations carried out policies in World War II that resemble the *Kriegsraison* approach that necessity knows no law. Necessity was kept open throughout the war notwithstanding the increasing certainty of the defeat of the Axis, and strategic bombing policies were pursued in a manner that can only be defended plausibly by supreme-emergency arguments.

In effect, Churchill's version of supreme necessity lasted for the duration and justified continued countervalue attacks on German population centers right down to the final defeat of Hitler, as well, by extension of comparable attacks on Japan ending with the use of the atomic bomb. Churchill's version, if one may attribute the collective United Nations strategy to him—or, more accurately, the Churchill-Roosevelt-Truman strategy—justified all measures of total war to defeat the Axis. This strategy thereby fell into the pattern mentioned by Mara of turning exceptional measures into standard operating procedure to the long-term detriment of prospects for conducting just war.[36] In summary, the United Nations supreme-emergency policies differed from those of the German proponents of *Kriegsraison* of World War I in that their justification was much more plausible, but they resembled the Germans in their propensity to use exceptional and morally impermissible means beyond the point where they could be justified by even a bona fide argument of necessity.

Walzer's version of supreme necessity, on the other hand, has a built-in limitation. Emergency measures must continue only as long as the emergency truly exists. When the emergency is no longer so stark and imminent that exceptional measures are truly necessary to deal with it, the belligerent must revert to the normal limits of just war.[37] This is such an important element of Walzer's supreme-emergency concept that it probably warrants specification as a third criterion to follow those of real threat and imminence. Abatement of the threat is implied as a component of imminence, but it is so important that it should be identified explicitly. Thus, the fact that the Western allies in World War II did not see the need to return to just war standards insofar as strategic bombing was concerned indicates the risks of the supreme-emergency approach. Moreover, it cannot be repeated too often that the effect of World War II countervalue bombing precedents on the decisions to use the atomic bomb and on subsequent nuclear deterrence and defense policies bears out all too clearly the dangers of establishing a supreme-emergency mentality at the heart of strategic planning and policies. Just as state of siege is an exceptional condition that tends to become pernicious if perpetuated in a political society, supreme emergency is a very dangerous basis for moral justification of acts of war.

Nevertheless, supreme emergency has been proposed as the most appropriate, or least inappropriate, basis for justifying nuclear deterrence. Is this the best approach to moral analysis of nuclear deterrence and defense? Before answering that question, it should first be observed that all of the preceding arguments of necessity, with which Walzer's supreme emergency has been compared, were addressed primarily to the issue of justifying exceptions to positive law, domestic or international. It should be further acknowledged that international law has provided only very imperfect and uncertain rules for the conduct of war in the total-war era of this century. Thus the British-U.S. countercity bombings of World War II were violative of the just war principle of discrimination and, very likely, of the principle of proportion. The international law principle of noncombatant immunity, however, was so widely violated in both world wars that one cannot say that the United Nations forces clearly violated international law with their strategic bombing policies.[38]

In the case of nuclear deterrence, conventional international law has been developed so as to exclude reference to nuclear means.[39] The practice of states *is* nuclear deterrence and preparations for nuclear war. To be sure, the principles of proportion and discrimination are principles of international law as well as of just war. But the normative character of the just war principles stands independently of the practice of states. In brief, invoking supreme emergency or necessity in order to justify exceptions to rules of the international law of war is an extreme and controversial step, but it is not as serious as claiming the right to violate moral rules such as the principles of just war doctrine. State practice, including retrogressions from earlier standards, can change international law. But state practice cannot change or "explode" basic moral principles. If, by *explosion,* we mean that these principles are so massively violated as to vitiate their effectiveness, the conclusion is that great wrongs are being done, not that the moral principles are inadequate.

Nevertheless, the dilemmas of nuclear deterrence and defense are so intractable that their relevance to supreme-emergency concepts should be examined. Of Walzer's criteria, the first, a real threat to the continued existence of a polity and the fundamental values of its people, is satisfied. In my view, it exists in the threat of forcible imposition by the Soviet Union and other communist states of *gulag* societies on the rest of the world. As I remarked earlier, in chapter 7, not everyone is so clear about this threat. I am also convinced that the threat is a transcendent one, potentially dangerous to many nations not presently suffering under communist totalitarian regimes. To deter and defend against this threat is to assume a posture and responsibilities very much like those of the principal United Nations belligerents in World War II. The agenda of security issues for the 1980s must include a renewed effort to assure consensus on this point. Establishment of a credible threat has been shown to be the essential starting point for just war justifications of deterrence and defense. A fortiori, it is the indispensable foundation for invocation of an ethics of distress or supreme emergency.

As to Walzer's second criterion, imminence of the threat, it would appear that Soviet and other communist military power, as well as a record of aggression and intervention in many parts of the world, make the communist threat to the noncommunist world imminent, of open-ended duration, and widespread. At this point in the analysis, however, it appears that there is an implied third criterion in the supreme-emergency concept. Growing out of the requirement for imminence in order to *initiate* measures justified by supreme emergency, it is required to *terminate* the abnormal license of supreme emergency or necessity when it appears that the normal just war prerogatives of a just belligerent should suffice to protect the existence and fundamental values of the threatened polities.

Thus Walzer objects to the continuation of countervalue city bombing in World War II beyond the point when the danger of Nazi victory was imminent. From that point, he argues, it was possible to win the war within the bounds of his "war convention"—that is, within the limits of just war doctrine.[40] Note that in taking this position Walzer is distinguishing his supreme-emergency doctrine from the *Kriegsraison* doctrine. The *Kriegsraison* claims operate constantly to the benefit of the state claiming necessity, whereas Walzer's supreme-emergency claims are limited to periods of extraordinary necessity that will presumably end. With their end, emergency powers cease.

The state of emergency or necessity may end because the threat that engendered it is ended or withdrawn, by whatever means. The state of emergency may also end because, although the threat remains great and imminent, the means available to the threatened state or states are decisively enhanced, making possible the relinquishment of the blank check of emergency powers and the resumption of defense in consonance with the normal moral and legal restraints of just war. At whatever point it could be said that the supreme emergency of Britain and its allies ended in World War II, the point would not be that of the absolute certainty of the defeat of the Axis. It would be the point, for example, at which the likely survival of its Soviet ally and the entrance of the United States into the war assured Britain that its supreme emergency was over.

The same logic applies to the case of applying supreme-emergency or ethics of distress reasoning to the moral analysis of nuclear deterrence and defense. If it be granted, for the sake of argument, that there is a plausible, imminent threat of a magnitude warranting invocation of the supreme-emergency justification, is it necessary to do so? If we hold that the reality of the threat and its imminence are relatively constant, the issue becomes that of evaluating whether there are prospects for bringing new options, decisively improving the capabilities of the threatened state to deal with the threat. If the means assumed in Walzer's analysis—essentially countervalue deterrence-only nuclear deterrence—could be so enhanced as to alter the prospects for successful deterrence and/or defense within just war limits, the warrant for invoking supreme emergency would not hold.

We are brought back, then, to the fact that the choice of moral approach to nuclear deterrence turns on one's estimate of the character and potentialities of nuclear war and one's choice of deterrent posture. If one believes that nuclear war inevitably escalates beyond any practically and morally acceptable level, one adopts a deterrence-only posture and works for relief through arms control and mitigation of international conflict. If one believes that nuclear war may be controlled and that nuclear deterrence requires the capability and intention to conduct controlled, limited nuclear defense, one adopts a deterrence-plus posture and works for the development of strategies and capabilities maximizing the limited nuclear war option. From such a deterrence/defense posture arms control progress and conflict avoidance and mitigation may be pursued, but the priority requirement is establishment of a just and limited nuclear security base.

If one's understanding of the limits of rational and moral use of nuclear weapons leads to a deterrence-only posture, a supreme-emergency rationale is probably the only moral position available short of pacifism. The desperate, abnormal character of the supreme-emergency rationale is required for a posture that cannot speak to the contingency of failed deterrence in terms other than the alternatives of uncontrollable nuclear war or surrender. Note, however, that although Walzer's version of supreme emergency insists that the actual doing of the immoral acts ("murder") threatened in nuclear deterrence as he understands it are not justified by extreme emergency, acts that he condemns as violative of just war standards (strategic bombing) were continued by the United Nations forces in World War II under the Churchill-Roosevelt-Truman version of supreme emergency. Although it is appropriate to condemn the German *Kriegsraison* doctrine because of its open-ended and unrestrained character, we should remember that the invocation of *any* supreme-emergency doctrine is more likely to resemble *Kriegsraison,* or the Churchill-Roosevelt-Truman doctrine of supreme emergency, than the Walzer doctrine.

If, on the other hand, one believes that the limitation of nuclear war is a possibility, particularly if it is made a priority policy objective and a moral imperative, then one takes a deterrence-plus approach that may be consonant with just war principles. The link between deterrence-plus and just war is not, however, automatic. This is a point properly brought out by the U.S. Catholic bishops and Father Hollenbach.[41] One might take a deterrence-plus, war-fighting approach and *not* intend to conform to all just war limits. I have done so in justifying selective countervalue attacks on population centers as the only means of intrawar deterrence against continuation of such attacks on one's own population centers.[42]

My 1981 position reflects my view that it is possible to violate just war conduct rules without necessarily vitiating the overall claim to be fighting a just war. What is wrongly done remains wrong, but even serious violations of war-conduct law do not, in my view, preclude the possibility that an overall assessment of compliance with just war conditions may conclude that a belligerent is just.[43] I would still prefer to deal with exceptional measures within just war doctrine than to suspend operations of that doctrine and rely on an ethics of distress or supreme-emergency justification for such acts. Even so, I have now abandoned my justification of any countervalue, counterpopulation attacks. By so doing I raise the perennial question of loss of deterrence potential as the price for threatening only what is permissible under just war standards. As usual, the choices are between undesirable alternatives.

To reject the possibilities of a deterrence-plus just and limited deterrence/ defense approach is to remain in the deterrence-only supreme-emergency posture described by Walzer. As he points out, this is an unstable position, resting on the exigencies of an extreme and volatile predicament.[44] As has been indicated in the survey of other doctrines of necessity, the normative justification of supreme emergency is a very exceptional one, usually considered to be tolerable only for the duration of an extreme crisis. Whether in domestic or international law and politics, long-term reliance on the extraordinary plea of supreme emergency or necessity is considered regrettable at best and morally suspect at worst. It is not too much to say that there is a third criterion for invocation of supreme emergency, beyond those of real threat and their imminence. This is the requirement that the emergency powers claimed must be relinquished as soon as they are not clearly required.

Walzer's evaluation of our predicament in 1977, when our deterrent posture was still in a kind of neo–mutual assured destruction phase, concluded that nuclear deterrence was morally explicable only in terms of the concept of supreme emergency. Are we condemned forever to reliance on such a deterrent and to the grim justification of supreme emergency or ethics of distress? We need not be if we can alter the facts of our predicament. That might be done by abating the underlying conflicts that give rise to our situation and/or by some extraordinary breakthrough in arms control. Absent success in such efforts, escape from the kind of situation requiring appeal to supreme-emergency justifications must be in the direction of developing alternative means of deterrence and defense that would permit return to the normal morality of just war doctrine.

One other possibility is suggested by the implications of the Churchillian supreme-emergency doctrine of World War II. That doctrine was invoked to justify extraordinary measures to protect Britain's existence and fundamental values. It was also invoked on behalf of a much broader array of threatened nations. The World War II generation learned from the experience of the 1930s that collective deterrence and defense are necessary against aggression. Since then that lesson has been applied in the concept of the U.S. strategic nuclear umbrella that must be coupled with the theater and local deterrence/defense systems, nuclear and conventional, that bar Soviet and other aggression and intimidation.

As I have suggested briefly in chapter 7, the strategic and moral debates in which we are now engaged may force reconsideration of the post–World War II maxim, institutionalized in NATO and various collective defense arrangements, that "an attack against one is an attack against all."[45] If the more pessimistic deterrence-only view is taken, the United States ought not permit itself to be drawn into a nuclear war because of a Warsaw Pact attack on NATO countries, or an attack by the Soviet Union or some other aggressor against South Korea or Japan, or any attack against a U.S. ally. If the prospects for controlled nuclear defense are so hopeless, the United States certainly should not consider any recourse to nuclear weapons except in a last-ditch retaliation for Soviet nuclear aggression against the U.S. homeland.

A strategic predicament so desperate as to warrant invocation of an ethics of distress or supreme emergency is perhaps unavoidable with respect to one's own existence and the survival of one's own way of life, but it is certainly possible to limit the scope of the predicament by excluding others from the strategic nuclear umbrella of extended U.S. deterrence. I have already proposed this by joining those who urge a policy of no first use of nuclear weapons, even with respect to conventional aggression against NATO.[46]

The consequences of withdrawal, in whole or in part, of the U.S. nuclear deterrent umbrella from collective defense systems around the world might well be very bad. As chapter 8 by Keegan points out, conventional defense, though perhaps preferable to limited nuclear defense with its risks of escalation, is already terribly destructive and may well be difficult to conduct within just war limits.[47] Moreover, the unlikelihood of U.S. nuclear intervention may very probably increase the temptations for aggression against nations formerly protected by the U.S. strategic and theater nuclear deterrence umbrellas. Other problems could and should be raised in the debates ahead. Should a moralist encourage the United States to divest itself of its worldwide collective defense responsibilities in order to narrow sharply the immediate prospects for confrontations leading to superpower nuclear war? If so, what are the implications for the abandoned nations? Would they face even more imminent threats? Would they, in turn, develop nuclear capabilities less amenable to an effort to conduct controlled, limited nuclear war than seems possible for the United States? Is a world in which the United States takes on the practical and moral responsibilities for strategic nuclear deterrence and defense of the noncommunist world, bad as it is, preferable to one in which abandonment of those responsibilities produces a rush to local nuclear deterrence/defense capabilities, most of them probably in the form of minimum deterrence posture of the most countervalue, counterpopulation variety?

Whether the United States continues to offer extended nuclear deterrence to nations threatened by aggression, or withdraws to Fortress America to defend its own existence and values against direct attack, some form of nuclear defense must be developed against the contingency of failed deterrence. Walzer's extreme-emergency concept does not apply to nuclear defense. One does not know what, if any, guidance can be derived from recent ethics of distress positions with respect to the actual conduct of nuclear war. If nuclear war ever becomes a reality, just war doctrine will remain the moral basis for efforts to limit it. I have discussed in chapter 7 the requirements for a just and limited nuclear war and have assessed the difficulties and possibilities involved.[48] The agenda for the continuing debate, in my view, consists in two empirical questions. First, can prospects for controlling nuclear war be improved so that the war-fighting contingencies of a nuclear deterrence/defense posture do not threaten escalation and destruction of the very societies and values defended? Second, even if limited nuclear war can be shown to be feasible, will a nuclear deterrence/ defense posture confined to the threat to retaliate with limited nuclear means, and only limited nuclear means, be adequate to deter nuclear aggression? These questions will be considered briefly in setting the agenda for future debates on strategic doctrine.

Strategic Doctrine in the Post-MAD World

There is little point in speculating about the possibility of just and limited nuclear deterrence and defense if expert opinion rules it out. The difficulties in developing a counterforce nuclear posture sufficient to deter and defend against nuclear aggression are formidable. Only a very strong and continuing set of efforts on a number of fronts can overcome these difficulties. If there is not a strong consensus on the necessity of attempting to develop just and limited nuclear war strategies to replace existing strategies, the judgment that the task is impossible will become a self-fulfilling prophecy.

To obtain such a consensus, it will be necessary to achieve recognition that arms control is not a panacea; that nuclear weapons will exist in someone's hand for a long time, possibly forever; and that some kind of effective nuclear deterrent, consonant with just war requirements, must be made a reality. We are far from that consensus today. The U.S. Catholic bishops, for their part, have contributed to the propensity to condemn as futile as well as dangerous any effort to develop limited nuclear strategies and capabilities. They, together with many former national security officials and experts, echo Walzer's conclusion that "Nuclear war is and will remain morally unacceptable, and there is no case for its rehabilitation."[49]

In this symposium, Walzer chose to speak to the issues of the future of the nuclear debate in the U.S. political process rather than to the further elaboration of his supreme-emergency concept. His suggestion that there must be a dual track in the debate in the streets and in the corridors of power probably reflects realistic expectations of the forms of nuclear debate.[50] If such a dual track approach does in fact eventuate, however, it seems likely to favor a deterrence-only approach that will emphasize arms control efforts to the detriment of concern for limited nuclear defense as a requirement of deterrence-plus. The prospects for alleviating the dangers of nuclear war through the magic of arms control will predictably inspire the debate, if it can be called that, in the streets among peace activists, nuclear freeze proponents, and the like. To the extent that those in the corridors are influenced by the streets, the development of a consensus supporting efforts to make limited nuclear deterrence and defense first respectable and then feasible is unlikely. As Walter Lippman observed years ago, public opinion in the democracies tends to prefer the extremes of unrealistic international idealism and chauvinistic support of total war to the kind of balanced perspectives that would support limited deterrence/defense strategies.[51] The task of achieving consensus sufficient to develop such strategies is one for political leadership that can be effective irrespective of the ebbs and flows of street opinion and activism.

If a continuing commitment were made by successive U.S. administrations to develop counterforce nuclear deterrence capabilities that could conform to just war conditions in war and serve as the basis for credible nuclear deterrence, the agenda would reflect the discussion I have offered in chapter 7. Just and limited nuclear deterrence and defense require that targeting be limited to military targets that could be attacked without excessive collateral damage. Clearly, long study by experts would be needed to determine what those targets should be and how *excessive* collateral damage could be defined. Such efforts would include study of ways to decrease foreseen collateral damage. Concomitantly, serious thought would have to be given to the minimum sets of targets the assured destruction of which would likely present the aggressor with too high a price to pay for nuclear aggression. Although such an effort might seem to be hopelessly speculative, the art of defining how much is enough is required in all defense planning and operations.

It may well be taken as given that the United States will not initiate a nuclear war. That being the case, the requirement for just and limited nuclear deterrence and defense is for retaliatory weapons systems and supporting C^3I capabilities that can survive any enemy first strike and retain the capability to inflict unacceptable damage with counterforce means. In other words, we would still have the same requirement of survivable second-strike capabilities, but it would be a much more demanding requirement since the capabilities must be for limited counterforce strikes, not countervalue countercity strikes. Dougherty discusses some of these problems in chapter 5.[52] Note that neither optimism nor pessimism regarding strategic missile defense, discussed by Dougherty, alters the basic requirement for survivable counterforce second-strike capabilities serviced by survivable C^3I. The object of strategic missile defense is not to prevent 100 percent of incoming missiles from striking their targets but to assure early destruction in space of a sufficiently high percentage of enemy missiles as to render impossible a disarming first strike. Under any scenario, some enemy missiles will strike their targets, and the requirement will then be for retaliation. A just and limited nuclear deterrence/defense policy would insist that the retaliation be with counterforce means. The empirical issue is whether such means can be effective.

An additional requirement of just and limited war will be to find ways to improve the ability of the government and the military chain of command to operate in the horrendous environment of a nuclear war. This would involve maximization of prewar planning to provide for as many contingencies as possible so that decisions may be made quickly, under great pressure, to put into effect counterforce strategies worked out in peacetime. In other words, we must plan seriously for the conduct of limited nuclear war, something that is currently denounced as obscene war-mongering and discouraged by some of our most informed and responsible former officials and military commanders.

At this point it is also necessary to emphasize the need to separate planning and preparations for retaliation for nuclear attacks against the United States and more limited and selective recourse to nuclear weapons in response to aggression against our allies. The hardest problem is that of developing a credible limited nuclear response to a strategic nuclear attack against the United States. No matter how committed we may become to avoidance of countervalue, counterpopulation attacks, the sheer magnitude of any significant nuclear response would raise the issues of possible uncontrolled escalation and of widespread, if not global, damage resulting from a major nuclear exchange.

Would a major superpower nuclear exchange inevitably explode the bounds of just war, as Walzer contends? Perhaps not inevitably, but the chances of keeping such a war within just war limits are probably less than 50–50. It is at this point that the new possibilities of strategic defense may prove critical. If a limited nuclear deterrence/defense posture were supplemented with a strategic missile defense system that reduced substantially the damage of a nuclear exchange, then perhaps the odds on keeping such a war within just war limits would improve. If, despite all efforts to control nuclear war, to eschew countervalue attacks on cities, and to defend against an aggressor's strategic nuclear attacks on the United States, it appears that damage violative of any reasonable definition of proportionality and discrimination is probable, then just war doctrine has been *exploded* in the sense that it can offer no further warrant for just defense. In such circumstances an ethics of distress or supreme emergency is all that is left, short of surrender and/or pacifism.

The case for limited nuclear deterrence and defense would seem to be stronger in the case of a response to nuclear attacks on a U.S. ally. My own view, expressed in chapter 7, is that the United States and its allies should not initiate nuclear war, that only nuclear aggression warrants a nuclear response. If such a policy were adopted, at least some of the problems of outlining a credible scenario for limited use of nuclear weapons might be set aside. One problem with the mixed nuclear/conventional deterrence/defense posture, as in NATO, is that the range of contingencies is so great that it is difficult to plot courses that could respect the kind of nuclear thresholds essential to any effort to limit nuclear war. The contingencies of a mixed nuclear-conventional war present all too many occasions for use of nuclear weapons. If there is to be any chance at all to conduct limited nuclear war, the number of weapons employed must be small, the targets must be selected with a view to discouraging continued use by the enemy of nuclear weapons, and the use of nuclear means must be discontinued as soon as this is possible consistent with deterrence of the enemy from continued use and/or resumption of use of nuclear weapons.

Difficult as it may be to envisage a limited nuclear war fought in response to a theater or local aggression against U.S. allies, the possibility of keeping such a war within the bounds of just and limited war appears to be much greater than in the case of a strategic nuclear exchange between the United States and the Soviet Union. In the debates ahead, it will be important to make this distinction. The U.S. Catholic bishops, for example, tend to treat the issue of limited nuclear war in terms of the highest strategic level—for example, with references to MX and other "hard kill" weapons.[53] It is, of course fair and necessary to confront limited nuclear war with the ultimate question on which all security depends—the viability of strategic nuclear deterrence. Nevertheless, to discount *any* possibility of limited nuclear war because of the difficulties of keeping a strategic nuclear exchange between the superpowers limited is not justifiable.

For whatever small comfort it may be, it seems likely that the threat of actual nuclear war is not greatest at the strategic superpower level at the present time. Moreover, a theater nuclear war in the NATO area, the most discussed contingency, is not necessarily the most likely one. Quite possibly, a nuclear war, if one ever occurs, will more likely arise out of some confused sequence of local aggression and defense in an area like the Middle East or Northeast Asia, followed by a series of escalations leading to a limited nuclear exchange. This is one "shadow on conventional conflicts" that Keegan does not discuss. A decision to initiate war, even at a very low level of intensity, may trigger a series of escalations predictably reaching the nuclear level. If this were to occur, a strong counterforce, limited nuclear deterrence/defense posture at the strategic and NATO levels might well make possible confinement of the conflict and its nuclear dimensions to the locale of the aggression.

Given all the uncertainties and risks of even the most limited nuclear war, nuclear deterrence is still the goal of nuclear strategy. Would U.S. and allied forces be able to deter nuclear aggression and intimidation if they relied entirely on a counterforce nuclear deterrence/defense posture consonant with just and limited war principles? In addressing this question, it is better to assume that we will be loyal to our commitment to just and limited war in the event that deterrence fails and that the adversary will believe in our commitment. Some may be tempted by the possibilities of a bluff deterrent, based in whole or in part on the assumption that the enemy will not believe that moral constraints will limit responses to aggression and will, accordingly, take a worst-case view of our actions should he attack.

Plausible as this may seem from the psychological standpoint, this is an approach that should not be relied on. Deterrence based on uncertainty on the part of the enemy will, in my view, eventually begin to raise uncertainty in our own minds about what we would actually do if deterrence failed. It would take a tremendous effort—and careful indoctrination and training of personnel—to limit a nuclear response to aggression to actions consistent with just war. To cloud that determination in advance with uncertainty about the just and limited character of responses to aggression is likely to confuse ourselves as much as the adversary. In any event, introduction of this angle blurs the issue of limited nuclear deterrence, which ought to be confronted cleanly without the moral crutch of reliance on the possible benefits of a bluff deterrent.

Viewed starkly, and without benefit of bluff ploys, will limited nuclear deterrence deter? It may. In the first place, it may deter because it makes more sense. In addition to being immoral, a nuclear war fought outside the bounds of just war doctrine would be so destructive that it would make no political or military sense. Indeed, that is the very characteristic of such a war that has been thought to render the threat of it an effective deterrent to it. The Soviets, followers of Clausewitz as interpreted by Lenin, should not be expected to discount the idea of limited nuclear warfare, whatever their propaganda rhetoric.[54]

Second, it is interesting that not even those moralists who enjoin respect for our own moral tradition seem to think that a deterrence/defense posture based on dedication to our own principles might be more credible and effective than one based on the abdication of our moral principles. It is true that for years many in the West avoided the issue of morality in nuclear deterrence, and during those years a posture developed that we now acknowledge to be based on threats to do things that would be immoral if carried out. But that time of looking the other way is over now. There has been an extended public debate about the morality of nuclear deterrence and defense. Countervalue, countercity nuclear war has been widely condemned as morally unacceptable. For many in the West the question is no longer whether the old deterrence/defense posture was immoral: it is agreed that it was. The issue now is how to move to a morally acceptable posture. If our enemies take at all seriously our need for a moral consensus to sustain the political consensus necessary in free societies for support of national security policies, they will see that deterrence based on policies we now reject as immoral may well be less credible than policies based on our own just war values.

As the debate continues, it will become a matter of empirical fact and prudential judgment whether a just and limited nuclear deterrent/defense posture is feasible and how well such a posture can be expected to deter aggression. Concomitantly, it will be a matter of fact and of judgment whether parallel efforts to mitigate the sources of conflict and to achieve effective and meaningful arms control progress will ameliorate the nuclear predicament. It can be expected that the conflict resolution/arms control agenda will be more popular. But if our situation is really so desperate as to warrant reliance for moral guidance on Walzer's supreme emergency or the European bishops' ethics of distress, it should be clear that some kind of effective and morally permissible alternative to our present nuclear deterrence/defense policies is badly needed. The less popular agenda will be to work for the realization of that practical and moral alternative.

Notes

1. Michael Walzer, *Just and Unjust Wars* (New York: Basic Books, 1977), p. 282.

2. I cite some former high U.S. officials' doubts about the escalatory propensities of nuclear war in chapter 7, note 57.

3. In addition to their chapters in this book, see, for example, James Turner Johnson, *Just War Tradition and the Restraint of War* (Princeton, N.J.: Princeton University Press, 1981), esp. chap. 10, pp. 327–366; James E. Dougherty, *The Bishops and Nuclear Weapons* (Hamden, Conn.: Archon, 1984), pp. 171–177, 181–190, 201–202.

4. Walzer, *Just and Unjust Wars,* pp. 274–283.

5. See my discussion in chapter 7, this book.

6. Langan, chapter 6, this book.

7. Walzer, *Just and Unjust Wars,* p. 283.

8. Ibid.

9. In continental international law texts, sections on international delinquencies (*delits*) treat *titre justificatif exceptionel,* for example: "Le délit suppose le caractère illégal de l'action. Or, ce caractère illégal peut être écarté par les titres justificatifs exceptionnels. Ce sont le droit de conservation et la représaille." Robert Redslob, *Traité de droit des gens* (Paris: Sirey, 1950), p. 243. Redslob discusses two forms of the "droit de conservation," "la légitime défense," and "le droit de nécessité." Ibid.

Similar treatments are to be found in Franz von Liszt, *Das Voelkerrecht, systematisch dargestellt* (Sechste umgearbeitete Auflage) (Berlin: Verlag von O. Haring, 1910), p. 177; Jean Spiropoulos, *Traité theorique et practique de droit international public* (Paris: Librairie Generale de Droit et de Jurisprudence, 1933), p. 286; Albéric Rolin, *Le droit moderne de la guerre,* 2 vols. (Brussels: Albert de Writ, 1920), vol. I, pp. 32, 37.

10. Professor H. Donnedieu de Vabres, the French judge on the Nuremberg International Military Tribunal, discusses necessity as follows:

> L'état de nécessité est un sujet à la fois très ancien et très nouveau. Lorsqu'en 1898 le président du Tribunal de Chateau-Thierry—le bon juge—pronounca l'acquittement d'une femme qui, pour sauver la vie de son enfant mourant de faim, avait soustrait un pain à la devanture d'un boulanger, sa décision parût empreingé d'une hardiesse significative de temps nouveau; elle comptait, en réalité, de précédents qui remontent jusqu'à l'Antiquité et au Moyen Age.

Preface to Edouard Twafik Hazan, *L'État de nécessité en droit pénal interétatique et international* (Paris: Pedone, 1949), p. 1.

11. In *Regina* v. *Dudley and Stephens,* 14 Q.B.D. 273 (1884), a man who killed and ate the flesh of his shipmate while they were adrift in a small boat a thousand miles from land and without food was convicted of murder and sentenced to death, but the sentence was commuted by the crown to six months imprisonment. On necessity in British and

American criminal law, see Rollin M. Perkins, *Cases and Materials on Criminal Law and Procedure* (Brooklyn: Foundation Press, 1952), chap. 8, section 2, "Compulsion or Necessity," pp. 489–498: Alan Donagan, *The Theory of Morality* (Chicago: University of Chicago Press, 1977), pp. 175–180.

12. The Nazi argument that Norway was invaded out of necessity to forestall an alleged British incursion into that country was rejected by the Nuremberg Tribunal in the light of evidence that Germany had long planned the invasion. Nuremberg International Military Tribunal, *Opinion and Judgment,* in *Nazi Conspiracy and Aggression* (Office of United States Chief of Counsel for Prosecution of Axis Criminality; Washington, D.C.: U.S. Government Printing Office, 1947), pp. 34–38.

13. See Clinton Rossiter, *Constitutional Dictatorship: Crisis Government in the Modern Democracies* (Princeton, N.J.: Princeton University Press, 1948); Aaron Klieman, *Emergency Politics: The Growth of Crisis Government* (London: Institute for the Study of Conflict, 1976).

14. On Lincoln's wartime measures, see Edward S. Corwin, *The President, Office and Powers, 1787–1948* (New York: New York University Press, 1948), chap. 6, pp. 275–318, esp. pp. 275–283, 317–318; Clinton Rossiter, *The Supreme Court and the Commander in Chief* (Ithaca, N.Y.: Cornell University Press, 1976), pp. 26–39; *Ex-parte Milligan* 4 Wall 2 (1866).

15. See Edward S. Corwin, *Total War and the Constitution* (New York: Knopf, 1947); Corwin, *The President, Office and Powers,* chap. 6, pp. 275–318; Rossiter, *The Supreme Court.*

16. On the exploitation of Article 48 of the Weimar Constitution and the rise of Hitler, see Rossiter, *Constitutional Dictatorship,* pp. 31–73.

17. See, for example, John M. Goshko, "Chile's 'Siege' Discomfits White House," *Washington Post,* November 18, 1984, A32, cols. 1–2; "Government by Intimidation," *Newsweek,* November 26, 1984, p. 67.

18. On the positive principle of military necessity, see Charles Cheny Hyde, *International Law, Chiefly as Interpreted and Applied by the United States,* 2nd ed., rev., 2 vols (Boston: Little, Brown, 1947), vol. III, pp. 1801–1802; U.S. Department of the Army, *The Law of Land Warfare, July 1956,* FM 27-10 (Washington, D.C.: Department of the Army, 1956), p. 4; Robert W. Tucker, *The Law of War and Neutrality at Sea,* U.S. Naval War College, International Law Studies, 1955, vol. 50 (Washington, D.C.: U.S. Government Printing Office, 1957), pp. 33, 364, 368–369; Myres C. McDougal and Florentino P. Feliciano, *Law and Minimum World Public Order* (New Haven, Conn.: Yale University Press, 1961), pp. 72–76; U.S. Department of the Air Force, *International Law—the Conduct of Armed Conflict and Air Operations, 19 November 1976,* AFP 110-31 (Washington, D.C.: Department of the Air Force, 1976), 1-5-6.

I review the military manuals and publicists' literature in "Legitimate Military Necessity in Nuclear War," *World Polity* 2(1960):35–120. I discuss the place of military necessity as a principle of the law of war in *The Conduct of Just and Limited War* (New York: Praeger, 1981), pp. 64–67.

19. I summarize and provide major examples of the *Kriegsraison* theorists in " 'Military Necessity' in International Law," *World Polity* 1(1957):119–128. See John Westlake, *International Law,* part I: *War* (Cambridge: The University Press, 1913), vol. 2, pp. 126–128; Charles de Visscher, "Les lois de la guerre et la théorie de nécessité," *Revue générale de droit international public* 24(1917):74–108; Paul Weiden, "Necessity in

International Law," *Transactions of the Grotius Society* 24(1939):113 ff.; N.C.H. Dunbar, "Military Necessity in War Crimes Trials," *British Yearbook of International Law* 29(1952):442.

20. See, for example, General Julius von Hartmann, *Militarische Notwendigkeit und Humanitat,* in *Deutsche Rundschau,* vols. XIII, XIV (1877–1878); E. Ullmann, *Voelkerrecht* (Frieburg: Verlag von F.C.B. Mohr, 1898), pp. 316–317; E. Lueder, "Kireg und Kriegsrecht in Allgemeinen," in Franz von Holtzendorf, *Handbuch des Voelkerrechts* (Hamburg: Verlagsanstelt und Druckerei, 1899), vol. IV, pp. 169–367.

21. See Prussia, Gorsser Generalstab, *Kriegsgeschichtliche Abteilung—The German War Book, Being the "Usage on Land" Issued by the Great General Staff of the German Army,* trans. with Critical Introduction by J.H. Morgan (London: John Murray, 1915), pp. 52–54; von Liszt, *Das Voelkerrecht, systematisch dargestellt,* 6th ed. (1910). Von Liszt altered his view somewhat to take cognizance of the binding character of the emerging conventional law in his sixth edition. The previous five editions reflected the *Kriegsraison* view.

For extreme applications of the *Kriegsraison* doctrine during World War I, see, for example: Josef Kohler, "Notwehr und Neutralitat," *Zeitschrift fuer Voelkerrecht* 8(1914): 576 ff.; Kohler, *Not kennt kein Gebot—Die Theorie des Notrechtes und die Ereignisse unserer Zeit* (Berlin and Leipzig: Verlagabuchhandlund Dr. Walter Rothschild, 1915); Philip K.L. Zorn, *Die Beiden Haager Friendenskonferenzen von 1899 und 1907* (Stuttgart: Verlag Von W. Kohlammer, 1915), pp. v–vi.

22. Hegel's political thought is clearly at the foundation of the *Kriegsraison* doctrine. The characterization of the state as having no superior, free to pursue its destiny regardless of international law, is reflected in the doctrine. See, for example, Georg Friederich Hegel, *Philosophy of Right,* with notes by T.M. Knox, trans. (Oxford: The Clarendon Press, 1942), pp. 213–218.

Perhaps equally influential is the political-military doctrines of General Carl von Clausewitz. See note 24.

Field Marshal Helmuth von Moltke, highly successful and influential field commander in the Franco-Prussian War, epitomized the German attitude toward war and the laws of war in several letters to the *Revue de Droit International.* He became famous for the proposition that "Sans la guerre le monde sombrerait dans le materialism." Quoted in Colonel Eugene Carrias, *La Pensée militaire allemande* (Paris: Presses Universitaires de France, 1949), p. 291. General von Moltke summarized the case for what came to be known as *total war,* as against limited war, with the observation, "The greatest kindness in war is to bring it to a speedy conclusion." Quoted in Thomas Erskine Holland, *Letters to "The Times" upon War and Neutrality (1881–1909)—With Some Commentary* (London: Longmans, Green, 1909), p. 25.

The use of the *Kriegsraison* doctrine by Chancellor Bethmann-Hollweg accepted by much of the political and intellectual elite of Germany, is described later.

23. See Carl von Clausewitz, *On War,* Michael Howard and Peter Paret, eds. and trans. (Princeton, N.J.: Princeton University Press, 1976).

24. Quoted in James Wilford Garner, *International Law and the World War,* 2 vols. (London: Longmans, Green, 1920), vol. II, pp. 192–193.

25. See, for example, the authorities cited in note 20.

26. FM 27-10, p. 3.

27. See the account of the British and German aerial bombing policies, justifications, charges, and countercharges in the early part of World War II in Julius Stone, *Legal Controls of International Conflict* (New York: Rinehart, 1954), pp. 625–627.

28. See Walzer, *Just and Unjust Wars*, pp. 251–255. Walzer quotes Churchill's 1939 statement to the cabinet: "We are fighting to re-establish the reign of law and to protect the liberties of small countries. Our defeat would mean an age of barbaric violence, and would be fatal, not only to ourselves, but to the independent life of every small country in Europe. . . . The letter of the law must not in supreme emergency obstruct those who are charged with its protection and enforcement. . . . Humanity, rather than legality, must be our guide." Winston S. Churchill, *The Gathering Storm* (Boston: Houghton Mifflin, 1948), Book II, chap. 9, p. 547, as quoted in Walzer, *Just and Unjust Wars*, p. 245.

29. On British-American strategic bombing objectives and strategies, see: Sir Charles Webster and Noble Frankland, *The Strategic Air Offensive against Germany, 1939–1945* (London: Her Majesty's Stationary Office, 1961), particularly 2:12, and 4:128–129, 168, 323–324, 345; Wesley Frank Craven and James Lee Cate, eds., *The Army Air Forces in World War II* (Chicago: University of Chicago Press, 1948–1958), vol. 2, pp. 274–301, 715–755; Geoffrey Best, *Humanity in Warfare* (New York: Columbia University Press, 1980), pp. 271–285.

30. See AFP 110-31, 5-4-6.

31. Walzer, *Just and Unjust Wars*, pp. 251–255.

32. Ibid., p. 254.

33. Ibid., p. 253.

34. Ibid., pp. 255–263; O'Brien, *Conduct of Just and Limited War*, pp. 79–84.

35. Walzer, *Just and Unjust Wars*, pp. 261–263.

36. See Mara, chapter 4, this book.

37. Walzer, *Just and Unjust Wars*, pp. 261–263.

38. On the collapse of observance of the principle of discrimination or noncombatant immunity during World War II, see, for example, H. Lauterpacht, "The Problem of the Revision of the Law of War," *British Yearbook of International Law* 29(1952):360–369; McDougal and Feliciano, *Law and Minimum World Public Order*, pp. 79–80.

39. I discuss the possibilities for claiming regulation of nuclear weapons by analogy or inference from the principles, customary rules, and conventional provisions of the law of war in "Legitimate Military Necessity in Nuclear War," and conclude that there were not, as of 1960, any binding provisions of international law limiting nuclear weapons any more or less than conventional weapons. The 1949 Geneva Conventions do not deal with nuclear weapons. The 1977 Geneva Protocols to the 1949 Geneva Conventions do revise the war-conduct law. The United States has not yet ratified the protocols and, in any event, the protocols are clearly not intended to regulate nuclear weapons. Ambassador George M. Aldrich, chairman of the U.S. delegation to the Geneva Conference that produced the 1977 protocols, states in his report:

> During the course of the Conference there was no consideration of the issues raised by the use of nuclear weapons. Although there are several articles that could seem to raise questions with respect to the use of nuclear weapons, most clearly Article 55 on the protection of the natural environment, it was the understanding of the United States Delegation throughout the Conference that the rules to be developed were designed with a view to conventional weapons and their effects and that the new rules established by the Protocol [Protocol I, Relating to the Protection of Victims of International Armed

Conflicts] were not intended to have any effect on, and do not regulate or prohibit the use of nuclear weapons. We made this understanding several times during the Conference, and it was also stated explicitly by the British and French delegations. It was not contradicted by any Delegation so far as we are aware. Despite this clear record, however, the United States may wish to make a formal statement of understanding on this subject, given its importance, at the times of signature and of ratification.

U.S. Department of State, *Report of the United States Delegation to the Diplomatic Conference on the Reaffirmation and Development of International Humanitarian Law Applicable in Armed Conflicts,* Washington, D.C., September 8, 1977, p. 32.

40. Walzer, *Just and Unjust Wars,* pp. 259–263.

41. See National Conference of Catholic Bishops, *The Challenge of Peace: God's Promise and Our Response, A Pastoral Letter on War and Peace,* May 3, 1983 (Washington, D.C.: United States Catholic Conference, 1983) (hereinafter cited as *Challenge of Peace*), pars. 157–161, 188–199; David Hollenbach, S.J., *Nuclear Ethics: A Christian Moral Argument* (New York: Paulist Press, 1983); Hollenbach, chapter 2, this book.

42. O'Brien, *Conduct of Just and Limited War,* p. 135.

43. Ibid., pp. 35–36.

44. Walzer, *Just and Unjust Wars,* p. 283.

45. Article 5 of the North Atlantic Treaty, April 4, 1949, provides:

The parties agree that an armed attack against one or more of them in Europe or North America shall be considered an attack against them all; and consequently they agree that, if such an armed attack occurs, each of them, in exercise of the right of individual or collective self-defense recognized by Article 51 of the Charter of the United Nations, will assist the party or parties so attacked by taking forthwith, individually and in concert with the other parties, such action as it deems necessary, including the use of armed force, to restore and maintain the security of the North Atlantic area. . . .

T.I.A.S. no. 1964, U.S. *Department of State Bulletin* 20(1949):339.

46. O'Brien, chapter 7, this book.

47. Keegan, chapter 8, this book.

48. O'Brien, chapter 7, this book.

49. Walzer, *Just and Unjust Wars,* p. 283.

50. Walzer, chapter 9, this book.

51. Lippman observed:

The unhappy truth is that the prevailing public opinion has been destructively wrong at the critical junctures. The people have imposed a veto upon the judgments of informed and responsible officials. They have compelled the governments, which usually knew what would have been wiser, or was necessary, or was more expedient, to be too late with too little, or too long with too much, too pacifist in peace and too bellicose in war, too neutralist or appeasing in negotiation or too intransigent. Mass opinion has acquired mounting power in this century. It has shown itself to be a dangerous master of decisions when the stakes are life and death.

Walter Lippman, *Essays in the Public Philosophy* (Boston: Little, Brown, 1955), p. 20.

52. Dougherty, chapter 5, this book.

53. *Challenge of Peace,* par. 190.

54. See Marshal of the Soviet Union V.D. Sokolovskiy, *Soviet Military Strategy,* 3rd ed., with analysis and commentary by Harriet Fast Scott, ed. (New York: Crane, Russak, 1975), pp. 172–213; Mrs. Scott's comments, pp. 167–171.

Index

About the Contributors

James E. Dougherty is professor of political science at St. Joseph's University. He has written widely on international affairs, with a particular focus on international security. Among his many books are *The Bishops and Nuclear Weapons* (1984); *The Fateful Ends and Shades of Salt: Past ... Present ... and Yet to Come?* (1979, joint author); *How to Think about Arms Control and Disarmament* (1973); and *Arms Control and Disarmament: The Critical Issues* (1966). He is also coeditor of *Contending Theories of International Relations*, 2nd ed. (1981).

David Hollenbach, S.J., is associate professor of moral theology at Weston School of Theology. He is the author of *Nuclear Ethics: A Christian Moral Argument* (1983) and *Claims in Conflict: Retrieving and Renewing the Catholic Human Rights Tradition* (1979). Father Hollenbach has also served as consultant to the U.S. Catholic bishops on both international and domestic policy issues.

James Turner Johnson is professor of religion, Rutgers University. His most recent related books include *Can Modern War Be Just?* (1984); *Just War Tradition and the Restraint of War: A Moral and Historical Inquiry* (1981) and *Ideology, Reason and the Limitation of War* (1975). He has also published work on related topics in such journals as the *Journal of Religious Ethics, The Monist*, and *Parameters*. Professor Johnson was the recipient of a Guggenheim Fellowship in 1983–84 and was a Rockefeller Fellow in the humanities in 1976–77.

John Keegan is professor of military history in the Department of War Studies and International Affairs, The Royal Military Academy at Sandhurst. He serves as the general editor for the Rand McNally *Encyclopedia of World War II*. His books include *The Face of Battle* (1976) and *Six Armies in Normandy: From D-Day to the Liberation of Paris* (1982).

Gerald M. Mara is associate dean for research of the graduate school and professorial lecturer in goverment at Georgetown University. He has published work on political philosophers ranging from Plato to Jurgen Habermas in such journals as *Polity, Western Political Quarterly, Journal of Politics*, and *Journal of the History of Philosophy*.

Michael Walzer is the author of the widely acclaimed *Just and Unjust Wars* (1977). His other books include *The Revolution of the Saints* (1965), *Obligations* (1970), *Spheres of Justice* (1983), and most recently *Exodus and Revolution* (1985). He is currently a member of the permanent faculty in the School of Social Science, the Institute for Advanced Study, Princeton University.

About the Editors

William V. O'Brien is professor of government at Georgetown University. He has written widely on international relations, international law, and the moral dimensions of conflict. His most recent book, *The Conduct of Just and Limited War*, was published by Praeger in 1981. His previous books include *War and/or Survival* (1969) and *Nuclear War, Deterrence and Morality* (1967). He has contributed articles to such journals as *World Affairs, Virginia Journal of International Law, Strategic Review*, and *Theological Studies*. He is currently completing a book on the moral and political dimensions of the Israeli-PLO conflict.

John Langan, S.J., is senior research fellow at the Woodstock Theological Center, Georgetown University. His scholarly interests cover a wide range of issues connected with ethics and public policy. He has coedited *Human Rights in the Americas: The Struggle for Consensus* (1982) and has published articles on ethics and foreign affairs, the morality of nuclear deterrence, human rights, and social justice in such journals as *Theological Studies, Journal of Religious Ethics, Harvard Theological Review*, and *Thought*. Father Langan served as a consultant to the U.S. Catholic bishops in their development of the Pastoral Letter on war and peace.